| READING |

Basic

Intermediate

Advanced

Expert

| LISTENING |

Basic

Intermediate

Advanced*

Expert*

* To be released

Informative passages

HACKERS APEX READING includes informative and interesting passages on a variety of topics, such as science, art, and history.

Useful online study materials

HACKERS APEX READING provides access to quality online study materials at HackersBook.com. These include streaming audio recordings of all passages accessible through QR codes in the book.

HACKERS

APEX
READING
for the
TOEFL iBT®

Expert

HACKERS

Preface

Preface

Thank you for purchasing HACKERS APEX READING for the TOEFL iBT Expert. The TOEFL iBT is a highly challenging exam, so it is important to select an effective study guide. All of us at Hackers Language Research Institute are confident that this publication will be an invaluable resource as you prepare for the TOEFL iBT.

HACKERS APEX READING for the TOEFL iBT is a series of comprehensive study guides for students planning to take the TOEFL iBT or for those wanting to improve their general English reading skills. This series includes four books that progress in difficulty. Students can begin at the level that matches their current abilities and then move on to the higher ones. All of the books in this series provide step-by-step question-solving strategies for every TOEFL question type. These are based on thorough research and years of instructional experience. Each book also includes informative and interesting passages that enable students to improve their English reading skills and expand their background knowledge at the same time. Furthermore, students will receive access to quality online study materials that are designed to help them get the most out of the books in this series. Key features of HACKERS APEX READING for the TOEFL iBT books include:

- Detailed explanations and question-solving strategies for all TOEFL Reading question types
- A large number of high-quality TOEFL Reading passages and questions
- Two full-length TOEFL Reading tests
- Vocabulary exercises to review essential vocabulary that appeared in the passages
- An answer book with Korean translations and lists of key vocabulary
- Access to streaming audio recordings of all passages through QR codes
- Access to supplementary study materials online (www.HackersBook.com)

Thank you again for choosing HACKERS APEX READING for the TOEFL iBT Expert, and we wish you all the best whether you are preparing to take the TOEFL iBT in the near future or simply hoping to develop your English reading skills overall.

Table of Contents

How to Use This Book

1 Understand the Question Type

Each chapter includes an Overview page that provides essential information about the featured question type and key strategies for answering it. Make sure you fully understand the strategies before moving on to the Example section, which provides a short passage with up to three questions to apply the key strategies to.

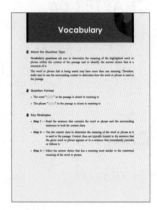

2 Improve Your Skills with Reading Practice Exercises

Each chapter includes three Reading Practice exercises. These will help you become more familiar with the featured question type, as well as other question types.

3 Take the iBT Reading Tests

Each chapter includes two iBT Reading Tests. Each consists of a longer passage and 10 questions that are similar to those that appear on the TOEFL iBT. Taking these tests will enable you to improve your reading comprehension skills and prepare for the TOEFL iBT.

4 Review Essential Vocabulary

At the end of each chapter is a Vocabulary Review, which includes questions on essential vocabulary from the chapter. You will be able to easily memorize the vocabulary words by seeing them in sentences with various contexts.

5 Evaluate Your Progress with Actual Tests

The book includes two Actual Tests, which are full-length reading tests that include passages and questions that closely match what appears on the TOEFL iBT. They provide an excellent opportunity to apply the skills you have learned and evaluate your progress.

6 Check the Answer Book

The Answer Book specifies the correct answer choice for all questions and provides Korean translations of all passages and questions. It also includes a list of key vocabulary words from each passage with definitions.

About the TOEFL iBT

What Is the TOEFL iBT?

The TOEFL (Test of English as a Foreign Language) iBT (Internet-Based test) includes Reading, Listening, Speaking, and Writing sections to comprehensively assess English ability. Although most tasks require the application of only one of these skills, some require the use of two or more. The TOEFL iBT is designed to measure a student's capacity to use and understand English at a university level and is, therefore, much more difficult than many other English proficiency tests.

TOEFL iBT Structure

Section	No. of passages and questions	Time (min.)	Score	Notable Features
Reading	• 3-4 Passages • 10 Questions/Passage	54-72	30	• Each passage is approximately 700 words long.
Listening	• 2-3 Conversations • 5 Questions/Conversation • 3-4 Lectures • 6 Questions/Lecture	41-57	30	• Speakers have various accents, including American, British, Australian, etc.
10-minute break				
Speaking	• 1 Independent Task • 3 Integrated Tasks	17	30	• Independent Tasks ask you to state your opinion about a specific topic. • Integrated Tasks ask you to provide a response based on reading and listening content.
Writing	• 1 Integrated Task • 1 Independent Task	50	30	• Integrated Tasks ask you to provide a response based on reading and listening content. • Independent Tasks ask you to write about a specific topic.

Total Time: Approximately 3 hours 30 minutes / Total Score: 120

TOEFL iBT Reading Section

The TOEFL iBT Reading Section evaluates a student's ability to read and comprehend English texts that are comparable to those encountered in a typical first- or second-year university class. Although the passages cover a wide variety of academic topics, there is no requirement to be familiar with the subject matter. The information in the passage is all that is needed to answer the questions.

TOEFL iBT Reading Question Types

Question Type	Description	Score	No. of Questions (per passage)
Vocabulary	Choose the answer choice that is closest in meaning to the given word or phrase.	1	1-2
Reference	Choose the answer choice that the given word or phrase refers to.	1	0-2
Sentence Simplification	Choose the answer choice that accurately and completely summarizes the key information in the given sentence.	1	0-1
Fact & Negative Fact	Choose the answer choice that restates (Fact) or contradicts (Negative Fact) the relevant information in the passage.	1	2-7
Inference	Choose the answer choice that can be inferred based on the relevant information in the passage.	1	1-2
Rhetorical Purpose	Choose the answer choice that best describes the function of a specific piece of information in relation to the immediate context or the passage as a whole.	1	1-2
Sentence Insertion	Choose the answer choice that corresponds to the correct location in the passage to insert the given sentence. Each possible location in the passage is marked by a square [■].	1	1
Summary	Choose three answer choices that best summarize the main points of the passage.	2	0-1
Category Chart	Choose the answer choices that match the given categories.	3	0-1

CHAPTER 01

Vocabulary

Vocabulary

About the Question Type

Vocabulary questions ask you to determine the meaning of the highlighted word or phrase within the context of the passage and to identify the answer choice that is a synonym of it.

The word or phrase that is being tested may have more than one meaning. Therefore, make sure to use the surrounding context to determine how the word or phrase is used in the passage.

Question Format

- The word "   " in the passage is closest in meaning to

- The phrase "   " in the passage is closest in meaning to

Key Strategies

- **Step 1** — Read the sentence that contains the word or phrase and the surrounding sentences to look for context clues.

- **Step 2** — Use the context clues to determine the meaning of the word or phrase as it is used in the passage. Context clues are typically located in the sentence that the given word or phrase appears or in a sentence that immediately precedes or follows it.

- **Step 3** — Select the answer choice that has a meaning most similar to the contextual meaning of the word or phrase.

Example

Answer Book p. 2

Amnesia

All cases of amnesia are further divided into three main types: immediate, intermediate, and long-term memory loss. A person suffering from the first cannot recall any event that occurred during the preceding few seconds. The second involves an inability to recall events that took place between a few seconds and a few days prior to the onset of amnesia. The last is the most serious type and entails an inability to recall events further back in time.　5

Amnesia has various causes, including a blow to the head or damage to the brain as a result of disease. In the case of the former, a head injury such as a concussion can result in unconsciousness for a short period of time and a subsequent inability to recall the events that preceded the head blow. In the case of the latter, serious ailments such as a brain tumor, a degenerative disorder, or a stroke can cause memory loss.　10

Amnesia is often confused with dementia, a condition that affects approximately 3 percent of the population between the ages of 70 and 79 and is significantly more common among older age groups. In conjunction with memory loss, dementia typically results in impairment of language, visual and spatial abilities, judgment, and emotional control. Although there is a common misperception that dementia is an unavoidable part of the aging process, it is actually　15 caused by damage to or loss of nerve cells in the brain.

Glossary
· concussion: an injury caused by a blow to the head

1　The word "onset" in the passage is closest in meaning to

(A) termination　　　　(B) worsening　　　　(C) beginning　　　　(D) realization

2　The word "subsequent" in the passage is closest in meaning to

(A) prevailing　　　　(B) delinquent　　　　(C) prominent　　　　(D) ensuing

3　The phrase "In conjunction with" in the passage is closest in meaning to

(A) Because of　　　　(B) By means of　　　　(C) Along with　　　　(D) Contrary to

Answer Book p. 2

Desert Life

The desert receives, on average, less than 250 millimeters of precipitation annually. The diurnal temperature gradient is extreme, ranging from a high of 50 degrees Celsius at noon to a low of 0 degrees Celsius during the night. This is because of the extremely low humidity levels of these ecosystems. In the daytime, a large amount of solar radiation is absorbed by the land because there is no water vapor in the air to scatter it. However, this heat dissipates quickly once the sun sets because 5 water vapor also has insulating qualities.

The limited moisture and severe temperatures shape the desert landscape, usually composed of rocky or sandy surfaces, along with wind erosion, which is responsible for weathering bedrock outcrops and transporting loose particles from one place to another. Soil is, therefore, only minimally developed, and fluvial deposits, containing pebbles and cobbles, are scattered across the bottomlands. 10 These compounding factors make it very difficult for any life to survive in a desert without substantial morphological and behavioral adaptations to cope with the inherent environmental stresses.

Water management is the primary concern for organisms because the available moisture is either stored in deep underground reservoirs or falls irregularly and in sparse quantities. Desert vegetation, therefore, has evolved several innovative strategies for obtaining and retaining moisture from such 15 limited sources. Some of these plants have developed extensive radial root systems that can quickly acquire vast quantities of precipitation when it falls and store it in core structures protected by a waxy outer tissue; a single rainfall can sustain them for years. Many have thorns instead of leaves; these narrow, pointed structures limit the amount of water lost to the air and protect the plant from animals. 20

Further up the food chain, insects thrive in the desert climate wherein entire populations of ants and butterflies, among others, can subsist on only one or a few plants. Beetles, for example, play a large role in the decomposition of vegetation by devouring soft fruits and invading larger woody shrubs. Their thick exoskeletons trap moisture, and their body cavities store extra water supplies otherwise lost to respiration. 25

Several small herbivorous rodent species, such as the kangaroo rat and the hamster, manage to overcome the scarcity of water in a different way. They produce water as a by-product of digesting dry seeds and recycle it from their urine back into their bloodstreams via microscopic tubes attached to their kidneys. They then retire to snug subterranean dens, where they can recover moisture that might be lost during the process of respiration by using specialized organs within the nasal cavities. Often, 30 these dens are sealed off with sand to prevent hot, dry wind from sweeping through and soaking up moisture.

Burrowing underground during the day also limits exposure to the sun, and this nocturnal behavior helps these small rodents to evade heat, a second major concern. Alternatively, certain species of mammals and reptiles are active only in the twilight hours of the day when they are exposed to 35 minimal solar radiation. Others avoid overheating by remaining entirely dormant during the summer months and coming out only after a fall or winter rain cools the air. Those few that do stay active throughout the year have adaptations that allow them to either absorb less heat or lose it rapidly.

Glossary

·diurnal: having a daily cycle
·fluvial deposits: sediments deposited by the flowing water of a stream

1 The word "dissipates" in the passage is closest in meaning to

(A) dilutes

(B) accumulates

(C) vanishes

(D) escalates

2 According to paragraph 1, all of the following are characteristics of the desert EXCEPT

(A) intense heat through the day and night

(B) extreme temperature variations

(C) increased absorption of solar energy

(D) a lack of water vapor in the air

3 According to paragraph 4, why do insect populations flourish in the desert?

(A) They can consume a wide variety of vegetation.

(B) They do not dehydrate by breathing heavily.

(C) Minimal resources can support whole communities.

(D) Indigenous vegetation is particularly vulnerable to them.

4 According to paragraph 5, how do small rodents cope with the lack of water?

(A) They consume seeds that contain significant quantities of fluids.

(B) They produce moisture during the digestion process and then reuse it.

(C) They drink their own urine immediately after producing it.

(D) They control the flow of blood in their bodies using an efficient kidney system.

5 The word "evade" in the passage is closest in meaning to

(A) compel

(B) escape

(C) preserve

(D) detect

6 According to paragraph 6, what is true of the desert animals that are active throughout the year?

(A) They grow thick fur during the cool winter months.

(B) They have adapted to limit heat absorption or expedite heat loss.

(C) They remain in the shade during the summer months.

(D) They have evolved the capacity to retain large amounts of water.

Reading Practice 2

Japan

As an island nation, Japan has an important advantage that has enabled it to maintain its political and cultural autonomy throughout a significant portion of its history. This has led to the development of a somewhat insular society that has come to view its seclusion as both a positive and defining characteristic. However, external forces have had a substantial impact on its development, as many of the basic elements of the Japanese state were created as a direct result of religious, legal, and cultural 5 concepts contributed by civilizations on the Chinese mainland and the Korean peninsula.

Buddhism was introduced to Japan during the latter half of the Yamato period, from roughly AD 538 to 710, via the Korean kingdom of Baekje, which often served as a conduit for the dissemination of Chinese culture. At this time, the Yamato state was heavily involved in Baekje's struggle for hegemony on the Korean peninsula, due to its desire for access to advanced metallurgical and 10 agricultural technologies. Consequently, Korean monks, who often served as advisors to the imperial family, were highly respected and endowed with a great deal of authority. Their successful conversion of Empress Suiko in AD 594 resulted in the official state recognition of Buddhism. This led to a dramatic increase in the level of cultural exchange between Japan and its neighbors, due to scholars frequently traveling back and forth during the course of their studies. In addition, the Japanese gained 15 access for the first time to philosophical books from distant lands, such as India and Persia, as these teachings were transmitted along the Silk Road with the spread of Buddhism.

During the same period, contact between the Yamato state and the Tang dynasty of China intensified, with many elements of Chinese society being directly transplanted by the Japanese. These included architecture, arts, calligraphy, culinary practices, and clothing, among others. However, the 20 most important adaptations concerned politics and law, with Yamato rulers making a conscious effort to imitate both the structure and vocabulary of mainland institutions. The establishment of a court rank system in AD 603 was part of a concerted effort to create a highly centralized state firmly under the control of the royal family. The Taika Reforms of AD 646 took the process one step further, with the establishment of an absolute monarchy and the curtailment of the power and prerogatives of 25 regional authorities by the Imperial Court. In order for these edicts to be enacted, the Chinese writing system was formally adopted and numerous scholars were sent to China to study this discipline.

Japan has always been very pragmatic in its response to contact with foreign cultures, in that it is willing to adopt ideas and practices that are useful but assimilates them in a manner that ensures core social values are not affected. This is illustrated by Japan's attempt to isolate itself from outside 30 contact during the seventeenth and eighteenth centuries following an extended period of internal and external conflict. The shogunate, the military government that had seized power from the emperor, encouraged Japanese society to reject aspects of Chinese thought that were perceived as destabilizing. Neo-Confucianism, a later school of philosophy that was widespread throughout Asia, was subtly altered by scholars to make it applicable to the political and social climate of the time. In particular, 35 emphasis was placed on the requirements for loyalty and personal honor, two important concepts in the samurai code of bushido.

Glossary
· hegemony: the dominance of one group over another
· metallurgical: relating to the branch of science that deals with metals

1 The word "seclusion" in the passage is closest in meaning to

(A) expansion

(B) isolation

(C) confusion

(D) reputation

2 The word "its" in the passage refers to

(A) the Yamato state

(B) Baekje

(C) hegemony

(D) the Korean peninsula

3 According to paragraph 2, which of the following facilitated cultural exchanges between Japan and its neighbors?

(A) The imperial succession of Empress Suiko

(B) The recognition of a religion by the state

(C) Transfer of advanced technologies from Baekje

(D) Contact with Asian neighbors through the Silk Road

4 In paragraph 3, all of the following are mentioned as a political or legal adaptation EXCEPT

(A) the establishment of a centralized government

(B) formal adoption of the Chinese script

(C) the elimination of absolute monarchy

(D) a reduction in the power of regional authorities

5 The word "pragmatic" in the passage is closest in meaning to

(A) problematic

(B) preeminent

(C) proactive

(D) practical

6 According to paragraph 4, why did Japanese scholars modify Neo-Confucianism?

(A) To encourage the study of Chinese philosophy

(B) To establish rules of behavior for the emperor

(C) To ensure it conformed to Chinese ideology

(D) To make it compatible with contemporary culture

Reading Practice 3

Academic Art

Academic art is the painting and sculpture produced under the influence of the French Royal Academy of Painting and Sculpture, founded during the reign of Louis XIV in an effort to distinguish artists from artisans. Modeled on Italian principles, the institution maintained a strict hierarchical structure for its membership. A 5 prospective student submitted a piece for review and, if the work was accepted, was sponsored by a benefactor as the student moved up the ranks of the institution. The most talented were conferred with the Prix de Rome (Rome Prize) upon completion of preliminary training and sent to Rome to study the works of Renaissance masters, especially those of Raphael, firsthand. Artists returned to France when commissioned by a 10 member of the aristocracy or a religious figure to create works for either private collections or public infrastructure.

Considered not only a preeminent learned society but also a means to protect, monitor, and foster French culture, the academy swiftly gained a monopoly on the arts; until its ultimate decline, patronage outside of the institution was unattainable with few exceptions. As a result, academic 15 fine art, which encompasses both painting and sculpture, tends to be uniform in style and thematic presentation. According to the tenets of classical art, the purpose of artistic creation was the actualization of perfection in five areas: invention, proportion, color, expression, and composition. A good artist, therefore, was able to blend all of these elements into a creative and unique display by portraying a utopian version of the world. Thematically, allegory grew to be a dominant focus of all 20 media, wherein line and color summoned an emotional response from viewers familiar with religious mythology. The intention of the artist was to synthesize the feelings, thoughts, and emotions into one cohesive representation; that is, each painting or sculpture told a complete story.

Once deemed a master able to reproduce these standard themes in innovative ways, a graduate could build a career as a professional artist without ever having his or her credentials challenged. **A** 25 The artist would also retain membership in the academy as long as he or she agreed to periodically show pieces at the Palace of the Louvre's Salon Carré, a public gallery in Paris. **B** Over time, these exhibitions transitioned into sensational biannual events known as Paris Salons, attracting crowds as large as half a million people over the course of their two-month runs. **C** The field of professional art criticism originated with published descriptions of the Salon offerings, including the occasional 30 scathing review. **D**

For almost two centuries, Salons had an undisputed influence over French society and culture; however, by the mid-nineteenth century, a group of fringe painters began to raise serious doubts about the dominance of the academy with regard to the conception and production of fine art. Many of them regarded the Salon as a symbol of the elitism in society that revolutionaries had fought against. 35 These artists, now known as Impressionists because they painted their subjective impressions of the world rather than attempting to recreate objective reality, instituted a series of independent exhibitions that marked the birth of the avant-garde movement in Europe and the decline in the authority of the academy. Academic art, nevertheless, continues to be taught, appreciated, and purchased, throughout the Western world. 40

1 The word "conferred" in the passage is closest in meaning to

(A) associated

(B) granted

(C) guaranteed

(D) nominated

2 The word "unattainable" in the passage is closest in meaning to

(A) at a loss

(B) by all means

(C) beyond reach

(D) in demand

3 According to paragraph 2, the motivation for creating art according to classical principles was

(A) the invention of a unique style

(B) a realistic portrayal of the world

(C) the fulfillment of perfection

(D) a critique of religious myths

4 Look at the four squares [■] that indicate where the following sentence could be added to the passage.

They also became social affairs where elite members of society could meet and discuss art trends or discover up-and-coming young artists.

Where would the sentence best fit?

5 The word "their" in the passage refers to

(A) exhibitions

(B) events

(C) crowds

(D) people

6 According to paragraph 4, how did many fringe painters view the Salon?

(A) They thought it was too revolutionary for its time.

(B) They considered it to be a representation of elite culture.

(C) They believed it failed to sufficiently compensate artists.

(D) They regarded it as the greatest venue for artistic expression.

Dust Storms on Mars

➡ Mars is characterized by an arid environment mostly dominated by rock and dust. As in desert environments on Earth, the processes governing erosion on the Martian surface are largely *aeolian*—a term meaning "related to or caused by wind" and derived from the name of the Greek god of wind, Aíolos. Just like on Earth, winds on Mars can push sediments across the landscape to form dunes, lift minute particles into the air to create haze, or, if they are strong enough, produce dust storms. Major dust storms persisting for days or weeks on Mars were observed through telescopes in the early twentieth century and wrongly assumed to be extraordinary events, but further observation and exploration revealed that they are in fact common occurrences on the Red Planet.

➡ In 1971, NASA launched its Mariner 9 spacecraft to map the topography of Mars as well as measure changes on the surface and in the atmosphere. Initially, the mapping had been planned for Mariner 8, but, due to its failure to launch, both tasks were left to Mariner 9. This initial setback was followed by another challenge during Mariner 9's approach to Mars when a dust storm began and soon blossomed into a massive storm. **A** The storm encircled the entire planet and completely obscured its surface except for the summits of four volcanoes, including that of Olympus Mons, the tallest on Mars. **B** Because the storm was truly global, with clouds of dust stretching from pole to pole, scientists referred to it as a global dust storm. **C** Two subsequent expeditions by Viking Orbiters (Viking 1 and Viking 2) in 1976 also discovered large dust storms. **D**

These findings shed new light on the frequency and scale of the dust storms on Mars, but the precise details of their formation remained murky. However, substantial progress in understanding how they form occurred in 2001 with the help of the Mars Global Surveyor's Mars Observer Camera (MOC), which was a photographic instrument with a narrow-angle camera and two wide-angle cameras attached. The MOC sent vivid photos of the precise moments in which a global dust storm formed, and soon researchers discerned that the global storm's origin was actually a series of disturbances that occurred in close proximity to Hellas Planitia, the easily recognizable impact crater in Mars's southern hemisphere.

➡ Astronomers hypothesized that surface dust was displaced as cold air from the south pole pushed north toward the warmer air at the equator, and, as it reached the warmer, less-dense air, it was lifted high into the atmosphere. Within several weeks, a thick layer of dust covered virtually the whole planet in an opaque cloud. In the end, the MOC's images provided scientists with the understanding that global dust storms on Mars begin locally and that multiple small disturbances can increase in size and coalesce with great rapidity.

Scientists continue to study the storms for the sake of knowledge, but they are also keenly interested in the useful implications of this knowledge. In reality, scientific measurements have proven that the winds on Mars are not extreme enough to create such damage and are actually far less intense than the strongest winds on Earth. Still, the storms and winds do present some practical challenges, so scientists planning any mission to Mars must always prepare for their regular occurrence.

1 The word "they" in the passage refers to

- (A) winds
- (B) sediments
- (C) dunes
- (D) particles

2 According to paragraph 1, which of the following is a misconception that was held in the early 1900s?

- (A) Wind is not a major factor in shaping the Martian landscape.
- (B) The physical environments on Earth and Mars have nothing in common.
- (C) Large and lasting dust storms on Mars are unusual occurrences.
- (D) Dust storms on Mars cannot be seen from Earth even with telescopes.

Paragraph 1 is marked with an arrow [➡].

3 The word "setback" in the passage is closest in meaning to

- (A) achievement
- (B) endeavor
- (C) obstacle
- (D) scheme

4 It can be inferred from paragraph 2 that Mariner 9

- (A) was not originally intended to map the Martian landscape
- (B) was less sophisticated than its predecessor, Mariner 8
- (C) experienced some technical malfunctions due to the dust storm
- (D) lost communication with NASA during its approach to Mars

Paragraph 2 is marked with an arrow [➡].

5 The word "murky" in the passage is closest in meaning to

(A) pristine

(B) obscure

(C) faulty

(D) apparent

6 Why does the author mention "Hellas Planitia" in the passage?

(A) To show that craters are common throughout the southern hemisphere of Mars

(B) To identify the location of emerging storms using a clear geographical landmark

(C) To suggest that the displacement of dust may have been caused by an impact

(D) To pinpoint the spot at which the cold polar air met the warm equatorial air

7 According to paragraph 4, the photographs from the MOC ultimately allowed scientists to comprehend that

(A) extensive dust storms on Mars are common but do not happen every year

(B) global dust storms arise exclusively in Mars's northern regions

(C) the vast majority of small disturbances do not result in large-scale storms

(D) multiple local outbreaks can combine quickly to form global dust storms

Paragraph 4 is marked with an arrow [➡].

8 The phrase "for the sake of" in the passage is closest in meaning to

(A) in response to

(B) in accordance with

(C) by means of

(D) for the purpose of

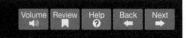

9 Look at the four squares [■] that indicate where the following sentence could be added to the passage.

However, one of them impacted only a single hemisphere, and another affected both hemispheres but was not fully planetary in scale like the one in 1971.

Where would the sentence best fit?

> Click on a square [■] to add the sentence to the passage.

10 Directions: An introductory sentence for a brief summary of the passage is provided below. Complete the summary by selecting the THREE answer choices that express the most important ideas in the passage. Some sentences do not belong in the summary because they express ideas that are not presented in the passage or are minor ideas in the passage. **This question is worth 2 points.**

> Drag your answer choices to the spaces where they belong.
> To remove an answer choice, click on it. To review the passage, click on **View Text**.

Observations with telescopes and later expeditions led scientists to develop an interest in learning more about dust storms on Mars.

- ●
- ●
- ●

Answer Choices

(A) The first mission to study dust storms on Mars was hampered by technical difficulties as one spacecraft failed to launch, so the other had to gather all of the data.

(B) During the 1970s, NASA conducted several missions to Mars and observed a few large dust storms, including one of global scale.

(C) Despite sponsoring numerous missions to Mars, NASA was unable to gather conclusive evidence of a dust storm actually covering the planet.

(D) Missions undertaken during the early twenty-first century revealed a wealth of information about the scale of dust storms and also where and how they form.

(E) Not only are scientists interested in the dust storms for scientific reasons but they are also motivated by practical concerns related to current and future expeditions.

(F) Measurements made by high-tech equipment have led scientists to the conclusion that dust storms on Mars are not as severe as those on Earth.

Answer Book p. 5

Answer Book p. 6

TOEFL Reading

Genetically Modified Organisms

For centuries, humans have been modifying the genetic makeup of plants and animals through selective breeding, resulting in the enhancement of desirable traits in modern-day domesticated species, such as sweetness in corn and speed in racehorses. To achieve favorable results with traditional breeding methods can take many reproductive cycles and is often tremendously time consuming and laborious. However, recent advances in biotechnology afford a more expedient 5 means of genetic modification. Desirable genes from a donor organism can be transferred directly to a host organism so that the resulting genetically modified organism (GMO) expresses the selected trait.

➡ The prospective environmental benefits imparted by GMOs cannot be dismissed. Modifying crop species to resist insect pests reduces or altogether eliminates the need for chemical 10 pesticides. For example, scientists have effectively transferred the toxin-producing genes of Bt, a soil-dwelling bacterium, to corn. Previous efforts to selectively breed corn varieties that exhibit resistance to pests such as the European corn borer, an insect that causes extensive damage to crops and decreases yields, had been only moderately successful. Farmers were thus forced to protect their corn from harmful pests by spraying them with insecticides, the environmentally 15 destructive effects of which have been well documented. However, since Bt manufactures toxic proteins that kill the corn borer, transferring Bt genes to corn allows the Bt-modified corn to produce its own defensive proteins against the pests without the need for excessive chemical pesticides. Cultivation of Bt corn has resulted in a sharp decrease in global pesticide use; application of pesticides has decreased by fifty million kilograms per year worldwide since 1995 20 when Bt corn was first introduced.

➡ Genetically modified plants not only reduce the use of harmful chemicals by farmers, but they also may be more resistant to crop-damaging insects than chemically treated ones, and, as fewer plants are lost to pests, crop yields increase. With the world's population predicted to double by 2050, finding ways to increase food production is expected to become one of the most 25 critical issues facing humanity. And since pests are responsible for the destruction of an estimated 50 percent of all food grown on the planet, GMO advocates point to genetic modification of crops as a potential way to alleviate the problem.

➡ Yet, despite the myriad benefits associated with genetic modification, not everyone is enamored with the biotechnology revolution. In fact, many critics fiercely oppose any genetic 30 modification of living things, derisively referring to GMOs as "Frankenstein food." **A** They argue that it is far too soon to assume that GMOs are safe since sufficient time has not passed for long-term studies on the impact on human health. **B** Moreover, they fear that modified organisms could spread outside of agricultural areas and breed with wild organisms, resulting in genetic pollution of the natural world. **C** They also point to scientific studies that have demonstrated 35 negative effects in animals that were fed a strict GMO diet; symptoms have included weakened

immune systems, stunted growth, and diminished reproductive health. **D**

➡ While opponents of GMOs have frequently publicized this research along with their concerns about the safety of the practice, supporters of GMOs assert that no scientific studies have confirmed any ill effects on humans. In fact, most agriculturalists and researchers have expressed ⁴⁰ frustration at the widespread popular opposition to GMOs, which they view as unscientific and ultimately detrimental to human health. This is because, while opponents advocate a complete ban on genetic food alteration, food shortages continue unabated around the world.

1 Which of the sentences below best expresses the essential information in the highlighted sentence in the passage? *Incorrect* choices change the meaning in important ways or leave out essential information.

- Ⓐ People have long been selectively breeding domestic plants and animals to express certain desirable characteristics.
- Ⓑ The prevalence of certain qualities in cultivated organisms is a consequence of natural selection over centuries.
- Ⓒ Enhanced sweetness in corn and increased speed in racehorses are results of genetic modification using modern technology.
- Ⓓ For many years, people have been enhancing the genetic makeup of plants and animals for the purpose of domesticating them.

2 The word "laborious" in the passage is closest in meaning to

- Ⓐ indigenous   Ⓑ lonesome   Ⓒ expeditious   Ⓓ arduous

3 According to paragraph 2, what are TWO characteristics of Bt corn? Choose TWO answers.

- Ⓐ It has been modified using a gene from a bacterium found in the ground.
- Ⓑ Its ability to resist pests is the result of years of selective breeding.
- Ⓒ It has the capacity to manufacture proteins that kill harmful bacteria.
- Ⓓ Its use has played a role in reducing global pesticide usage.

Paragraph 2 is marked with an arrow [➡].

4 The word "ones" in the passage refers to

- Ⓐ plants   Ⓑ chemicals   Ⓒ farmers   Ⓓ insects

5 According to paragraph 3, why is food production expected to become a serious concern?

    Ⓐ The percentage of arable land is predicted to decrease by 50 percent in the next few decades.

    Ⓑ Pests will likely adapt rapidly enough to wipe out any increase in yields from using GMOs.

    Ⓒ The number of people in the world is forecast to be twice its current size by the middle of the twenty-first century.

    Ⓓ Damaging insects have the potential to become far more numerous due to global warming.

Paragraph 3 is marked with an arrow [➡].

6 The word "myriad" in the passage is closest in meaning to

    Ⓐ sensible

    Ⓑ foreseeable

    Ⓒ innumerable

    Ⓓ formidable

7 Why does the author discuss scientific studies in paragraphs 4 and 5?

    Ⓐ To indicate that GMOs have negative effects on animals

    Ⓑ To suggest that GMOs pollute the natural gene pool

    Ⓒ To emphasize that the benefits of GMOs have been confirmed

    Ⓓ To show that the safety of GMOs is subject to debate

Paragraphs 4 and 5 are marked with arrows [➡].

8 What can be inferred from paragraph 5 about agriculturalists and researchers?

    Ⓐ Few of them believe GMOs are better than conventional crops.

    Ⓑ Most of them are opposed to raising controversial GMO food crops.

    Ⓒ The majority of them are in favor of incorporating GMOs into food production.

    Ⓓ Some of them support a complete ban on the use of GMO crops.

Paragraph 5 is marked with an arrow [➡].

9 Look at the four squares [■] that indicate where the following sentence could be added to the passage.

This concern is not unfounded, as genetically modified crop plants have already been reported outside of their original confines.

Where would the sentence best fit?

Click on a square [■] to add the sentence to the passage.

10 Directions: An introductory sentence for a brief summary of the passage is provided below. Complete the summary by selecting the THREE answer choices that express the most important ideas in the passage. Some sentences do not belong in the summary because they express ideas that are not presented in the passage or are minor ideas in the passage. **This question is worth 2 points.**

Drag your answer choices to the spaces where they belong.
To remove an answer choice, click on it. To review the passage, click on **View Text**.

Genetically modified organisms offer numerous advantages over traditional crop breeds, but some people have raised safety concerns.

- ●
- ●
- ●

Answer Choices

(A) Since modifying the genetic structure of crops will result in greater food production, it is widely regarded as the most effective way to solve the pressing issue of global hunger.

(B) GMOs contribute to a healthier environment because they reduce the amount of damaging chemicals that farmers apply to crops.

(C) Since Bt corn is far more resistant to pests than unmodified corn, scientists expect that its cultivation will result in a drastic cutback in worldwide pesticide usage.

(D) Critics of genetically modified food are not enthusiastic about the agricultural revolution, citing studies that show GMOs have long-term negative effects on human health.

(E) Genetic modification increases food production by making plants more resilient to pest infestation, thereby increasing crop yields.

(F) Some people argue that genetically modified foods are detrimental to humans and the environment, although GMO advocates contest their claims.

Answer Book p. 6

Vocabulary Review

A. Fill in the blanks with the appropriate words from the box.

conduit	unabated	subsist
undisputed	dormant	preeminent

1 He was the _____ literary scholar of his day, having won several awards in his field.

2 The alumni office acts as a(n) _____ between the university and its former students.

3 That the painting is a fine example of expressionism is _____; the only controversy is whether it is the finest ever made.

4 If carbon emissions continue _____, the planet will likely endure more regular instances of extreme weather.

5 Raccoons have been known to _____ on human garbage through the winter.

6 While bears are _____ during the winter months, they do not technically hibernate because their body temperature remains constant during their period of inactivity.

B. Choose the closest meaning for each highlighted word or phrase.

7 The dinosaurs disappeared suddenly after having dominated the earth during the preceding 165 million years.
(A) progressive   (B) latter   (C) previous   (D) subsequent

8 In an authoritarian country, the dissemination of propaganda to the masses is fairly common.
(A) opposition   (B) transmission   (C) rejection   (D) admission

9 I was hired for the position at the bank because of my impressive credentials.
(A) treatments   (B) approaches   (C) opportunities   (D) qualifications

10 While education was once a prerogative of the wealthy, scholarships now provide opportunities for people of all classes.
(A) privilege   (B) regret   (C) choice   (D) dilemma

11 Even though I had known the twins for years, I could still discern no difference between them.
(A) propose   (B) associate   (C) perpetuate   (D) differentiate

12 Constant exposure to sunlight is known to be detrimental to skin health.
(A) exhausting   (B) harmful   (C) essential   (D) indifferent

13 Due to his speech impairment, the stutterer was unable to convey the urgency of the situation.
(A) proficiency   (B) collapse   (C) advantage   (D) disability

14 Despite their respective talents, the individual players somehow failed to coalesce into a championship-winning team.
(A) represent   (B) focus   (C) fuse   (D) cultivate

CHAPTER 02

Reference

Reference

About the Question Type

Reference questions ask you to identify what the highlighted word or phrase refers to in the passage.

The highlighted word or phrase is usually a pronoun (*it, they, this*, etc.). The correct answer choice will be the noun that the highlighted word or phrase refers to. The incorrect answer choices will be nouns that appear in the preceding sentences but are not referred to by the highlighted word or phrase.

Question Format

- The word "_____" in the passage refers to

- The phrase "_____" in the passage refers to

Key Strategies

- **Step 1** — Read the sentence that contains the highlighted word or phrase and the sentences that immediately precede it.

- **Step 2** — Find the noun that the highlighted word or phrase refers to. Determining whether the highlighted word or phrase is singular or plural can make it easier to identify its referent.

- **Step 3** — Substitute your answer choice for the highlighted word or phrase, and confirm that it makes sense.

Example

Know-Nothing Movement

In the 1840s, a large number of immigrants coming into America triggered the formation of an anti-immigrant movement known as the Know-Nothing Movement. Its members were not allowed to talk about their secret organization. The group earned the nickname "Know Nothings" because whenever its members were questioned about their organization, they would usually say, "I know nothing." 5

Many of the native-born Americans who were the descendants of the early settlers opposed immigrants for their sheer numbers and their willingness to work for meager wages. Others simply did not trust the more recent arrivals because everything about them was different—their appearance, language, customs, and religion. A number of secret anti-immigrant organizations were formed, and, essentially, their purpose was to combat what they considered foreign 10 influences and to uphold what they believed was the established American way of life. The Know-Nothing Movement was the most successful of these.

By the 1850s, the Know-Nothing Movement had attracted followers in many states and placed 43 members in Congress. In an effort to take over the leadership of the country, the group selected Millard Fillmore as its candidate for the 1856 presidential election. However, 15 this objective could not be attained, due in large part to the nationwide debate over slavery. People who opposed slavery voted for the Republican candidate, while those who supported it cast their votes for the Democratic representative. Choosing to remain neutral on the issue, Fillmore performed extremely poorly in the election. Following this failure, the influence of the Know-Nothing Movement began to decline. 20

---

1 The word "their" in the passage refers to

(A) native-born Americans
(B) descendants
(C) early settlers
(D) immigrants

2 The word "they" in the passage refers to

(A) arrivals   (B) customs   (C) organizations   (D) influences

3 The phrase "this objective" in the passage refers to

(A) attracting followers in many states
(B) placing 43 members in Congress
(C) taking over leadership of the country
(D) selecting a candidate for an election

Reading Practice 1

Answer Book p. 8

Desert Hydrology

Almost one third of the planet's surface is covered by extensive areas of exposed soil that are largely devoid of vegetation. Known as deserts, these ecosystems can be found anywhere on Earth, although they are most common in the mid-latitudes, which are located between the tropics and the polar regions. There is a great deal of variance in temperatures between different desert types. However, a defining feature of all is a lack of rainfall, with most of these areas receiving less than 250 millimeters 5 per year.

Despite their aridity, deserts have long been home to human population groups, with inhabitants usually adopting nomadic lifestyles to cope with the harsh conditions they encounter. But, as the population of adjacent regions continues to rise, desert ecosystems are increasingly being utilized for the purpose of agriculture, placing increased pressure on the limited water available. Consequently, it 10 has become imperative to maximize the efficiency with which available water sources are utilized, as well as to develop and exploit reservoirs of this resource that have until now remained untapped.

The most important sources of water in most arid areas are ephemeral river systems, which are actually just intermittent streams that are formed as a result of flash floods. **A** Although deserts receive minimal precipitation, when rain does occur it is likely to be quite heavy, with the entire annual 15 rainfall taking place over a very brief period of time. **B** This results in the rapid erosion of channels that will continue to serve as conduits for any future floods. **C** While the high probability that specific geographic locations will be deluged every year makes them an integral part of the existence of many desert dwellers, the sporadic nature of these streams significantly limits their utility. **D**

Perennial rivers are water sources with a much greater potential for application, especially regarding 20 the requirements of large populations. River systems such as these, including the Nile, the Tigris, and the Euphrates, are all characterized by the fact that they are replenished by sources outside of the desert environment. In the case of the Nile, seasonal rains in the African Equatorial Lake Region are augmented by the monsoons that occur in the highlands of Sudan to create a flow that continues year round. The same pattern holds true for the Tigris-Euphrates river system, which depends on 25 the winter snowmelt of the Taurus and Zagros mountains. The importance of these rivers to desert communities cannot be overstated, and, in fact, many of the earliest known civilizations arose along their banks.

Yet, dependence on these rivers limits human habitation to the narrow swaths of fertile land along their edges, as it is a challenge to transport the water any significant distance from the original course 30 of the river. Recently, there has been an increased focus on the aquifers deep below the surface of the planet and recognition of the need to develop technologies and methods to enable the utilization of these water sources. Many scientists believe that access to these caches of water could vastly increase the desert's capacity to support human life. People have made limited use of these in the past because a significant portion of the water either is located too far below the surface or contains elevated levels 35 of salt. It is hoped that improvements in drilling techniques, combined with advances in desalinization technologies, will enable this important resource to be used in the future.

Glossary
· aquifer: a layer of rock or sand underneath the surface of the earth that contains water

1 The word "they" in the passage refers to

(A) deserts

(B) inhabitants

(C) nomadic lifestyles

(D) the harsh conditions

2 According to paragraph 2, why is there increased pressure on desert water resources?

(A) The areas that border the ecosystem are becoming more populous.

(B) More and more people are shifting to a nomadic way of life.

(C) The efficiency of water usage in the area has increased significantly.

(D) The number of reservoirs that are suitable for human use is limited.

3 Look at the four squares [■] that indicate where the following sentence could be added to the passage.

This drawback is compounded by the difficulties associated with the long-term storage of water in a desert environment.

Where would the sentence best fit?

4 The word "their" in the passage refers to

(A) the Taurus and Zagros mountains

(B) these rivers

(C) desert communities

(D) the earliest known civilizations

5 According to paragraph 4, what is the defining trait of a perennial river system?

(A) It is surrounded by many large human settlements.

(B) It is restricted to regions that are flooded annually.

(C) It is supplemented by seasonal rainfall in the higher altitudes.

(D) It is supplied with moisture from non-arid regions.

6 According to paragraph 5, what are TWO reasons that people have made limited use of the water in aquifers in the past? Choose TWO answers.

(A) A substantial part of it is deep underground.

(B) Most of it disappears in the dry season.

(C) Much of it contains manmade pollution.

(D) A large amount of it has high quantities of salt.

Reading Practice 2

Women's Suffrage Movement

Suffrage, or the right of citizens to vote for candidates to represent them in government, is generally extended to all adult citizens in modern democracies. However, voting rights were at one time far more restricted, with women not being permitted to vote.

For most of England's history, voting rights were reserved for males who owned property of a certain value, and women were perpetually prevented from participating in elections. The issue of ⁵ women's right to vote was sometimes raised. However, it was not until the Reform Act of 1832, which made sweeping changes to the electoral system but failed to extend voting rights to women, that the women's suffrage movement began to develop significant momentum. In response to the legislation, many wealthy women argued that any person who owned property and thereby paid taxes should not be excluded from the democratic process. ¹⁰

Initially, suffrage groups were local in nature, springing up in various communities, both rural and urban, across England. In 1897, Millicent Fawcett, a leading campaigner for equal rights for women, established the National Union of Women's Suffrage Societies (NUWSS). It brought together several smaller organizations and provided the first public forum for the growing number of property-holding women in England to voice their desire to be enfranchised. ¹⁵

One of the groups included in the NUWSS was the London-based Women's Franchise League, which had, under the leadership of Emmeline Pankhurst, already won voting rights for women in elections for local offices. As time went on, however, and with no further progress having been made, she became increasingly impatient and, in 1903, founded a breakaway organization called the Women's Social and Political Union (WSPU). Unlike the NUWSS, Pankhurst's organization excluded men but ²⁰ recruited more working-class women; the organization demanded rights for all women, regardless of marital or social status. The tactics of the WSPU members were militant: campaigns involved deliberate acts of violence against members of Parliament as well as government buildings and other public structures that they believed represented agents of women's oppression. Some members were destroying property and chaining themselves to the gates of Parliament. ²⁵

In America, women organized under the National American Woman Suffrage Association (NAWSA) were as interested in suffrage as their English counterparts but were much less confrontational than the WSPU. Their lobbying efforts, spearheaded by Susan B. Anthony, were also distinguished by the fact that they did not include the ownership of property as a prerequisite for suffrage, as the right to vote was considered a basic individual right that should not be limited to landowners. In addition, ³⁰ Anthony quickly distanced herself from Pankhurst's militant acts; she championed amendments to the Constitution and peaceful acts of civil disobedience. When the Nineteenth Amendment was ratified in 1920, granting the right to vote to all persons regardless of sex, it was due, in no small part, to the writing, petitions, and protests of Anthony and her collaborators.

Pankhurst, on the other hand, would struggle for eight more years before all disenfranchised ³⁵ English women earned the right to vote. Some historians believe that the militancy of the WSPU soured the earlier efforts of Fawcett and her contemporaries; others maintain that Pankhurst's actions were instrumental in achieving universal suffrage in England and, without them, no change would have been implemented.

Glossary

·enfranchise: to grant a right to vote

1 According to paragraph 2, how did many rich women respond to the Reform Act of 1832?

(A) They were angry about the effect the law had on taxation.

(B) They argued that voting rights should be extended to all adult women.

(C) They insisted that all property owners be allowed to vote.

(D) They were satisfied by the changes to the electoral system.

2 The word "their" in the passage refers to

(A) various communities

(B) equal rights

(C) smaller organizations

(D) property-holding women

3 The word "they" in the passage refers to

(A) WSPU members

(B) deliberate acts

(C) members of Parliament

(D) public structures

4 According to paragraph 4, what was a difference between the NUWSS and the WSPU?

(A) The NUWSS had a significantly larger membership.

(B) The NUWSS recruited more working-class women.

(C) The WSPU did not allow males in the organization.

(D) The WSPU excluded women who were not married.

5 According to paragraph 5, what differentiates the American suffrage movement from the NUWSS?

(A) It did not view suffrage as a right that was restricted to property owners.

(B) It held those who committed acts of violence in contempt.

(C) It was politically aligned with several other groups who were seeking enfranchisement.

(D) It employed strategies that attempted to earn the respect of government officials.

6 The word "instrumental" in the passage is closest in meaning to

(A) essential

(B) pervasive

(C) successive

(D) drastic

Reading Practice 3

Mountain Climates

Most meteorologists are conscious of major climatological influences, such as tropical storms or urban heat islands. But they also stress that local weather patterns are additionally affected by smaller-scale phenomena related to regional wind patterns, topographical features, and location. For this reason, the experts have developed a system of general classification that can help explain overarching characteristics present in particular biomes. 5

One regional category is the North American mountain climate system, which describes the prevailing weather found in alpine regions and surrounding valleys. The presence of any significant landmass can cause a temperature gradient of as much as 28 degrees Celsius between north- and south-facing slopes. Consequently, regions shaded by a north face tend to support cool, wet spruce forests, while a walk to the other side reveals an arid microclimate, usually bearing aspen and poplar 10 trees.

This temperature change is the end result of a couple of factors. The first of these is latitude, which describes the angle at which land is exposed to the Sun's rays. At the equator, for example, sunlight strikes the planet nearly perpendicular to the surface, but as one moves farther north, the angle becomes increasingly shallow. Therefore, any mountainous range located in the Northern Hemisphere 15 receives light at a maximum 66.5 degree angle, never from straight above, and the north face becomes the sheltered side. This explains why the Rockies, situated along the continental divide, facilitate a wide range of boreal ecosystems that display great divergence in plant species depending on the relative positions of slopes.

The second factor is elevation. Higher terrain is dramatically affected by solar radiation, so any 20 surface exposed to the sun quickly heats up; however, surfaces in the shade remain cold. Thus, the presence of sunlight or shade directly contributes to the temperature gradient in the air at high elevations. This difference in solar radiation is one of the main reasons why remnant northern face glaciers have been able to survive the trend of global warming; they melt at a slower rate than others. The Columbia Icefield, for instance, is a thick ice mass that covers an elevated plateau in Jasper 25 National Park in Canada and remains a stable glacier because it is shielded by three-quarters of the highest peaks. Furthermore, as elevation increases, barometric pressure is reduced, and because a less dense atmosphere has lower heat retention capabilities, there is an accompanying decrease in temperature roughly equivalent to one or two degrees for every 300 meters ascended. An increasing impact of winds accents this variance in temperature as winds are colder at high altitudes and lower 30 regions are sheltered from icy winds.

The movement of winds also profoundly affects the moisture levels in the mountainous regions. In Western Canada, the prevailing winds originate off the coast of British Columbia and sweep inward toward the prairies. They are forced over the Rockies, and as the air rises, it cools and condenses. Clouds form, and vapor precipitates out on the western slopes in substantial quantities, enough to 35 support the country's only tracts of temperate rainforests. As the air pushes further eastward, it is depleted of moisture, creating a rain shadow effect, whereby the eastern slopes receive very little rainfall. The remaining dry air descends, heating up to a temperature as high as 30 degrees Celsius in just a short period of time.

1 According to paragraph 3, latitude is related to

(A) the diameter of Earth's orbit

(B) a calculation of accumulated sunlight

(C) the distance between the equator and a mountain

(D) the incline of Earth's surface toward the Sun

2 The word "it" in the passage refers to

(A) The Columbia Icefield

(B) elevated plateau

(C) Jasper National Park

(D) Canada

3 The author's description of the effect of solar radiation on higher terrain mentions all of the following EXCEPT

(A) the accelerated rate at which surfaces get warmer

(B) the role of shade in keeping the ground cool

(C) the variance in air temperature at different elevations

(D) the increase in barometric pressure

4 According to paragraph 4, what is true of a less dense atmosphere at higher elevations?

(A) Its barometric pressure fluctuates.

(B) It leads to glaciers melting at a faster rate.

(C) It is less affected by solar radiation.

(D) Its capacity to retain heat is reduced.

5 The word "They" in the passage refers to

(A) moisture levels

(B) mountainous regions

(C) prevailing winds

(D) prairies

6 According to paragraph 5, which of the following is true of the rain shadow effect in Western Canada?

(A) It causes clouds to form and substantial rains to fall on the eastern slopes.

(B) It results in drier air on the east side of the mountains.

(C) It is amplified by strong winds sweeping in from the prairies.

(D) It is responsible for severe droughts that occur throughout British Columbia.

iBT Reading Test 1

TOEFL Reading

Health Benefits of Soy

➡ The extent to which the health-care sector has been able to ameliorate suffering from disease in developed countries has been constrained by the inability to eliminate several illnesses, including certain types of cancer and heart disease, and the fact that they have become increasingly prevalent. Medical professionals recognize 5 a multiplicity of causes for these conditions, and extensive analysis has been conducted on the genetic, environmental, and behavioral factors that contribute to their development.

An avenue of study that has garnered a great deal of interest is the relationship between certain foods and disease prevention. One such food is soy, a member of the legume family, 10 which has been extensively cultivated throughout Asia for over 13,000 years and has become a dietary staple of many Asian nations. Initially domesticated in northern China, the crop had been disseminated throughout southern China, Korea, Japan, Southeast Asia, and India by the first century AD. The success of this agricultural product can be in part attributed to its texture, which makes it adaptable to an assortment of culinary styles. It can be consumed in its natural state, in 15 the form of whole soybeans or soy sprouts, or processed into tofu, milk, and flour.

In countries such as China and Japan, which have the highest rates of soy consumption, incidences of certain types of cancer are dramatically lower than in North America, where animal proteins are ingested more regularly. Soybeans contain compounds that have been identified as anticarcinogens, and while many of these substances are available in other sources of nutrition, 20 particularly in plant-based foods, soybeans are the only known source of isoflavones, which are structurally similar to estrogen. This close relationship enables isoflavones to bind to estrogen receptors in the body, thereby dampening the physical effects of this hormone. As both breast and prostate cancer are hormonally triggered, isoflavones effectively inhibit the expansion of these malignant growths. 25

➡ Soy-based food products have been shown to lower both cholesterol and blood pressure, factors that are significant contributors to heart disease. **A** There are two types of cholesterol produced in the human body: Low-Density Lipoprotein (LDL), which is harmful, and High-Density Lipoprotein (HDL), which is beneficial. **B** The evidence suggests a strong correlation between the consumption of soy and a reduction of LDL levels. **C** This results from the manner in which soy 30 fibers bond with the bile salts generated by the liver as it processes this LDL cholesterol. **D** The bonding facilitates the elimination of waste products, allowing the liver to increase its capacity.

➡ In addition to these specific ailments, the medicinal properties of soy are useful in the treatment of the wide variety of health issues faced by women during and after menopause, which stem from the dramatic drop in estrogen production that occurs at this stage of life. It 35

has long been recognized that women in regions where soy products are a dietary staple do not seem to suffer the negative physical effects of menopause to the same degree as their Western counterparts. The reason for this is again related to the estrogenic properties of the isoflavones, which provide enough stimulation to the receptors of those with lower estrogen levels to alleviate common symptoms such as hot flashes, fatigue, and depression. For many women, 40 the consumption of soy has proven to be an alternative to more extreme treatments, such as hormonal replacement therapy, demonstrating that a carefully regulated diet is an important component of health management.

Glossary	☒

anticarcinogen: a substance that inhibits the development of cancer

1 The word "ameliorate" in the passage is closest in meaning to

Ⓐ mitigate   Ⓑ worsen   Ⓒ terminate   Ⓓ emphasize

2 The word "their" in the passage refers to

Ⓐ professionals   Ⓑ causes   Ⓒ conditions   Ⓓ factors

3 Which of the following can be inferred from paragraph 1 about certain types of cancer and heart disease?

Ⓐ They have been eradicated by doctors in several advanced countries.

Ⓑ They are limited to those people who possess certain hereditary traits.

Ⓒ They have affected more patients in recent years than in the past.

Ⓓ They are easily treated once the causal agent has been identified.

Paragraph 1 is marked with an arrow [➡].

4 Why does the author mention "the highest rates of soy consumption" in the passage?

Ⓐ To specify the most common protein sources in Asia

Ⓑ To demonstrate the superiority of the typical Eastern diet

Ⓒ To highlight the role of diet in susceptibility to some cancers

Ⓓ To compare the respective disease rates of China and Japan

5 Which of the sentences below best expresses the essential information in the highlighted sentence in the passage? *Incorrect* choices change the meaning in important ways or leave out essential information.

(A) Although most of the cancer-fighting compounds in soy are found in other foods, isoflavones occur only in soy.

(B) The elements of the soybean that fight cancer are not unique, although the estrogenic qualities of the isoflavones are usually not found in vegetables.

(C) Although isoflavones are considered important, there are many other nutrients found in soybeans that have also proven effective against cancer.

(D) While many edible materials are utilized to prevent cancer, vegetables such as the soybean contain isoflavones that imitate estrogen.

6 The word "correlation" in the passage is closest in meaning to

(A) antagonism

(B) association

(C) distinction

(D) balance

7 According to paragraph 4, how does soy reduce the amount of harmful cholesterol in the body?

(A) Soy transforms the cholesterol into a material that is less dangerous.

(B) Soy improves the function of the organ that processes the cholesterol.

(C) Soy disrupts the production of cholesterol by destroying certain byproducts.

(D) Soy produces a substance that absorbs and eradicates the cholesterol.

Paragraph 4 is marked with an arrow [➡].

8 According to paragraph 5, why are isoflavones effective in the treatment of the symptoms of menopause?

(A) They reduce the amount of estrogen generated by the body.

(B) They allow estrogen to easily circulate in the body.

(C) They compensate for the decrease in estrogen production.

(D) They encourage the creation of estrogen in the body.

Paragraph 5 is marked with an arrow [➡].

9 Look at the four squares [■] that indicate where the following sentence could be added to the passage.

The dangerous form is commonly produced as the result of bad dietary habits, such as eating large amounts of fatty foods.

Where would the sentence best fit?

Click on a square [■] to add the sentence to the passage.

10 Directions: An introductory sentence for a brief summary of the passage is provided below. Complete the summary by selecting the THREE answer choices that express the most important ideas in the passage. Some sentences do not belong in the summary because they express ideas that are not presented in the passage or are minor ideas in the passage. **This question is worth 2 points.**

Drag your answer choices to the spaces where they belong.
To remove an answer choice, click on it. To review the passage, click on **View Text**.

The soybean is a versatile source of nutrition that has many health benefits.

- ●
- ●
- ●

Answer Choices

(A) The characteristics of isoflavones that are similar to estrogen result in a reduction in the negative effects of menopause.

(B) The production of estrogen in the body is often stimulated by the consumption of tofu and other foods that contain soy.

(C) Isoflavones have been shown to be able to prevent certain types of cancer.

(D) The ability of the liver to process LDL is augmented by certain aspects of soy-based food products.

(E) The soybean is the only known source of the many types of cancer-fighting substances it contains.

(F) The replacement of hormones in menopausal women is facilitated by the ingestion of soy.

Answer Book p. 11

Answer Book p. 12

Merce Cunningham

➡ Before 1950, dance choreography tended to stress a tightly scripted performance with stage construction, musical accompaniment, and movements designed together to relay a theatrical narrative. **A** Classical ballet, which permeated the public consciousness, was the standard dance form; however, methods of composition, as well as attitudes toward setting and music evolved rapidly throughout the early twentieth century as several choreographers began experimenting with improvisational techniques. **B** Instructors who subscribed to this new approach, including Martha Graham and Jerome Robbins, encouraged their students to move freely based on basic instructions. **C** This venturesome period, in turn, fostered an entire generation of performers keen on abandoning the confines of traditional ballet to produce fresh and innovative works. **D** Merce Cunningham, in particular, is considered the most pioneering and talented dancer to come of age during this time.

➡ Taking up dancing at a young age, Cunningham grew up performing with a number of repertory companies, including the Martha Graham Dance Company, to audiences throughout Oregon and California. But he soon revealed himself as a virtuoso lead by incorporating modern dance techniques into roles he created on his own. His works de-emphasized the presence of Pas de Deux, the standard narrative of ballet, consisting of a short introduction, dramatic dances by male and female ballet dancers, followed by a conclusion that repeated themes from earlier in the performance. In fact, Cunningham removed the concept of storytelling altogether and focused on the tension evoked by the movements themselves, infuriating many critics but impressing others. Cunningham's approach to dance was influenced by Dadaism, an art movement that called for the need to shift away from traditional art forms and to embrace free-spirited creation based on commonplace objects and actions. Years later, Cunningham explained that observations of everyday movements, such as a cat stretching or a man stepping off a curb, inspired him early in his career.

➡ Dadaism also played out in Cunningham's use of chance in his choreography and the relationship between his movements and the integrated aural and visual atmosphere. Encouraged by both Albert Einstein's declaration that there are no fixed points in space and the work of avant-garde composer John Cage, Cunningham developed a method known as Chance Operations. Using dice, cards, coins, or other probability devices, he determined the type and repetition of movements at random. Meanwhile, a musician was invited to write a score, and a set designer created a visual environment, all in isolation. In this sense, Cunningham avoided traditional collaborative approaches; the elements were united only during the premiere performance on stage in front of a live audience. Those works that received immediate acclaim were kept and performed again, and those that did not were dropped from the repertoire.

It should not be assumed, however, that because Cunningham encouraged his dancers to make impromptu movements, his final works were completely spontaneous. On the contrary, all the steps of his performances were carefully planned out and drilled so that the dancers knew exactly where they were supposed to be at each moment. That way, Cunningham could record them in standard dance notation, and they could be performed again by the same performers or another troupe. This also served to legitimize his Chance Operations as a true choreographic method, one that opens up options for all choreographers and at the same time ensures that they maintained a high quality of standards in their work. 35

40

1 The word "permeated" in the passage is closest in meaning to

(A) distracted

(B) compelled

(C) filled

(D) bothered

2 Which of the following can be inferred from paragraph 1 about choreography prior to the mid-twentieth century?

(A) It highlighted the skills of veteran performers over those of students.

(B) It was based on basic combinations taught visually by an instructor.

(C) It did not emphasize spontaneous creativity during performances.

(D) It had fallen out of favor with contemporary audiences.

Paragraph 1 is marked with an arrow [➡].

3 The word "infuriating" in the passage is closest in meaning to

(A) appealing   (B) enraging   (C) obligating   (D) isolating

4 According to paragraph 2, Pas de Deux is

(A) a conclusion that resolves the plot of a performance

(B) a traditional form of choreography criticized by Merce Cunningham

(C) the suspense evoked between male and female ballet dancers

(D) the sequence in which traditional ballet told a story

Paragraph 2 is marked with an arrow [➡].

5 Why does the author mention Cunningham's observation of everyday movements in paragraph 2?

(A) To identify the source of his inspiration in his early career

(B) To explain why his choreography was not popular at the time

(C) To suggest that his performances depicted common situations

(D) To show that his style conformed with traditional expectations

Paragraph 2 is marked with an arrow [➡].

6 According to paragraph 3, all of the following are aspects of Chance Operations EXCEPT:

(A) All elements of the performance are created in seclusion.

(B) The selection of movements occurs without a definite pattern.

(C) Only praised works are retained for subsequent performance.

(D) Musicians and designers are invited to observe rehearsals.

Paragraph 3 is marked with an arrow [➡].

7 The word "them" in the passage refers to

(A) works   (B) steps   (C) performances   (D) dancers

8 Which of the sentences below best expresses the essential information in the highlighted sentence in the passage? *Incorrect* choices change the meaning in important ways or leave out essential information.

(A) Chance Operations provide choreographers with a real opportunity to promote the advantage of innovative pieces.

(B) The worth of Chance Operations is situated in its ability to help choreographers develop a new repertoire in a typical manner.

(C) Chance Operations were confirmed as a viable tool for choreographers to produce inventive works at a superior level.

(D) Chance Operations merit attention by choreographers who wish to produce excellent works using established criteria.

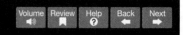
9 Look at the four squares [■] that indicate where the following sentence could be added to the passage.

These elements were constructed simultaneously by a group of people working in constant contact with one another.

Where would the sentence best fit?

Click on a square [■] to add the sentence to the passage.

10 Directions: An introductory sentence for a brief summary of the passage is provided below. Complete the summary by selecting the THREE answer choices that express the most important ideas in the passage. Some sentences do not belong in the summary because they express ideas that are not presented in the passage or are minor ideas in the passage. **This question is worth 2 points.**

Drag your answer choices to the spaces where they belong.
To remove an answer choice, click on it. To review the passage, click on **View Text**.

Merce Cunningham's experimentation with new forms of dance revolutionized the art of choreography.

- ●
- ●
- ●

Answer Choices

(A) Influenced by the Dada movement, he applied observations from everyday life as well as elements of chance in his choreography.

(B) His new randomly generated choreographic style isolated the three elements of performance and brought them back together on stage.

(C) Ideas from people as diverse as Albert Einstein and John Cage inspired Cunningham to develop a new approach to ballet.

(D) Cunningham's commitment to honoring traditional choreography assured that his work would be used by other choreographers.

(E) His pieces ignored the tradition of Pas de Deux by eliminating narrative themes from dances and focusing on improvisational techniques.

(F) He frequently collaborated with artists of other disciplines, including musicians and stage designers.

Answer Book p. 12

Vocabulary Review

A. **Fill in the blanks with the appropriate words from the box.**

divergence	confines	momentum
prerequisite	meager	prevailing

1 The court has restricted itself from challenging precedent, staying within the _____ of past decisions.

2 Jeff supplements his _____ income by working part-time at a café.

3 The candidate began to gain _____ in the polls, making victory seem possible after all.

4 The jurors had a sharp _____ of opinion on the defendant's guilt and were not able to agree on a verdict.

5 Appearing in several feature films was a _____ for membership in the organization of professional actors.

6 For almost 2,000 years before Copernicus, the idea that the Sun revolved around Earth was the _____ view.

B. **Choose the closest meaning for each highlighted word or phrase.**

7 The Alzheimer's patient grew so absentminded that losing her wallet became a commonplace occurrence.
   (A) disordered   (B) ordinary   (C) defining   (D) rare

8 The radio signal cut in and out, providing intermittent information about the developing storm.
   (A) crucial   (B) discouraging   (C) profound   (D) sporadic

9 The president made an impromptu appearance at the luncheon, startling many of the attendees.
   (A) spontaneous   (B) perfunctory   (C) gracious   (D) magnetic

10 The reduction of greenhouse gas emissions is imperative for the survival of the planet.
   (A) problematic   (B) necessary   (C) uncertain   (D) tentative

11 As the singer's health worsened, her musicians began to notice that she was perpetually late for rehearsals.
   (A) continually   (B) legally   (C) slightly   (D) previously

12 The death of the American dream was an overarching theme in the writer's work.
   (A) peculiar   (B) encompassing   (C) optimal   (D) emerging

13 Demand for gasoline continues to exceed supply, but for now the nation's oil reserves remain untapped.
   (A) commanding   (B) elusive   (C) precipitous   (D) untouched

14 Patients with Tourette's Syndrome are known to utter profanities at random throughout the day.
   (A) completely   (B) substantially   (C) arbitrarily   (D) amusingly

CHAPTER 03

Sentence Simplification

Sentence Simplification

About the Question Type

Sentence Simplification questions ask you to choose the sentence that best summarizes the highlighted sentence in the passage.

Incorrect choices often change the original meaning of the highlighted sentence or leave out essential information. Therefore, make sure that your answer choice paraphrases the key information of the sentence.

Question Format

Which of the sentences below best expresses the essential information in the highlighted sentence in the passage? *Incorrect* choices change the meaning in important ways or leave out essential information.

Key Strategies

- **Step 1** — Read the highlighted sentence in the passage and identify its essential information.

- **Step 2** — Select the answer choice that most accurately paraphrases the essential information of the sentence. Keep in mind that an answer choice that does not fully restate the essential information cannot be the correct one.

Example

Cloud Formation

Clouds form as the result of a cycle in which liquid water turns into a gas and is then transformed back into liquid droplets that become attached to particles in the air. The cycle begins with evaporation. Some of the water in oceans, lakes, and rivers changes into a gas called water vapor and rises into the atmosphere.

The water vapor in the atmosphere is converted back into liquid through condensation, which occurs in two ways. First, the air cannot hold an infinite amount of water vapor—when it becomes saturated, the excess water vapor has to change back into liquid form. Second, atmospheric vapor sometimes cools below the dew point and condenses into droplets of liquid water. [1]This process can be seen with a glass of ice water: the temperature in the glass is cooler than the dew point of the atmosphere, so the vapor surrounding the glass turns into liquid and clings to the glass.

The droplets of water in the air cling to particles such as dust or pollen. [2]The water droplets clinging to the particles cluster together into a cloud, but the droplets initially weigh so little that they remain suspended in the air, drifting with the wind instead of falling as rain. Only when the water droplets in the clouds combine into larger droplets do they fall as precipitation.

---

1 Which of the sentences below best expresses the essential information in the highlighted sentence in the passage?

(A) When the air is warmer than the water in a glass, the surrounding water vapor condenses into droplets on the glass.

(B) As the liquid clings to the glass of ice water, the temperature in the glass becomes cooler than the dew point.

(C) When the weather is hot, liquid water in a glass of ice water transforms into water vapor in the atmosphere, clinging to the glass.

(D) Water vapor present in the atmosphere condenses into droplets if the temperature on the outside of a glass of ice water is cooler.

2 Which of the sentences below best expresses the essential information in the highlighted sentence in the passage?

(A) As the water droplets increase in size and weight, they begin to form clusters around particles.

(B) The water droplets attached to particles that first form a cloud are not heavy enough to become rain.

(C) In order for water droplets to produce rain, they must absorb particles that are concentrated within a cloud.

(D) Because the water droplets in a cloud are so small, many of them are quickly dissipated by the wind.

Answer Book p. 14

Early Building Materials

Building construction emerged in prehistoric times as a practical means to moderate the effects of climate—essentially, to create a barrier between people and the elements. It originally started with rudimentary shelters created in natural structures, such as caves, and from found objects, such as tree branches and leaves. From those first makeshift shelters, humans gradually evolved to build free-standing structures, and these included not only dwellings but also buildings for food storage 5 and ceremonial functions. Still, for much of pre-agrarian history, most of these were meant to be used temporarily and thus were not constructed with long-term settlement in mind. However, with the advent of agriculture and the formation of permanent settlements, people began erecting buildings in a more systematic and organized manner and with a more complex set of natural and manmade materials. 10

[3]A widespread building technique that connected many Neolithic cultures was the manipulation of earth, usually in the form of baked or unbaked clay, and wood, typically small saplings, to erect simple edifices. The universality of the use of these natural materials for residential buildings, with examples ranging from the mud homes of the Middle East to the wooden longhouses of northern Europe, is attributable to their widespread availability, as well as the Stone Age tools available to early architects. 15 The classic example of this style is the wattle-and-daub method, in which young trees were cut and driven into the ground, and then tied together with fibers. This simple wall was then plastered with clay to provide added strength and weatherproofing.

But as civilizations became more advanced and cities grew, new methods appeared, and a significant one was the manufacture of brick. The use of brick for construction can be traced to the early 20 civilizations of the Fertile Crescent, and, by AD 1200, the technology had spread throughout Africa, Asia, and Europe. [5]Brick represented a substantial advancement in the development of architecture, as for the first time a functional and durable material was available that was both easy and inexpensive to produce, which made it particularly well suited for regions with large urban populations. Moreover, the prefabricated rectangular design made the bricks easy to stack vertically, so buildings of notable 25 size began to appear; in Mesopotamia, for instance, some temples made of masonry exceeded 25 meters in height.

By the Bronze Age, advances in metallurgy provided builders with metal tools, and, in turn, opened up the opportunity for the exploitation of timber and quarried stone. With metal tools, people in forested areas could fell large trees and use the timber for frames or, in the case of log homes, entire 30 buildings. Where timber was sparse and stone was plentiful, workers used hammers and chisels to painstakingly cut out massive chunks of stone from quarries. Quarried stone is differentiated from other natural materials by the fact that it requires a high level of skill and vast resources in terms of wealth and labor to be exploited, and these are usually only found in advanced cultures with well-developed economies. As a result, it has been employed almost exclusively for the construction of 35 public structures or the residences of the extremely affluent. The ancient Greeks made extensive use of limestone to build a wide range of religious and civil structures, including the Parthenon and the Temple of Hephaestus.

1 The word "moderate" in the passage is closest in meaning to

(A) trigger

(B) compensate

(C) alleviate

(D) replenish

2 According to paragraph 1, what was a characteristic of the majority of pre-agrarian buildings?

(A) They had a shape similar to a natural cavern.

(B) They were used for a limited period of time.

(C) They were designed for public ceremonies.

(D) They had extensive areas for storing goods.

3 Which of the sentences below best expresses the essential information in the highlighted sentence in the passage?

(A) Many Neolithic cultures utilized earth, typically baked or unbaked clay, in their simple buildings.

(B) As a building method, the use of earth and wood was not widespread prior to the Neolithic period.

(C) In Neolithic times, a common method of building basic structures was the use of earth and wood.

(D) Most Neolithic cultures had the same simple building technique because building materials were limited.

4 The word "their" in the passage refers to

(A) materials

(B) examples

(C) mud homes

(D) wooden longhouses

5 Which of the sentences below best expresses the essential information in the highlighted sentence in the passage?

(A) Regions with large cities were the primary places where brick production began to develop.

(B) Brick architecture developed rapidly in urban areas because it required far less labor.

(C) Because brick was practical and efficient to produce, it was a major step in architectural progress.

(D) Even though brick was durable and functional, its cost was prohibitive for use in big urban areas.

6 According to paragraph 4, all of the following are required to make use of stone EXCEPT

(A) significant funds

(B) great proficiency

(C) many workers

(D) international commerce

Redwoods

Extensive forests of giant redwoods once covered vast areas of Asia, Europe, and North America. Despite the considerable extent of their ancient range, all modern representatives of the giant trees now occupy a limited geographic area, primarily a narrow strip of the coast spanning northern California and southern Oregon. The 5 unique physiology of the redwood makes it particularly well suited for this ecological niche and has allowed it to maintain its position as the dominant form of vegetation in the region.

Redwoods have developed several evolutionary adaptations that assure their biological success, including the ability to reproduce both sexually and asexually. In the case of the former, seed 10 production may begin as early as ten to fifteen years of age, and each individual tree produces a large quantity of seeds annually. Although seed viability is quite low, with only 20 percent of the yearly yield being fertile and the rest consisting of empty shells, scientists speculate that this strategy may have a reproductive benefit. It serves as a means to discourage seed predators that are daunted by the time required to find the small proportion of edible seeds. 15

While sexual reproduction is the norm, physical stress may trigger the process of asexual replication, which results in multiple genetic copies of an individual tree. In the event that the parent has been knocked over, usually as the result of high winds, a series of new vegetative shoots will spring up along the length of the fallen trunk. The shoots may also sprout from the main trunk or the underlying root system in response to a dramatic worsening of the health of the original tree. In each 20 instance, a significant percentage of the shoots survive until maturity, due largely to the remarkable speed at which they grow, often averaging a meter per year for the first twenty years of their life cycle.

The massive size of the redwood necessitates an elaborate system to make certain the moisture and nutrients required for survival reach all areas of the tree. A redwood draws groundwater through its extensive root system into a network of internal conduits that is comparable to the vascular system of 25 the human body, and it uses variations in pressure to transport the fluid up the trunk. [4]On its own, it is unlikely that the system would be able to support the extreme vertical growth achieved by the redwood, as gravity places limits on the distance that moisture can be transported in this manner. However, the species has incorporated a unique adaptation to augment the water received through the primary underground root system. The redwood has evolved the capacity to utilize the moisture from 30 mist and rain by absorbing it directly through its needles and by way of specialized roots that actually rise up the trunk for this purpose.

The success of the redwood in the ecosystem is also facilitated by its imperviousness to the effects of fire. Once the tree matures, the bark begins to thicken, eventually developing into a substantial protective shell over eight centimeters deep. As wildfires are an annual occurrence in most forests, 35 this is a trait that provides the redwood with a significant advantage over most other plants. In addition, the charred remains of the burnt undergrowth enrich the soil and are an important source of nutrients. [6]Research into the redwood's dependence on fire for its survival has led scientists to reexamine the role that forest fires play in maintaining the overall health of other wooded areas.

1 According to paragraph 2, what is a potential advantage of low seed viability in redwoods?

(A) It hastens reproduction because animals distribute the seeds faster.

(B) It results in lower competition among germinating seedlings.

(C) It makes locating edible seeds more time consuming for predators.

(D) It allows the empty shells to enrich the forest floor with nutrients.

2 According to paragraph 3, what is the distinguishing characteristic of the saplings produced by asexual reproduction?

(A) They are clones of the original specimen.

(B) They grow rapidly after reaching maturity.

(C) They are produced by healthy trees.

(D) They cause physical damage to the parent.

3 The word "comparable" in the passage is closest in meaning to

(A) vulnerable   (B) responsible   (C) relevant   (D) analogous

4 Which of the sentences below best expresses the essential information in the highlighted sentence in the passage?

(A) The system is so efficient that it can successfully transport moisture vertically all the way up the redwood on its own.

(B) As the redwood becomes extremely tall, the system must overcome gravity in order to carry the water to the top of the tree.

(C) Due to the distance that moisture must travel to reach the vertical extremes of the redwood, gravity must be weaker than the system.

(D) The system probably could not move water up the great height of the redwood by itself due to limitations imposed by gravity.

5 The word "it" in the passage refers to

(A) redwood   (B) moisture   (C) mist   (D) rain

6 Which of the sentences below best expresses the essential information in the highlighted sentence in the passage?

(A) The need to better understand the influence of fires on this species has necessitated additional studies in other areas.

(B) The relationship between redwoods and forest fires has resulted in a plan to use flames to aid the growth of other species.

(C) The need to ensure that the redwoods thrive has prompted extensive research on the impact of forest fires on the region.

(D) As a result of studying fire dependence in redwoods, scientists are taking a closer look at how fires sustain forest health elsewhere.

Reading Practice 3

Wind and Water Erosion

Each year, millions of tourists visit the stunning natural wonder known as the Grand Canyon, a massive channel carved into the Colorado Plateau by the Colorado River and its tributaries. While geologists are certain that the ancient water system is responsible for the gorge's 1,600-meter depth and 466-kilometer length, its width, ranging from five to twenty kilometers, is more likely related to the combination of agents that continue to move almost half a million tons of sediment each year. 5 This process by which landforms are shaped and molded is known as erosion, and it is defined as the removal of material from the earth's crust or surface and the transportation of such substances by natural agencies, such as fluvial, marine, and glacial processes.

Moving air is the most important agent of erosion in arid and desert environments, where wind can frequently drive sand at velocities higher than 240 kilometers per hour. This action, called aeolian 10 erosion, is exacerbated by the lack of vegetation, which would normally fuse topsoil to root structures and protect against the removal of small particles. **A** Loosely formed dunes, thus, are particularly vulnerable to sweeping blasts of wind that can pick up the sand and transport it for hundreds of kilometers in many directions. **B** When the force of these powerful winds dissipates, the sand is deposited onto the ground. **C** This explains the phenomenon of drifting sand dunes that is prevalent 15 in the desert and is a major obstacle to building housing or other structures in affected regions. **D**

[3]The suspended particles carried by the wind will also sandblast any landform with which they collide, weathering rock faces, for instance, or alternatively, clinging to the surface and causing buildup. An example of this form of weathering can be observed in Egypt, where the Great Sphinx of Giza was buried up to its shoulders in sand after the region was abandoned prior to 1400 BC. 20 Although archeologists attempted to restore the Sphinx in the early twentieth century, it had already suffered significant damage to its face and body due to sandblasting.

In most coastal regions, however, water movement is the primary cause of erosion, as it is wave action, in addition to other atmospheric conditions, including rain that causes the wastage of shorelines. [4]Incoming waves impact the coastal topography, breaking up large rocks into smaller 25 particles, while the hydraulic pressure of outgoing waves constantly agitates pebbles along the beaches, weathering them down to smooth surfaces as they tumble to and fro along the beach. Additionally, waves contribute to the erosion of shoreline cliffs to the point of collapse. Shorelines composed of bedrock or other highly jointed material are particularly susceptible because the water can enter the fractures between sedimentary layers and break away large chunks of rock. 30

The destructive force of waves is also compounded by the construction of artificial coastal structures, including breakwaters, which are designed to protect human populations from environmental hazards. In Lagos, Nigeria, for example, massive works of masonry and large stones were laid in the sea around the dredged entrance to the narrow harbor to prevent silting of the entrance by drifting sand. However, this barrier also inhibits waves from depositing particles onto 35 the shore but does not limit hydraulic suction. Therefore, sand is removed from the beach but is not replaced. Even though the coastline has been nourished with three million cubic meters of imported sand, severe erosion continues to degrade the area's beach, which is the focal point of the country's lapsing tourist industry.

1 Look at the four squares [■] that indicate where the following sentence could be added to the passage.

This is one of the reasons that, until fairly recently, desert inhabitants tended to live a nomadic lifestyle.

Where would the sentence best fit?

2 According to paragraph 2, the absence of plants in the desert

(A) reduces the quality of topsoil

(B) facilitates increased wind speeds

(C) limits the movement of rock particles

(D) intensifies aeolian erosion

3 Which of the sentences below best expresses the essential information in the highlighted sentence in the passage?

(A) Windblown sand will either wear down or accumulate upon the surrounding land.

(B) When particles are carried by the wind, they burst through surfaces that have previously built up.

(C) Sand carried by the wind attaches itself to rocks and creates layers that cannot be removed.

(D) Wind runs into the outside of rock formations, causing sand to stick to the rock and blast through the air.

4 Which of the sentences below best expresses the essential information in the highlighted sentence in the passage?

(A) Pebbles on the beach are coarsened by incoming waves and leveled by outgoing waves.

(B) The features of a coastline are altered by waves that can either break down or build up rock, depending on their direction.

(C) Inbound waves crumble rocks into pieces, while outbound waves polish smaller rocks.

(D) Waves, regardless of their direction, reshape the coastline by reducing large rocks into pebbles.

5 The word "compounded" in the passage is closest in meaning to

(A) augmented   (B) compressed   (C) reduced   (D) implemented

6 According to paragraph 5, all of the following contribute to the degradation of natural beaches in Lagos EXCEPT

(A) the unrestrained hydraulic drag of incoming waves

(B) a synthetic blockade built to guard against silting

(C) the introduction of sand from other regions

(D) a reduction in the accumulation of sand

Answer Book p. 17

Tang Dynasty

The Tang dynasty (AD 618-907) is regarded by historians as the pinnacle of ancient Chinese civilization. During the almost three centuries of rule by the Tang emperors, successful military campaigns enlarged the territory under imperial control, extending it east toward Korea and south and west to the fringes of 5 Indochina.

➡ Early in the Tang dynasty, a Chinese Buddhist monk, Xuanzang, explored the Silk Road, an interconnected series of pathways stretching more than 8,000 kilometers from Chang'an, the Tang capital, to Antioch, Asia Minor. By caravan, he traversed the continent, stopping at several major centers along the way to record his observations of foreign culture, including the different styles 10 of Buddhism that were flourishing along the main route. Xuanzang then rested in India, where he obtained Buddhist literature.

Xuanzang's return to Chang'an heralded the beginning of a creative renaissance in China, sparked by greater exposure to Buddhism through the literature he brought back. Chinese writers benefited from exposure to the documents, and they incorporated Buddhist ideals in a form of 15 poetry called *shi*, which had previously conveyed Taoist themes in a five-line narrative structure. When poets began adding Buddhist ideals into their works, the poems became relaxed in tone and more imaginative, reaching their zenith around the end of the Tang dynasty. The popularity of *shi* was also heightened by the invention of block printing, which could quickly and efficiently reproduce texts for mass dissemination.
20

➡ A piqued interest in the arts proved instrumental in the stabilization of China. Emperor Gaozong saw the opportunity to bring intelligent and creative personnel into government, so he had a series of objective civil servant examinations developed to test the talents of all male children, recruiting the highest scorers for court positions. This ushered in a long era of relative stability because it created a class of scholar-officials unaffiliated with any of the feudal families 25 that frequently staged coups and assassinations of key political figures.

➡ The benefits of this extended period of stability were most prevalent in the capital city, Chang'an. Because the Tang emperors maintained a policy of open trade routes to the east and west, many of the inhabitants of the capital were foreigners. Some were missionaries and others were pilgrims seeking escape from their own oppressive homelands. A few represented 30 their native countries as ambassadors, and there were scholars learning from Chinese masters. Most, however, were merchants who worked in the many bazaars, dealing in rare plants, spices, medicines, and novelty goods. In fact, their prosperity was so widely known that historical records reporting the economic advantages of doing business in China have been uncovered as far away as Turkey.
35

The country's good fortunes continued until An Lushan, who had risen to the ranks of military governor, staged a rebellion. **A** Soldiers under his command moved into Chang'an, almost seizing control of the capital city. **B** The weakened central government was no longer able to properly police the vast Chinese countryside and to supply enough guards to provide security for merchants traveling along the Silk Road. **C** Discouraged by the high risk of travel, fewer and fewer merchants entered China and their absence slowed the transfer of ideas and knowledge that had characterized the Tang dynasty, signaling an end to the era of prosperity. **D**

40

1 According to paragraph 2, what did Xuanzang do during his exploration of the Silk Road?

(A) He established a number of new towns along the main route.

(B) He walked thousands of miles to cross the continent.

(C) He collaborated with Buddhist philosophers on several works.

(D) He witnessed the practices of a variety of religious traditions.

Paragraph 2 is marked with an arrow [➡].

2 The word "heralded" in the passage is closest in meaning to

(A) signaled

(B) assumed

(C) prepared

(D) determined

3 Which of the sentences below best expresses the essential information in the highlighted sentence in the passage? *Incorrect* choices change the meaning in important ways or leave out essential information.

(A) New printing technology resulted in a heightened interest in *shi*.

(B) The use of printing technology was promoted to ensure new works of *shi* were written.

(C) Distributed copies of poetry were made using a rapid new process for printing text.

(D) Block printing was invented as a way to mass-produce *shi*.

4 The word "piqued" in the passage is closest in meaning to

   Ⓐ mandated

   Ⓑ stimulated

   Ⓒ flawed

   Ⓓ diminished

5 According to paragraph 4, Emperor Gaozong initiated the civil servant exams

   Ⓐ to evaluate young men who were already working for the government

   Ⓑ to distinguish the government officials from the scholars

   Ⓒ to determine which boys were well suited to a career in the creative arts

   Ⓓ to identify the best possible employees who could serve the imperial court

Paragraph 4 is marked with an arrow [➡].

6 The word "others" in the passage refers to

   Ⓐ emperors

   Ⓑ trade routes

   Ⓒ inhabitants

   Ⓓ missionaries

7 Why does the author mention "historical records" in the passage?

   Ⓐ To support the claim that the capital was a sophisticated urban center

   Ⓑ To demonstrate that China had a favorable reputation in distant lands

   Ⓒ To show that trade occurred between Tang China and other nations

   Ⓓ To illustrate the importance of merchants to the Tang emperors

8 According to paragraph 5, the capital city was home to many foreigners because

   Ⓐ Chinese instructors attracted many students from distant lands

   Ⓑ government officials permitted anyone to make use of a trading network

   Ⓒ devout individuals were attracted by the strict enforcement of religious doctrine

   Ⓓ other states established embassies to house their representatives

Paragraph 5 is marked with an arrow [➡].

9 Look at the four squares [■] that indicate where the following sentence could be added to the passage.

The imperial government successfully defended Chang'an and put down the coup, but the distraction provided feudal lords with the chance to increase their own power by attacking their neighbors.

Where would the sentence best fit?

Click on a square [■] to add the sentence to the passage.

10 Directions: An introductory sentence for a brief summary of the passage is provided below. Complete the summary by selecting the THREE answer choices that express the most important ideas in the passage. Some sentences do not belong in the summary because they express ideas that are not presented in the passage or are minor ideas in the passage. **This question is worth 2 points.**

Drag your answer choices to the spaces where they belong.
To remove an answer choice, click on it. To review the passage, click on **View Text**.

China underwent a major cultural revival under the leadership of the Tang dynasty.

-
-
-

Answer Choices

Ⓐ Artists thrived and adopted a more creative approach to their work after Buddhism was introduced into China.

Ⓑ Scholars regularly visited religious sites along the Silk Road to learn about the customs of foreign cultures.

Ⓒ The development of an impartial exam system led to the creation of a talented bureaucracy, which increased national stability.

Ⓓ The royal government began testing all young men in China to determine their intellectual abilities.

Ⓔ Chang'an developed into a wealthy and densely populated urban center that attracted a range of people from distant lands.

Ⓕ The invention of block printing facilitated the spread of literature throughout the country.

Answer Book p. 17

Voodoo Death

    According to the Haitian spiritual system known as voodoo, a mixture of West African folklore and a selection of traditions adopted from the Roman Catholic Church, people may die as a result of any number of mystical causes. For example, the cause of death may be a malicious gesture made toward them by someone they had previously offended or one of several known death-knell hexes designed to produce malevolent results. In other words, sickness and ⁵ subsequent death can be initiated solely by sorcery without any evidence of direct physical harm. Western anthropologists began studying this phenomenon—commonly referred to as *voodoo death*—in earnest during the mid-nineteenth century but often did so with much skepticism, as few initially believed that death could be invoked through psychosomatic means.

➡ Early reports attributed voodoo death to mental processes and hypothesized that if the ¹⁰ power of suggestion were strong enough, the victim would die. These explanations were rejected, however, because they did not comply with the prevailing model of human motivation studies, the James-Lange theory of emotion. The theory suggests that emotions are the results of physiological responses to a specific situation. An automobile accident, for instance, will increase the victim's heart rate and adrenaline output. This, in turn, is detected by the brain and stimulates fear. ¹⁵ Therefore, the physical reactions to the accident cause the expression of emotion, a relationship in direct opposition to the notion of voodoo death.

➡ The phenomenon continued to puzzle anthropologists until the dawn of the twentieth century, when physiologist Walter Cannon made startling claims that suggested emotions were not, in fact, the result of bodily changes, but the reason for them. Using observational data he collected in ²⁰ case studies of healthy European soldiers who had died of severe psychological trauma during the First World War, Cannon realized that the body had a natural fight-or-flight response mechanism that was triggered by perceived danger. Emotion, he believed, was the agent responsible for the physiological changes, such as muscular tension and enhanced visual acuity, necessary for people to either flee from danger or defend themselves. As such, voodoo death, a term that he ²⁵ broadened to include all instances of death caused by severe mental trauma, is the delayed physiological response to fear, anxiety, and panic.

➡ Cannon's work supported the early anthropological studies of Haitian spirituality and offered insight into a broad range of disorders. However, it remained hypothetical until the mid-twentieth century when physicians uncovered the function of the pituitary and adrenal glands and identified ³⁰ several chemical compounds, called hormones, that produce the fight-or-flight response. **A** It is now known that the nervous system possesses a sympathetic division, which is interconnected with the cardiovascular system and regulates homeostasis in the human body. **B** Normally, a person is at rest until he or she is provoked by an environmental stimulus. **C** Then the information is relayed from the sensory cortex of the brain to the brain stem. **D** These signals ³⁵ cause blood vessels to contract and sugar (energy) to be released into the body. Research into

this process has formed an entirely new scientific discipline, endocrinology, the study of the hormone system, which continues to fill out the details of Cannon's theories, but not overturn them.

Glossary	☒
psychosomatic: of a physical disorder caused by emotional factors **homeostasis:** process used by living organisms to maintain stable internal conditions	

1 The phrase "in earnest" in the passage is closest in meaning to

  Ⓐ responsibly

  Ⓑ voluntarily

  Ⓒ seriously

  Ⓓ dismissively

2 The phrase "comply with" in the passage is closest in meaning to

  Ⓐ prepare for

  Ⓑ dispense with

  Ⓒ abstain from

  Ⓓ conform to

3 Why does the author mention an automobile accident in paragraph 2?

  Ⓐ To illustrate how real-life experiences led to the formation of a hypothesis

  Ⓑ To demonstrate the underlying principles of a theoretical model

  Ⓒ To highlight a common occurrence during this period of time

  Ⓓ To confirm the validity of the James-Lange Theory

Paragraph 2 is marked with an arrow [➡].

4 According to paragraph 2, why were the initial hypotheses of voodoo death dismissed?

  Ⓐ They suggested that only feeble members of society were affected.

  Ⓑ They were documented by fringe members of the scientific community.

  Ⓒ They went against the principal psychological theory of emotion.

  Ⓓ They were not conducted under the scientific model of research.

Paragraph 2 is marked with an arrow [➡].

5 The word "them" in the passage refers to

(A) anthropologists

(B) claims

(C) emotions

(D) bodily changes

6 According to paragraph 3, the fight-of-flight response is

(A) an innate human reaction to an apparent threat

(B) a typical ordeal experienced by military personnel

(C) the explanation for all physiological changes

(D) the process whereby emotions are expressed

Paragraph 3 is marked with an arrow [➡].

7 Which of the sentences below best expresses the essential information in the highlighted sentence in the passage? *Incorrect* choices change the meaning in important ways or leave out essential information.

(A) Although studies continue to be performed, new research into the endocrine system confirms Cannon's suppositions.

(B) Cannon's theory on endocrinology is not devalued by the plethora of modern research into the hormone system.

(C) Endocrinology, a consequence of further research, has revealed facts that reinforce the existence of the hormone system.

(D) The evolution of endocrinology as a distinct field of study both legitimizes and strengthens Cannon's work.

8 Which of the following can be inferred from paragraph 4 about Cannon's work prior to the mid-twentieth century?

(A) There was no physical evidence to support his claims.

(B) Experts rejected it because the James-Lange Theory was regarded as correct.

(C) It was considered too general to provide specific answers for doctors.

(D) It incorporated aspects of religion that were deemed unscientific.

Paragraph 4 is marked with an arrow [➡].

9 Look at the four squares [■] that indicate where the following sentence could be added to the passage.

This would include seeing a bear in the wild or being reprimanded by a parent.

Where would the sentence best fit?

Click on a square [■] to add the sentence to the passage.

10 Directions: An introductory sentence for a brief summary of the passage is provided below. Complete the summary by selecting the THREE answer choices that express the most important ideas in the passage. Some sentences do not belong in the summary because they express ideas that are not presented in the passage or are minor ideas in the passage. **This question is worth 2 points.**

Drag your answer choices to the spaces where they belong.
To remove an answer choice, click on it. To review the passage, click on **View Text**.

> **Voodoo death has long perplexed researchers who study human emotions and physiology.**
>
> •
>
> •
>
> •

Answer Choices

(A) Cases of dead soldiers coincide with stories of death by spiritual means, leading some to believe that they are interconnected.

(B) A well-researched theory that introduced an instinctive desire to flee from peril or defend oneself provided an explanation for voodoo death.

(C) The theory that the body could react to an altered mental state was originally rejected, as it was not in accordance with the idea that emotions were the result of physiological changes.

(D) With the discovery of particular physiological processes and their influence on the body, scientists have augmented previously documented studies.

(E) In Haiti, sufferers of serious diseases were believed to have been inflicted with undetectable physical harm by sorcery.

(F) The connection between a medical condition and voodoo death gave researchers the impetus to continue research into both phenomena.

Answer Book p. 19

Vocabulary Review

Answer Book p. 20

A. Fill in the blanks with the appropriate words from the box.

precipitation	painstakingly	pinnacle
malevolent	edible	hypothetical

1 She is convinced that oatmeal is barely _____ without a spoonful of sugar.

2 The archaeologists _____ excavated the tomb, often spending twelve hours on a single artifact.

3 Dickens novels are regarded as the _____ of Victorian literature.

4 The president declined to comment on the matter, insisting that the situation was _____ because it had not happened yet.

5 The prosecutor declared that the defendant had entered the house with a(n) _____ intention to harm the owner.

6 The forecast called for _____, which was expected to bring the drought to an end.

B. Choose the closest meaning for each highlighted word or phrase.

7 People are reading far less than they did prior to the advent of the Internet.
   (A) appearance   (B) advancement   (C) awareness   (D) application

8 The Dadaists hoped to usher in a new era in which the meaninglessness of life was reflected in the meaninglessness of their art.
   (A) advise   (B) introduce   (C) question   (D) supplant

9 Due to their low cost and imperviousness to water, plastics have been used everywhere.
   (A) availablility   (B) resistance   (C) fabrication   (D) benefit

10 After the first three surfers wiped out, the remaining surfer felt daunted and swam to shore.
   (A) morose   (B) empowered   (C) discouraged   (D) respected

11 The nation emerged from poverty after the exploitation of its mineral reserves.
   (A) conservation   (B) utilization   (C) preparation   (D) installation

12 In order to augment the country's existing military presence, the president ordered thousands more troops into the region.
   (A) enhance   (B) predict   (C) laud   (D) prepare

13 The contagious nature of the virus necessitates aggressive action such as mask mandates.
   (A) abides by   (B) makes up   (C) comes in   (D) calls for

14 The court voted six to three in opposition to gun control legislation that kept concealed weapons off the streets of the nation's largest cities.
   (A) rejection   (B) reference   (C) support   (D) ignorance

CHAPTER 04

Fact

Fact

About the Question Type

Fact questions ask you to identify specific information that is explicitly stated in the passage.

The correct answer choice restates specific information in the passage that directly answers the question. Incorrect answer choices include information that is contradicted by the passage, irrelevant to the question, or not mentioned in the passage.

Question Format

- According to paragraph #, which of the following is true of X?

- According to paragraph #, what/how/why . . . ?

- The author's description/discussion of X mentions which of the following?

Key Strategies

- **Step 1** — Read the question and identify the keywords. If the question indicates a specific paragraph, you can ignore the rest of the passage.

- **Step 2** — Scan the passage for the keywords, and locate the relevant information.

- **Step 3** — Select the answer choice that correctly paraphrases the relevant information in the passage.

Example

Pelagic Ecosystem

The open ocean, or the pelagic region, includes all ocean waters away from shores and comprises roughly 65 percent of the total volume of the world's oceans. Although the region lacks the biotic density and diversity of the coastal waters, primarily because of the absence of complex forms of vegetation and suitable surfaces for the formation of coral reefs, it is inhabited by a wide variety of species. The pelagic region is divided into distinct strata. 5

Extending from the surface of the ocean to a depth of approximately 200 meters is the euphotic zone, also known as the sunlight zone because it defines the limit to which sufficient solar radiation for photosynthesis can penetrate. As a result, the area includes over 90 percent of all aquatic life in the pelagic region, supporting a wide range of organisms from microscopic bacteria to massive creatures such as whales and sharks. The biotic potential of this section of 10 the ocean is further enhanced by the relatively high temperature and low pressure of the water.

Although the disphotic zone, beginning at a depth of 200 meters, is unable to support photosynthesis, it is occupied by a range of aquatic organisms that have developed specialized adaptations. Many resident species of fish rise to the upper regions of the ocean to feed on phytoplankton, which are photosynthetic aquatic plants. Other species make efficient use of 15 the limited sustenance available through adaptations such as bioluminescence, in which light is generated by an organism to attract prey.

1   According to paragraph 1, what limits the life-supporting capacity of the open ocean?

(A) The absence of advanced forms of marine vegetation

(B) The reduced assortment of aquatic animals

(C) The moderate extent of the geographic area

(D) The close proximity of more suitable aquatic habitats

2   According to paragraph 3, which of the following is a feeding method used in the disphotic zone?

(A) Predators use light to ensnare phytoplankton.

(B) Deep-dwelling organisms lure prey from the euphotic zone.

(C) Fish acquire nutrients by consuming photosynthetic plants.

(D) Phytoplankton rise to upper regions to feed on microscopic bacteria.

Overtone Singing

Overtone singing, also known as harmonic singing or throat singing, is a highly specialized vocal technique, whereby the singer is able to generate two different pitches simultaneously. While there are many different styles, the most common method involves the production of a single underlying note, over which a melody is imposed through the selective reinforcement of specific harmonics or "overtones," and the most well-known form is from Central Asia. 5

In particular, the traditional folk music of the people of Tuva, a Russian republic in southern Siberia, has been the focus of a great deal of scrutiny by both scientists and musicians alike due to its beauty and distinctive characteristics. **A** Geographically and politically isolated from other civilizations for most of their history, the Tuvan people have developed a unique cultural heritage that is centered on a strong relationship with the natural world. **B** The Tuvan people claim that their singing style, 10 known as *khoomei*, is inspired by sounds found in nature, with specific tones corresponding to sounds made by birds singing, the wind traversing the mountains, and the water moving over the rocks of a riverbed. **C** The perceived connection between khoomei and the natural world has resulted in a widely held conviction that it is an ability that should be acquired intuitively rather than formally studied, much in the same way that a child develops the capacity to speak his or her native language. 15 **D** The lack of a standardized system of instruction has made it difficult for outsiders who wish to learn this style of singing.

However, the increase in international attention has led to several research projects that have provided insight into the manner in which khoomei is produced. Scientists began by examining the fundamental aspects of sound. Sound energy travels in waves through a conductive medium, such as 20 air, and oscillates at a particular frequency depending on several variables. When sound is produced by the human voice, the most important factors are how the tones are generated by the larynx and the manner in which they are altered by the vocal folds. Notes produced by the vocal tract include both the fundamental pitch as well as a series of harmonics that oscillate through a scale of higher frequencies. 25

In conventional forms of singing, harmonics have an auxiliary function in relation to the actual note and are used primarily to add timbre. They are not deliberately manipulated, however, and are instead viewed as an inherent quality of an individual's voice rather than an aspect of the composition. In contrast, overtones are the most important element of the Tuvan style of singing, and the ability to manipulate them is a basic requirement to master the technique. In khoomei, the process begins by 30 generating a single buzzing note that is held for an extended period of time. Using the vocal tract, the singer forms a vowel sound known as a formant and then merges that sound with multiple formants.

In order to achieve the best results, khoomei vocalists must exercise a high degree of control over the actions of the vocal folds, as overtone frequencies are amplified by the rapid opening of these and are extended by delaying their closure. This unique physical procedure enables the singer to single 35 out specific harmonics to strengthen or weaken, facilitating the creation of an overtone melody that is generated at the same time as the original fundamental pitch.

Glossary

·formant: a resonance frequency of the vocal tract

1 The word "simultaneously" in the passage is closest in meaning to

(A) consequently

(B) subsequently

(C) accordingly

(D) concurrently

2 The word "its" in the passage refers to

(A) traditional folk music

(B) Tuva

(C) Russian republic

(D) scrutiny

3 Look at the four squares [■] that indicate where the following sentence could be added to the passage.

Many feel that these naturally produced sounds are able to positively or negatively affect those who hear them.

Where would the sentence best fit?

4 According to paragraph 2, what do the Tuvan people believe about khoomei?

(A) It must be performed outdoors in a natural setting.

(B) It should use sounds that are not found in nature.

(C) It must be shared with other geographically isolated cultures.

(D) It should be acquired through intuition rather than study.

5 According to paragraph 3, what is the function of the vocal folds?

(A) They modify the sounds produced by another organ.

(B) They make the basic pitch required to create sound.

(C) They cause the harmonics to fluctuate up a scale.

(D) They increase the frequency of the overtones.

6 According to paragraph 4, conventional singers

(A) do not intentionally control the harmonics of a note

(B) manipulate harmonics to increase timbre

(C) reproduce the timbre specified by the composer

(D) utilize their vocal range to influence harmonics

Reading Practice 2

The Diving Bell Spider

The diving bell spider is a small arachnid native to mainland Europe and northern Asia, where it can be found among the aquatic vegetation of freshwater habitats. These spiders are unique amongst arachnids because of their propensity to spend most of their lives in water, despite lacking the biological organs necessary to breathe underwater. To survive in these conditions, this arachnid constructs the diving bell, or air bubble, from which its name is derived. These spiders can endure 5 approximately 24 hours in a bubble of average size without having to return to the surface, depending on water conditions such as temperature and pollution levels.

Although lacking a water-breathing apparatus, this species breathes through the lungs in its abdomen, meaning that only the bottom half of the body needs access to oxygen at any given time. This area is cloaked in fine hairs that ensnare air when the abdomen is pushed out of the water 10 and retain a thin film of air as the spider travels through the water. Before creating its air reservoir, the spider must first find a suitable location, such as an underwater plant. At this point, it has an inadequate amount of oxygen available and must endure frequent, risky trips to the surface, where it has little defense from predators. When an ideal site has been selected, it begins creating the air reservoir by constructing an amalgamation of overlapping thick and thin silk threads. 15

The size and structure of the air bubble are dependent on the gender of the individual spider. These spiders feature atypical sexual size dimorphism for arachnids, as normally the male is diminutive compared to the female, but the opposite is true for this species. Consequently, females create comparatively small bubbles, while males must build larger structures to accommodate their bulkier bodies. 20

First, the air bubble is assembled with silk threads in a tight crescent shape around a tiny pocket of air, with an open underside to permit the spider to enter and exit unimpeded. The air bubble functions by maintaining an internal pressure that is greater than the external pressure, causing it to remain despite the force of the surrounding water. Then, the spider affixes thick anchor threads between the bubble and the aquatic plant, using pieces of dirt to plug the narrow space between the 25 threads. In this way, it strengthens the links to the plant matter used to stop the bubble from being washed away by the water currents. Next, it progressively inflates the reservoir with air through repeated trips between the surface and the bubble. As the bubble is expanded with air, it effectively becomes an external gill.

When the air reservoir is large enough, the spider begins to hunt in the water. The majority of the 30 time, it waits patiently with its abdomen situated inside the bubble in a stasis, consuming little oxygen or energy. The differences between the genders are further exhibited in hunting. Females hunt close to the bubble, whereas males may hunt further away and actively pursue their prey. After the prey has been captured, it is subdued before being dragged inside the bubble and ingested. In some cases, the prey is too large, and the spider must expend some effort expanding the bubble before eating its prey. 35 In this way, this species can survive for approximately two years underwater, as its habitat grants it protection from terrestrial predators.

Glossary

· sexual size dimorphism: the difference in size between males and females of the same species

1 The word "propensity" in the passage is closest in meaning to

(A) capacity
(B) inability
(C) reluctance
(D) tendency

2 According to paragraph 1, how are diving bell spiders different from other spider species?

(A) Diving bell spiders have gills used for breathing underwater.
(B) Diving bell spiders obtain strong leg muscles from swimming.
(C) Diving bell spiders have the ability to survive in aquatic habitats.
(D) Diving bell spiders are capable of hunting freshwater species.

3 Which of the following is mentioned in paragraph 2 as a physical trait of the diving bell spider?

(A) It evolved lungs for breathing in high-pressure habitats.
(B) It produced special threads to repel water from the reservoir.
(C) It developed hairs for capturing air from the atmosphere.
(D) It expelled the air reservoir from its lungs.

4 The word "their" in the passage refers to

(A) females
(B) bubbles
(C) males
(D) structures

5 According to paragraph 4, how are aquatic plants used by the diving bell spider?

(A) They restrict the movement of the bubble in water.
(B) They block predators from damaging the bubble.
(C) They prevent the bubble from drying out.
(D) They provide a source of oxygen for the bubble.

6 According to paragraph 5, which of the following is NOT true of the hunting practices of diving bell spiders?

(A) They exhibit different hunting habits depending on their gender.
(B) They can consume prey outside their bubble.
(C) They pull the prey into their bubble before they eat.
(D) Some of them leave their bubble to go search for food.

Oil

Petroleum is the product of ancient organic material, typically the remains of single-cell planktonic plants that inhabited primeval marine environments in vast quantities, that has been subject to a prolonged period of exposure to thermal and compressive energy. As a result, regions that were covered by large bodies of water millions of years ago contain the majority of the world's oil reserves. Of these, the Arabian-Iranian sedimentary basin is the most significant, with over two-thirds of the   5
known liquid petroleum reserves being situated in this area.

Although initially used as a source of illumination, over the course of the last one hundred years industrialized nations have come to depend on petroleum products as the primary form of energy for all aspects of their economies. This transition can be largely attributed to the advent of the automobile, as the need to develop a reliable fuel for the technology provided the financial impetus for   10
the exploitation and commercialization of the resource. However, dependence on this energy source, combined with the rapid industrialization of developing nations, has resulted in a dramatic depletion of existing reserves. Consequentially, there has been extensive research into developing technologies to increase the efficiency of current extraction methods and to facilitate the recovery of less-accessible deposits.   15

Most of the oil produced is drawn from large underground reservoirs that can be accessed by conventional drilling methods. As these fields usually include large volumes of natural gas, they exist under extreme pressure, ensuring that once a well has been drilled, the oil will move up to the surface of the planet easily. This phase of the process, known as primary recovery, is the most cost-effective for the producer and accounts for about 20 percent of the overall production from a   20
specific location. Nevertheless, once the pressure within the subterranean chamber decreases to a certain level, secondary recovery methods must be employed. These traditionally include the use of pump systems, although more recent methods involve the injection of carbon dioxide to repressurize the deposit.

Conventional methods have also been successfully applied in order to exploit less-accessible   25
deposits, such as those located under the surface of the ocean. In order to achieve this, marine drilling platforms must be utilized, which usually consist of fixed platforms attached to the continental shelf, although floating platforms are now being designed to allow deep-water drilling. While the structures are incredibly expensive both in terms of initial construction and ongoing maintenance, the technology has made it possible for several northern European nations to utilize the North Sea reserves, which   30
have proven to be among the largest on the planet. Due to the vast outlays of funds required, marine oil drilling is only employed when prices have risen to a point that renders it profitable.

As the price of oil increases, researchers have begun to focus on the development of alternatives to conventional oil supplies. **A** Considerable interest has been shown in the possibility of producing petroleum products from oil sands that include sand, water, and bitumen, a semisolid, crude form   35
of oil. **B** Bitumen has a very high viscosity, making it impossible to remove by conventional drilling methods, which means that it must be extracted by a procedure resembling that used to mine minerals. **C** However, using current technology, the process is prohibitively expensive and has a significant negative impact on the environment, as it produces high volumes of greenhouse gases and waste products. **D**   40

1 Which of the sentences below best expresses the essential information in the highlighted sentence in the passage?

(A) Large amounts of living organisms are required for the creation of petroleum because of the high temperatures and pressures involved.

(B) Single-cell aquatic species generated the vast quantities of energy required for the formation of the extensive petroleum deposits.

(C) The prehistoric oceans determined the location of areas with the necessary geological conditions to produce petroleum.

(D) The lengthy application of heat and pressure on the remains of long-dead sea creatures is responsible for the creation of petroleum.

2 The word "these" in the passage refers to

(A) regions

(B) bodies of water

(C) years

(D) oil reserves

3 According to paragraph 2, petroleum became the main fuel source because of

(A) the expansion of industry in agrarian societies

(B) the widespread use of a new method of transit

(C) the need for a reliable source of lighting

(D) the dramatic economic growth of developing nations

4 According to paragraph 3, what necessitates the use of secondary recovery methods?

(A) The loss of chamber pressure

(B) The presence of harmful gases

(C) A drop in overall output

(D) An increase in the volume of oil

5 Look at the four squares [■] that indicate where the following sentence could be added to the passage.

Once this is done, the bitumen can then be processed by specialized refineries into synthetic petroleum.

Where would the sentence best fit?

6 According to paragraph 5, what is a consequence of the high viscosity of bitumen?

(A) It allows the oil to flow more easily once the drilling into the reservoir is completed.

(B) It precludes the use of traditional drilling techniques for extracting bitumen.

(C) It causes the removal of bitumen to result in substantial pollution of seawater.

(D) It results in an inferior oil that is inefficient as a primary energy source.

TOEFL Reading

Lateralization of the Brain

The lateralization of the brain, the asymmetry between the right and left hemispheres of brain, is a crucial area of neuroscience research and is subject to common misconceptions. If people were asked whether they were right- or left-handed, most would answer, "right-handed." This is because, for certain tasks, approximately 90 percent of humans use their right hands. And because the left side of the brain controls and receives information from the right side of the 5 body, the same popular assumption is that most people are left-brain dominant.

➡ However, to propose such a strict dichotomy is an overstatement because, in fact, people demonstrate no preference for one side or the other when performing many everyday tasks. Numerous studies have shown that in humans and other primates, the type of task determines whether there is a dominance of one side of the brain or the other. For example, complex tasks 10 that require more dexterity, such as using a tool, show a strong tendency toward left-brain priority in most people. But simple ones, like picking up an object, demonstrate no favorability of one side or the other in populations as a whole.

➡ A feature that separates the bilateral brains of humans from those of lower organisms is that the two hemispheres are connected with a series of nerve bundles that span the separation 15 between them. These "bridges" allow for information that is received by one side of the brain to be shared with the other side, and the most significant of them is the corpus callosum. We know that the corpus callosum aids in bilateral communication due to its role in language processing, which had traditionally been considered a left-brain endeavor because the two primary language areas are both located in the left hemisphere. However, the reality that language involves more 20 than brain activity from a single hemisphere was discovered after surgeons began the occasional practice of severing the corpus callosum of people with epilepsy to provide relief from seizures. Usually, this procedure had no serious side effects on brain function. However, in some patients, their language ability was negatively impacted after the surgery, suggesting that both hemispheres must play at least some role in linguistic functioning. 25

➡ The fact that most people can maintain normal brain function even after the corpus callosum is severed illustrates just how independently the two sides can operate; yet, the two hemispheres interact more than was previously assumed. Advances in brain-imaging technology have allowed researchers to see precisely where stimuli activate the brain. By using an electroencephalogram (EEG), scientists can see particular areas of the brain light up when they are activated. They have 30 found that many tasks require engagement between hemispheres in the form of simultaneous activity or rapid switching back and forth between the two halves of the brain.

➡ Speech, for example, uses each hemisphere of the brain. **A** Similarly, in math, although the right hemisphere is utilized for tasks like estimating the quantity of a set of objects and the left one is usually responsible for counting or memorizing data, both sides are used when solving 35

complicated problems that require multiple categories of tasks to be conducted together. **B** By operating together, whether in alternation or in unison, the two sides can efficiently divide the workload to multitask. **C** This prevents the brain from becoming overwhelmed when meeting the challenge of rigorous mental activity. **D**

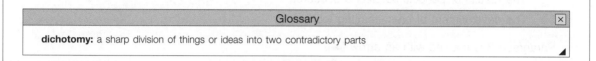

Glossary	☒
dichotomy: a sharp division of things or ideas into two contradictory parts	

1 The word "dexterity" in the passage is closest in meaning to

  Ⓐ agility   Ⓑ confidence   Ⓒ determination   Ⓓ strength

2 According to paragraph 2, which of the following is true of most people?

  Ⓐ They use their right hand more often regardless of the task.

  Ⓑ They tend to be left-brain dominant when performing complicated tasks.

  Ⓒ They are likely to be right-brain dominant if raised to be left-handed.

  Ⓓ They show no favorability at all between using their left or right hand.

Paragraph 2 is marked with an arrow [➡].

3 In paragraph 2, what point does the author make about right- and left-handedness?

  Ⓐ The ratio of each is equal in human and other primate populations.

  Ⓑ The preference for one or the other has a genetic basis.

  Ⓒ The division between them is commonly exaggerated.

  Ⓓ The dominance of one over the other occurs in 90 percent of people.

Paragraph 2 is marked with an arrow [➡].

4 The word "them" in the passage refers to

  Ⓐ bilateral brains

  Ⓑ lower organisms

  Ⓒ two hemispheres

  Ⓓ nerve bundles

5 According to paragraph 3, which of the following led to the understanding that language entailed participation from both sides of the brain?

(A) The discovery of the corpus callosum

(B) The effects of epileptic seizures on brain function

(C) The results of periodic surgical procedures

(D) The development of brain-imaging technology

Paragraph 3 is marked with an arrow [➡].

6 According to paragraph 4, brain-imaging equipment has revealed all of the following EXCEPT

(A) the extent to which the brain's hemispheres cooperate

(B) the specific parts of the brain employed for different tasks

(C) the manner in which the brain's left and right sides interact

(D) the type of stimuli that affect each half of the brain equally

Paragraph 4 is marked with an arrow [➡].

7 Why does the author discuss speech and math in paragraph 5?

(A) To show that the two sides of the brain can operate independently

(B) To highlight tasks that necessitate participation of both brain hemispheres

(C) To give some examples of how brain-imaging technology works

(D) To introduce the main areas of research where electroencephalograms are used

Paragraph 5 is marked with an arrow [➡].

8 The word "rigorous" in the passage is closest in meaning to

(A) demanding

(B) consequential

(C) rewarding

(D) elementary

9 Look at the four squares [■] that indicate where the following sentence could be added to the passage.

One side ensures correct sentence syntax, while the other is responsible for proper stress and intonation.

Where would the sentence best fit?

Click on a square [■] to add the sentence to the passage.

10 Directions: An introductory sentence for a brief summary of the passage is provided below. Complete the summary by selecting the THREE answer choices that express the most important ideas in the passage. Some sentences do not belong in the summary because they express ideas that are not presented in the passage or are minor ideas in the passage. **This question is worth 2 points.**

Drag your answer choices to the spaces where they belong.
To remove an answer choice, click on it. To review the passage, click on **View Text**.

> **The lateralization of the brain is a phenomenon that is generally misunderstood by the public.**
>
> ●
>
> ●
>
> ●

Answer Choices

(A) The vast majority of people in the world have dominant left brains, which results in them being right-handed.

(B) Research has conclusively proven that language ability is not hindered even when the corpus callosum is severed.

(C) An important aspect of the bilateral brain is the network of neural pathways that allow for the passage of information from one hemisphere to the other.

(D) Although the left and right sides of the brain have the capacity to work alone, they actually work together more than was previously believed.

(E) It is unlikely that people would be able to process complex speech and math without the cooperation of both hemispheres.

(F) The tendency of most people to have a dominant hand is real, but handedness does not fit into simple divisions like right- or left-handed.

Answer Book p. 23

Tornadoes

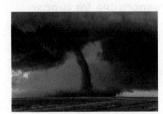

The spring of 1974 was one of the most devastating in US history in terms of tornado damage. For two days in April, 148 individual tornadoes ravaged the American Midwest, resulting in numerous casualties and over $3 billion in damages. Although outbreaks of this magnitude are rare, with recent research suggesting they are tied to a recurring 500-year cycle, tornadoes are a regular occurrence in many regions of the planet.

➡ Local and national governments have engaged in a concerted effort to devise means to alleviate the impact of these storms on the affected communities. It has long been noted that the best way to assure that casualties are limited is to provide residents of threatened areas with advance notice of an incoming tornado. Consequently, related research has focused on indicators of tornado formation and classifying the characteristics of fully developed storms, as well as developing methods to accurately measure their intensity.

The huge lowlands of the American interior, known colloquially as "Tornado Alley," include numerous geological and climatic features that combine to make the region an unparalleled breeding ground for extreme weather conditions. Of particular importance is the lack of variation in land elevation, as it facilitates the easy passage of cold dry air from the north and warm humid air from the south. The collision of two distinct air fronts results in a transfer of heat that provides the necessary energy for the continuous circulation of air that leads to the creation of tornadoes. As the cold and warm fronts meet, air in the atmosphere begins to rotate, forming an extended cylinder that runs parallel to the ground along a horizontal axis. If it encounters a strong enough updraft, the rotation of the winds may shift to form a vertical axis. Consequently, large volumes of air are forced into the higher altitudes where spinning air columns, which are prerequisites for tornadoes, can form.

➡ If a tornado does develop, it will have several distinguishing physical characteristics, with the most important being that it is almost always cyclonic. In the Northern Hemisphere, tornadoes rotate counterclockwise, while in the Southern Hemisphere they turn clockwise. **A** Wind speeds within the tornado vary depending on location, with peripheral winds reaching a maximum of 160 meters per second, and 80 meters per second being the limit for the vertical updraft at the core. **B** The distinctive shape of a tornado, referred to by climatologists as a condensation funnel, is in fact a mixture of water droplets and sediment in the form of a tapered column that extends down from the parent cloud. **C** The taper becomes less pronounced when the storm intensifies, with the most powerful examples of the phenomenon resembling broad cylinders. **D**

➡ Although such visual indicators provide a rough guide to the relative strength of different tornadoes, scientists rely on the Fujita scale to accurately judge their intensity. The Fujita system does not directly measure wind speed but estimates it based on the damage tornadoes

Volume Review Help Back Next

inflict upon engineered structures, such as buildings and bridges. In the Fujita scale, tornado classifications follow a graduated series, with F1 being the weakest and F5 the strongest. Very few reach the level of violence required to be categorized as an F5, which is fortunate because these storms are capable of almost unimaginable destruction. With wind speeds of more than 418 kilometers per hour, they are able to lift cars and other massive objects and hurl them distances in excess of 100 meters.

40

1 Why does the author mention "a recurring 500-year cycle"?

- (A) To emphasize the infrequency of certain severe weather events
- (B) To stress the destruction that results from a type of storm
- (C) To suggest that tornadoes are not difficult to predict
- (D) To illustrate recent developments in the field of climatology

2 The word "concerted" in the passage is closest in meaning to

(A) prepared   (B) structured   (C) unified   (D) revised

3 According to paragraph 2, what is the most effective way to limit casualties from tornadoes?

- (A) Evacuating residents from areas near an incoming tornado
- (B) Providing people with advanced notice of an approaching tornado
- (C) Accurately measuring the intensity of storms that might cause a tornado
- (D) Installing an automatic warning system in as many communities as possible

Paragraph 2 is marked with an arrow [➡].

4 Which of the sentences below best expresses the essential information in the highlighted sentence in the passage? *Incorrect* choices change the meaning in important ways or leave out essential information.

- (A) Tornadoes generate such a large amount of energy that distinct air masses often collide, resulting in a dramatic increase in temperature.
- (B) As heat is exchanged between the air fronts, the resulting energy causes the air to rotate in a manner that facilitates tornado development.
- (C) Once the tornado has been formed, the circular motion of the wind results in hot and cold air currents that must transmit energy to gain intensity.
- (D) Although tornadoes require large amounts of energy, they are also dependent on the heat that results from the movements of large volumes of air.

5 The word "it" in the passage refers to

   (A) atmosphere

   (B) cylinder

   (C) ground

   (D) axis

6 According to paragraph 4, what is a characteristic of the tapered column of a condensation funnel?

   (A) The strongest winds are at the lower end of it.

   (B) It changes shape as the storm strengthens.

   (C) It expels sediment and water droplets from the cylinder.

   (D) The tornado's rotation direction depends on its size.

Paragraph 4 is marked with an arrow [➡].

7 The word "graduated" in the passage is closest in meaning to

   (A) exemplary

   (B) advanced

   (C) restrictive

   (D) progressive

8 According to paragraph 5, tornado intensity is determined by

   (A) comparing the strengths of different storms

   (B) inferring air speed from resulting destruction

   (C) measuring the rate of rotation directly

   (D) examining the tornado's physical shape

Paragraph 5 is marked with an arrow [➡].

9 Look at the four squares [■] that indicate where the following sentence could be added to the passage.

This circular pattern of movement is also found in other storms of this type, such as hurricanes.

Where would the sentence best fit?

Click on a square [■] to add the sentence to the passage.

10 Directions: An introductory sentence for a brief summary of the passage is provided below. Complete the summary by selecting the THREE answer choices that express the most important ideas in the passage. Some sentences do not belong in the summary because they express ideas that are not presented in the passage or are minor ideas in the passage. **This question is worth 2 points.**

Drag your answer choices to the spaces where they belong.
To remove an answer choice, click on it. To review the passage, click on **View Text**.

The destructive potential of tornadoes has resulted in extensive research on this extreme weather phenomenon.

- ●
- ●
- ●

Answer Choices

(A) The number of tornadoes that occur in the American interior has increased significantly in recent years.

(B) The destruction caused by tornadoes is less severe in regions that have developed an extensive warning system.

(C) Tornadoes form in areas where the terrain and climate are conducive to certain interactions between cold and warm fronts.

(D) Tornadoes are easy to predict because their formation follows a consistent timetable.

(E) A tornado has a number of physical and behavioral properties that make it easy for observers to identify.

(F) Tornado strength is determined indirectly by classifying tornadoes based on the architectural damage they cause.

Answer Book p. 25

Vocabulary Review

A. Fill in the blanks with the appropriate words from the box.

diminutive	unimpeded	overstatement
subterranean	auxiliary	counterclockwise

1 To say that I am broke is a(n) _____, as I still have a few thousand dollars in the bank.

2 The telescope requires a number of _____ components in addition to the main part in order to function properly.

3 The increase in interest rates permits economic growth _____ by financial constraints.

4 This electric car is _____ in size but surprisingly spacious and powerful.

5 The skunks emerge from their _____ homes at night, burrowing their way back when morning comes.

6 The game continues with the dice being passed _____, that is, to the right of the first player.

B. Choose the closest meaning for each highlighted word or phrase.

7 The depletion of the ozone layer leads to higher levels of harmful UV radiations reaching the earth's surface.
   (A) attainment   (B) penetration   (C) reduction   (D) discovery

8 Years of war have ravaged most of the nation's cities, leaving little in the way of infrastructure.
   (A) seized   (B) stolen   (C) awakened   (D) destroyed

9 Psychologists believe that violence is a learned behavior rather than an inherent one.
   (A) innate   (B) acquired   (C) quiet   (D) destitute

10 Despite the administration's promises to clean up corruption, the number of scandals has been unparalleled.
   (A) strange   (B) consistent   (C) shameful   (D) exceptional

11 Because it is a nation of immigrants, the culture of the United States is an amalgamation of numerous cultures.
   (A) agreement   (B) mixture   (C) refutation   (D) concentration

12 The nation's healthcare system can be prohibitively expensive for those without insurance.
   (A) relentlessly   (B) reluctantly   (C) extremely   (D) catastrophically

13 Media scrutiny of celebrities' personal lives is a significant disadvantage of fame.
   (A) examination   (B) disapproval   (C) emergence   (D) greed

14 His silence is atypical for a guy who usually doesn't know when to stop speaking.
   (A) immediate   (B) unfashionable   (C) abnormal   (D) amoral

CHAPTER 05

Negative Fact

Negative Fact

About the Question Type

Negative Fact questions ask you to identify specific information that is NOT true according to the passage or NOT mentioned in the passage.

These questions usually contain the words *NOT* or *EXCEPT*. Be careful to select the answer choice that includes information that is contradicted by the passage or not mentioned in the passage.

Question Format

- According to paragraph #, which of the following is NOT true of X?

- According to paragraph #, all of the following are true of X EXCEPT

- The author mentions all of the following EXCEPT

Key Strategies

- **Step 1** — Read the question and identify the keywords. If the question indicates a specific paragraph, you can ignore the rest of the passage.

- **Step 2** — Scan the passage for the keywords, and locate the relevant information.

- **Step 3** — Verify each answer choice. Select the answer choice that includes information that is contradicted by the passage or not mentioned in the passage.

Example

Answer Book p. 26

Aquatic Carnivorous Plants

All plants are autotrophic, meaning that they are able to generate their own food. The most common method is photosynthesis using chlorophyll, a green photosynthetic pigment that absorbs sunlight and transforms its blue and red electromagnetic spectrum into energy. While this process requires sunlight, water, and carbon dioxide, most people erroneously believe that these are the sum of a plant's requirements; however, it also requires a certain set of vitamins 5 and nutrients, and if a plant cannot attain those through soil or rainfall, then it may seek them through other means.

Where access to some nutrients, particularly nitrogen, is diminished, plants may obtain them by digesting insects or other small organisms and absorbing the required nourishment from their bodies. These plants, which usually grow in swampy moist conditions, some underwater and 10 some on land, are carnivorous or <u>insectivorous</u> in that they attract, capture, and consume prey.

Underwater insectivorous plants are generally found in the shallow water along the margins of lakes and streams. Bladderworts, for example, catch aquatic insects with a complex mechanism whereby curled but stiff hairs situated along the delicate leaves hide a special hinged flap on the stem. When touched by an organism, the hairs act as triggers to alert the plant to its presence. 15 Like a trapdoor, the hatch springs open, and water rushes into an empty bladder, the force of which propels the victim inside the vascular structure and then snaps the hatch shut, trapping the insect inside. The action takes place in less than one-hundredth of a second and makes a distinct popping sound. The trapped prey eventually dies, is broken down by bacteria, and the chemical compounds are absorbed by cells in the walls of the bladder. 20

Glossary
· insectivorous: of an animal that eats insects

1　According to paragraph 2, all of the following are true of carnivorous plants EXCEPT that they

(A) grow in regions that are characterized by high humidity

(B) can be found on both land and water

(C) gain nitrogen from insects and small animals

(D) cooperate with other organisms to acquire food

2　Which of the following is NOT mentioned about bladderworts?

(A) They make a unique sound when they capture their prey.

(B) They use water to force insects into their traps.

(C) They use delicate leaves to attract insects.

(D) They ensnare their prey within a fraction of a second.

Answer Book p. 27

Evolution of Flight in Birds

The dominant scientific theory for the origin of birds is that they evolved from dinosaurs, and there is strong anatomical and paleontological evidence supporting this. Most notably, the fossil record makes it clear that some theropods—a diverse group of small dinosaurs that walked upright on two feet—represent a morphologically intermediate stage between certain carnivorous dinosaurs and birds. *Archaeopteryx*, often referred to as "the first bird," was one such creature that maintained dinosaur   5 features, such as teeth and a lengthy tail, but also assumed bird-like traits, including wings and large feathers.

At first glance, it might seem apparent that birds and their ancestors developed feathers specifically for flight, but, logically, there is no inevitable correlation between the two; after all, bats are excellent fliers but lack feathers, and ostriches are feathered but cannot fly. Whatever the case, feathers offered   10 a survival advantage and ultimately became useful for generating lift and creating stability and maneuverability in powered flight. Yet they were just part of a wide range of anatomical changes that led to birds becoming such skillful aviators. To generate enough thrust to keep their bodies aloft, birds had to develop powerful chest muscles. In turn, it was necessary for the breastbone to become larger and stronger to support the larger muscles. Other flight-optimizing modifications to the skeletal   15 system included a highly flexible wishbone, a shortened thigh bone, elongated bones in the lower arm, and modified wrist bones. Overall, the bones became narrow and hollow, and thus lighter, but without losing strength.

Physiological alterations were equally as important because sustained, powered flight is an energy-intensive activity that requires a high metabolism. **A** In modern vertebrates, such a high   20 metabolic rate is limited to endotherms (warm-blooded animals) like mammals and birds. **B** Though scientists debate whether dinosaurs were ectotherms (cold-blooded animals) or endotherms, what they generally agree upon is that either the ancestors of birds had already become endotherms prior to taking flight or endothermy arose along with the ability to fly. **C** As endotherms, the first birds had high enough metabolism to flap their wings for considerable periods without having to stop repeatedly   25 to let their muscles recover. **D**

Still, these physical changes and characteristics do not explain precisely how birds first began to fly. Opinions on the origin of this ability have traditionally come from two competing groups. The first contends that a tree-dwelling, bird-like creature underwent a gradual behavioral progression that commenced with leaping from and between trees. Over time, this primordial creature learned to glide   30 and steer and to flap its wings, and, ultimately, to fully perform winged flight. The other faction holds that the bird ancestors were two-legged ground dwellers, often exploiting their running and jumping ability to grasp prey before it escaped. For example, leaping would have been beneficial for these predators when attacking taller animals or prey that was situated on the branches of trees or perched on a large rock.   35

Regardless of how birds developed the ability to fly, progress initially remained gradual. *Archaeopteryx* almost certainly could fly like a bird, but it was not a powerful flier, and *Hesperornis*, an aquatic diving bird, along with *Diatryma*, an avian land predator that stood over two meters tall and was able to run extremely fast, remained flightless. Later in the Cretaceous period, however, avian flight

became considerably more varied as more species evolved. Birds became excellent fliers and dispersed 40
to every corner of the earth, honing their flight skills and modifying them to maximize their chance
of survival in each particular niche they have come to occupy today.

1 The word "assumed" in the passage is closest in meaning to

(A) acquired
(B) mimicked
(C) duplicated
(D) produced

2 According to paragraph 1, the fossil record indicates which of the following about some theropods?

(A) They were the first dinosaurs to lose their tails and teeth.
(B) Their behavior was more similar to birds than that of dinosaurs.
(C) Their body structure was in between that of birds and dinosaurs.
(D) They were among the last dinosaurs to develop feathers.

3 The word "they" in the passage refers to

(A) bats
(B) fliers
(C) ostriches
(D) feathers

4 Which of the following is NOT mentioned in paragraph 2 as an anatomical change that contributed to flight in birds?

(A) The chest muscles became stronger.
(B) The breastbone was enlarged.
(C) The lower arms were shortened.
(D) The bones became thin and hollow.

5 Look at the four squares [■] that indicate where the following sentence could be added to the passage.

This increased endurance was largely due to their development of a very high proportion of red muscle fiber, which provided the aerobic respiration needed for flight.

Where would the sentence best fit?

6 According to paragraph 5, which of the following is NOT true of Diatryma?

(A) It was taller than a typical human.
(B) It was capable of moving quickly on land.
(C) It never developed the capacity to fly.
(D) It primarily hunted aquatic animals.

Answer Book p. 28

Nomadic Pastoralism in Iran

    In ancient Iran, agriculture was hampered by geographic constraints. The Iranian plateau lacked major rivers and other natural water sources necessary for large-scale farming settlements. Since much of the country could not be cultivated and was only suitable for grazing, nomadic pastoralism became the only lasting agricultural practice during Iran's early history.

    Pastoralism had many economic advantages for its practitioners. Where rainfall was sufficient, 5 nomads could settle for periods of time. However, because vegetation was sparse across the majority of the arid landscape, one pasture could never sustain their herds for very long. The herds were crucial because they provided not only meat and dairy products for the pastoralists but also wool and hides for the production of various textiles. These goods were traded for other products, such as grain, from Sumer. As producers of essential goods and materials, pastoralists played an important role in the 10 development of permanent settlements in Iran. Their exchanges with sedentary communities created an economic interdependence between migrant and settled people that remained consistent throughout much of Iranian history.

    At some point (perhaps around 2700 years ago), the people of the Persian Empire made a technological breakthrough that allowed them to farm areas of land without a local water source. 15 This was the *qanat*, an irrigation and water management system that used canals to divert water from underground sources at points of higher elevation to outlets at points of lower elevation. The qanat system included a number of vertical shafts, which were positioned at intervals and connected to an underground channel. Pumps were not necessary because the natural slope of the land allowed gravity to transport water down the hillside. 20

    Although the qanat system made it easier to form permanent or semi-permanent agricultural communities, pastoral nomads continued to be the primary driving force behind Iranian political affairs. They made their mark on Iranian history and culture through their tribal confederations, some of which were autonomous and highly organized. Tribes with strong leadership had a significant amount of influence in traditional Iranian politics, and their power was dependent upon their capacity 25 to raise and maintain a substantial cavalry. The skills of pastoral nomads were easily converted into martial activity, and the most successful tribes were able to gain control of large territories— along with the essential water resources of those lands—through conquering rival tribes. Settled communities were unable to match the power of the nomadic tribes, largely due to their low numbers and reluctance to participate in military campaigns. 30

    By the end of the nineteenth century, much of Iran was under the authority of powerful nomadic tribes. However, after the first quarter of the twentieth century, the nomadic populations came under increasing pressure both from internal and external forces. Many pastoralists were attracted to permanent settlements, and the rise of a national Iranian consciousness created factions of Iranian leadership that were in favor of national unity and sedentary communities. These groups viewed the 35 nomadic tribes as threats to stability and sought to suppress the nomadic lifestyle by issuing land rights to individual families. In addition, the advent of modern mechanized military technology made it possible for a strong centralized government to exert its will upon the nomadic population, and these efforts to centralize power and establish a sedentary civilization were overwhelmingly successful. As a result, the nomadic majority that had traditionally made up the Iranian populace shrank to less 40 than 5 percent of the population in the late twentieth century.

1 The word "hampered" in the passage is closest in meaning to

(A) facilitated

(B) impeded

(C) expanded

(D) inspired

2 According to paragraph 2, which of the following was constantly maintained throughout much of the history of Iran?

(A) The local people depended heavily on foreign products, such as Sumerian grain.

(B) Traders from various neighboring countries visited local Iranian markets.

(C) Pastoralists and settled communities relied upon one another for commerce.

(D) Migrants and settled people tended to have conflicting economic goals.

3 According to paragraph 3, why was it unnecessary to use pumps in the qanats?

(A) The water was easily diverted into natural canals.

(B) The force of gravity moved the water downhill.

(C) The vertical shafts were shallow enough to be accessed by hand.

(D) The channels were kept full by seasonal rains.

4 The word "their" in the passage refers to

(A) large territories

(B) water resources

(C) settled communities

(D) nomadic tribes

5 In paragraph 4, all of the following are mentioned as ways that nomadic pastoralists impacted society EXCEPT

(A) overwhelming competing tribes with military force

(B) exerting political influence by keeping a sizeable cavalry

(C) taking command of crucial water resources

(D) developing superior agricultural techniques

6 Which of the following is NOT mentioned in paragraph 5 as a reason for the declining power and influence of nomadic tribes?

(A) International leaders pressured Iranians to form sedentary communities.

(B) Nomadic people settled in permanent communities.

(C) Iranian leaders promoted nationalist policies that favored settled communities.

(D) Land rights were granted to single family units.

Reading Practice 3

Historical Perspectives on Air

Today, chemists think of air as a mixture of gases, but in the seventeenth century, only a few scientists were beginning to view air as a measurable entity similar to liquids and solids. After all, it was a simple matter to observe water or rocks, but gases were considered to be outside the range of experimental possibility. Conceptually, Van Helmont's distinction between gas and air was a monumental breakthrough, but it was tempered by many chemists' belief that it was impossible to 5 manipulate gases.

Nonetheless, an early step in the understanding of air was taken in the seventeenth century by John Mayow, who revealed that plants and animals as well as flames would eventually expire when enclosed beneath an airtight cup. He concluded that the volume of air was reduced by respiration and combustion, and he inferred that both processes deprived air of the same particles. Mayow's 10 experiments led him to believe that there was a common constituent of the air that was necessary for life and combustion. It seems that Mayow was on the verge of discovering oxygen and carbon dioxide. However, his work was largely ignored for nearly a century during which no comparable progress was made.

With regard to experimental apparatuses, an important innovation in chemistry was furnished by 15 Stephen Hales in the early 1700s. For Hales, measurement was a fundamental tool for understanding the natural world, and he urged other scientists to view air quantitatively. Hales was particularly interested in determining the amount of air that was given off by assorted substances when they were burned. To perform these measurements, he developed an instrument called the pneumatic trough. It was a system where gases were passed through a glass tube to an inverted flask that was submerged 20 in a bucket of water to transfer the discharge from burned substances into the flask where it would displace the water. The volume of air trapped in a substance could thus be released and measured.

Hales' device inspired a wave of experiments in the eighteenth century, and it was discovered to have a second convenient application—containing gases. A group of scientists collectively known as pneumatic chemists began to isolate and describe different "airs" using similar devices. Mayow's 25 "nitro-aerial particles" (oxygen), Joseph Black's "fixed air" (carbon dioxide), and Henry Cavendish's "inflammable air" (hydrogen) all represented a conceptual shift away from the perspective of air as "the air" to one of "airs." Cavendish was able to create water vapor by mixing hydrogen and oxygen in the presence of an electric spark, clearly demonstrating that neither air nor water was a fundamental element as had been assumed since ancient times. 30

The legacy of the pneumatic chemists was not lost to posterity. Their methods and instruments are still used in laboratories and have become staples of educational and experimental chemistry. Yet, for all their accomplishments, these Englishmen were unable to fully grasp the gaseous state of matter, and this incapacity was due to the fact that they still operated within the widely accepted theory of phlogiston. According to the phlogiston theory, a fundamental fire-like essence was liberated 35 from all flammable substances through combustion. The pneumatic chemists were thus confused by the realization that when combusted, some metals gained rather than lost weight. Despite leaving oxidation completely unaccounted for, phlogiston remained the dominant theory throughout much of the eighteenth century. It was left for the French chemist Antoine Lavoisier to take the momentous leap forward that would usher in the era known as the chemical revolution. 40

1 The word "monumental" in the passage is closest in meaning to

(A) original

(B) relative

(C) controversial

(D) significant

2 In paragraph 1, the author mentions which of the following as a reason that chemists did not view air as measurable?

(A) They were skeptical of Van Helmont's conclusions.

(B) They did not believe that gases could be controlled.

(C) Experimental methods were frowned upon.

(D) Chemistry was viewed as a mere superstition.

3 According to paragraph 2, Mayow's experiments led to the discovery that

(A) combustion was caused by the release of particles from air

(B) oxygen and carbon dioxide were basic components of air

(C) neither organisms nor flames could survive without air

(D) both plants and animals died quickly when deprived of air

4 Which of the following is NOT mentioned in paragraph 3 about Hales in relation to his scientific views and experimentation?

(A) He sought to refute the conclusions of other scientists.

(B) He considered nature as something that should be measured.

(C) He created an instrument to perform experiments.

(D) He encouraged other scientists to observe air in a quantitative fashion.

5 Which of the sentences below best expresses the essential information in the highlighted sentence in the passage?

(A) Because of their achievements with matter in a gaseous form, these Englishmen were unable to move beyond a widely supported theory.

(B) These Englishmen, though accomplished, failed to incorporate gases into their theory of phlogiston, which was widely accepted at the time.

(C) Their achievements notwithstanding, these Englishmen could not completely comprehend gases because they were limited by the theory of phlogiston.

(D) Even given their accomplishments, these Englishmen contributed little to the understanding of the gaseous state of matter because they believed in phlogiston.

6 According to paragraphs 4 and 5, all of the following were true of the pneumatic chemists EXCEPT:

(A) They used instruments to separate gases.

(B) They made a lasting impact on chemical science.

(C) They could not explain the oxidation of metals.

(D) They collaborated on their experiments.

TOEFL Reading

Inuit Art

➡ *Inuit* is a general term used to describe the culturally homogenous indigenous peoples who inhabit the Arctic regions of Canada and Alaska. The late 1700s marked a significant change in the cultural history of these people. This was the first time European fur traders began to move north to profit from a lucrative white fox fur   5 trade with the Inuit, whose rudimentary economy had been centered on trapping, whaling, and hunting for hundreds of years.

➡ However, when overhunting of the white fox eventually led to the collapse of the trade, the Inuit faced both economic hardships and mass starvation. This dire situation lingered until a Supreme Court of Canada ruling granted the Inuit the same rights and privileges as those   10 of other indigenous people in Canada covered under treaties—including education and health care. Unfortunately, it did not provide them with a new source of income, and as they swiftly transitioned from their traditional nomadic ways of life into permanent villages, elders looked for a new way to support the communities.

➡ One option revealed itself when renowned Toronto artist James Houston visited some of the   15 northern settlements and took an interest in the amulets and tools crafted by the villagers. The Inuit did not have a concept of art as a commodity. Their carvings and etchings were produced on a small scale for decorative purposes, and Houston was impressed with the pieces and believed they held intrinsic aesthetic value. He brought several of these back to his gallery and exhibited them to critical acclaim.   20

➡ Initially, the works were crude and utilized material available in the Arctic: ivory, stone, and infrequently, wood. **A** Most importantly, these works were small enough to be easily transported from place to place along with the rest of the nomadic people's personal items. **B** The majority of art was done to decorate practical objects, such as the handles of knives, but there were also simply designed cribbage boards to facilitate the play of a card game that had been introduced   25 to them by the English. **C** A few pieces were created as tokens to be given to kin or trustworthy trade partners, and these were cherished possessions. **D**

This latter category of items, in particular, proved highly marketable, mainly because they featured "primitive" themes of whales, polar bears, seals, and mothers with their children, which many consumers perceived as representative of the Inuit lifestyle. Therefore, young men and   30 women, instead of pursuing trapping or other traditional means of survival, honed their carving skills to become full-time craftspeople. Many helped to set up an Inuit art guild to both standardize their practices and provide training opportunities for up-and-coming artists. By the mid-1970s, entire villages of people were producing these small ivory and stone carvings while setting up trade partnerships with a variety of sales portals, ranging from fine art galleries to souvenir shops   35

around the country.

➡ Controversy surrounds the notion of Inuit art as fine art, as the term usually conveys the sense that the work is done for purposes other than commercial gain. The argument, nevertheless, is merely academic, because the works do attract a wide range of admirers from all over the world based on their aesthetic qualities. They have also been praised as exceptionally 40 emotional and expressive, allowing outsiders to feel a connection to a people who are undergoing an incredible transition to the Western way of life.

Glossary	☒
amulet: an ornament worn for protection against evil, danger, or unhappiness	

1 The word "dire" in the passage is closest in meaning to

   Ⓐ irrelevant   Ⓑ repugnant   Ⓒ critical   Ⓓ reckless

2 The word "it" in the passage refers to

   Ⓐ situation   Ⓑ ruling   Ⓒ education   Ⓓ health care

3 According to paragraphs 1 and 2, all of the following factors contributed to major changes in Inuit culture EXCEPT

   Ⓐ the conversion of local villages into Inuit communities
   Ⓑ the demise of the traditional economy
   Ⓒ the legal decision to provide the Inuit with various rights
   Ⓓ the exposure of the Inuit to foreign traders

Paragraphs 1 and 2 are marked with arrows [➡].

4 According to paragraph 3, why was James Houston impressed by Inuit crafts?

   Ⓐ He believed they had artistic worth.
   Ⓑ He thought they were important spiritual instruments.
   Ⓒ He expected to capitalize on their sale.
   Ⓓ He thought they could serve decorative purposes.

Paragraph 3 is marked with an arrow [➡].

5 Which of the following is NOT mentioned in paragraph 4 as a feature of early Inuit art pieces?

   (A) They were typically created to adorn other items.

   (B) They were designed to be easy for people to move.

   (C) They were primarily made from natural materials.

   (D) They were intended for use in various Inuit games.

Paragraph 4 is marked with an arrow [➡].

6 The word "honed" in the passage is closest in meaning to

   (A) documented

   (B) improved

   (C) propagated

   (D) displayed

7 Why does the author mention "fine art galleries" and "souvenir shops"?

   (A) To show the dedication of the craftspeople to marketing their skills

   (B) To stress the range of economic opportunities available to Inuit artists

   (C) To give examples of businesses that hire indigenous craftspeople

   (D) To illustrate the narrow range of consumers who purchase Inuit art

8 According to paragraph 6, why do some critics question the categorization of Inuit art as a fine art?

   (A) Craftspeople are not trained in an institutional setting.

   (B) Works are produced primarily as economic commodities.

   (C) Creators lack the motivation to introduce new ideas.

   (D) The subject matter is archaic.

Paragraph 6 is marked with an arrow [➡].

9 Look at the four squares [■] that indicate where the following sentence could be added to the passage.

This was not only convenient but also reduced waste as having portable objects meant that fewer belongings had to be left behind.

Where would the sentence best fit?

Click on a square [■] to add the sentence to the passage.

10 Directions: An introductory sentence for a brief summary of the passage is provided below. Complete the summary by selecting the THREE answer choices that express the most important ideas in the passage. Some sentences do not belong in the summary because they express ideas that are not presented in the passage or are minor ideas in the passage. **This question is worth 2 points.**

Drag your answer choices to the spaces where they belong.
To remove an answer choice, click on it. To review the passage, click on **View Text**.

The Inuit developed an industry based on traditional art in response to cultural and economic crises.

- ●
- ●
- ●

Answer Choices

(A) Customers preferred primitive themes, as they assumed these were symbolic of the traditional Arctic communities.

(B) New legislation bestowed basic rights on the Inuit akin to those of other indigenous Canadians.

(C) The commodification of Inuit art has led some people to undervalue it, but its artistic value has been widely recognized.

(D) The marketability of crafts encouraged the Inuit to concentrate on their creation and to seek out places to sell them.

(E) Without a cultural understanding of art, decorative works were originally created utilizing materials native to northern Canada.

(F) The idea to sell crafts was inspired by the success of a famous Inuit artist who introduced his carvings to art galleries.

Answer Book p. 30

Answer Book p. 31

TOEFL Reading

Solar Power

The fuel sources commonly used by humans, such as oil, coal, and natural gas, are finite, and the rate at which they are being depleted has necessitated the search for a viable alternative fuel source. While a variety of options have been considered, it is widely recognized that solar power is the best prospect to satisfy the world's current and future energy needs.

➡ The radiation that reaches the periphery of the atmosphere surrounding Earth—known as the solar constant because it never varies—averages 1,400 watts per square meter. Due to interference, the amount that arrives at the surface of the planet is much less, and there is a great deal of variation between different geographic locations. That said, the total is still exponentially greater than the sum production of all conventional methods of generating electricity. Widespread recognition of the potential of the resource has led to the development of a variety of technologies to facilitate the effective utilization of its vast renewable energy.

➡ The simplest way to harness the radiation of the Sun is to use it to heat water, a technique that has been employed in many countries for over a century. In the United States, the method was actually more prevalent in the early twentieth century than it is now. This was due to the fact that the high cost of coal and the inability to access wood made these fuels unattractive to urban dwellers. By the 1920s, a significant number of private residences were equipped with simple solar water heaters to reduce energy bills. The technology was largely discarded with the discovery of extensive natural gas deposits in the United States, which provided a reasonably priced alternative that was much more convenient. However, as fuel costs have continued to rise since the 1970s, there is a renewed interest in this solar apparatus.

Although solar heat is an example of a successful and practical employment of the Sun's energy, its utility is somewhat limited in that it is only congruent with small-scale endeavors, usually isolated to one structure or location. Scientists have therefore begun to develop ways to transform the energy of the Sun into more generally applicable electricity.

➡ Thermal power plants represent the first attempt to achieve this goal, and while they take a variety of forms, all are based on the same underlying technology. **A** In order to capture solar energy, large parabolic mirrors are set out in formation so that the rays of the Sun are concentrated on a pipe or boiler containing water. **B** As the water is heated, it eventually transforms into steam, which creates enough pressure to turn a turbine, leading to the production of electricity. **C** This is only possible in daylight, and, as a result, most generators are hybrids, meaning they use solar power during the day and conventional fuels at night. **D** The infrastructure demands of the technology make it best suited for bulk energy production, and it has been successfully included in several existing electrical grids.

A more recent technique has incorporated the advantages of both solar heat and thermal electricity, as it is adaptable to large-scale electricity generation and able to serve as a localized

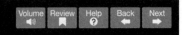

power source. Initially developed for satellites, photovoltaic cells convert solar radiation directly into electricity. As sunlight strikes the cell, electrons are transferred between the numerous silicon panels, producing positive and negative charges that generate an electrical current, which can be utilized immediately or stored for future use. Although this method is much more efficient than thermal electricity generation, the high cost and complexity of the technology have limited its 40 application.

1 The word "finite" in the passage is closest in meaning to

  (A) extended   (B) limited   (C) finished   (D) modified

2 Which of the following can be inferred from paragraph 2 about solar radiation?

  (A) Much of it that reaches the atmosphere is not transferred to Earth's surface.

  (B) Some of it is reflected back into space, but most of it eventually arrives at the surface.

  (C) The variation in amounts between different geographical locations is minimal.

  (D) Most of it is absorbed by energy-trapping particles in the atmosphere.

Paragraph 2 is marked with an arrow [➡].

3 According to paragraph 3, heating water with solar radiation in the US

  (A) was more common in the past than in the present

  (B) was more expensive than using fossil fuels

  (C) was more popular in rural areas than in the cities

  (D) was more advanced than traditional heating methods

Paragraph 3 is marked with an arrow [➡].

4 According to paragraph 5, all of the following are steps in the process by which thermal power plants convert solar energy to electricity EXCEPT:

  (A) A turbine is rotated.

  (B) Fossil fuels are modified.

  (C) Water is converted into vapor.

  (D) Solar rays are targeted.

Paragraph 5 is marked with an arrow [➡].

5 According to paragraph 5, thermal power plants

(A) only function during periods of sunlight

(B) are not used in current power systems

(C) generate large quantities of electricity

(D) are not as efficient as regular power generators

Paragraph 5 is marked with an arrow [➡].

6 The word "incorporated" in the passage is closest in meaning to

(A) instituted   (B) intensified   (C) inverted   (D) integrated

7 Why does the author mention "satellites" in the passage?

(A) To demonstrate a benefit of a technology

(B) To suggest a possible use for a technology

(C) To explain the origins of a technology

(D) To point out a limitation of a technology

8 Which of the sentences below best expresses the essential information in the highlighted sentence in the passage? *Incorrect* choices change the meaning in important ways or leave out essential information.

(A) Electricity that can be used right away or later is generated by a chemical reaction caused by sunlight hitting silicon panels.

(B) The transfer of electrons from sunlight to solar panels results in the production of a powerful electrical current.

(C) An electrical charge is created when the energy stored in solar panels comes into contact with direct sunlight.

(D) The long-term storage of electricity is an obstacle that must be overcome before silicon solar panels can be widely utilized.

9 Look at the four squares [■] that indicate where the following sentence could be added to the passage.

While there is a great deal of variation among different plants, these commonly include oil, coal, and gas.

Where would the sentence best fit?

Click on a square [■] to add the sentence to the passage.

10 Directions: An introductory sentence for a brief summary of the passage is provided below. Complete the summary by selecting the THREE answer choices that express the most important ideas in the passage. Some sentences do not belong in the summary because they express ideas that are not presented in the passage or are minor ideas in the passage. **This question is worth 2 points.**

Drag your answer choices to the spaces where they belong.
To remove an answer choice, click on it. To review the passage, click on **View Text**.

Many different technologies have been created to make use of solar energy.

-
-
-

Answer Choices

(A) The invariable nature of the solar energy that reaches the surface of Earth has facilitated the development of new power generation mechanisms.

(B) The direct conversion of solar radiation to electricity involves a complicated technology that requires many expensive components.

(C) The use of the Sun's thermal energy to heat water is the oldest method, as well as the simplest.

(D) The heat of the Sun can be employed to convert water to steam, which is then used to generate electricity.

(E) Satellite technology was a significant contributor to the invention of large-scale solar power generators.

(F) It is likely that all future solar energy methods will rely on fossil fuels to supplement the radiation received from the Sun.

Answer Book p. 31

Vocabulary Review

Answer Book p. 32

A. Fill in the blanks with the appropriate words from the box.

acclaim	periphery	endeavor
nomadic	reasonably	commence

1 The crowd spent almost an hour waiting for the concert to _____ with the opening act.

2 The tightrope walker tried to stay on the rope, but his _____ failed, and he plummeted toward the net below.

3 The work of Steven Spielberg has achieved as much critical _____ as public popularity.

4 Hunter-gatherers lived a(n) _____ lifestyle and did not have permanent residence.

5 When one suffers from tunnel vision, the objects in the center will be visible, while anything in the _____ will be obscured.

6 With a 20 percent discount, the food at the restaurant is as _____ priced as it is tasty.

B. Choose the closest meaning for each highlighted word or phrase.

7 Bob Dylan is famous for his reluctance to engage with audiences at his concerts.
(A) enthusiasm   (B) pressure   (C) unwillingness   (D) tendency

8 Hydrogen peroxide has more than one application—it can be used to clean, to sterilize, and even to whiten teeth.
(A) utilization   (B) drawback   (C) example   (D) exception

9 The banning of a particular pesticide was momentous in the removal of the bald eagle from the endangered list.
(A) relevant   (B) emotional   (C) significant   (D) brief

10 The Global Economic Recession came to end in 2009, but its effects lingered for many years.
(A) dwindled   (B) remained   (C) extinguished   (D) brightened

11 The party was concerned about its ability to find a viable candidate who had a chance of defeating the incumbent.
(A) feasible   (B) reliable   (C) qualified   (D) dignified

12 As cases of the disease grew exponentially, scientists raced to test vaccines capable of limiting its impact.
(A) ideally   (B) occasionally   (C) prodigiously   (D) glacially

13 Fossil fuels such as petroleum and natural gas are made from the remains of primordial organisms that died millions of years ago.
(A) manufactured   (B) complex   (C) disgusting   (D) ancient

14 A breathing apparatus assists those working in a confined space without access to clean air.
(A) merchandise   (B) device   (C) diversion   (D) relief

CHAPTER 06

Inference

Inference

About the Question Type

Inference questions ask you to identify information that is implied but not explicitly stated in the passage.

These questions require you to draw a logical conclusion based on the information in the passage. Be careful to use only the information presented in the passage to select the correct answer choice. Do not draw any conclusions based on what you know about the topic from other sources.

Question Format

- Which of the following can be inferred from paragraph # about X?

- In paragraph #, what does the author imply about X?

- It can be inferred from paragraph # that

Key Strategies

- **Step 1** — Read the question and identify the keywords.

- **Step 2** — Scan the passage for the keywords, and locate the relevant information.

- **Step 3** — Select the answer choice that is a logical conclusion based on the information in the passage.

Example

Navajo Code Talkers

For the US Armed Forces, communications had become a bewildering problem during World War II. Japanese cryptographers were proving themselves amazingly adept at breaking top-secret military codes almost as rapidly as these could be devised. Many of the Japanese code breakers had been educated in the United States, where they had learned to speak English and had become familiar with American colloquialisms, including slang terms and 5 profanity. As a result, American battle plans became known to the enemy almost immediately, often before they had become operational, and there appeared to be no workable solution.

In 1942, Philip Johnston, a World War I veteran, formulated a plan to create a secret military code based on the Navajo language. Johnston, who was fluent in this language, chose it because it includes many words that change in meaning depending on the inflection used. As a 10 result, the language is virtually incomprehensible to most people who were not raised speaking it. The use of native Navajo speakers, known as code talkers, proved to be a great success. By basing codes on Navajo words, the US army could be confident that exchanges between military personnel would not be understood by the enemy. The effectiveness of the code talkers is demonstrated by their role in the Battle of Iwo Jima, which was a major turning point in the 15 Pacific campaign. It is generally accepted that without the six Navajo code talkers who put themselves at great personal risk to provide secure communications during the battle, the US forces would have faced defeat.

Glossary

·inflection: a change in vocal pitch or volume

---

1 Which of the following can be inferred from paragraph 1 about early American codes during World War II?

(A) They were created by Japanese soldiers.

(B) They were used chiefly to communicate battle plans.

(C) They contained slang terms and profanity.

(D) They could not be transmitted over great distances.

2 In paragraph 2, the author implies that Philip Johnston

(A) was one of the six Navajo code talkers

(B) had experience speaking Navajo as a child

(C) interpreted codes during the Battle of Iwo Jima

(D) served as a code talker in World War I

Chimpanzees

Chimpanzees are the species of ape most closely related to Homo sapiens. Their relatively similar physiological structure, as well as their notable level of intelligence, has captured the interest of ethologists, who have studied the behavior of animals in their natural habitats since a breakthrough study was published in the 1970s by British researcher 5 Jane Goodall. Living among a population of chimps in Tanzania's Gombe National Park, Goodall observed behavior that had never before been documented. In an effort to collect protein for their otherwise herbivorous diet, female chimps capitalize on the plentiful termite nests, a feat that requires the use of manufactured tools. Her research stood in direct conflict with the firmly entrenched belief that humans were the sole tool-making animals, a behavioral trait 10 that separated Homo sapiens from primates that merely made use of available objects to forage for food, build shelter, and defend territory.

According to Goodall's notes, the Gombe chimpanzees consciously gather material and fashion it to their needs in order to go "fishing" for termites. First, they locate a long branch and shear off its bark and leaves to create a smooth stick. They will drill holes into sunbaked mounds, probing for a 15 subterranean chamber that will yield the most insects. Then, they use a second instrument, often a long blade of grass that has been pulled through their mouths and frayed at one end by their canine teeth, to harvest the exposed termites. When the utensil's paintbrush-like tip is covered with nutritious bugs, they are consumed immediately. The entire process shows foresight as the chimps search out nests with ample inhabitants and always arrive with the correct tools in hand. They even favor 20 particular species of vegetation to construct their tools, for which they frequently must travel a good distance to acquire.

To fabricate a new implement, chimps must mentally conceptualize all conditions related to their objective and acquire material to satisfy this goal. If a particular material does not function as intended, then they may choose a different one and try again. Their inventive and flexible thinking 25 skills allow them to move on to plan B should plan A fail. Such is the case with chimpanzees living in the Tai Forest, Ivory Coast. They use rocks to smash open hard husks to reach the nutritive kernels inside and often try one stone after another until they find one that works efficiently in opening the nuts.

Quick-witted intelligence notwithstanding, chimpanzees are highly influenced by a gradual form of 30 learning, imitating the behavior of their parents and other members of the community as they procure tools. Adroitness is reinforced over time as babies receive feedback from their mothers, correcting inappropriate or ineffectual application. Older chimps may point to trees that will provide the best raw materials or bring back good rock samples to school the youngsters on their appealing qualities. This social interaction is the foundation of chimpanzee enculturation, and even chimps in their fourth or 35 fifth years, far more experienced than the babies, receive assistance from their mentors on an ongoing basis.

Spurred on by Goodall's findings and those of her colleagues, modern researchers have implemented infrared, motion-triggered video cameras in an effort to capture previously undocumented chimpanzee tool use. As the data continue to accumulate, scientists will likely be forced to reexamine old 40 assumptions about the capabilities of these apes, which are apparently far more sophisticated than experts once thought.

1 The word "capitalize" in the passage is closest in meaning to

(A) demolish
(B) exploit
(C) substantiate
(D) proliferate

2 According to paragraph 1, which of the following is true of Jane Goodall?

(A) She was the first person to live among chimpanzees in the wild.
(B) She was the first to record evidence of tool use in chimpanzees.
(C) She was the first to enter Gombe National Park for scientific field research.
(D) She was the first person to do research on the diet of chimpanzees.

3 According to paragraph 2, chimpanzees use a long blade of grass

(A) to get the termites from their nest
(B) to make a hole in the termite mounds
(C) to sharpen their teeth for feeding
(D) to discover where termites are located

4 It can be inferred from paragraph 3 that the chimpanzees living in the Tai Forest

(A) are able to compare the efficiency of different tools
(B) will shape rocks to ensure they function properly
(C) prefer kernels that are easier to remove from husks
(D) suffer from a shortage of nutritious foodstuffs

5 The word "their" in the passage refers to

(A) older chimps
(B) trees
(C) rock samples
(D) youngsters

6 The author implies that the special cameras that modern researchers have put into action will

(A) reveal that much of the talk about the skill of chimps is hyperbole
(B) generate data that is consistent with older studies of tool use in chimps
(C) revolutionize scientific views on the abilities of chimpanzees
(D) allow scientists to track the behavior of chimpanzees at all times

HACKERS APEX READING for the TOEFL iBT Expert

Reading Practice 2

Empire State Building

Standing 1,454 feet high, the Empire State Building opened on May 1, 1931, as the tallest building in the world. It became an icon of New York City and a symbol of humankind's attempts to achieve the impossible.

When the Eiffel Tower was built in Paris in 1889 at a height of 984 feet, architects around the world were taunted to build something taller. By 5 the early twentieth century, a skyscraper race was on, as the Metropolitan Life Tower rose to 700 feet in 1909 and was quickly followed by the Woolworth Building in 1913 at 792 feet. The Bank of Manhattan Building exceeded this height in 1929 by reaching 927 feet and 71 stories. Determined to eclipse these other structures, Walter Chrysler, the founder of the Chrysler Corporation, began constructing the Chrysler 10 Building, the height of which he kept secret until the structure's completion. The former vice president of General Motors, John Jacob Raskob, decided to enter the race and better his former rival, and he purchased a parcel of property at 34th Street and Fifth Avenue for approximately $16 million.

After obtaining a site for the Empire State Building, Raskob hired an architectural firm, Shreve, Lamb & Harmon, for his new skyscraper and asked them to make it as tall as technologically possible. 15 Lamb devised a simple and logical plan by creating an inner pyramid of shared space, containing the air-circulation system, mail chutes, toilets, and corridors. He surrounded this core with a perimeter of office space 28 feet deep, ensuring that all offices in the building were close to a window. The building was designed to be 80 stories tall, but the Chrysler building was redesigned to be taller, so the Empire State Building was lifted to 85 stories. 20

Raskob was still worried that Chrysler would pull a trick to further increase the height of his building at the last minute. Therefore, he decided to add a docking station for the inflatable airships called dirigibles that were commonly used for air travel at this time. The idea was that these massive vessels would dock at the top of the Empire State Building, and then the passengers would disembark and take an elevator down to street level. Although this would prove to be impossible due to the need 25 for a large ground crew to secure a landing dirigible, the inclusion of the docking station gave the Empire State Building the additional height it needed to be the tallest building in the world. It would hold this distinction until the opening of the World Trade Towers in 1972.

The landmark status that the Empire State Building has enjoyed over the years is a result of not only its immense size but also its beautiful exterior. It is considered by many to be an iconic representation 30 of Art Deco architecture, a design style popular in the 1920s and 1930s that emphasized bold geometric shapes and well-defined lines. The basic form of the building is highly symmetrical and tapers significantly, with the top floors being much narrower than the bottom ones. This is achieved through the use of setbacks, which are step-like recessions that reduce the profile of a building as it increases in height. Although the architects embraced the use of setbacks to create the series of highly 35 visible, rectangular blocks that give the Empire State Building its distinctive appearance, these were initially incorporated into the design of the building in response to a New York City zoning regulation. The purpose of the regulation was to ensure that that sunlight would reach the smaller buildings surrounding the Empire State Building.

1 The word "eclipse" in the passage is closest in meaning to

(A) surpass

(B) impress

(C) undermine

(D) imitate

2 The author implies that the Eiffel Tower in Paris was

(A) built to challenge American architecture

(B) the tallest structure in the world upon completion

(C) designed by American architects

(D) erected as a monument to the Industrial Revolution

3 According to paragraph 3, the inner pyramid of the Empire State Building

(A) includes facilities shared by all tenants

(B) provides office staff with access to windows

(C) is off-limits to everyone except maintenance workers

(D) is surrounded by residential space

4 The word "his" in the passage refers to

(A) Harmon

(B) Lamb

(C) Raskob

(D) Chrysler

5 It can be inferred from paragraph 4 that dirigibles

(A) could not land without supervision from air traffic control

(B) were unable to land at the Empire State Building

(C) landed at the top of the World Trade Towers after 1972

(D) carried ground crew staff to assist with landings

6 According to paragraph 5, the setbacks incorporated into the Empire State Building's design

(A) softened the lines of the rectangular elements

(B) were mandated by a government body

(C) were initially rejected by the architects

(D) reduced the visibility of a nearby structure

Reading Practice 3

Answer Book p. 35

Thermoregulation

Heat management is one of the key factors that determine whether an organism will be able to survive in a particular biome. Also known as thermoregulation, it is the ability to maintain body temperature within certain boundaries, even when the ambient temperature fluctuates greatly. The methods employed by organisms to achieve this depend on whether they are ectothermic (cold-blooded) or endothermic (warm-blooded), with the latter able to regulate body temperature much more 5 effectively than the former. Endothermic animals, such as mammals and birds, utilize a variety of advanced regulatory mechanisms that allow them to inhabit a diverse assortment of climatic zones.

One of the primary advantages possessed by endothermic animals is the ability to use metabolic processes to maintain their body temperature regardless of external conditions. Known as thermal homeostasis, the process results from the conversion of fats and sugars into energy, which is then used 10 to generate heat within the body. This is made possible by the presence within each cell of a large number of mitochondria: a membrane-enclosed structure commonly referred to as the "cellular power plant." Endothermic mitochondria are also significantly different than those found in ectothermic organisms in that they are much more efficient energy converters, able to produce up to eight times as much heat. 15

The thermal energy produced on the cellular level is distributed by way of the circulatory system, which assures the relative uniformity of temperature throughout the body by carrying warm blood to the extremities. This process is controlled by the hypothalamus, a component of the brain that functions like a thermostat. In response to thermal variations, it gives off nerve impulses that control the diameter of the blood vessels in the skin, and the constriction or dilation of these determines the 20 rate at which blood flows through the body.

Insulation is another mechanism employed by endothermic animals to retain heat, and it includes the fat under the skin as well as external coverings such as fur and feathers. **A** Although internal insulation systems cannot be consciously manipulated by the organism, both fur and feathers can be influenced through a method known as piloerection. **B** This involves the use of specialized muscles 25 to adjust the intensity of the insulation by altering the angle of the individual hairs or feathers. **C** The function is particularly important for aquatic birds in cooler ecosystems as the continual transition from water to dry land leads to dramatic fluctuations in body temperature. **D**

Conversely, endothermic animals that dwell in the warmer climatic zones possess equally effective methods to assure that they do not overheat. The most efficient and common approach is to make 30 use of evaporation, the dissipation of heat through the conversion of water to vapor. One way that this is achieved is through the use of sweat glands—specialized cell clusters located in the skin that secrete moisture. Animals that do not possess these glands or have only a limited number will usually experience a marked increase in the production of saliva, which will then be dissipated through a distinctive breathing technique called panting. 35

While evaporation is the most common method employed by endothermic animals to lower their body temperature, it is not the only one. The process of natural selection has endowed individual species with unique adaptations—ranging from the fanning motion of an elephant's ears to the emission of heat through the long tails of certain rodents—that are specifically tailored for their habitats. 40

1 Which of the following can be inferred from paragraph 1 about ectothermic animals?

(A) They cannot manipulate their body temperature.

(B) Their geographic range is limited.

(C) They are unaffected by climate fluctuations.

(D) Their blood temperature never changes.

2 Which of the sentences below best expresses the essential information in the highlighted sentence in the passage?

(A) Metabolic processes are accounted for via the maintenance of internal temperatures using a procedure unique to endothermic creatures.

(B) Metabolic processes benefit warm-blooded organisms by ensuring thermal stability despite environmental fluctuations.

(C) The permanence of body temperature in warm-blooded species results from ambient circumstances rather than internal metabolic processes.

(D) The metabolic processes endothermic animals use to maintain their body temperature can be influenced by external conditions.

3 According to paragraph 2, thermal homeostasis is dependent on

(A) the consumption of certain nutrients

(B) the production of sufficient heat

(C) the existence of a cellular structure

(D) the transformation of energy into food

4 Look at the four squares [■] that indicate where the following sentence could be added to the passage.

This could negatively affect the health of the organism without some way to compensate for it.

Where would the sentence best fit?

5 In paragraph 5, the author implies that panting

(A) occurs when skin cells with a single function are activated

(B) causes breathing problems as body temperature increases

(C) increases the amount of saliva in the mouth

(D) results in water transforming from a liquid to vapor

6 Why does the author mention elephant ears and rodent tails in paragraph 6?

(A) To suggest that certain cooling methods are preferable to others

(B) To demonstrate why evaporation is ineffective in certain biomes

(C) To provide examples of distinctive traits related to thermoregulation

(D) To illustrate the genetic diversity of endothermic organisms

TOEFL Reading

Spanish Representations of the Inca

➡ After Spanish adventurer Francisco Pizarro heard stories about *Pirú* (known today as Peru)—a place that fellow explorers from his homeland had described as "rich with gold"—he organized a new expedition to sail along the Pacific coast of South America. His first attempt to find this treasured land was hampered by inclement weather, insufficient rations, and skirmishes with natives, so the ship failed to reach its destination. However, subsequent operations were 5 successful and ultimately led to the subjugation of Peru in 1532. At the time, Peru was the seat of the Inca Empire, which ruled the continent's Pacific coast regions, including the Andes. While the Spanish conquest helped to enlighten the Western world about the existence of this once-powerful society, it also created confusion regarding what actually happened before, during, and after the takeover. 10

➡ The first written records were composed by the conquistadors themselves. They conducted interviews with locals using Spanish-trained interpreters whose competence in bilingualism will never be known because the Inca never developed a written language. To complicate matters further, native stories were substantially different from one another. The variation was so significant that the early Spanish chroniclers recorded in excess of fifty different versions of Inca 15 oral history. And when the various accounts did concur, the facts were skewed by the lenses of mythology, religion, and propaganda. The official story that the Spaniards wrote down indicated that the Inca had spread throughout the region and brought civilized life to primitive people devoid of culture, and that the expansion of the Inca was inspired by the gods.

➡ This narrative was eerily similar to the Spanish explanation of their own invasion of Peru, 20 whereby they cited divine providence as justification for subduing a barbaric society in hopes of converting it to Catholicism. Indeed, most Spanish historians were not motivated by anthropological accuracy; their goal was to please their audience, whether it was the Spanish crown, clergy, or administrative officers. This is reflected in Pedro Pizarro's *Discovery and Conquest of Peru*, in which he praised his cousin Francisco's conquest, the capture and execution of the Inca emperor 25 Atahualpa, and the expansion of the Spanish Empire. **A** Pedro did include some details about Inca customs, such as descriptions of their dances, but, overall, he never presented the native people in a very respectful manner. **B** In a letter to King Charles I of Spain, Francisco himself praised the Peruvian capital of Cuzco as a city so exquisite that it was worthy of comparison with any contemporary European municipality, but this remark was self-serving. **C** He sought credit 30 for obtaining this valuable possession and did not intend to highlight the prior achievements of the Inca. **D**

➡ Complicating the representations of the Inca further were the later accounts by mestizos. Mestizos had both Spanish and Inca parentage, typically via a Spanish father and indigenous mother. Such intermarriages became common practices and led to the proliferation of mixed-race 35

progeny. Usually, mestizo chroniclers showed sympathy for their Spanish heritage, but it was their empathy for Inca perspectives that set them apart. For example, *An Inca Account of the Conquest of Peru*, which was written by a mestizo assistant of a missionary in 1570, described the abusive treatment of the locals by the Spanish. The text was suppressed by the Spanish government until 1916, and a full English translation did not appear until 2005.

40

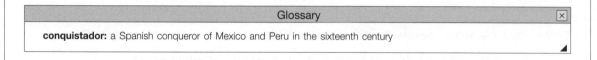

Glossary	☒
conquistador: a Spanish conqueror of Mexico and Peru in the sixteenth century	

1 The word "it" in the passage refers to

   (A) conquest

   (B) Western world

   (C) existence

   (D) society

2 According to paragraph 1, all of the following contributed to the failure of Pizarro's first mission EXCEPT

   (A) conflicts with locals

   (B) inadequate food supplies

   (C) primitive sailing ships

   (D) adverse weather conditions

Paragraph 1 is marked with an arrow [➡].

3 Which of the following is NOT mentioned in paragraph 2 as a complication of the Spanish records?

   (A) The Inca people did not possess a written language.

   (B) The Spanish had no access to bilingual interpreters.

   (C) The natives offered accounts that differed from one another.

   (D) The details presented through oral history were distorted.

Paragraph 2 is marked with an arrow [➡].

4 The word "subduing" in the passage is closest in meaning to

(A) dismissing

(B) recruiting

(C) astounding

(D) suppressing

5 Why does the author include the discussion of Pedro Pizarro's work in paragraph 3?

(A) To demonstrate the ability of some Spanish writers to remain objective

(B) To show that correct information was not the goal of Spanish chroniclers

(C) To point out how selfish the motives of the Pizarro family were

(D) To suggest that the Inca distrusted the Spanish

Paragraph 3 is marked with an arrow [➡].

6 The word "progeny" in the passage is closest in meaning to

(A) ancestry

(B) prodigy

(C) offspring

(D) heritage

7 According to paragraph 4, what was distinctive about the mestizo chroniclers?

(A) They were hostile in their depictions of the Spanish.

(B) They were the first South Americans to adopt Catholic theology.

(C) They conducted extensive interviews with Inca descendants.

(D) They demonstrated a sensitivity toward the Inca perspective.

Paragraph 4 is marked with an arrow [➡].

8 Which of the following can be inferred about *An Inca Account of the Conquest of Peru*?

(A) Its content was considered undesirable by Spanish rulers in Peru.

(B) It was first translated into the Spanish language in the eighteenth century.

(C) Its tone conveyed a strong opposition to the native uprisings.

(D) It became widely distributed in the Western world after 2005.

9 Look at the four squares [■] that indicate where the following sentence could be added to the passage.

A similar assessment could be suggested about the attitude of his cousin in regard to the locals.

Where would the sentence best fit?

Click on a square [■] to add the sentence to the passage.

10 Directions: An introductory sentence for a brief summary of the passage is provided below. Complete the summary by selecting the THREE answer choices that express the most important ideas in the passage. Some sentences do not belong in the summary because they express ideas that are not presented in the passage or are minor ideas in the passage. **This question is worth 2 points.**

Drag your answer choices to the spaces where they belong.
To remove an answer choice, click on it. To review the passage, click on **View Text**.

The historical record of the period surrounding the Spanish conquest of Peru is shrouded in uncertainty.

- ●
- ●
- ●

Answer Choices

(A) Inca accounts of the Spanish portrayed them as a primitive people without sophisticated culture.

(B) Mestizos, who were the mixed-race progeny of the Spanish, began to portray a different picture of Peruvian history.

(C) Prior to the Spanish invasion, Inca accounts suggest that they were subject to conquest by another powerful Andean tribe.

(D) Pedro Pizzaro's narrative shows an appreciation of Inca civilization that other historians never had.

(E) As with the stories of the Incan rise to power, Spanish histories depict the subjugation of an uncivilized people.

(F) The conquering Spaniards initiated the writing down of historical accounts, and these were characterized by ambiguity and distortion.

Answer Book p. 36

Answer Book p. 37

El Niño and the Southern Oscillation

➡ Every few years, the complex interactions between the atmosphere and the ocean creates warmer-than-average water temperatures in the eastern Pacific Ocean. This occasional oceanic warming was noticed by South American fishermen along the coast of Ecuador and Peru more than a century ago, and they named it *El Niño*, meaning "the boy" in Spanish and referring to the Christ child, as it seemed to typically occur around Christmas. It is particularly noticeable to ₅ members of that industry due to the fact that it severely hampers the otherwise profitable anchovy harvest. Although the full range of causes of the phenomenon remains only partially understood, several principal factors have been identified as representative of El Niño.

➡ An El Niño event has its origin in the accumulation of an exceptionally vast layer of warm surface water in the western Pacific. An enormous quantity of warm water gradually becomes ₁₀ concentrated in the west because of the prevailing tropical east-to-west winds, or trade winds, which in the absence of El Niño blow continually in that direction due to the rotation of the earth. **A** As the trade winds whisk across the ocean's surface, the topmost layer of water, which is naturally heated by solar radiation, literally gets pushed across the sea, resulting in a higher sea level in the west than in the east. **B** Over the period of many months, this discrepancy grows to ₁₅ approximately a half meter of seawater covering an area thousands of kilometers wide. **C** When the winds weaken, as they inevitably do, they can no longer continue to push the mass of warm water westward, and the vast reservoir sloshes back toward the west coast of South America, triggering an El Niño event. **D**

➡ It is also apparent that a reversal of the normal pattern of barometric pressure develops ₂₀ in the earth's atmosphere during El Niño as a result of the temperature gradient. Typically, barometric pressure is higher in the eastern Pacific and lower in the western Pacific, but this pattern of atmospheric pressure tends to switch every three to eight years, and this see-saw pattern is known as the *Southern Oscillation*. The change in air pressure is so inextricably linked to El Niño that the two are often joined together under the acronym ENSO. According to ₂₅ meteorologists, the change in atmospheric pressure is attributable to the eastward movement of the mass of warm seawater, which works in conjunction with the intense solar rays in the tropics to cause the surrounding air to ascend.

➡ In recent decades, some evidence has surfaced that suggests explosive volcanic activity in the tropics may greatly increase the probability of an El Niño event. This theory first emerged ₃₀ in the winter of 1982 only months after El Chichón, a previously presumed dormant volcano in Mexico, unexpectedly erupted. Because an El Niño episode followed that historic eruption, climatologists theorized that the cooling effect that occurs when large amounts of sulfur dioxide and particulate matter are released into the air by volcanoes may shift the direction of trade winds, triggering El Niño. ₃₅

Although a comprehensive picture of what exactly causes El Niño is not yet on the horizon, scientists have a sound understanding of how the phenomenon evolves once it has begun, and this knowledge may have far more practical value because it helps them forecast the events with reasonable accuracy—as far as six or nine months in advance. Because El Niño can give rise to devastating consequences, such as unseasonal droughts, the advance notice may help impacted communities prepare for aberrant weather patterns well before they occur. 40

1 Which of the following can be inferred from paragraph 1 about the periodic warming of seawater?

Ⓐ It was previously so uncommon that it went unnoticed for over a century.

Ⓑ It is heavily relied upon by fishermen in some South American countries.

Ⓒ It has a profound impact on the flow of ocean currents around the world.

Ⓓ It results in far fewer numbers of certain fish than usual in some places.

Paragraph 1 is marked with an arrow [➡].

2 The word "discrepancy" in the passage is closest in meaning to

Ⓐ offense   Ⓑ inconsistency   Ⓒ ambiguity   Ⓓ frequency

3 According to paragraph 2, which of the following is a result of the normal motion of trade winds?

Ⓐ The water on the surface of the ocean cools.

Ⓑ The warm water in the western Pacific is pushed to the east.

Ⓒ The sea level in the western Pacific rises.

Ⓓ The topmost layer of water becomes more turbulent.

Paragraph 2 is marked with an arrow [➡].

4 The phrase "attributable to" in the passage is closest in meaning to

Ⓐ caused by   Ⓑ accompanied by   Ⓒ connected to   Ⓓ incorporated in

5 According to paragraph 3, which of the following is true about the Southern Oscillation?

Ⓐ It occurs in a predictable pattern year after year.

Ⓑ It reverses areas of low air pressure between east and west.

Ⓒ Its association with El Niño is doubted by most researchers.

Ⓓ Its causes are unrelated to oceanic water temperatures.

Paragraph 3 is marked with an arrow [➡].

6 In paragraph 4, why does the author mention the Mexican volcano El Chichón?

Ⓐ To point out a historical eruption that climatologists did not predict

Ⓑ To indicate that there is limited evidence for a theory

Ⓒ To provide support for one explanation of a phenomenon

Ⓓ To show how volcanic eruptions can directly impact trade winds

Paragraph 4 is marked with an arrow [➡].

7 Which of the sentences below best expresses the essential information in the highlighted sentence in the passage? *Incorrect* choices change the meaning in important ways or leave out essential information.

Ⓐ Researchers do not completely understand what causes El Niño, but they do know how this climatic anomaly develops, and this is useful because it enables them to predict El Niño occurrences in advance.

Ⓑ The precise causes of El Niño remain a mystery, but scientists now understand the process well enough to predict the precise duration of El Niño events once they have begun.

Ⓒ El Niño, which typically lasts for six to nine months, is not yet totally understood by experts, but they have made useful discoveries that enable them to anticipate El Niño events more accurately.

Ⓓ Climatologists can identify the first signs of an El Niño event approximately six to nine months before it fully develops, but they are as of yet unable to determine any of the underlying causes of the phenomenon.

8 The word "they" in the passage refers to

Ⓐ consequences   Ⓑ droughts   Ⓒ communities   Ⓓ patterns

9 Look at the four squares [■] that indicate where the following sentence could be added to the passage.

In other words, seawater in the eastern Pacific becomes significantly warmer.

Where would the sentence best fit?

Click on a square [■] to add the sentence to the passage.

10 Directions: An introductory sentence for a brief summary of the passage is provided below. Complete the summary by selecting the THREE answer choices that express the most important ideas in the passage. Some sentences do not belong in the summary because they express ideas that are not presented in the passage or are minor ideas in the passage. **This question is worth 2 points.**

Drag your answer choices to the spaces where they belong.
To remove an answer choice, click on it. To review the passage, click on **View Text**.

Scientists do not fully understand the root causes of El Niño, but they have discovered several occurrences that may contribute to it.

-
-
-

Answer Choices

(A) Warm water is pushed west across the Pacific Ocean by prevailing trade winds, and then flows back east when the winds die down.

(B) Research performed in recent years indicates that there is a relationship between volcanic activity in the tropics and the later emergence of El Niño events.

(C) A switch in barometric pressure patterns in the Pacific Ocean causes an extensive wall of warm water to accumulate in the western tropics.

(D) The eruption of a large Mexican volcano in 1982, shortly before an El Niño outbreak, conclusively demonstrated that volcanic activity and El Niño are linked.

(E) The changes in weather patterns due to the El Niño effect are partially responsible for the bountiful fish harvests off the west coast of South America.

(F) By identifying the root causes of the phenomenon, scientists have learned to predict when El Niño episodes will occur, helping affected communities ready themselves.

Answer Book p. 37

Vocabulary Review

Answer Book p. 39

A. Fill in the blanks with the appropriate words from the box.

skewed	skirmishes	dilation
barbaric	incomprehensible	aberrant

1 Several people were arrested in _____ between two groups of protestors.

2 Until the Rosetta Stone was used to translate them, hieroglyphics were _____ to Western scholars.

3 It was _____ of him to behave that way considering he was usually very polite.

4 Watching biased news media may promote a(n) _____ view on politics.

5 When some stimulants such as caffeine are taken in excess, it can cause _____ of pupils.

6 Though colonial governments viewed indigenous people as savages, their own actions were far more _____ than anything the natives ever did.

B. Choose the closest meaning for each highlighted word or phrase.

7 Even on casual fridays, tank tops are considered inappropriate attire for the workplace.
(A) irreparable   (B) symmetrical   (C) improper   (D) adequate

8 Copernicus overturned the entrenched belief that Earth was at the center of the universe.
(A) speculated   (B) established   (C) assessed   (D) designated

9 The government has unveiled its plans for reforming education, but critics say they are not comprehensive enough to fulfill the public's needs.
(A) persistent   (B) deliberate   (C) obvious   (D) extensive

10 This area was once a low-income neighborhood, but now it is where the young and hip dwell.
(A) accrue   (B) linger   (C) reside   (D) arrive

11 Most businesses provide credit cards to their employees, allowing them to procure work-related goods at the company's expense.
(A) acquire   (B) covet   (C) embrace   (D) admire

12 Folk and country music seem to have little in common, but the two are inextricably linked.
(A) excitingly   (B) inseparably   (C) implausibly   (D) superficially

13 These new wireless earbuds are designed to effectively block ambient noise so that users can enjoy their music.
(A) surrounding   (B) emphatic   (C) dim   (D) morose

14 The company is fabricating its products at a factory in China because of the low production costs.
(A) alternating   (B) gratifying   (C) manufacturing   (D) distributing

CHAPTER 07

Rhetorical Purpose

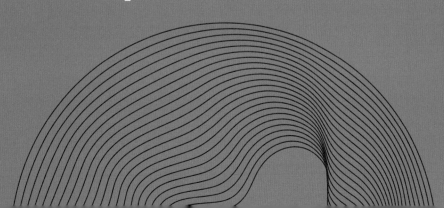

Rhetorical Purpose

About the Question Type

Rhetorical Purpose questions ask you to identify the function of a particular piece of information presented in the paragraph or the passage. Possible functions include explaining a concept, suggesting an option, illustrating a point, making a comparison, and providing an example.

Rhetoric refers to the writing techniques that an author uses to make his or her point effectively. Make sure to understand why the specified piece of information was presented by the author.

Question Format

- Why does the author mention "   " in the passage?

- In paragraph #, the author mentions/discusses/includes "   " in order to

- What is the author's primary purpose in paragraph #?

Key Strategies

- **Step 1** — Read the question and locate the specified piece of information in the passage.

- **Step 2** — Use the surrounding context to determine its purpose.

- **Step 3** — Select the answer choice that best describes the rhetorical function of the piece of information.

Example

Answer Book p. 39

Climatic Change in the Quaternary Period

During the course of the Quaternary Period, which began approximately two million years ago and continues until the present, Earth has undergone repeated cycles of glacial and interglacial periods. During a period of glaciation, the most recent of which ended approximately 10,000 years ago, massive ice sheets cover much of the temperate zones. A glacial period typically lasts for between 70,000 to 90,000 years before temperatures begin to rise and the ice sheets recede back to the poles. Due to their great size, the movement of these ice sheets fundamentally alters the landscape; for example, the Great Lakes of North America were formed as a result of this process. An interglacial period typically lasts for only 10,000 years, meaning that the current one is likely to end fairly soon.

The explanation for this phenomenon that is most widely accepted among scientists is related to the cyclic variances in Earth's orbit around the Sun. The planet's orbital path alternates from oval-shaped to circular and back again every 100,000 years. When it is oval-shaped, Earth is much farther from the Sun than usual for much of the year. Another factor is that the tilt of Earth's axis varies over a 41,000-year period. The greater the tilt, the less solar radiation the Northern and Southern Hemispheres receive during winter. In 1920, Serbian mathematician Milutin Milankovitch proposed that the onset of past glacial periods corresponded with the points at which Earth's orbit was oval-shaped and the axial tilt was most pronounced.

---

1   Why does the author mention "the Great Lakes of North America" in the passage?

(A) To provide a description of an unusual outcome of a geological process

(B) To emphasize the extent to which the ice sheets have receded

(C) To illustrate the impact that ice sheets have on the planet's surface

(D) To show how temperature changes can affect large bodies of water

2   What is the author's primary purpose in paragraph 2?

(A) To present a theory to account for a long-term climatic pattern

(B) To demonstrate that a variety of factors can affect Earth's climate

(C) To offer arguments against an explanation of weather patterns

(D) To describe an ongoing debate about the causes of glacial periods

Reading Practice 1

MBTI

In many North American secondary schools, students are given the opportunity to take the Myers-Briggs Type Indicator (MBTI), a standardized test first developed in the 1940s by a mother-daughter team of psychologists, Katharine Cook Briggs and Isabel Briggs Myers. The MBTI is unique: unlike other standardized examinations, it does not measure traits such as intelligence or math skills, but instead helps identify temperament based on responses to a series of questions designed 5 to assess preferences. For example, one question may ask test takers to indicate whether they feel energized or exhausted by intense social interaction, the answer to which shows whether they display extroverted or introverted tendencies.

The criteria used to develop these questions are derived exclusively from the work of Carl Jung, a Swiss psychiatrist and the founder of analytical psychology. Jung's approach to studying the human 10 mind placed emphasis on the exploration of nonscientific sources of knowledge, such as dreams, religion, and mythology. His writings, often radical and rarely accepted by his contemporaries including Sigmund Freud, suggested that cognition is the sum of all unconscious and conscious experiences. He also presented a number of theories about the development of personality as it relates to the balance and interaction between these two realms of thought. 15

According to Jung, one way that personality is affected by the unconscious is through a *complex*, which includes feelings and morals related to both typical and traumatic events in childhood. He described a complex like a knot in one's mind that manifests itself in behavior that is otherwise bizarre or difficult to explain. Jung's key complexes, which he called the *anima* (male) and the *animus* (female), are bundles of preconceived notions associated with gender, which cause a man, for example, 20 to behave in an irrational manner toward a woman. Jung's conclusion was that if the man had been inundated with negative representations of women throughout his childhood, regardless of his adult conception of women, his mannerisms toward women could indicate an unconscious rejection or discomfort with women.

To analyze these complexes further, Jung used word-association tests, as does the MBTI, in which 25 the subject is provided with a random word and asked to immediately respond with the first thing that comes to mind. With the answers, Jung created maps of his patients' psyches to outline the underlying complexes that are stimulating conscious behavior. After reviewing hundreds of cases, Jung noticed that there were obvious patterns in his patients' personalities marked by these complexes. He referred to these modes of thought and their typical representations as archetypes. Interestingly, the MBTI 30 incorporates these archetypes in its evaluations by situating responses into four categories of cognitive functions—sensing, intuition, thinking, and feeling—which are utilized in the overall descriptions of temperament. As a result, each respondent is classified into one of a limited number of personality types.

Skeptics of the test argue that it is accurate only because test-takers perceive it to be accurate due 35 to the Forer effect. It is an observation that people give validation to descriptions of personality that are supposedly tailored to them, but are, in fact, vague and applicable to a wide range of people. Meanwhile, a multitude of career counselors, employee trainers, and leadership coaches view it as an essential tool in understanding which jobs and lifestyles would be most likely acceptable to a particular person. 40

1   According to paragraph 1, what is unusual about the Myers-Briggs Type Indicator?

(A) It was developed by a mother and her daughter.

(B) It examines characteristics that relate to personality.

(C) It provides information about human cognition.

(D) It was designed to measure social interaction.

2   Which of the following can be inferred from paragraph 2 about Jung's contemporaries?

(A) They believed that Jung intentionally falsified data.

(B) They were unaware of the importance of the unconsciousness.

(C) They did not value nonscientific tools in the understanding of the human mind.

(D) They thought that dreams had no connection to human experiences.

3   The word "manifests" in the passage is closest in meaning to

(A) replaces

(B) distinguishes

(C) absorbs

(D) reveals

4   Why does the author mention "negative representations of women"?

(A) To explain a male subject's illogical behavior

(B) To suggest why females behave in an irrational manner

(C) To provide evidence to support a gender bias

(D) To suggest a reason why men cannot understand women

5   Why does the author mention the "Forer effect"?

(A) To provide an example of an MBTI alternative

(B) To cast doubt on a common usage of the MBTI

(C) To support the claim that the MBTI is accurate

(D) To present the basis of a criticism of the MBTI

6   In paragraph 5, which of the following is stated about some descriptions of personalities?

(A) They lack distinctiveness and can be applied to many people.

(B) They are accurate as long as they are provided by competent professionals.

(C) They are particular enough to be tailored to specific individuals.

(D) They inevitably fail because test-takers do not consider them reliable.

Reading Practice 2

Etching

The renowned artist Rembrandt van Rijn (1606-1669) is best remembered for his stunning visual portrayals of biblical scenes. His skill was particularly well suited to illustrating religious and allegorical themes with a sense of power and energy unmatched by his contemporaries. Using oil on canvas, he created more than 600 works during his lifetime, many of which are considered classical masterpieces.

In addition, he was one of the first artists to experiment with etching, a chemical printmaking method developed by goldsmiths in the Middle Ages to decorate their metalwork. This required Rembrandt to learn <u>metallurgical</u> techniques and have a working knowledge of chemistry, as well as to develop advanced papermaking skills, in order to complete a number of complicated steps involved in the process. First, the artist must create an etching, a piece of metal incised with an image. To do this, a copperplate is painted with a substance, usually a compound of beeswax, bitumen, and resin, which can resist the <u>corrosive</u> effects of acid. Then, using a sharp tool, the artist carves a design into the coating, referred to as an etching ground, exposing the metal to the air. Upon completion, the plate is dipped into nitric acid, which reacts with the exposed copper to form a pattern of recessed lines. The copperplate is then scrubbed off to remove the remaining coating, leaving a clean piece of metal displaying an incised illustration.

Once this is done, the artist moistens a piece of paper (usually made from local resources, such as tree bark, straw, or cornstalk-fiber pulp), and brushes the plate with ink (usually black or blue in color). Because the recessed lines can hold more ink than the smooth surface of the metal, when the plate is pressed onto the paper, the illustration appears darker than the rest of the transferred ink, creating a mirror-image impression of the artist's original carving.

Rembrandt and his contemporaries soon realized that there were two major benefits to making etchings: the printmaking process, known as *intaglio*, was adaptable to many kinds of surfaces as long as they could absorb ink, and the artwork created with this method was reproducible. The former encouraged artists to try out new ways to present their works, resulting in an increased interest in the decorative arts. For example, textiles could be printed with more detailed images, leading to a greater demand for intaglio fabrics. The latter, however, was arguably more important since it was the key factor in the method's proliferation throughout Europe over the next century. Reusable incised plates provided artists with a tool to make copies of their works and reap more wealth from a single creation. In addition, it facilitated the growth of private and public art collections by making available more pieces.

Intaglio continued to inspire artists during the nineteenth and twentieth centuries, as it does today. In the early 1800s, Goya, a court painter to the Spanish Crown, perfected a variant of etching called *aquatint* that supplements the carved incisions with raised lines drawn with an acid-resistant powdered resin to give the print a tonal effect. His work, in turn, paved the way for later generations, notably Pablo Picasso and his friend and rival Henri Matisse. Picasso, in particular, used aquatint intaglio to contribute to the avant-garde art movement Cubism.

Glossary
·metallurgical: of the technique or science of metals
·corrosive: able to cause damage by chemical action

1 According to paragraph 2, all of the following are necessary to create an etching EXCEPT

(A) getting rid of the excess material from the piece of metal

(B) submerging the copperplate into a chemical solution

(C) chiseling an illustration onto a metallic surface

(D) applying a coating that is vulnerable to the effects of acid

2 In etching, why is the illustration darker than the remainder of the transferred ink?

(A) The pressure of the metal infuses the ink deep into the paper.

(B) Recessed lines contain a higher ink volume than smooth metal.

(C) Two different shades of ink are used to generate contrast.

(D) The moisture in the paper causes some of the ink to spread.

3 The author's primary purpose in paragraph 3 is to

(A) suggest an alternative method of producing images

(B) point out a serious shortcoming of an etching technique

(C) show the end result of a complex preparation process

(D) explain a preference for using materials from local sources

4 The word "they" in the passage refers to

(A) contemporaries

(B) benefits

(C) etchings

(D) surfaces

5 According to paragraph 4, why did intaglio spread throughout Europe?

(A) It allowed artists to make multiple reproductions of their work.

(B) It facilitated experimentation by a number of different artists.

(C) It enhanced the interest in textile design and fashion.

(D) It resulted in pieces that could be easily imitated by other etchers.

6 Why does the author mention "Goya" in the passage?

(A) To give evidence that etching spread into the country of Spain

(B) To illustrate one way in which etching influenced artists after Picasso

(C) To provide an example of an artist who was influenced by intaglio

(D) To suggest that etching achieved its greatest popularity in the nineteenth century

Reading Practice 3

Louis Pasteur

Louis Pasteur is frequently cited as one of the most influential scientists in history, responsible for laying the foundation of numerous branches of science, including immunology and microbiology, as well as for introducing the germ theory of disease to modern epidemiology. He is also single-handedly responsible for medical breakthroughs that have saved the lives of millions around the globe. 5

Pasteur initially sought to investigate alcoholic fermentation to solve a common problem in the liquor industry, the souring of beer and wine due to lactic acid formation. At the time, it was known that yeast cells were present in alcohol, but this was attributed to spontaneous generation, the prevailing scientific model of the day. According to this theory, any organic molecules in the mixture were by-products of the chemical reactions occurring during fermentation. 10 Pasteur, however, suspected that yeast was, in fact, the catalyst for fermentation and that other microorganisms could negatively affect this process. Using a microscope, he determined that when fermentation was successful, only healthy yeast cells were present. However, soured alcohol contained small, rod-like microbes as well. **A** Pasteur believed that these microbes were responsible for lactic acid formation. **B** To test his idea, he heated the juice of grapes to sterilize it to kill off any microbes and 15 then added yeast cells to initiate fermentation. **C** Pasteur's experiment produced untainted alcohol. **D**

The success of this process had great implications for human-health professionals because it suggested that the introduction of foreign microorganisms, or germs, could be responsible for maladies as well, such as infectious diseases. Inspired by Pasteur's work, several European doctors began systematically sterilizing their operating instruments prior to surgery, a practice that dramatically 20 reduced post-surgery mortality rates. Yet many were hesitant to admit that microbes could be responsible for greater illnesses, such as cholera, diphtheria, and syphilis, which were still causing deaths in pandemic proportions.

Seeking definitive proof, Pasteur began working with anthrax bacteria, a type of microbe suspected of sickening sheep and cattle in France. He isolated the anthrax by adding a drop of infected sheep's 25 blood to a sterile culture, and after allowing time for the anthrax to multiply, a drop of the mixture was added to a new culture. This process of dilution was repeated until nothing was left of the original blood except anthrax, and the resulting substance was then tested on healthy sheep, which became ill when injected. The final culture remained as potent as the original, showing that the anthrax microbes were, beyond a doubt, responsible for the disease, and their ability to be transferred from one sheep to 30 another thus proved the germ theory of contagion.

Limiting exposure to anthrax, however, proved a difficult task as the bacterium was traced back to fields where it was easily transported through airborne spores. This encouraged Pasteur to look in another direction: following the example set by Edward Jenner's smallpox vaccine, he turned his attention to developing a treatment that could provide the animals with immunity to the disease, 35 rather than attempting to prevent its spread. Pasteur experimented with a variety of techniques to develop an anthrax vaccine, finally producing a heat-treated serum of carbolic acid. This method proved successful, and, in turn, opened up a new field of scientific exploration into the treatment of diseases caused by microbial agents. It also earned Pasteur professional and public accolades, some even hailing him as one of the greatest benefactors of humanity. 40

1 Why does the author mention "spontaneous generation" in the passage?

(A) To explain how alcohol was produced in the past

(B) To present an explanation that Pasteur invalidated

(C) To specify an idea that inspired Pasteur's experiments

(D) To indicate how lactic acid was first discovered

2 Look at the four squares [■] that indicate where the following sentence could be added to the passage.

More evidence was needed to confirm the hypothesis.

Where would the sentence best fit?

3 Which of the following can be inferred from paragraph 3 about operating instruments?

(A) They had not yet been invented prior to Pasteur's initial experiments.

(B) They were not typically sterilized before Pasteur's time.

(C) They were redesigned after Pasteur's work was published.

(D) They had caused the majority of mortalities in European hospitals.

4 According to paragraph 4, what did Pasteur learn about anthrax microbes through his experiments?

(A) That they were not related to the illnesses of sheep and cattle in France

(B) That they were the cause of disease in certain human communities

(C) That they were not effectively countered by a vaccine

(D) That they were responsible for an illness that occurred in certain animals

5 Why does the author mention "Edward Jenner's smallpox vaccine" in the passage?

(A) To show the model of treatment on which Pasteur based his work

(B) To provide background information about the state of contagion studies in the 1800s

(C) To illustrate a treatment for an infectious disease that was common in Pasteur's time

(D) To demonstrate how Pasteur's experiments motivated another scientist

6 The word "accolades" in the passage is closest in meaning to

(A) notices

(B) directions

(C) honors

(D) proposals

Answer Book p. 42

TOEFL Reading

The Celtic Oral Tradition in Ireland

➡ During the Celtic Iron Age and throughout the first four centuries AD, the history of Ireland was not recorded in written form. The Celts did not feel the need to write because they committed their stories to memory and transmitted them orally. There was also a practical problem. The only writing system they had was the ogham alphabet, which was an extremely cumbersome system of representing letters with lines of varying length and number. This could explain why extant   5 stone inscriptions are exclusively of names and genealogies. It would have made sense to use inscriptions to mark gravestones and property, but using them to record historical events or literary prose would have been futile.

➡ Most of the historical knowledge we have about early Ireland comes from Roman authors, who must have received information about the Celts indirectly. Just how reliable those early   10 records are is a matter of debate, as historical events were typically written down long after they actually occurred. However, from AD 500 onward, some Celts converted to Christianity and traveled to Europe to study. Upon their return, they composed religious texts in Latin. As a result, the number of textual resources grew from the sixth century. For instance, the *Book of Kells*, a beautifully illustrated Christian manuscript from around AD 800, stands as one of the highest   15 examples of early Irish literature. Eventually, written histories began to appear, but, early on, literacy was largely limited to religious organizations.

➡ It might be tempting to associate this relative absence of literacy prior to the sixth century with a lack of cultural sophistication. **A** However, such a view underestimates the eloquence of the Celtic oral tradition, the techniques of which were not confined to any particular class. **B** In   20 terms of their skillfulness in oratory, the Celts were on par with their contemporaries, the Gauls, who were described by Roman chroniclers of the time as a people who emphasized excellence in oratory as much as they did military glory. **C** Likewise, the Celts viewed oral poetry, speech, and song as the most powerful of human achievements. **D**

Memorization and oratory were imperative for the maintenance of Celtic tradition during the Iron   25 Age because they were the only vehicles through which the Celts could pass along their collective wisdom to subsequent generations. Clarity and factual accuracy were not the primary goals of transmission. Oral histories sometimes took the form of panegyrics, which were lyrical discourses that exaggerated certain qualities of eminent persons. Past leaders were often extolled for their generosity and concern for the people's welfare, while warriors were praised for their heroism and   30 dexterity in handling weaponry.

➡ Most often, the oral tradition was used as educational propaganda to promote the concerns of the ruling class. It is therefore understandable that lively and vivid detail was used by poets in order to captivate the audience. In addition, orations were constructed in metrical forms meant to be sung. The Celts knew very well the benefit of metrical verse as a medium for conveying   35

historical information. Sung verse, with its metrical patterns, easily stuck in the memories of Celtic youth, and it also had the advantage of not requiring the poet to be an expert in written language. Poets thus served as vessels of knowledge and were central to the education of future generations. It was the spoken word that ensured that the corpus of learning would be disseminated to succeeding generations and safeguarded against dissipation.

40

1 The word "cumbersome" in the passage is closest in meaning to

   Ⓐ atypical

   Ⓑ inconvenient

   Ⓒ irrelevant

   Ⓓ substantial

2 According to paragraph 1, which of the following is true of the ogham alphabet?

   Ⓐ It was transmitted to Ireland from the European mainland.

   Ⓑ It was mainly used in prose and to record historical events.

   Ⓒ It was first developed during the Celtic Iron Age.

   Ⓓ It was primarily used to denote names and genealogies.

Paragraph 1 is marked with an arrow [➡].

3 What can be inferred from paragraph 2 about early historical records about Ireland?

   Ⓐ They are considered unreliable by most scholars in the field of Irish history.

   Ⓑ They were usually written by people with no firsthand experience in Ireland.

   Ⓒ They were typically compiled by religious clerics in European monasteries.

   Ⓓ They are believed to be the inspiration for the *Book of Kells*.

Paragraph 2 is marked with an arrow [➡].

4 According to paragraph 3, which of the following did the Celts and Gauls have in common?

   Ⓐ They were known for their military prowess.

   Ⓑ They represented mostly illiterate populations.

   Ⓒ They had oral traditions that transcended social classes.

   Ⓓ They placed a strong emphasis on oration.

Paragraph 3 is marked with an arrow [➡].

5 Why does the author discuss "panegyrics" in the passage?

   Ⓐ To identify the primary means through which collective knowledge was passed on

   Ⓑ To highlight changes that occurred in Celtic oral history during the Iron Age

   Ⓒ To dispute that the Celts were primarily concerned with clear and accurate accounts

   Ⓓ To show that oral histories were not necessarily intended to be taken literally

6 The word "extolled" in the passage is closest in meaning to

   Ⓐ praised

   Ⓑ compensated

   Ⓒ imitated

   Ⓓ compared

7 The word "disseminated" in the passage is closest in meaning to

   Ⓐ offered

   Ⓑ spread

   Ⓒ discharged

   Ⓓ permitted

8 According to paragraph 5, what was an advantage of using metrical patterns in sung verse?

   Ⓐ They allowed verse to better convey lively details to the audience.

   Ⓑ They made it easy for young people to remember what they heard.

   Ⓒ They facilitated the conversion of traditional song into written form.

   Ⓓ They enabled poets to creatively elaborate on chronicles of past events.

Paragraph 5 is marked with an arrow [➡].

9 Look at the four squares [■] that indicate where the following sentence could be added to the passage.

The tales told by the educated elite were certainly heard and repeated by commoners.

Where would the sentence best fit?

> Click on a square [■] to add the sentence to the passage.

10 Directions: An introductory sentence for a brief summary of the passage is provided below. Complete the summary by selecting the THREE answer choices that express the most important ideas in the passage. Some sentences do not belong in the summary because they express ideas that are not presented in the passage or are minor ideas in the passage. **This question is worth 2 points.**

> Drag your answer choices to the spaces where they belong.
> To remove an answer choice, click on it. To review the passage, click on **View Text**.

During their early history, Irish Celts emphasized an oral over a written tradition.

-
-
-

Answer Choices

(A) The ogham script required considerable space for compositions, so it was not appropriate for major written works.

(B) The Celts considered oral communication to be among the most important facets of a civilization.

(C) The factual accuracy of oral histories was of secondary importance because their main functions were to praise notable figures and serve as educational propaganda.

(D) Although the written tradition was not well developed prior to the sixth century, the Celts had a sophisticated oral tradition.

(E) Panegyrics are characterized by overblown praise for a notable figure.

(F) Because they were responsible for educating the youth, poets who were skilled in lyrical verse held the highest rank in Celtic society.

Answer Book p. 42

iBT Reading Test 2

Answer Book p. 44

TOEFL Reading

Overexploitation and Animal Extinctions

According to eminent biologist E. O. Wilson, half of all living species on earth will become extinct by the end of the twenty-first century should the present rates at which they are disappearing be maintained. While organisms sometimes disappear due to natural factors, such as natural disasters that destroy habitats and interspecies competition, overexploitation by humans— the harvesting of so many individuals from a population that it can no longer sustain itself—has caused many organisms to die out or become endangered.

➡ Since prehistoric times, hunting and fishing have profoundly benefited humans by providing vital sources of sustenance. Unfortunately, they have contributed to the extinction or near extinction of some formerly prolific species. For instance, the passenger pigeon was a North American bird that used to be so populous that a flock of them was once witnessed flying overhead in a continuous stream for three days. However, the species became increasingly popular as a cheap source of meat in the nineteenth century, and the growing demand encouraged large-scale commercial hunting of the birds. As a result, the last passenger pigeon died at the Cincinnati Zoo in 1914.

Aside from capturing animals for food, humans have also targeted specific body parts of certain animals for their purported medicinal properties. Unsustainable collection has resulted in precipitous population declines of some medically valuable species. One example is the Chinese bahaba, a massive fish that used to be widespread in the waters off the coast of China from Shanghai to Hong Kong. With the aid of specialized fishing gear, fishermen caught this fish intensively for its swim bladder, an organ that is greatly valued as a general health tonic and is believed to cure heart and lung diseases. Since the market value of its highly sought-after swim bladder now exceeds that of gold, the Chinese bahaba has become scarce even though females of this species are highly fertile, releasing millions of eggs annually.

The desire for exotic pets is another avenue through which humans have exploited certain species, and, as with creatures hunted for food or medicine, the market demand for captive specimens increases their price and encourages even more poaching. Some exotic pets are bred in captivity, but many are taken directly from their natural habitats. **A** Following the discovery of the Roti Island snake-necked turtle in 1994, it quickly became exceedingly popular among exotic pet owners due to its unusually long neck, and many of the turtles are captured and sold each year. **B** As a result, the turtle is on the edge of extinction. **C** Only three populations exist on one small island, and this exclusivity has had the outcome of making it more coveted than ever. **D** Protective laws have been established to halt the trade of the endangered turtles for recreational purposes, but transactions involving these turtles have proven too lucrative for poachers to resist.

➡ As the human population has exploded and technology has advanced in recent history, the overexploitation of animal species has grown exponentially and is now a major contributor to species extinctions. If humans are concerned about the permanent loss of species, they will

need to modify their current behaviors to make use of natural resources including animal species in a more sustainable manner. In addition to improved natural resource management, necessary changes include greater control of invasive species and more aggressive measures to combat climate change.

1 According to the passage, what are TWO natural factors contributing to species extinction? Choose TWO answers.

- Ⓐ Habitat loss from natural disasters
- Ⓑ Alterations in weather patterns
- Ⓒ Competition between species
- Ⓓ Reproductive problems

2 The word "sustenance" in the passage is closest in meaning to

- Ⓐ comfort
- Ⓑ rudiments
- Ⓒ nourishment
- Ⓓ hazard

3 The word "they" in the passage refers to

- Ⓐ prehistoric times
- Ⓑ hunting and fishing
- Ⓒ humans
- Ⓓ vital sources

4 Which of the following can be inferred from paragraph 2 about the extinction of species?

- Ⓐ Extinctions caused by human activity were common in prehistoric times.
- Ⓑ An enormous population is not an effective safeguard against extinction.
- Ⓒ A high reproductive rate is necessary to avoid human-induced extinction.
- Ⓓ Extremely prolific species are less likely to die out in the short term.

Paragraph 2 is marked with an arrow [➡].

5 The word "precipitous" in the passage is closest in meaning to

(A) obvious

(B) gradual

(C) random

(D) sharp

6 Which of the sentences below best expresses the essential information in the highlighted sentence in the passage? *Incorrect* choices change the meaning in important ways or leave out essential information.

(A) As a result of its scarcity, the Chinese bahaba has evolved to survive by releasing millions of eggs a year.

(B) The swim bladder of the Chinese bahaba commands very high prices, even though the fish are close to extinction.

(C) Although the Chinese bahaba is highly fertile, it has become so scarce in the wild that it is now rarer than gold.

(D) Despite having a high reproductive potential, the Chinese bahaba is endangered because of high demand for its prized swim bladder.

7 Which of the following is NOT mentioned in paragraph 5 as a necessary modification to human behavior?

(A) More substantial restriction of invasive species

(B) More serious legal penalties for species exploitation

(C) Better administration of resources

(D) Stronger action to fight climate change

Paragraph 5 is marked with an arrow [➡].

8 What is the author's primary purpose in paragraph 5?

(A) To highlight some popular misconceptions about an issue

(B) To make a connection between overexploitation and extinctions

(C) To emphasize the need for more effective resource management

(D) To urge readers to understand the severity of a problem

Paragraph 5 is marked with an arrow [➡].

9 Look at the four squares [■] that indicate where the following sentence could be added to the passage.

Due to this increased demand, the turtles are still collected and taken off of the island to be sold overseas.

Where would the sentence best fit?

Click on a square [■] to add the sentence to the passage.

10 Directions: An introductory sentence for a brief summary of the passage is provided below. Complete the summary by selecting the THREE answer choices that express the most important ideas in the passage. Some sentences do not belong in the summary because they express ideas that are not presented in the passage or are minor ideas in the passage. **This question is worth 2 points.**

Drag your answer choices to the spaces where they belong.
To remove an answer choice, click on it. To review the passage, click on **View Text**.

A leading cause of animal extinctions is overexploitation by humans.

- ●
- ●
- ●

Answer Choices

(A) Demand for rare and exotic pets has led to the unsustainable collection of some species, such as the Roti Island snake-necked turtle.

(B) Certain animals are endangered because they are harvested intensively for the perceived medical value of specific body parts.

(C) The popularity of recreational hunting has increased to the point that many animals are in danger of extinction.

(D) The swim bladder of the Chinese bahaba is highly prized by humans for its health benefits.

(E) Because the illegal pet trade has become a major environmental concern, lawmakers have created legislation banning the distribution of exotic pets.

(F) Excessive hunting and fishing have caused some species to go extinct and greatly reduced the populations of other organisms.

Answer Book p. 44

Vocabulary Review

A. Fill in the blanks with the appropriate words from the box.

tailored	contemporaries	captivity
irrational	immunity	sustainable

1 A phobia refers to a(n) _____ fear of something that is unlikely to cause any harm.

2 Scientists maintain that _____ achieved through vaccination is longer lasting than the kind that comes from becoming infected.

3 Welfare programs are _____ to the needs of the impoverished population.

4 Salvador Dali's paintings have little in common stylistically with his Surrealist _____.

5 Acquiring electricity from sources that cannot be depleted, such as sunlight and wind, is more _____ than getting it from finite fossil fuels.

6 Elephants raised in _____ are far more calm than those that come of age in the wild.

B. Choose the closest meaning for each highlighted word or phrase.

7 The director did not even pay attention to auditions; he selected his cast based on preconceived ideas of who was right for each part.
   (A) biased   (B) sincere   (C) pathetic   (D) shady

8 Although merbromin is a potent antiseptic, it has fallen out of favor with doctors because it can cause mercury poisoning.
   (A) strong   (B) subtle   (C) neutral   (D) ineffectual

9 Elton John is dismissed by serious rock fans today, but, in the 1970s, he was hailed as the greatest songwriter since the Beatles.
   (A) corroborated   (B) acclaimed   (C) desired   (D) declaimed

10 The Greek playwrights likely wrote a thousand plays, but only 32 extant manuscripts remain in the libraries of the world.
   (A) monumental   (B) extra   (C) surviving   (D) urgent

11 The Democrats tried to pass a gun control bill, but the effort was futile without the support of Republicans.
   (A) pointless   (B) arrogant   (C) catastrophic   (D) laudable

12 Individual differences in temperament influence the way people handle emotions.
   (A) facade   (B) personality   (C) enthusiasm   (D) impracticality

13 The Palme d'Or is the most coveted award at the Cannes Film Festival.
   (A) consumed   (B) eliminated   (C) celebrated   (D) desired

14 Effective communication is one of the most highly sought-after skills in the workplace.
   (A) popular   (B) elusive   (C) invisible   (D) profound

CHAPTER 08

Sentence Insertion

Sentence Insertion

About the Question Type

Sentence Insertion questions ask you to identify the best place within a paragraph to insert the given sentence.

Pay attention to words or phrases that indicate the logical relationships between the sentences before and after the squares. These include, among others, conjunctive adverbs such as *however, therefore, nevertheless, yet,* and *moreover,* as well as pronouns like *it, they, this,* and *that.*

Question Format

Look at the four squares [■] that indicate where the following sentence could be added to the passage.

[A given sentence]

Where would the sentence best fit?

Click on a square [■] to add the sentence to the passage.

Key Strategies

- **Step 1** — Read the given sentence and look for transitional words or phrases. Use these to determine the logical relationships between the given sentence and the rest of the paragraph.

- **Step 2** — Determine the location the sentence should be placed in the paragraph.

- **Step 3** — Confirm that the paragraph has a logical flow with the sentence inserted.

Example

Answer Book p. 45

Plow Society

Prior to the development of sedentary agricultural societies, most population groups consisted of hunters, gatherers, and herders. **A** Such groups naturally had to be relatively small because their food sources were limited. **B** At some point, agrarian societies appeared, and they depended on knowledge about the cultivation of plants as well as sufficient means of preparing the soil for planting. **C** The earliest implements used were pointed sticks, which primitive 5 farmers used to stab and scrape the ground, but these gradually transformed into the hoe, a better tool with a blade that could be used to till the soil. **D**

A major breakthrough that was associated with agrarian settlements was the invention of the plow, which could be dragged in the fertile land to create many rows of long furrows for sowing seeds or planting. **A** Two people could work together to pull the plow across the field, but even 10 though using a plow was a huge advantage over previous methods, it nonetheless required a tremendous amount of physical might. **B** Moreover, it was arduous, so innovative farmers turned to beasts of burden to help reduce their toil. **C** Nevertheless, the physical strength needed to control the plow and these unwieldy beasts was substantial. **D**

Thus, with the invention of the plow, the job of preparing fields became the responsibility 15 of men as the work of women in preparing fields became less valuable in terms of economic productivity. Before that, women had shared the responsibility of breaking up the soil, but freed from this task, they had time to devote to other activities, and thus the plow was influential in altering gender roles.

1　Look at the four squares [■] in paragraph 1 that indicate where the following sentence could be added to the passage.

In addition, they had to move around from place to place because otherwise there would have been an inevitable exhaustion of resources.

Where would the sentence best fit?

2　Look at the four squares [■] in paragraph 2 that indicate where the following sentence could be added to the passage.

The ox-drawn plow permitted a single person to till a comparatively vast plot of land in less time.

Where would the sentence best fit?

Answer Book p. 45

Mammal Migration Practices

In biology, the practice of periodically migrating to and from a location is commonly associated with flying and aquatic animals. However, numerous mammal species also engage in migration in response to the changing availability of resources and mates. Three prominent examples of mammals that migrate are northern fur seals, North American pronghorns, and African elephants.

The largest species of eared seal found in the North Pacific region, the northern fur seal migrates 5 for the purpose of procreation. As an amphibious species, northern fur seals have a significant advantage over migratory land mammals in that they are able to swim great distances. As a result, the migration of the northern fur seal can extend up to three thousand miles. Each year, the seals return to rookeries on the Pribilof Islands in the Bering Sea to meet a mate. Male seals reach the breeding grounds first, in May, and the females arrive slightly later. Near the end of November, after the seal 10 pups have been weaned, the seals spread in a southerly direction for the winter.

While males generally spend their winters in the Bering Sea and upper Pacific, females swim as far as the southern tip of California. After exhaustive research, scientists believe that the reason for this disparity in migratory range lies in the size differences in the species—males can grow up to 40 percent longer and 370 percent heavier than females. The significantly smaller females are unable to 15 withstand the brutally cold winters of the upper Pacific and must travel thousands of miles to warmer regions in the winter. However, the migration of the seals is under threat of disruption by human activities. For example, excessive fishing can interfere with their migration, as females that cannot obtain enough prey do not have enough energy to complete the journey back to the breeding grounds.

The North American pronghorn completes a short migration in just three days. Pronghorn herds 20 in the Grand Teton National Park in Wyoming travel over one hundred miles south to reach the milder climate of the Green River Basin. Their path spans fragmented private and public lands, each of which is lined with manmade obstacles. Despite having the ability to run at 55 miles per hour, pronghorn cannot easily jump over barriers. **A** Consequently, agricultural and security fences create a serious impediment, and pronghorn must attempt to squeeze through or under the fences, an action 25 that leaves them highly vulnerable to predation. **B** In recognition of these difficulties, nonprofit and governmental organizations have joined forces to create pronghorn-friendly areas. **C** Grass overpasses have been constructed to facilitate the safe passage of the pronghorn across highways. **D**

In comparison to other mammal species, the migration of the African bush elephant is poorly understood. These animals are highly unpredictable, and their disparate migratory patterns pose 30 a challenge for conservationists. Moreover, unlike other migratory mammals, elephants do not appear to be driven by a biological imperative to breed in a particular area, nor is their movement prompted by the location of food resources. Instead, research performed at Hwange National Park in Zimbabwe found that some elephants traveled over sixty miles to visit water sources during droughts. Unfortunately, these migrations frequently exit protected parks, putting the elephants in danger when 35 they cross into an area with a high poaching risk.

Glossary

·amphibious: living in both land and water

1 The word "exhaustive" in the passage is closest in meaning to

(A) thorough

(B) accurate

(C) supreme

(D) noticeable

2 According to paragraph 3, all of the following are differences between male and female northern fur seals EXCEPT:

(A) Males are substantially larger than females.

(B) Females are the first to arrive at the rookeries.

(C) Males spend the winter in cooler areas.

(D) Females travel greater distances in winter.

3 Look at the four squares [■] that indicate where the following sentence could be added to the passage.

With the ability to cross roads smoothly, pronghorn in several areas have suffered virtually no fatalities due to vehicle collisions.

Where would the sentence best fit?

4 According to paragraph 4, what restriction limits the movement of pronghorns?

(A) They are unable to run through snow.

(B) They can only move in groups.

(C) They cannot identify a migratory route.

(D) They find it difficult to navigate obstacles.

5 Which of the sentences below best expresses the essential information in the highlighted sentence in the passage?

(A) The location of food is the primary reason for elephant movement.

(B) Elephants are not motivated by breeding or food sources in their migrations.

(C) Compared to others, elephants are not driven by biological necessity.

(D) Different species' migratory habits can be readily compared to those of elephants.

6 According to paragraph 5, why does elephant migration disrupt conservation efforts?

(A) They do not want to remain in one country.

(B) They travel to areas that are unknown to conservationists.

(C) Their feeding habits occur at unpredictable times.

(D) Their routes lead out of secure zones.

HACKERS APEX READING for the TOEFL iBT Expert

Reading Practice 2

Atlantis

Utopia is usually defined as a perfect community that represents the human desire for peace and equality. One of the most famous stories about a utopia comes from the Socratic dialogues *Timaeus* and *Critias*, in which Plato tells the story of an island called Atlantis that is swallowed up by the sea in a profound natural disaster. In his writing, Plato laments the loss of the former Atlantean empire, an advanced civilization that had an imperial palace constructed of ivory, gold, and silver as well as   5 infrastructure that included bridges, temples, and a stadium for horse-racing.

Because Plato's story of Atlantis is embedded in his philosophical works and intended to support invented theories, few scholars believe the author intended to convey a true history. There remains, however, the possibility that the myth of Atlantis was inspired by memories of an actual past event.

One common hypothesis holds that the destruction of Atlantis is based on the volcano Thera that   10 erupted in the Mediterranean Sea during the Bronze Age around 1650 BC. This natural disaster would have been the single most important incident in the Aegean region prior to the Trojan War, and Plato would certainly have been aware of the devastation that it brought about. Some archaeologists believe that this cataclysmic geologic event triggered the downfall of the Minoan civilization, a powerful seafaring culture that was centered on the Greek island of Crete. The explosion dropped roughly   15 ten centimeters of ash on the island, smothering all indigenous vegetation and, in turn, leading to mass starvation among the animal and human populations. At the same time, a series of tidal waves, generated when the eruption caused the collapse of the Santorini caldera, devastated the Cretan coastline. Minoan navy fortresses and merchant ports were washed away. With their ability to produce food severely diminished and their seafaring livelihood effectively destroyed, the Minoans struggled to   20 survive and their civilization eventually disappeared 200 years later.

Others postulate that a coastal region in southern Spain was the Atlantis described in Plato's works. This hypothesis is largely based on satellite images that show what appears to be a sunken city, which some scholars believe to be the ancient city of Tartessos. **A** According to ancient Greek and Egyptian literature, the people of Tartessos were wealthy traders of precious metals from the western extremes   25 of the Mediterranean, and this description is consistent with Plato's depiction of Atlantis. **B** One issue with this theory, however, is that Tartessos was not an island, while Plato's Atlantis was. **C** Still, proponents of the theory explain the contradiction by suggesting that Plato, who frequently used Egyptian historical texts in his dialogues, confused the hieroglyphic for "coastline" with the one meaning "island," a mistake that was quite common in other Greek works. **D**   30

A third claim is that when Plato spoke of the Ocean of Atlantis, he was actually referring to the sea now known as the Atlantic Ocean. In his account, Plato mentions that Atlantis was located in a vast sea beyond the Pillars of Hercules, where the Mediterranean flows into the Atlantic Ocean. Therefore, the doomed utopian city could have been located outside of the Mediterranean. Supporters of this theory propose that the legend incorporates historical accounts of the Neolithic cultures of   35 Ireland, who left megalithic stone tombs. Moreover, Ireland is the only island in the world that fits the geographical description of Atlantis (roughly 300 miles long and 200 miles wide), and its landscape was fundamentally changed by natural disasters related to climate change at the end of the last ice age.

Glossary

·hieroglyphic: the pictorial script of the ancient Egyptians

1   According to paragraph 1, Plato's dialogues describe the Atlantean empire as

(A) a wealthy group of people

(B) a classless community

(C) a peaceful society

(D) a highly developed civilization

2   The word "embedded" in the passage is closest in meaning to

(A) integrated

(B) discovered

(C) isolated

(D) implied

3   Why does the author mention the "Trojan War" in the passage?

(A) To suggest that Plato could have used the Trojan War as a foundation for Atlantis

(B) To emphasize how significant Thera's eruption was in the ancient Greek world

(C) To support the claim that the major armed conflict occurred after the geological disaster

(D) To give an example of another historical event that may appear in Plato's dialogues

4   Which of the following can be inferred from paragraph 3 about the Minoan people?

(A) They lived on a volcanic island.

(B) They did not have any agricultural technology.

(C) They utilized many ships.

(D) They relied on animals for food.

5   Look at the four squares [■] that indicate where the following sentence could be added to the passage.

This has led to a fair amount of skepticism regarding the Tartessos theory.

Where would the sentence best fit?

6   All of the following evidence is used to support the theory that Ireland could be the location of Atlantis EXCEPT:

(A) Its size is similar to the island Plato described.

(B) It was home to a society that built large stone structures.

(C) It was altered by a devastating natural event.

(D) Its inhabitants worshipped the god Hercules.

Answer Book p. 47

Geoengineering

In the past one hundred years, the average surface temperature of the earth has increased by 0.6 °C. While the climate of the planet has undergone similar changes in the past, there is a growing body of research that shows human activity is responsible for the most recent rise in global temperatures. This notion is bolstered by the fact that the increase in temperature has occurred during a period that has seen industrialized societies vastly increase emissions of gases such as carbon 5 dioxide, methane, and nitrous oxide. These substances are widely considered to be the primary causes of the greenhouse effect, whereby gases trapped in the atmosphere prevent the radiation of heat into space.

The consequences of global warming have been the subject of extensive conjecture, with some long-term projections showing a dramatic rise in sea levels, changes in ocean currents, and 10 fluctuations in precipitation. These forecasts have led to concerns about widespread desertification and mass extinctions that could result from habitat alteration. There is also a growing consensus that the negative effects of global warming are not limited to the distant future. Many climatologists assert that it is responsible for the recent increased prevalence of extreme weather systems such as hurricanes, typhoons, and tornadoes. As a result, scientists have begun to explore alternative methods to deal with 15 global warming, with the most prominent of these being geoengineering, which is the use of human technology to modify the physical properties of the planet.

In 1990, a British physicist John Latham argued that the simplest solution to the problem of rising temperatures was to increase the reflective capacity, or albedo, of the earth. Although many factors contribute to the planet's capacity to reflect light, low-altitude stratocumulus clouds have always been 20 considered particularly important. Latham's proposal would capitalize on this by using a specialized device to atomize seawater in a manner that would project particles of salt into existing clouds. **A** This would have the dual effect of increasing the overall volume of cloud coverage by providing a nucleus around which droplets of moisture would form, while simultaneously raising the albedo of existing clouds by increasing their density. **B** The plan calls for multiple apparatuses to be attached 25 to several automated vessels, powered by the wind and navigated by satellite, which would continually crisscross the oceans. **C** While proponents emphasize the fact that the scheme would have a low environmental impact and would be easily reversible, some experts have expressed concern about whether it would have intended effect. **D**

A more recent method for limiting the amount of solar radiation reaching the earth has proven 30 much more controversial, as it would result in changes to the atmosphere of the planet that would last for a duration of multiple years. Scientists have long recognized that increased levels of certain airborne particles result in a drop in global temperatures, a fact confirmed by climatic studies following large volcanic eruptions. Working from this data, a Nobel-winning chemist Paul Crutzen suggested that the albedo of the earth could be increased by injecting sulfur particles into the stratosphere. 35 Although there is little debate regarding the effectiveness of this idea, there is grave concern regarding its safety. Not only would the effects take several years to reverse in the case that there were negative consequences, but there is also a high probability that the sulfur particles will return to the planet's surface, posing a potential health hazard. As a result, the plan has been presented as a last resort, best suited to deal with a situation in which climatic conditions deteriorate dramatically. 40

1 According to paragraph 1, the recent rise in the earth's average temperature is attributable to human activity because

(A) developed nations have expanded their production of certain air pollutants
(B) modern factories generate gases that absorb the energy of the sun
(C) wealthy countries create products that are dependent on harmful substances
(D) many industries have increased the amount of goods they manufacture

2 The word "conjecture" in the passage is closest in meaning to

(A) consequence
(B) pledge
(C) prerequisite
(D) speculation

3 Look at the four squares [■] that indicate where the following sentence could be added to the passage.

As a renewable energy source would be used, they would be able to operate for extended periods of time.

Where would the sentence best fit?

4 According to paragraph 3, how would the apparatus invented by Latham lower the temperature of the planet?

(A) It would increase the number of water droplets, leading to more precipitation.
(B) It would draw oceanic water into the clouds, resulting in currents of cooler air.
(C) It would propel matter into clouds, raising their density and volume.
(D) It would traverse the oceans, reducing the effects of certain weather systems.

5 The word "it" in the passage refers to

(A) method
(B) amount
(C) radiation
(D) earth

6 Why does the author mention "a duration of multiple years"?

(A) To illustrate the effectiveness of a proposed course of action
(B) To explain why a project is considered by many to be unsuitable
(C) To emphasize the need for long-term solutions to global warming
(D) To show the extent to which solar radiation reaches the earth

Pottery

➡ Pottery is an example of a relatively simple technology that had a profound impact on those cultures that became proficient in its application. Prior to the invention of the pottery wheel, production methods involved the use of coils and balls of clay that were shaped by hand to create the finished product. Due to its unique properties 5 and widespread availability, clay was the predominant material used in the creation of early pots, as the substance is malleable when wet, hardens when dry, and with the application of intense heat becomes as hard as concrete.

Once the expertise and knowledge required to create a durable and utilitarian baked clay vessel for storage, transportation, and cooking was acquired, the structure of a society was 10 transformed in a manner that altered many of its fundamental features. As early cultures became more technologically and economically advanced, greater effort and resources were devoted to the adornment of containers, resulting in these items serving both an artistic and a functional role.

➡ The earliest known example of the widespread use of pottery is the Jomon period in Japan, with estimates for the age of the fragments unearthed by archeologists ranging from 10,000 to 15 15,000 years. The name Jomon, which means "cord pattern" in Japanese, is taken from the manner in which the people of this Neolithic culture decorated their ceramics. Jomon pottery was formed with a variety of materials, including plant fibers and crushed shells. As with most Neolithic pottery, the vessels were fashioned by women, and they were made without the aid of a wheel.

➡ Extensive research has provided a great deal of insight into the significance of pottery to 20 early societies, with the most important contribution being that ceramic vessels made it possible to boil or steam foodstuffs, a necessity if a group is to be able to adjust to a diet more dependent on plant-based sources of nutrition. This shift in diet, and the primitive form of agriculture that developed in response, led to a dramatic increase in population during the Neolithic period, as humanity made the transition from a nomadic to a semi-sedentary lifestyle. 25

The utility of ceramics was not, however, limited to primitive cultures, and it was a significant contributor to the growth of the complex social, cultural, and political systems that arose in what is commonly referred to as the Fertile Crescent. **A** In order for the process of urbanization to occur, it was necessary to be able to store vast quantities of food in a manner that protected it from rodents and other pests that might consume the community's reserves of provisions. **B** Safe food 30 storage was made possible by the invention of the pottery wheel, which allowed for the production of a large number of standardized containers, and the specialized expertise required to make use of the technology led to a new class of artisans. **C** Eventually, certain regions began to focus on pottery as their primary economic activity, with the result that the clay vessels themselves became important trade goods. **D** 35

➡ As the manufacturing of ceramics became increasingly commercialized, the focus shifted to the creation of unique ornaments intended for the luxury market. This resulted in an increased awareness of the potential for ceramics to act solely as a vehicle for creative expression, a trend that reached its peak with the rise of Greek culture. Rather than simply serving pragmatic purposes, Greek vases were often elaborately decorated and served as works of art in affluent 40 households.

1 According to paragraph 1, all of the following are characteristics of clay EXCEPT:

- Ⓐ Moisture makes it pliable.
- Ⓑ High temperatures make it durable.
- Ⓒ Dehydration makes it inflexible.
- Ⓓ Glazing makes it heat-resistant.

Paragraph 1 is marked with an arrow [➡].

2 The word "utilitarian" in the passage is closest in meaning to

- Ⓐ influential
- Ⓑ practical
- Ⓒ appropriate
- Ⓓ controversial

3 The word "its" in the passage refers to

- Ⓐ expertise
- Ⓑ knowledge
- Ⓒ vessel
- Ⓓ society

4 According to paragraph 3, which of the following is NOT true of Jomon pottery?

- Ⓐ It was typically produced by females.
- Ⓑ Its name came from its rope-like designs.
- Ⓒ It was made with various natural materials.
- Ⓓ Its production was aided by the use of a wheel.

Paragraph 3 is marked with an arrow [➡].

5 According to paragraph 4, how did pottery influence Neolithic society?

(A) It facilitated the consumption of different types of foods.

(B) It contributed to the effectiveness of cultivation activities.

(C) It diminished the harmful effects of overpopulation.

(D) It enabled groups to travel further in search of provisions.

Paragraph 4 is marked with an arrow [➡].

6 Why does the author mention "rodents and other pests" in the passage?

(A) To show that cities required such large volumes of food

(B) To suggest a problem associated with high population densities

(C) To explain the role ceramics played in the formation of early cities

(D) To demonstrate a shortcoming of the clay pots used in the Middle East

7 Which of the sentences below best expresses the essential information in the highlighted sentence in the passage? *Incorrect* choices change the meaning in important ways or leave out essential information.

(A) The need for safe food vessels made it necessary for potters to work in unison in order to create the necessary technology.

(B) Specialization within the pottery industry led to the development of safer technologies, such as the pottery wheel.

(C) As craftsmen with specific knowledge became more skilled in the use of the pottery wheel, the quality of pottery improved dramatically.

(D) The invention of the pottery wheel made safely storing food feasible, and a new category of craftspeople emerged from mastering its use.

8 Which of the following can be inferred from paragraph 6 about Greek ornamental ceramics?

(A) They were among Greece's leading commercial exports.

(B) They were usually used as storage containers.

(C) They were found in the majority of households.

(D) They were not affordable to all families.

Paragraph 6 is marked with an arrow [➡].

9 Look at the four squares [■] that indicate where the following sentence could be added to the passage.

This was an issue in many cities and acted as an impediment to significant population increases.

Where would the sentence best fit?

Click on a square [■] to add the sentence to the passage.

10 Directions: An introductory sentence for a brief summary of the passage is provided below. Complete the summary by selecting the THREE answer choices that express the most important ideas in the passage. Some sentences do not belong in the summary because they express ideas that are not presented in the passage or are minor ideas in the passage. **This question is worth 2 points.**

Drag your answer choices to the spaces where they belong.
To remove an answer choice, click on it. To review the passage, click on **View Text**.

Ceramics have played an important role in the development of human civilization.

-
-
-

Answer Choices

(A) The artistic potential of pottery was exploited in the classical world, and this resulted in the creation of new modes of expression.

(B) With the advent of the pottery wheel, craftspeople began to produce products that contributed to economic growth.

(C) Early examples of pottery show its importance to the establishment of permanent agrarian communities.

(D) The availability of suitable vessels for food storage contributed to the rise of ancient cities.

(E) Nomadic peoples depended on clay vessels to transport perishable food items.

(F) Pottery became an artistic medium, as practitioners experimented with more sophisticated designs.

Answer Book p. 48

The Host-Parasite System

Insect ectoparasites are those that subsist on the exterior of animals, consuming the iron-rich hemoglobin or bodily secretions of their hosts. They are not to be confused with carnivorous mosquitoes, as these creatures, although they survive off the blood of others, do not actually live on their prey. True ectoparasites make their primary home on hosts and are highly adapted to these niche environments, often evolving concurrently with the animal on which they live. Most 5 have developed morphological modifications, such as strong claws, sucking mouthparts, and the loss of functional wings, as a result of this coevolution—a complex relationship that scientists call a host-parasite system.

➡ Bats, a widely distributed flying mammal, provide a good example of this form of coevolutionary interaction because they are associated with numerous parasitic species, most of 10 them ectoparasitic. There are several main causative factors that promote the development of ectoparasites on bats, all of which are crucial to understanding the host-parasite system. Although they vary considerably in mass and can be separated into almost one thousand distinct species, all bats exhibit social behavior that makes them favorable hosts and distributors of disease. For example, they live in colonies ranging in size from several hundred up to a million individuals 15 and prefer to remain in close proximity to other members to facilitate successful foraging. The large numbers of bats per colony provide a fitness advantage for ectoparasites; specifically, they have multiple hosts from which to feed while they evolve to cope with the bats' morphological or behavioral changes. The development of ectoparasites is additionally encouraged by the predilection of bats to roost communally with others of the same sex in isolated structures, such 20 as caves, culverts, or abandoned buildings, where temperatures are stable, and humidity is elevated. All of these factors contribute to the high transmission rate of ectoparasites from host to host.

➡ **A** Bat flies, which inhabit several species of bats, exemplify an ectoparasitic organism that thrives on bat hosts. **B** These wingless insects are highly specialized, with modified body 25 segments, hind tibiae, and strong bristles used to latch onto the fur of bats. **C** The reproductive season for bat flies lasts for several months in the spring and summer, and metamorphosis from puparia in bat roosts takes thirty days, resulting in a plethora of insects emerging in July. **D**

➡ To combat the flies, bats participate in extended grooming sessions during the summer, when they will utilize several methods of cleaning and maintaining their fur. Despite some 30 evidence to suggest that this activity is related to mating behavior, the fact that bats roost mainly with members of the same sex suggests that it is more likely done for the purpose of removing ectoparasites from the bodies of kin, with increased reproductive success being an indirect result. Young bats spend most of their waking hours self-grooming; however, as they age, they shift their efforts to the grooming of other colony members. The more ectoparasites in a particular colony, 35

the longer the bats will spend grooming themselves and others in response, until the population of flies, for instance, is reduced to a comfortable level.

Coevolution, however, has allowed bat flies to develop their own strategies to cope with the constant threat of removal by grooming. A large number cling to each host and can switch from a male bat to a female while the hosts are engaged in mating activities. This allows them to alternate between sex-specific roosts to reduce exposure to one type of grooming, as well as to avoid exhausting any one particular host, which improves their own chance for long-term survival.

─ 40

1 Why does the author mention "mosquitoes" in the passage?

  Ⓐ To illustrate the type of organism ectoparasites consume

  Ⓑ To provide an example of an ectoparasite

  Ⓒ To identify a particular trait of insect ectoparasites

  Ⓓ To distinguish between two types of ectoparasites

2 The word "concurrently" in the passage is closest in meaning to

  Ⓐ ambiguously   Ⓑ proportionately   Ⓒ simultaneously   Ⓓ inadvertently

3 The word "predilection" in the passage is closest in meaning to

  Ⓐ weakness   Ⓑ preference   Ⓒ attraction   Ⓓ thoughtfulness

4 According to paragraph 2, all of the following traits make bats suitable ectoparasite hosts EXCEPT:

  Ⓐ They sleep together in large sex-specific groups.

  Ⓑ They congregate in great numbers to search for food.

  Ⓒ Their preferred resting places are moist.

  Ⓓ Their bodies adjust quickly to temperature changes.

Paragraph 2 is marked with an arrow [➡].

5 Which of the following can be inferred from paragraph 3 about bat flies?

   Ⓐ They live for about one year.

   Ⓑ They are unable to fly.

   Ⓒ They are more common in spring than summer.

   Ⓓ They live on mammals other than bats.

Paragraph 3 is marked with an arrow [➡].

6 Why do experts reject the idea that grooming is an aspect of mating behavior?

   Ⓐ The practice begins after the summer mating season.

   Ⓑ Bats tend to clean others of the same gender.

   Ⓒ Bats are inclined to clean family members of the identical age.

   Ⓓ The conduct has not been shown to improve sexual reproduction.

7 According to paragraph 4, what determines the amount of time bats devote to grooming?

   Ⓐ The size of a population group of ectoparasites

   Ⓑ The number of hours that colony members remain awake

   Ⓒ The proximity of bats willing to engage in reciprocal grooming

   Ⓓ The type of ectoparasites infesting the colony

Paragraph 4 is marked with an arrow [➡].

8 The word "them" in the passage refers to

   Ⓐ bat flies

   Ⓑ strategies

   Ⓒ hosts

   Ⓓ activities

9 Look at the four squares [■] that indicate where the following sentence could be added to the passage.

In particular, their mouthparts are adapted to pierce the skin and suck blood.

Where would the sentence best fit?

Click on a square [■] to add the sentence to the passage.

10 Directions: An introductory sentence for a brief summary of the passage is provided below. Complete the summary by selecting the THREE answer choices that express the most important ideas in the passage. Some sentences do not belong in the summary because they express ideas that are not presented in the passage or are minor ideas in the passage. **This question is worth 2 points.**

Drag your answer choices to the spaces where they belong.
To remove an answer choice, click on it. To review the passage, click on **View Text**.

The interaction between bats and parasitic organisms exemplify the host-parasite system.

- ●

- ●

- ●

Answer Choices

(A) Bats sleep and forage in groups, which provides good opportunities for gender-specific ectoparasites populations to prosper.

(B) Bats have developed self-cleaning practices that reduce the number of ectoparasites on their bodies and will perform these tasks as necessary.

(C) Ectoparasites flourish in bat populations, as they thrive in the same remote environments that bats use as roosts.

(D) Insects with adapted morphologies live on the skin and fur of bats by consuming waste products of their host.

(E) Small parasitic organisms continually modify their behavior to cope with any changes that their bat hosts make to defend themselves.

(F) Because bats exhibit a variety of social behaviors, they provide an excellent host for parasitic species, which evolve concurrently.

Answer Book p. 50

Vocabulary Review

A. Fill in the blanks with the appropriate words from the box.

devastated	sedentary	unwieldy
resort	reversible	expertise

1　Nomadic hunter-gatherers became _____ farmers after forming agricultural societies.

2　With exercise and dietary restrictions, mild cases of type two diabetes can be _____.

3　I was determined to find the answer for myself and to ask my sister for help only as a last _____.

4　Writing a blog can be a lucrative enterprise if you have _____ in a field that readers are interested in.

5　We tried to maneuver the _____ sofa through the door, but its size made that effort pointless.

6　The tsunami _____ the island, destroying hundreds of houses and motor vehicles.

B. Choose the closest meaning for each highlighted word or phrase.

7　Adornment of the body is a universal human practice with numerous cultural variations.
　(A) Decorating　　　　(B) Protecting　　　　(C) Recognizing　　　　(D) Maintaining

8　The effect of human activity on biodiversity has been cataclysmic, with 150 species going extinct each day.
　(A) creative　　　　(B) destructive　　　　(C) celebratory　　　　(D) gradual

9　I made my way up the mountain, but the hike was arduous because the path was so steep.
　(A) laborious　　　　(B) inspiring　　　　(C) picturesque　　　　(D) grating

10　A poor diet is a causative factor in the development of numerous diseases.
　(A) unseemly　　　　(B) salubrious　　　　(C) embarrassing　　　　(D) contributing

11　The disparity in wealth between urban and rural areas has become wider than ever.
　(A) choice　　　　(B) discrepancy　　　　(C) realm　　　　(D) earnings

12　Lack of infrastructure has been a major impediment to the economic development of African countries.
　(A) accompaniment　　(B) path　　　　(C) hindrance　　　　(D) symbol

13　DNA is the vehicle through which a trait can pass from one generation to the next.
　(A) premise　　　　(B) fashion　　　　(C) automobile　　　　(D) means

14　The opening strains of Mozart's *The Magic Flute* exemplify the playful tone that continues throughout the opera.
　(A) illustrate　　　　(B) portray　　　　(C) synthesize　　　　(D) exclude

CHAPTER 09

Summary

Summary

About the Question Type

Summary questions ask you to complete a summary of the passage by selecting three out of six sentences that best express the major ideas in the passage.

Correct answer choices are restatements of the main idea of one or more paragraphs in the passage. Incorrect answer choices often express inaccurate information, minor points (examples, supporting ideas, etc.), or details that are not mentioned in the passage.

Question Format

Directions: An introductory sentence for a brief summary of the passage is provided below. Complete the summary by selecting the THREE answer choices that express the most important ideas in the passage. Some sentences do not belong in the summary because they express ideas that are not presented in the passage or are minor ideas in the passage. **This question is worth 2 points.**

> Drag your answer choices to the spaces where they belong.
> To remove an answer choice, click on it. To review the passage, click on **View Text**.

[An introductory sentence]
-
-
-

Answer Choices

Key Strategies

- **Step 1** — Read the introductory sentence that represents the main idea of the passage.

- **Step 2** — Scan the passage to see if each answer choice is supported by the passage.

- **Step 3** — Select the three answer choices that express the major ideas in the passage.

Example

Sumerian Cuneiform

Sumer was the earliest documented civilization in Mesopotamia, founded around 4000 BC and located in the southern part of modern Iraq. The society was recorded in Sumerian cuneiform, a system of writing that emerged without any precursors at some point before 3000 BC. Cuneiform marks were pushed into clay tablets to document large trade transactions and other important information. 5

Over time, Sumerian pictograms became precise and practical. This was beneficial because laws that were previously orally recited were transcribed onto clay to be preserved and spread throughout the Sumerian cities. Additionally, descriptions of the food and other resources collected for taxes were recorded for bureaucratic purposes. This recording system bolstered the 10 wealth of the civilization as the contribution of every household was carefully checked to reduce tax avoidance and ensure that everyone was contributing the correct amount of tax.

Through writing, with each subsequent generation of scholars, the accumulated knowledge of Mesopotamia could be utilized and built upon. This prevented wastage, as fundamental workers, such as farmers and potters, did not forget essential information or lose specialized skills. One 15 example is the Sumerian Farmer's Almanac, which is a small clay tablet containing lines of detailed agricultural instructions. These lines describe the methods for irrigating fields, the best tools to use, and the optimal depth for seed planting.

The creation of cuneiform played a crucial role in advancing the culture of the Sumerians and humanity as a whole. The development of written language granted an extension to the 20 limits of human knowledge, allowing information to be reliably shared across the generations. Lacking writing, the entirety of human history would have been different. Furthermore, the use of clay has allowed millions of documents to survive from the ancient Mesopotamian kingdoms, providing historians with a wealth of information about ancient society.

1 **Directions:** An introductory sentence for a brief summary of the passage is provided below. Complete the summary by selecting the THREE answer choices that express the most important ideas in the passage.

The invention of cuneiform allowed Sumerians to become a record-keeping society that benefited from storing and passing down knowledge.

(A) The use of cuneiform for tax and legal purposes offered advantages to Sumerian society.

(B) Cuneiform provides insight for scholars into the daily activities of Sumerian households.

(C) The sharing of written information permitted skilled workers to transfer key techniques over multiple generations.

(D) Clay was adopted for a variety of bureaucratic and educational reasons in the cities of Mesopotamia.

(E) Cuneiform played a key role in the development of both Sumerian and human culture.

(F) Cuneiform was useful because it could document knowledge that was not preserved orally.

Answer Book p. 51

Italian Renaissance Architecture

Thinking men and women of the Italian Renaissance were fascinated with the remains of Greco-Roman antiquity, as they reasoned that the arts and humanities had undergone a significant decline from the Middle Ages until the beginning of their own time. Thus, to restore these disciplines to their original glory, 5 creators passionately emulated works of the ancients, endeavoring to match their quality or surpass it, and, as a result, Italy experienced a revitalization of culture.

The style of architecture during this period was therefore an amalgamation of Classical Roman elements, including columns, arches, and domes, and variations on these advanced by Renaissance 10 artists. The most important consideration was the notion of *symmetra*, or symmetry, which required any building to be geometrically balanced, a reflection of the concept of perfect parity as emphasized by the humanist movement. In addition, the component parts of a structure had to be built with *disposito*, or disposition, demanding that all must be congruous with one another. A church with a tall, acutely pointed pyramidal roof would be counterweighted with two smaller mathematically 15 proportionate steeples, one on either side, in compliance with these underlying rules.

A Yet, architects added their own innovations as well, and the first great architect of this era, Filippo Brunelleschi, produced new architectural forms in the Florentine churches of San Lorenzo and Santo Spirito. **B** Under the direction of the Pope, he also presented a revolutionary plan to build a massive dome on the Cathedral of Florence. **C** Most importantly, his works served as a model 20 for subsequent projects because they were not only prominent features of the cities in which they appeared, but their blueprints were described and analyzed in the writings of Leon Battista Alberti, a renowned architectural theoretician. **D**

The dissemination of works by Alberti and other influential writers had an incredible impact on the discipline, as it facilitated greater access to architectural theory for the growing number of artists 25 interested in the subject. Aided by the introduction of the movable type press, a groundbreaking invention that made possible the development of print culture, knowledge of architectural principles spread rapidly. Perhaps the most significant books, however, were the four volumes composed by Andrea Palladio, who outlined all known aspects of Classical Roman architecture and described the appropriation of those elements into contemporary buildings. It was an effort that was intended to 30 supplement the training of up-and-coming architects and inspire veteran artists.

The proliferation of such literature was also an essential tool that helped motivate citizens to become patrons of the arts, a role that was key to the continued success of any art form. Most Renaissance-era structures can be clearly traced back to private sources of funding, such as a wealthy banker or influential merchant, and many still bear the name of these patrons. For instance, the Palazzo Medici, 35 a palace located in the heart of Florence, was built with money donated by the powerful Medici family, whose generous patronage for a number of distinguished artists helped transform the city into the preeminent architectural center of Europe. It also encouraged some famous artists such as Donatello and Michelangelo, who created works to either decorate these structures or be the focal point of rooms within them, to take up residence in Florence. 40

1 Which of the sentences below best expresses the essential information in the highlighted sentence in the passage?

(A) Classical Roman architecture included a variety of elements that also defined the Renaissance style.

(B) The Renaissance approach incorporated all facets of Classical Roman architecture.

(C) Imitation of aspects of Classical Roman architecture led to the Renaissance form.

(D) Elements of Classical Roman design and modifications of these dictated the nature of Renaissance architecture.

2 Look at the four squares [■] that indicate where the following sentence could be added to the passage.

Although this was never actually realized, its bold design roused many other architects to attempt similar feats.

Where would the sentence best fit?

3 According to paragraph 4, what was a result of the development of movable type press?

(A) The quality of printed architectural books increased dramatically.

(B) The number of architectural schools and students grew rapidly.

(C) Ancient architectural techniques were replaced with new ones.

(D) Understanding of the standards of architecture spread quickly.

4 According to paragraph 5, which of the following is true of many of the structures from the Renaissance era?

(A) They were modeled on the architecture of Florence.

(B) They were paid for with public sources of funding.

(C) They were named after the people who financed them.

(D) They were designed by Donatello and Michelangelo.

5 **Directions:** An introductory sentence for a brief summary of the passage is provided below. Complete the summary by selecting the THREE answer choices that express the most important ideas in the passage.

The rediscovery of Classical Greek and Roman architectural elements sparked a revitalization of the field of architecture in Renaissance Italy.

(A) Funds from private backers were necessary to support artists, and, ultimately, this type of patronage was responsible for ensuring that great architectural works were erected.

(B) Promotion of the discipline was aided by the spread of literature that was intended to both document important ideas and inspire practicing artists.

(C) Whether novices or veterans, virtually all architects of the Renaissance learned about Classical Roman style through the works of Palladio.

(D) A combination of formal training and practical experience examining old structures provided the skills required to become a celebrated architect.

(E) Classical Roman architectural elements such as equilibrium and harmony were emphasized, but architects also included innovative elements.

(F) As more printed books became available, architects learned about the diversity of styles and began to reject Classical Roman forms.

Reading Practice 2

Feral Children

World mythology includes dozens of stories about children who were lost or abandoned and then discovered years later after being raised by animals in the wild. Perhaps the most famous of these is the one about Romulus and Remus, the mythical founders of Rome, who were supposedly raised by a wolf. Such fictional accounts of feral children usually depict them as having average or better than average human intelligence, great skills learned from their adoptive animal parents, and a special ability to survive in the wild. This makes their reintegration into culture relatively easy. 5

In reality, however, most reported cases of feral children do not include animal caregivers but involve a situation in which a child is purposely isolated from other humans. Once rescued, these youngsters face almost insurmountable obstacles when trying to adapt to society, and despite much effort to rehabilitate them, scientists are frequently unsuccessful when attempting to teach them basic 10 social skills.

Sociologists refer to the means by which an individual acquires knowledge of a culture's established norms as enculturation. It is through enculturation that a child learns appropriate behavior within a particular context as well as what is and is not permissible within the framework of a broader society. Raised without the enculturation derived from constant communication with other community 15 members, feral children never develop a sense of shared ideology or an understanding of expected forms of interaction. Moreover, they may not understand how to perform simple tasks, such as using the toilet or walking upright.

Scientists have also noticed that children brought up in an environment devoid of socialization tend to suffer from a condition known as psychosocial dwarfism. The disorder is brought on by 20 extreme emotional stress, not lack of nutrition, and is characterized by weight that is abnormally low, an immature skeleton, and a diminutive height. The disorder is progressive but can occasionally be reversed if the children are placed into a nurturing and caring home. Nevertheless, most of these children fail to respond favorably to the new environment and generally die young.

Yet, the most challenging obstacle to overcome in treating feral children is that, in most cases, the 25 young boys and girls have not been exposed to language or have been discouraged from learning how to talk. In these circumstances, researchers have noted that regardless of the children's level of general intelligence, they appear unable to grasp grammar or syntax. This was true of Genie, a thirteen-year-old girl who was rescued from a negligent parent and placed in Children's Hospital in Los Angeles, California in 1970. Although she quickly learned to use the toilet and her social skills improved 30 immediately, she could not manage to speak in full sentences even after years of instruction. She learned vocabulary words by pointing to objects and repeating what a therapist said, but she could only manage to utilize verbs and nouns in sentences like, "Applesauce buy store."

Because, on the whole, feral children seem to struggle with grammar, some researchers have suggested that there is a critical period of time in which people must learn how to communicate 35 verbally before losing their potential completely. Theoretical linguist Noam Chomsky proposed that this is related to a part of the brain called the Language Acquisition Device (LAD), which aids in language learning but requires data input from external sources in order to determine a structure. Thus, language is both inherent and learned, and requires a parent-child relationship to master.

Without this social interaction, a feral child misses this crucial step in human development that is not 40 possible to achieve later on in life.

1 According to paragraph 2, which of the following is true of most feral children?

(A) Their social skills often improve rapidly.

(B) They have extreme difficulty adjusting to society.

(C) Their rehabilitation is never successful.

(D) They typically develop emotional bonds with animals.

2 The word "diminutive" in the passage is closest in meaning to

(A) vague

(B) tiny

(C) unusual

(D) stable

3 Why does the author mention "Genie" in the passage?

(A) To provide an example of a feral child who could not master a language

(B) To illustrate a situation in which a feral child learned nouns and verbs

(C) To suggest that not all feral children can be integrated into society

(D) To explain how therapists can teach a feral child who cannot speak

4 Which of the following can be inferred from paragraph 6 about the human brain?

(A) It is naturally able to comprehend vocabulary.

(B) It is able to synthesize new information easily.

(C) It needs external stimuli to learn language.

(D) It is able to acquire language at any age.

5 **Directions:** An introductory sentence for a brief summary of the passage is provided below. Complete the summary by selecting the THREE answer choices that express the most important ideas in the passage.

Fictional accounts of feral children do not accurately portray the hardships they face.

(A) They do not have the genetic capability required to acquire and master verbal communication skills.

(B) Those denied a nurturing environment show a tendency to remain small in size, have a diminished intellect, and struggle when assimilating into society.

(C) Feral children are not taught normal patterns of behavior and, thus, lack a common social framework.

(D) Their language acquisition process is incomplete, and, frequently, they cannot formulate full sentences using proper grammar.

(E) Many feral children pass away before reaching the normal life expectancy of enculturated individuals within their society.

(F) Children raised without constant interaction with other people do not recognize the differences between social and anti-social behavior.

Reading Practice 3

Phases of a Supernova Explosion

Stars undergo a series of changes referred to as star death, and a small percentage of these deaths will result in an incredible supernova, wherein the star experiences rapid, intense combustion. To develop into a supernova, stars must acquire a certain mass. This was discovered in 1930, by Subrahmanyan Chandrasekhar, who found that the maximum mass for an active star is 1.4 times the mass of the Sun. 5

When a star's mass exceeds the Chandrasekhar limit, it will no longer be able to produce sufficient energy to support itself. Stars smaller than the Sun cannot generate the heat required to start fusion because of lower gravity. Therefore, this occurs predominantly in stars larger than the Sun, as these feature a hotter core temperature that prompts fusion to transpire at an increased rate. This increases the overall size and causes them to have a relatively shorter lifetime when compared to slower burning 10 small stars. When the Chandrasekhar limit is passed, the structure begins to disintegrate, and a supernova occurs.

Astronomer Rudolph Minkowski has categorized supernovas into two types, Type I and Type II. A Type I supernova develops from dormant stars that have exhausted the hydrogen in their core. Typically, this is a gradual process that causes the star to slowly transform into an inactive white dwarf 15 as the heat of its core is sapped away into space. However, in cases where two dying stars are located adjacent to one another, in what is known as a binary star system, a supernova can occur. For a Type I supernova to occur, the stars must be close enough that one can draw material from the other. When the white dwarf accrues enough matter to surpass the Chandrasekhar limit, it becomes unstable, and this results in a Type I supernova. 20

In Type II supernovas, unlike Type I supernovas, the internal fusion process remains active even after the hydrogen fuel in the core is exhausted. When this happens, core contraction creates extremely high temperatures that force the helium atoms to convert into carbon, which consumes additional energy, causing the outermost layer to expand to conserve energy. Through this expansion, the star becomes a red giant. Then, the Type II supernova produces heavy elements in its core, such as iron 25 and nickel, which require greater energy and add to the overall mass. As the fusion can no longer produce enough energy to support the additional weight, the red giant exceeds the Chandrasekhar limit and collapses upon itself in a supernova.

One major consequence of this explosion is the creation of a nebula, which is a tremendous cloud of dust and gas that consists of expelled material. Over millennia, the dense nebula will amass matter 30 because of its own gravitational pull, resulting in the formation of planets, stars, and other space objects partially composed of material from the exploded star. At the same time, the core cools down from the supernova and forms into a dense, cold neutron star. These are similar to white dwarfs in that they cannot generate heat or energy because they do not possess any ability to perform fusion. However, neutron stars have a much higher density than white dwarfs due to the compression of the 35 core during the supernova explosion. Astronomers postulate that there are an estimated one hundred million neutron stars in the Milky Way galaxy, indicating a high degree of supernova occurrences.

Glossary
·white dwarf: a star that has burned up all of its hydrogen
·red giant: a dying star in its final stage of stellar evolution

1 According to paragraph 2, what is the Chandrasekhar limit?

(A) It is the maximum temperature at which fusion can occur.

(B) It is the greatest mass that a star can maintain.

(C) It is the last stage that a star develops into a supernova.

(D) It is the biggest size that a star can be to produce elements.

2 The word "accrues" in the passage is closest in meaning to

(A) encompasses

(B) exhausts

(C) facilitates

(D) accumulates

3 According to paragraph 3, white dwarf stars are created through

(A) the production of helium atoms in the fusion process

(B) the progressive buildup of heat in the core

(C) the slow separation of stars in a binary star system

(D) the eventual depletion of hydrogen in the core

4 According to paragraph 4, one characteristic of a Type II supernova is

(A) the scarcity of hydrogen in the outer layer

(B) the shortage of helium atoms in the core

(C) the suspension of internal fusion

(D) the development of heavy elements in the core

5 **Directions:** An introductory sentence for a brief summary of the passage is provided below. Complete the summary by selecting the THREE answer choices that express the most important ideas in the passage.

Although all stars undergo a form of star death, stars must achieve certain requirements in order to generate a supernova explosion.

(A) Supernovas occur when a star loses the ability to produce enough energy to support its own mass.

(B) The two main supernova types are differentiated by the ability to perform fusion at the point of structural collapse.

(C) Supernovas can develop when a star has reached a stage in its lifecycle known as a red giant star.

(D) Neutron stars comprise the bulk of the stars that can be currently identified in the Milky Way galaxy.

(E) Supernovas contribute to the development of new stars and other celestial bodies because they result in the formation of nebulas.

(F) When two dying stars are close to one another, they can share material, causing a supernova.

Glaciation and the Ice Ages

➡ In the Swiss Alps in 1836, Louis Agassiz noticed boulders that bore no resemblance to the rocks nearby. Some of these boulders were heavily scratched and located high on the valley walls, as if they had been stranded there. Agassiz concluded that the heterogeneous rocky terrain could best be explained by past glacial activity. He claimed that the entire area from the North Pole to the European Alps had once been covered by an ice sheet, a phenomenon made possible, he argued, because of an extended period of cold temperatures, or an ice age. Later, Agassiz noticed similar deposits and terrain in a variety of different regions in the United States. This convinced him that the glaciation had not been confined to Europe but was far-reaching, perhaps even extending across the entire Northern Hemisphere. ⁵

Agassiz's radical idea was initially met with considerable opposition. After all, the prevailing ¹⁰ view at the time was that the earth had been gradually cooling since its creation. But soon other scientists found several distinct sediment layers deposited by glacial drifts. If there were multiple layers, there must have in fact been multiple ice ages over a long period. Careful study and comparison of glacial till in North America and Europe in the late nineteenth century led to the acceptance that there were four major periods of glacial advance and retreat. Subsequent ¹⁵ research in the twentieth century utilized radiocarbon dating to determine the precise dates of these ice ages, the last of which ended approximately ten thousand years ago near the end of the Pleistocene epoch.

➡ Geologists referred to the intervals between glaciations as interglacials. During glaciations, the ice expanded, and, during interglacial periods, it retreated. Between the layers of glacial drift, ²⁰ geologists found well-developed soils and the remains of plants that could only have grown in warm climates. These finds provided the ultimate proof that the climate had changed drastically during the intervening periods. No longer was it possible to accept that there had been continual cooling or just a single ice age. However, scientific understanding of ice ages and past climates was still incomplete, and evidence taken from marine sediments caused another revolution in ²⁵ thinking with regard to ice ages.

➡ The ocean floor is composed of relatively undisturbed sediment layers containing innumerable foraminifera—small single-celled organisms with shells made primarily of calcite. These microfauna absorb oxygen from the water, and tests can be run to determine the isotopic concentration of different forms of oxygen present in the shells. When seawater evaporates, the ³⁰ heavier oxygen-18 is less readily transferred to the atmosphere. Consequently, water that falls on land to form snow and ice is high in oxygen-16. During past ice ages, when much of this light oxygen was trapped in ice sheets on the planet's surface, levels of oxygen-18 in ocean water were comparatively greater, and foraminifera containing higher ratios of heavy oxygen are thus indicative of glacial periods. ³⁵

These deep-ocean core samples and isotope comparisons revolutionized how scientists viewed ice ages. Instead of the four classical glaciation periods differentiated in Europe and North America, the isotopic analysis of the oceans revealed no fewer than sixteen major glaciation events during the Pleistocene. **A** The earth is fundamentally a glacial environment characterized by continual cycles of ice growth and ice shrinkage and happens to occasionally undergo unusually warm periods like the one during the last ten thousand years. **B** Every corner of the earth is affected by glaciation, from the alpine environments at high latitudes to the tropics. **C** Ice ages dictate the distribution of plants and even the types of life forms found on earth. **D**

40

1 Which of the sentences below best expresses the essential information in the highlighted sentence in the passage? *Incorrect* choices change the meaning in important ways or leave out essential information.

- Ⓐ According to Agassiz, extremely cold temperatures caused ice sheets to form in various places from the North Pole to the European Alps.
- Ⓑ Agassiz declared that an ice age led to the formation of a sheet of ice that once covered the entire area from the North Pole to the European Alps.
- Ⓒ Agassiz argued that the ice sheet between the North Pole and the European Alps survived long after the ice age.
- Ⓓ Agassiz maintained that a large ice sheet resulting from an extended period of cold temperatures could have been formed only in the past.

2 According to paragraph 1, what convinced Agassiz that past glaciation had been extensive?

- Ⓐ The many boulders stranded high on the slopes of valley walls
- Ⓑ The existence of similar geologic phenomena in many different areas in America
- Ⓒ The presence of active glaciers in Europe and America
- Ⓓ The enormous ice sheet extending from the North Pole to the Alps

Paragraph 1 is marked with an arrow [➡].

3 The word "prevailing" in the passage is closest in meaning to

- Ⓐ dominant
- Ⓑ exhaustive
- Ⓒ accurate
- Ⓓ convincing

4 Why does the author discuss "glacial till" in the passage?

    (A) To provide further evidence that multiple periods of glaciation had occurred

    (B) To identify the discoveries that led to Agassiz's ideas being modified

    (C) To emphasize how much scientific knowledge changed in the nineteenth century

    (D) To confirm that the earth had not been gradually cooling since its creation

5 According to paragraph 3, which of the following is true of the well-developed soils and plants found by geologists?

    (A) They refuted the claim that alternating warm and cold periods were of equal duration.

    (B) They verified what geologists had always believed about the earth's climate.

    (C) They disproved the theory that glaciations originated in the north and spread toward the south.

    (D) They confirmed that dramatic climate changes had occurred between glaciations.

Paragraph 3 is marked with an arrow [➡].

6 Which of the following can be inferred from paragraph 3 about the ocean floor?

    (A) Its sediments offer a broader insight into glaciations than those on land.

    (B) Its chemistry is relatively stable even during periods of climate change.

    (C) Its chemical composition is largely determined by calcite deposits.

    (D) Its sediment layers are disturbed far more frequently than those on continents.

Paragraph 3 is marked with an arrow [➡].

7 The word "comparatively" in the passage is closest in meaning to

    (A) successively   (B) deliberately   (C) relatively   (D) assuredly

8 According to paragraph 4, scientists use foraminifera shells to learn about past ocean conditions by

    (A) comparing the amount of oxygen in the shells with average atmospheric oxygen levels

    (B) calculating the total amount of calcite absorbed by the shells over time

    (C) measuring the relative quantities of the oxygen isotopes the shells contain

    (D) counting the shells and estimating the effect glaciation had on other organisms

Paragraph 4 is marked with an arrow [➡].

9 Look at the four squares [■] that indicate where the following sentence could be added to the passage.

For example, scientists know from fossil records that animal extinctions have occurred as a result of ice ages.

Where would the sentence best fit?

Click on a square [■] to add the sentence to the passage.

10 Directions: An introductory sentence for a brief summary of the passage is provided below. Complete the summary by selecting the THREE answer choices that express the most important ideas in the passage. Some sentences do not belong in the summary because they express ideas that are not presented in the passage or are minor ideas in the passage. **This question is worth 2 points.**

Drag your answer choices to the spaces where they belong.
To remove an answer choice, click on it. To review the passage, click on **View Text**.

> **After the initial discovery of the ice ages, additional research led to new realizations.**
>
> ●
>
> ●
>
> ●

Answer Choices

(A) Louis Agassiz was convinced of the existence of a past ice age, but the theory was not accepted by his contemporaries.

(B) Continental research uncovered evidence that proved there were four periods of glaciation marked by major climate change.

(C) Studies involving deep sea core samples and oxygen isotope analysis helped scientists develop a more comprehensive understanding of glaciation during ice ages.

(D) The geological observations of Louis Agassiz led to the ice age hypothesis, which was later modified to accommodate multiple ice ages.

(E) Foraminifera taken from the ocean floor provided proof that there might have been multiple glacial timelines.

(F) Soil and plant fossils taken from interglacial strata indicate that Europe and North America had similar flora in the distant past.

Answer Book p. 54

Transcendentalism

   The first meeting of the American Transcendental Club was held on September 8, 1836, in Boston, Massachusetts. The group was composed of young intellectuals who were frustrated with the state of society at the time, and it provided an organizing ground for political activism. Among its core beliefs was the notion that humans can achieve spiritual enlightenment, or transcend the materialistic world and the limits of the senses and logic, through natural intuition without the ⁵ intervention of established religious doctrines. Radical at the time, the club gave rise to a new set of philosophical ideals, labeled as transcendentalism, which challenged authority and favored individualism.

   ➡ One important transcendental ideal was mentioned in the essays of Ralph Waldo Emerson, one of the most influential authors of the period. He expressed transcendentalism's main theme ¹⁰ as the "mystical unity of nature," meaning that the environment, including the people living within it, should be viewed as a whole entity, not as a sum of separate components. Inspired by the vast untamed terrain of the American continent, Emerson encouraged people to consider the delicate balance between civilization and wilderness and to protect the environment against decimation at the hands of humans. In addition, Emerson encouraged acts of quiet civil disobedience as a ¹⁵ form of moral opposition to legislation that was unjust or gave citizens power over nature. This underlying principle had a profound impact on later peace activists, such as Mahatma Gandhi and Martin Luther King Jr.

   ➡ A second notion that grew out of transcendentalism manifested as the Second Great Awakening, a period of spiritual revival that began with the work of club members who expanded ²⁰ on Emerson's works by incorporating their own religious beliefs. In their writings, they stressed the idea that care of the natural environment was not only necessary to maintain a holistic world, but also a duty outlined in the Bible. Aiming to promote this concept of people as earthly custodians, missionaries were quickly established in New England and throughout the Appalachians to great success. Sermons attracted as many as 20,000 people, inspiring social activism by emphasizing ²⁵ the power of the individual to evoke change. These missionaries are attributed as the source of the Temperance Movement, which sought to reduce the consumption of alcohol to improve society.

   ➡ This concept of personal empowerment, a third tenet of transcendentalism, is perhaps the most far-reaching, as it is the belief held in highest regard by modern American citizens, and it ³⁰ is observed in long-lasting legislation that protects the rights of individuals over those of a group. Prior to the mid-eighteenth century, the American population was comprised of immigrants who tended to identify primarily as a part of the ethnic or political group to which they belonged, not as American citizens. However, children born between 1792 and 1821, posthumously named the Transcendental Generation, represent the first set of offspring to be raised in the new nation. ³⁵

A As they matured, they became reformers, evangelists, and campus rioters, fighting for freedom from the oppressive British government. **B** In adulthood, they grew into staunch supporters of the abolitionist movement, which argued that the emancipation of slaves was spiritually mandated because, according to the Bible, all men are equal custodians of the earth. **C** Unyielding in their later years, some turned to poetry, literature, and other more creative pursuits 40 as a means to express themselves, but, above all else, they remained committed to freedom. **D** The changes advocated for by the Transcendental Generation, whether enacted or not, deeply affected the cultural landscape, particularly in the North. As a result, conflicts arose between Southern slave owners and abolitionists, and these provided the impetus for the American Civil War.

1 The word "decimation" in the passage is closest in meaning to

  (A) destitution

  (B) transformation

  (C) aspiration

  (D) destruction

2 According to paragraph 2, which of the following is true of Emerson?

  (A) The notion of nature as a totality rather than the sum of its parts was important to him.

  (B) The practice of civil disobedience was a method he learned from other peace activists.

  (C) The pristine natural environment in America motivated him to advocate for industrial utilization of its resources.

  (D) The essays he wrote argued for the superiority of transcendentalism over traditional religion.

Paragraph 2 is marked with an arrow [➡].

3 Why does the author mention "the Temperance Movement" in the passage?

  (A) To describe an organized activity that grew out of the Second Great Awakening

  (B) To illustrate one type of missionary who preached in the Appalachians

  (C) To give an example of the ramifications of a Christian education

  (D) To show how Emerson's writing attracted a diverse group of people

4 According to paragraph 3, missionaries set up in the eastern United States in order to

    (A) impart lessons outlining religious responsibilities to nature

    (B) encourage people to accept others despite their differences

    (C) dissuade community members from drinking alcohol

    (D) promote improvements in jails and healthcare facilities

Paragraph 3 is marked with an arrow [➡].

5 Which of the sentences below best expresses the essential information in the highlighted sentence in the passage? *Incorrect* choices change the meaning in important ways or leave out essential information.

    (A) Contemporary rules have been drafted to reflect the belief that individual people, not general society, should have control over their lives.

    (B) The most accepted and persistent conviction of the Transcendentalism, still seen in the legal system, is the emphasis on individual freedoms.

    (C) Citizens happily accepted the Transcendentalist dogma of exclusive power over oneself because it endowed them with more capabilities.

    (D) Stressing the role of the individual person, Transcendentalists developed a third theory that has not been incorporated into American law.

6 Which of the following can be inferred from paragraph 4 about the children born between 1792 and 1821?

    (A) They migrated away from their families to different parts of the country.

    (B) They did not refer to themselves as the Transcendental Generation.

    (C) They shared the same values and morals as their immigrant parents.

    (D) They did not identify themselves as American citizens.

Paragraph 4 is marked with an arrow [➡].

7 The word "staunch" in the passage is closest in meaning to

    (A) firm   (B) practical   (C) innovative   (D) valued

8 The word "impetus" in the passage is closest in meaning to

    (A) improvement   (B) consequence   (C) admission   (D) stimulus

9 Look at the four squares [■] that indicate where the following sentence could be added to the passage.

Many of their works are now considered among the most important artistic accomplishments in the history of the United States.

Where would the sentence best fit?

Click on a square [■] to add the sentence to the passage.

10 Directions: An introductory sentence for a brief summary of the passage is provided below. Complete the summary by selecting the THREE answer choices that express the most important ideas in the passage. Some sentences do not belong in the summary because they express ideas that are not presented in the passage or are minor ideas in the passage. **This question is worth 2 points.**

Drag your answer choices to the spaces where they belong.
To remove an answer choice, click on it. To review the passage, click on **View Text**.

> **The founding of the Transcendental Club resulted in the proliferation of unprecedented philosophical concepts.**
>
> ●
>
> ●
>
> ●

Answer Choices

(A) An emphasis on the ability of a single person to instigate change provoked a number of people to become activists who pushed for major social adjustments.

(B) Immigrants migrating to America before 1750 did not subscribe to the Transcendentalist philosophy but produced children who did.

(C) Based on ideas presented in Emerson's works, harmony between humans and their natural environment was adopted into the philosophy.

(D) The agitation of members of the Transcendental Generation led to armed conflict between those who agreed with slavery and those who opposed it.

(E) Transcendentalists argued that Christians had an obligation to care for the earth, triggering a revival of interest in spiritualism.

(F) Preachers traveled across the Eastern part of the country to tell people about their duty to God as proclaimed in the Bible.

Answer Book p. 56

Vocabulary Review

Answer Book p. 57

A. Fill in the blanks with the appropriate words from the box.

insurmountable	distinguished	emancipation
immature	antiquity	resemblance

1 The Louvre Museum in Paris is known for its _____ art collection, which includes Da Vinci's *Mona Lisa*.

2 China, India, the Middle East, and the Mediterranean contained the most advanced civilizations in _____.

3 Contrary to popular belief, many of Chinese dialects bear little _____ to each other.

4 Stem cells are young, _____ cells that are able to develop into different cell types.

5 The _____ of the slaves is considered to be one of President Lincoln's most important achievements.

6 I do not see this situation as a(n) _____ obstacle but as an adventure.

B. Choose the closest meaning for each highlighted word or phrase.

7 America has immigrants from all over the world, so its culture reflects the appropriation of many international elements.
   (A) allocation   (B) adoption   (C) amendment   (D) allowance

8 The young actress emulated the behavior of famous movie stars, hoping to one day become a celebrity herself.
   (A) justified   (B) imitated   (C) convinced   (D) provoked

9 The driver's negligent behavior put everyone else on the road in harm's way.
   (A) placid   (B) exaggerated   (C) cautious   (D) indifferent

10 Companies that are not in compliance with the environmental regulations can be fined.
   (A) optimization   (B) manifestation   (C) agreement   (D) resolution

11 The stars in the sky are innumerable; there are far more of them than can ever be recorded by astronomers.
   (A) bright   (B) countless   (C) gaseous   (D) colossal

12 Screaming is permissible at a rock concert, but it is considered rude at a classical concert.
   (A) debatable   (B) reasonable   (C) potential   (D) acceptable

13 In spite of his distaste for dispute, he was unyielding in his adherence to his principles.
   (A) steadfast   (B) impeccable   (C) sophisticated   (D) superficial

14 Extreme weather events have become a regular occurrence in recent years.
   (A) happening   (B) distraction   (C) disorder   (D) peculiarity

CHAPTER 10

Category Chart

Category Chart

About the Question Type

Category Chart questions ask you to complete a table by placing the relevant information in the appropriate categories.

When reading the passage, try to identify what is being compared or contrasted, and recognize the important information for each category.

Question Format

Directions: Select the appropriate phrases from the answer choices and match them to the type to which they relate. **This question is worth 3 points.**

Drag your answer choices to the spaces where they belong.
To remove an answer choice, click on it. To review the passage, click on **View Text**.

Answer Choices	Category 1
	•
	•
	•
	Category 2
	•
	•

Key Strategies

- **Step 1** — Check the categories in the table.

- **Step 2** — Scan the passage and identify the important information for each category.

- **Step 3** — Select the answer choices that best paraphrase the important information in the passage for each category. Answer choices that include information from the passage that is unrelated to the categories or inaccurate information can be eliminated.

Example

Dinosaur Extinction

One of the greatest mysteries in science is the disappearance of the dinosaurs approximately 65 million years ago, as this group of animals had dominated the earth for over 200 million years. At present, paleontologists are divided over what led to this mass extinction.

One hypothesis, known as gradualism, argues that the events that caused the dinosaurs to die off occurred over an extended period of time. Basically, proponents look to plate tectonics to unravel the enigma, suggesting that the shifting of plates under the earth's crust gradually increased volcanic activity. The gases emitted by global eruptions would have triggered frequent acid rain, damaging flora and fauna. The resulting breakdown of the food chain would have also made it increasingly difficult for many animals to meet their nutritional needs. However, opponents of this theory point out that it is not supported by the fossil record, which indicates that the disappearance of the dinosaurs was more abrupt than can be accounted for by these processes.

In contrast, catastrophism postulates that the extinction of the dinosaurs happened quickly due to the impact of a massive comet or asteroid. Beyond the immediate damage of the strike, global weather systems would have been fundamentally altered. Massive firestorms resulting from the forests and other flammable ecosystems being set ablaze and extremely powerful hurricanes would have been commonplace. Under these catastrophic conditions, most organisms that had survived the initial impact would have disappeared in a short period of time. This explanation seems to be supported by the presence of a massive crater in Mexico from around the time the dinosaurs went extinct, although opponents claim that the devastation caused by its creation was insufficient to kill off these animals around the world.

1 **Directions:** Select the appropriate phrases from the answer choices and match them to the theory with which they are associated.

Answer Choices	Gradualism
(A) Involved a collision with a large extraterrestrial object	•
(B) Triggered the release of toxic gases lethal to most organisms	•
(C) Resulted in severe food shortages for various organisms	•
(D) Stemmed from a rise in volcano eruptions around the world	**Catastrophism**
(E) Led to the development of powerful storms and wildfires	
(F) Caused acidic precipitation harmful to animals and plants	•
(G) Accelerated the movement of the planet's tectonic plates	•

Reading Practice 1

Answer Book p. 58

Temperate Climates

    About 40 percent of the earth's population lives in the narrow temperate climate zones between the
Tropic of Cancer and the Arctic Circle in the northern hemisphere and the Tropic of Capricorn and
the Antarctic Circle in the southern hemisphere. Despite the relatively small area of the globe that is
temperate (roughly 7 percent of all land), temperate regions provide the best conditions for human
survival. This is in large part due to their mild climate, plentiful precipitation, and adequate soil 5
fertility. These conditions are suited to intensive agriculture, and farmers in temperate regions are able
to grow a wide variety of crops.

    The favorable climate is able to support the production of sufficient food for locals and provide a
surplus that can be exported in exchange for goods and services from other regions. There is some
variation, however, within the temperate climate zone that can influence what kinds of weather 10
conditions will prevail, usually related to the geographical location of the areas. Climatologists tend to
divide these into two main categories: maritime temperate zones and continental temperate zones.

    Maritime temperate zones, or oceanic climates, are typically found along the west coasts of the
major continents at middle latitudes and at the southeastern edge of Australia. Proximity to the poles
exposes these regions to constant polar fronts, causing the weather to be frequently overcast. This 15
cloud coverage allows for adequate precipitation to fall at all times of the year. Hazy skies also lead
to summers that are cooler than those of other climates at the same latitude and winters that are
milder because the region retains much of its warmth throughout the year. The temperature range
for ocean climates is quite narrow, between -10°C and 25°C, but it still supports four distinct seasons,
the hallmark of all temperate zones. In addition, the seasons in a maritime climate are considered 20
mesothermal: the winters are too cool to allow for year-round photosynthesis but are not cold enough
to maintain continuous snow coverage for a fixed period of time.

    Continental temperate zones, on the other hand, are known for cooler winters and warmer
summers, which are characteristic of the middle-latitude interiors of the large, northern hemisphere
continents. They are far enough away from the coast to remain impervious to the moderating 25
effect of the ocean or are situated where winds blow the polar fronts offshore as opposed to inland.
Instead, these regions are infiltrated by cold air masses in the winter and warm or hot air masses
in the summer. Thus, they achieve warmer temperatures for two or three months but also become
much cooler than any climate zone at a comparable latitude, supporting a fixed period of stable snow
coverage. 30

    Precipitation in continental climates is not evenly spread throughout the year. Considerably more
falls in the winter and spring than in the summer, which is somewhat dry. Deciduous trees and shrubs
that can tolerate periods of little rain commonly grow in continental climate zones, as do tall grasses.
Agriculture in these regions tends to focus on grains and root vegetables, which can survive periods of
drought. These products flourish in the continental temperate climate and have been the basis for the 35
population boom in many cities in the American Midwest, China, and Russia.

Glossary

·mesothermal: of a type of climate characterized by moderate temperatures

1   Which of the following can be inferred from paragraph 2 about temperate regions?

(A) They support large human populations despite their extreme climatological conditions.

(B) They boast a mild climate and ample precipitation, though soil fertility is often poor.

(C) They are generally better suited for extensive rather than intensive farming.

(D) They have the capacity to produce more food than a population can consume.

2   According to the passage, the classification of climates as continental or maritime is primarily determined by

(A) the ability of the area to support intensive agriculture

(B) the location of the region within the temperate zone

(C) the density of the population in each region

(D) the presence of four distinct seasons

3   The word "impervious" in the passage is closest in meaning to

(A) unaffected

(B) discharged

(C) imbalanced

(D) indispensable

4   According to paragraph 4, characteristics of continental temperate climates include

(A) temperature gradients with a wide range of values

(B) cool winds that gust toward the interior territories

(C) large bodies of water that influence weather conditions

(D) ample amounts of snow that melt instantaneously

5   **Directions:** Select the appropriate phrases from the answer choices and match them to the type of temperate climate with which they are associated.

Answer Choices	Maritime Temperate Climates
(A) Receive more precipitation in the winter than in the summer	●
(B) Receive much snow in the winter, but it immediately melts	●
(C) Are characterized by often cloudy conditions due to polar fronts	●
(D) Provide inadequate soil for intensive agriculture	**Continental Temperate Climates**
(E) Experience little variation between summer and winter temperatures	
(F) Receive abundant rainfall throughout the year	●
(G) Produce a good environment for cultivating drought-tolerant crops	●

Interpreting Visual Art

The question of how to interpret visual art is the primary concern of art theorists. While a critic evaluates an individual work based on established criteria, an art theorist attempts to determine exactly what the criteria should be. In effect, the goal is not to determine the intrinsic artistic value of a particular piece; instead, it is to develop a conceptual 5 framework that can be used to do this. At present, there are two main theories by which art is interpreted: formalism and contextualism.

Formalism holds that one must concentrate on the work itself to determine the aesthetic experience its lines, shapes, colors, textures, and composition provides to the viewer. In fact, the term formalism stems from this emphasis on form. An analysis of a piece should be based solely on its visual qualities, 10 and any other factor, such as the motivation of the artist or the environment in which it was created, should be ignored. Critics of the formalist approach argue that this narrow focus is a negative rather than a positive—they claim that it dismisses out of hand valid considerations about who created the work and for what purpose. However, by insisting that attention be paid exclusively to stylistic elements, formalists encourage viewers to look closely and to respond with feeling to the sensuous 15 qualities of art.

In contrast, contextualism is concerned with the context in which a work was produced. This form of interpretation seeks to understand an artwork in relation to the external factors that led to its creation. Of particular interest is the motivation of the artist. A contextualist would want to know about an artist's position in society, personal life, views on social and ethical issues, and how these 20 stimulated the creation process. Another consideration is the relationship between the work of art being studied and other works from the same culture. This provides insight into the influences of the artist. Finally, patronage is looked at during a contextual analysis. Who was the artwork made for, and why was support provided to the artist to create it? By examining these elements, a contextual analysis makes it possible to determine and evaluate the underlying purpose and function of a work of art. 25

The difference between the two approaches is apparent when applied to a specific work of art. Vincent Van Gogh's painting *The Night Café* is one that has been studied intensively by proponents of both theories. The formalist interpretation focuses on the various techniques Van Gogh used to create the distinctive visual effect of the painting. For example, he applied very thick brushstrokes to certain objects in different parts of the painting and outlined these with black lines to make them 30 stand out. In addition, Van Gogh used clashing colors such as red and green to create an intense, almost discordant, mood. However, the contextualist analysis draws attention to the fact that this painting represents an attempt by Van Gogh to reveal the sordid conditions in which the socially and economically disadvantaged lived. The type of café depicted in the painting was frequently full of homeless people who had nowhere else to go. That Van Gogh was aware of this is made clear by a 35 letter he wrote to his brother, in which he stated that he wanted to depict a place where people with no money can take refuge. It can be argued that his aim with *The Night Café* was to show this aspect of French society to the wealthy, upper-class individuals who frequented galleries and purchased art.

1 The word "stems" in the passage is closest in meaning to

(A) inhibits

(B) interprets

(C) originates

(D) dismisses

2 The word "them" in the passage refers to

(A) brushstrokes

(B) objects

(C) parts

(D) lines

3 According to paragraph 4, Van Gogh created the atmosphere of *The Night Café* by

(A) outlining items with black paint

(B) using hues that contrasted

(C) applying paint unevenly

(D) depicting people that looked poor

4 In paragraph 4, why does the author mention a letter that Van Gogh wrote?

(A) To demonstrate that Van Gogh knew about a café's clientele

(B) To suggest that Van Gogh had experienced financial hardship

(C) To stress the connection Van Gogh felt to a family member

(D) To show that Van Gogh was a member of the upper class

5 **Directions:** Select the appropriate phrases from the answer choices and match them to the theory of art interpretation to which they relate.

Answer Choices	Formalism
(A) Encourages a viewer to respond emotionally to art	●
(B) Focuses on composition over other visual elements	●
(C) Explores the underlying motivations of an artist	**Contextualism**
(D) Reflects on the people for whom a work was made	●
(E) Considers only the appearance of a work	
(F) Compares different pieces of art from within the same tradition	●
(G) Assumes that internal and external factors are equal	●

Answer Book p. 60

Orcas

The orca, or killer whale as it is commonly known, is the largest cetacean in the Delphinidae family, a classification of aquatic mammals that includes all oceanic dolphins. It is a versatile and efficient predator that combines its vast size and incredible speed with cooperative group strategies to maintain its position at the pinnacle of the food chain. 5

Orcas are divided into two distinct populations, known as residents and transients, which react with extreme hostility towards each other and do not interbreed. Although comprising a single species, scientists estimate that they have been isolated from each other for over 100,000 years. One theory suggests that the behavioral idiosyncrasies related to predatory activities and social relations that differentiate each classification may in fact be manifestations of an ongoing 10 process of speciation that will eventually result in a genetic incompatibility.

Residents are distinguished from transients by the fact that they primarily inhabit coastal waters and usually remain within the same area year-round, although their dependence on a diet composed exclusively of squid and fish requires that they continually traverse their territory in search of nourishment, sometimes traveling as many as 100 kilometers in a day. When hunting, residents engage 15 in a series of concerted maneuvers to achieve their goals. In order to locate prey, individual orcas spaced evenly along an extended line will move forward slowly in the same direction while employing echolocation, clicking noises that act as a biological sonar. If one orca discovers a school of fish or squid, it communicates vocally with the others to make them aware of the presence of food. At this point, the group may employ a number of strategies, including circling the school of fish in order to 20 force it into a tight ball and maneuvering the fish into shallow water for easy consumption.

The degree of social interaction required to engage in these complex predatory activities is a dominant behavioral trait of residents, who spend their entire lives in close-knit groups. The fundamental social unit is the family, which is matrilineal and consists of a mother and her children. As orcas have been known to live for up to 90 years, a matriline may be comprised of up to five 25 generations, with the offspring of the female members continually adding to the numbers of the group.

While the social organization of transients closely resembles that of the residents, it is much less rigid, particularly with regard to the behavior of the males. In general, transients usually travel and live in small groups that rarely reach the same size as the resident matriline due to the likelihood that male offspring will disperse after adolescence. While the first son will almost always remain with his 30 mother after reaching adulthood, subsequent sons will frequently leave their families to live a solitary existence when they are fully grown.

Despite the relatively fractured social structure, scattered groups and individuals frequently join together when engaged in predatory activities. The dietary staple of transients is large aquatic sea mammals, such as dolphins, porpoises, sea lions, seals, and occasionally whales, and the search for 35 sufficient quantities of prey forces the orcas to travel vast distances, encompassing a geographic range that extends from Alaska to the southern extremities of California. While close cooperation is required to successfully complete a hunt, vocal communication is rare, as the sounds emitted during this process are easily detectable by the prey. For the same reason, echolocation is avoided, and the hunt is therefore conducted in silence. 40

1 The word "versatile" in the passage is closest in meaning to

(A) adaptable

(B) viable

(C) disposable

(D) durable

2 According to the passage, all of the following enable the orca to stay at the top of the food chain EXCEPT

(A) its extreme swiftness

(B) its substantial bulk

(C) its long life span

(D) its hunting tactics

3 What does the author imply about resident and transient orcas in paragraph 2?

(A) They may eventually become two separate species.

(B) They never come into contact with each other.

(C) They might be unable to breed with one another already.

(D) They have been genetically different for thousands of years.

4 Why does the author mention the "resident matriline" in the passage?

(A) To illustrate a behavioral trait associated with transients

(B) To emphasize the superiority of a specific species

(C) To suggest that transient males are more independent

(D) To compare the sizes of resident and transient groups

5 **Directions:** Select the appropriate phrases from the answer choices and match them to the type of orcas to which they relate.

Answer Choices	Residents
(A) Rely on vocalizations to hunt their prey	•
(B) Have a flexible community structure	•
(C) Do not commonly depart from a specific region	
(D) Often hunt large organisms	**Transients**
(E) Move primarily in pairs rather than in groups	•
(F) Include males separated from a group	•
(G) Are unable to use vocal forms of social interaction	•

Railway Development in Germany

➡ The Industrial Revolution in Germany has been broadly categorized by historians into two waves. The first wave occurred from 1770 to 1871, mostly in the prosperous northeastern Prussian state. The second wave, which lasted from 1871 to 1914, followed the merging of 27 states with Prussia, creating the German nation. An important feature of the post-unification period was the utilization of railways in opening up industrial opportunities. 5

Initially, industrialists and investors from the disparate German states relied on imported hardware from the industrial leader, Great Britain, for technological advancement. As a result, industrialization in the region lagged behind other European nations; however, the German states achieved a higher degree of efficiency, as slow and inefficient technology was avoided. For example, the first railways used wrought iron tracks that required replacement every six months. 10 In 1857, steel railways were invented by British metallurgist Robert Mushet. These railways could last for years without replacement and accommodated heavier trains with greater volumes of freight. As a result, when German investors began to build railways, they used steel tracks and efficient train engines.

➡ Unfortunately, as the German states were largely fragmented, railway construction remained 15 too expensive in many cases. This restricted the economic growth of the region, as locations rich in minerals, including coal reserves in the Ruhr and iron deposits in Upper Silesia, could not be developed without railway access. While the railways built prior to 1871 were useful for speeding communication and transportation between the states, they did not prompt improvements to industry, as the train lines were not linked to industrial areas. Yet, despite the limited routes, the 20 states conducted trade with each other successfully through the *Zollverein*, or German customs union, from 1834 to 1871. This functioned as an economic union, which instituted tariffs and customs agreements in the region and insulated German industries from the protectionist policies of Austria and France. The *Zollverein* laid the foundations for unification and incubated industrial growth for the later period. 25

By 1870, over 11,000 miles of railroads had been constructed. These railways were nationalized following unification in 1871. **A** Unification opened up new markets for local products and invited investment in underdeveloped regions. **B** German politicians and economists recognized the importance of railways in the economy, and so, unlike other European powers, German industrialization prioritized railroads. **C** Within ten years of unification, German trains 30 carried over forty-three thousand passengers and thirty thousand tons of freight, surpassing the volume transported by France and other continental European countries. **D**

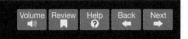
➡ The consolidation of wealth and mineral resources within one state, combined with rapid transportation, reignited industrialization throughout the country. Under the careful guidance of Chancellor Otto von Bismarck, rather than the German emperor, Germany became the leading 35 nation for steel production, increasing from one million metric tons in 1885 to ten million in 1905. The amount of coal mined was second only to Britain by 1905. Together with mechanical engineering, coal and iron became the prominent features of the second industrial revolution.

➡ Throughout the second phase, the government concentrated on competing with Britain in industrial, economic, and military matters. The well-integrated railway system supported this rivalry. 40 In an attempt to stay ahead, scientists and engineers switched to fields less researched by Britain. The country turned towards chemistry, electrical engineering, and motors. Altogether, it invested heavily in these areas, more than any other country, and this resulted in significant inventions and findings.

1 What is the purpose of paragraph 1 in the passage?

Ⓐ To outline the factors that expanded the borders of Germany

Ⓑ To detail the chronology of the German Industrial Revolution

Ⓒ To describe the effects of the regional development in Germany

Ⓓ To explain the methods used to start the German Industrial Revolution

Paragraph 1 is marked with an arrow [➡].

2 The word "disparate" in the passage is closest in meaning to

Ⓐ cooperative   Ⓑ diverse   Ⓒ autonomous   Ⓓ legitimate

3 The word "fragmented" in the passage is closest in meaning to

Ⓐ defeated   Ⓑ subdued   Ⓒ divided   Ⓓ nominated

4 The word "they" in the passage refers to

Ⓐ coal reserves   Ⓑ iron deposits   Ⓒ railways   Ⓓ states

5 Which of the following can be inferred from paragraph 3 about the mineral reserves in the Ruhr and Upper Silesia?

(A) They were not exploited in the early years of railway construction.

(B) They were not highly productive until they were owned by Prussia.

(C) They were not well known until they were linked to foreign exports.

(D) They were not mined until they were owned by the state.

Paragraph 3 is marked with an arrow [➡].

6 According to paragraph 3, how did the *Zollverein* benefit the German states?

(A) It rescued the states from economic depression.

(B) It defended the railway system from outdated technology.

(C) It regulated trade between the states.

(D) It strengthened relationships with foreign allies.

Paragraph 3 is marked with an arrow [➡].

7 According to paragraph 5, what revitalized industrialization in Germany? Choose TWO answers.

(A) the import of inexpensive steel

(B) the creation of a single nation

(C) the development of fast transport

(D) the improvement of mine safety

Paragraph 5 is marked with an arrow [➡].

8 According to paragraph 6, German scientists attempted to beat British rivals by

(A) boycotting British goods

(B) reproducing foreign research results

(C) becoming the biggest coal producer in the world

(D) focusing on different areas of study

Paragraph 6 is marked with an arrow [➡].

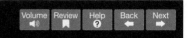

9 Look at the four squares [■] that indicate where the following sentence could be added to the passage.

Thus, new lines that connected industrial areas with major ports wrer constructed.

Where would the sentence best fit?

> Click on a square [■] to add the sentence to the passage.

10 Directions: Select the appropriate statements from the answer choices and match them to the period of German industrialization to which they relate. **This question is worth 3 points.**

> Drag your answer choices to the spaces where they belong.
> To remove an answer choice, click on it. To review the passage, click on **View Text**.

Answer Choices	First Period of Industrialization
Ⓐ Various types of materials were used to build railways.	•
Ⓑ Industry was dependent on imports from Great Britain.	•
Ⓒ The government took control of most railway lines.	
Ⓓ Steel production increased ten times over.	**Second Period of Industrialization**
Ⓔ Railways were primarily used for communication and transportation between states.	•
Ⓕ The amount of coal used declined significantly.	•
Ⓖ The focus was on competing with a foreign power.	•

Answer Book p. 61

The Dead Sea Scrolls

➡ In 1947, a Bedouin shepherd near Qumran, a small settlement situated on a dry plateau about a mile inland from the northwestern shore of the Dead Sea, discovered a collection of ancient pottery containing documents wrapped in linen in a cavern. Archeologists have since unearthed over 850 fragments of scrolls from this site, most of which were hidden in clay jars scattered throughout eleven different caves. This collection, referred to as the Dead Sea Scrolls, 5 is considered one of the most important discoveries of the twentieth century because it includes the earliest known biblical texts, including a copy of the Ten Commandments. It also consists of numerous non-biblical documents, such as songs and poetry, a list of caches containing valuable treasures, and other manuscripts describing ancient Hebrew culture.

➡ One of the controversial aspects of the Dead Sea Scrolls is the obscure location where they 10 were found and how they got there. These documents were found in a region far from any urban center and appeared to have been undisturbed for almost two thousand years. Since many Jewish groups from this era were destroyed by the Romans, leaving few clues about their cultures, it is possible that conclusive evidence linking the Dead Sea Scrolls to the people who produced them may never surface. 15

After early examinations of Qumran's geography, scholars began to make connections between the settlement and detailed accounts of the region provided by the Jewish historian Josephus. According to these ancient descriptions, the last people to live near the caves in the first century AD were the Essenes, a monotheistic group who followed the teachings set out in the Old Testament. Scholars speculate that the Essenes composed and deposited the Dead Sea 20 Scrolls in the caves to protect them. Around that time, the Romans initiated an era of violent anti-Semitic persecution, causing many Essenes to flee the region. The Essenes may have intended to retrieve the scrolls when it was safe to return, but the entire group was massacred in AD 68, leaving no ancestral knowledge of the hidden scriptures.

➡ Subsequent analysis of the scrolls using carbon dating has induced scholars to consider an 25 alternative theory that suggests the site is the remains of a monastery run by a different Jewish sect, the Sadducees. **A** Support for this viewpoint centers around several scroll fragments that have been dated to years before the Essene people inhabited the region, indicating that the previous residents, the Sadducees, wrote the scriptures. **B** One scroll clearly outlines purity laws that are identical to their rabbinic writings. **C** In addition, this document reproduces a calendar 30 that follows Sadducee principles, showing festival days that are known to have been celebrated by the Sadducees. **D**

➡ Recently, two Israeli archaeologists have asserted a third and more plausible theory. Based on the diversity of viewpoints offered in the texts written in several different languages, the archeologists argue that the scrolls represent the remains of a library of Jewish refugees, not 35

those of one single sect. Their supposition is supported by historical accounts of Jews carrying sacred texts from Jerusalem as they fled. They would have encountered the Qumran caves before descending to the shores of the Dead Sea.

According to this hypothesis, the significance of Qumran was not religious but practical. When the Romans destroyed the Jewish settlement in AD 68, the area was the center of the regional 40 pottery industry. Abandoned pottery kilns, clay vessels, and deposits of potter's clay have been unearthed, as well as a unique water-transport system that was designed to carry water into the caves. These findings indicate that the caves served as a pottery factory until the arrival of the Romans. The factory would have been the last secure place fleeing Jews could have hidden the scrolls prior to reaching the Dead Sea. 45

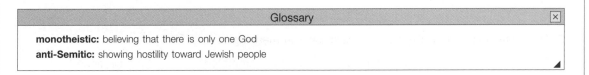

Glossary	☒
monotheistic: believing that there is only one God	
anti-Semitic: showing hostility toward Jewish people	

1 The word "caches" in the passage is closest in meaning to

Ⓐ exhibitions

Ⓑ stockpiles

Ⓒ selections

Ⓓ examples

2 According to paragraph 1, which of the following is true of the pottery first found at Qumran?

Ⓐ Some of it was located outside the caves.

Ⓑ Its contents were enveloped in fabric.

Ⓒ It had been hidden for a minimum of 850 years.

Ⓓ Much of it was broken at the time of discovery.

Paragraph 1 is marked with an arrow [➡].

3 According to paragraph 2, the discovery at Qumran was unusual because

Ⓐ it was verified in laboratories in an urban center

Ⓑ it was in a remote, sparsely populated region

Ⓒ it included structures used for religious ceremonies

Ⓓ it featured a catalog of important books

Paragraph 2 is marked with an arrow [➡].

4 Which of the sentences below best expresses the essential information in the highlighted sentence in the passage? *Incorrect* choices change the meaning in important ways or leave out essential information.

Ⓐ The Essenes were murdered before passing on information about the secret location, although the sect probably planned to reclaim the scrolls.

Ⓑ The Essenes left no clues as to the position of the written works because they were massacred.

Ⓒ The Jewish group had always planned to come back to the site and reacquire the scrolls but were prevented from doing so.

Ⓓ Even though the Essenes were not able to get back the documents, the old writings remained safe within the caves.

5 The word "induced" in the passage is closest in meaning to

Ⓐ reminded   Ⓑ directed   Ⓒ prompted   Ⓓ cautioned

6 According to paragraph 4, all of the following are mentioned as evidence attributing the scrolls to the Sadducee sect EXCEPT

Ⓐ similar scrolls that were discovered in the remains of a Sadducee monastery

Ⓑ fragments that have been dated to a time prior to the Essene occupation of the area

Ⓒ writings that are consistent with Sadducee religious doctrine

Ⓓ a document that details a schedule of Sadducee holidays

Paragraph 4 is marked with an arrow [➡].

7 In paragraph 5, the author implies that the scrolls were transported from

Ⓐ the city of Jerusalem

Ⓑ near the caverns where the scrolls were found

Ⓒ the settlement of Qumran

Ⓓ the coastline of the Dead Sea

Paragraph 5 is marked with an arrow [➡].

8 The author discusses a "unique water-transport system" in order to

    Ⓐ describe a technology that was known only to the Jewish people

    Ⓑ explain how clay was imported into Qumran from outlying regions

    Ⓒ provide evidence that the region was in close proximity to the Dead Sea

    Ⓓ show that the region was the main place for producing pottery

9 Look at the four squares [■] that indicate where the following sentence could be added to the passage.

Scholars have noted that some of the content of these fragments parallels that of Sadducee teachings.

Where would the sentence best fit?

> Click on a square [■] to add the sentence to the passage.

10 Directions: Select the appropriate phrases from the answer choices and match them to the people to which they relate. **This question is worth 3 points.**

> Drag your answer choices to the spaces where they belong.
> To remove an answer choice, click on it. To review the passage, click on **View Text**.

Answer Choices	Essenes
Ⓐ Celebrated festival days that are outlined in the scrolls	•
Ⓑ Brought the scrolls from Jerusalem in an effort to evade the Romans	•
Ⓒ Worshiped multiple gods, as documented in the scrolls	**Sadducees**
Ⓓ Wrote the songs that were found in the scrolls	•
Ⓔ Fled Qumran, leaving the scrolls behind for safe keeping	•
Ⓕ Were slaughtered by the Romans in the first century AD	**Jewish Refugees**
Ⓖ Were the earliest occupants of Qumran among the three groups	•

Answer Book p. 62

Vocabulary Review

A. Fill in the blanks with the appropriate words from the box.

incubate	conclusive	sordid
hallmark	frequent	supposition

1 I expected that she would clean her house before accepting guests, but it remained in its usual _____ state.

2 The novelist spent five years allowing the story to _____ in his imagination.

3 This restaurant is a favorite spot for stargazing because many actors _____ it.

4 Recent research findings provide _____ evidence that climate change is caused by human activity.

5 Based on the smell of baking cookies as I walked in the door, my _____ was that grandma had arrived.

6 The film has achieved a devoted following, usually a(n) _____ of a successful movie.

B. Choose the closest meaning for each highlighted word or phrase.

7 The nation has tried to insulate itself from political turmoil and conflicts in neighboring areas.
(A) harm   (B) alter   (C) isolate   (D) present

8 Gas prices dropped this week for the first time in months, falling approximately ten cents a gallon.
(A) roughly   (B) endearingly   (C) precipitously   (D) strangely

9 Inspiring students' intrinsic motivation to learn is the most effective strategy to get them engaged.
(A) impressive   (B) global   (C) healthy   (D) essential

10 The couple have long had a discordant relationship in which they cannot agree on almost anything.
(A) conflicting   (B) monotonous   (C) unpleasant   (D) elaborate

11 Sherlock Holmes used his powers of deduction to unravel another mystery.
(A) fix   (B) solve   (C) glean   (D) adopt

12 Like all geniuses he has idiosyncrasies, and one of them is that he eats raw pasta for breakfast.
(A) specialties   (B) oddities   (C) fondness   (D) processes

13 Some indigenous peoples are known to express high levels of hostility toward outsiders.
(A) fascination   (B) realism   (C) antagonism   (D) clarification

14 Most of the country's banks went through a consolidation with a larger bank, leaving a few giants and very few small banks.
(A) merger   (B) treatise   (C) stagnation   (D) compensation

Actual Test

Actual Test **1**

Actual Test **2**

History of Math

The Ishango Bone, an artifact estimated to be between 18,000 and 20,000 years old, is the earliest known example of the use of numbers by humans. Roughly ten centimeters in length, the bone tool is divided into three asymmetrical columns of notches organized in a manner that suggests they are functional rather than decorative. The notches on both the left and right columns are divided into several odd-numbered sets, the sum of which equals sixty, while the central column adds up to forty-eight. Although anthropologists disagree over the exact function of the artifact, with opinions ranging from a simple calculator to a primitive calendar, all agree that it clearly demonstrates the ability to recognize, count, and organize large numbers.

➡ From the Paleolithic to the Neolithic, the ancestors of modern humans made remarkable strides in the development of basic counting skills. **A** Prior to the invention of numbers as abstract concepts, early hunter-gatherers most likely used simple tallies that were based initially on the fingers and thumbs of the hands, often referred to as nature's abacus. **B** By the Mesolithic period, specific symbols were used to represent individual numbers, and the transition to the Neolithic is characterized by the use of simple calculations to assist with rituals and the construction of religious structures, such as Stonehenge. **C** This period marked an important milestone in the intellectual growth of humans and laid the foundation for the development of the advanced disciplines that would influence and shape the course of human civilization. **D**

➡ Much of this early knowledge was accumulated and consolidated by the cultures that flourished in the region known as the Fertile Crescent. The various peoples that arose between the Tigris and Euphrates Rivers made extensive use of numbers to manage their complex urban societies, particularly to inventory residents, provisions, and goods, as well as to keep track of taxes and commercial activities. To facilitate this, a new system of numerical representation was created, allowing for the inscription of mathematical records on clay tablets. Using a sexagesimal system (based on the number sixty), complex astronomical data was documented, leading to the development of sophisticated means to trace the passage of time that is still used today in the form of a sixty-minute hour and a sixty-second minute.

➡ Many of these early advances were adopted by the Egyptian civilization, with one notable exception. Rather than use sixty as a base, the Egyptians created a numerical system centered on the number ten, which was the first known use of the metric system. As this greatly expanded the range of equations that could be computed easily, they were able to apply mathematics to a wider range of purposes. In particular, it was used with great effectiveness in the field of engineering, allowing for the construction of the massive monuments for which the Egyptians are known, with the most impressive of these being the Great Pyramid of Giza.

Although the advances made by these early civilizations were significant, it was the scholars of ancient Greece that made the transition from the pragmatic application of numbers to the abstract numerical disciplines that are so important to modern science. The attitude of the Greeks towards mathematics is best summarized by the philosopher Philolaus, who argued that all things could be represented by a number and that the universe could only be conceived once the relationship between these figures was identified and understood. An example of this premise was Aristotle's belief that all commercial exchanges could be broken down into fundamental and unvarying equations. 40

The Greek scholars made significant advances in a variety of fields, including number theory, complex equations, and early calculus, although they are most well known for their work in geometry. Greek philosophical thought and geometry were closely linked, with each being focused on the classification and representation of idealized abstract forms. The effectiveness of this technique is illustrated by the work of Eratosthenes, who applied Greek principles to the study of geography and was the first to calculate the curvature of the planet with any accuracy, in the process devising a precursor to the modern system of longitude and latitude. 45

1 The word "asymmetrical" in the passage is closest in meaning to

   (A) inordinate   (B) uneven   (C) transient   (D) unfinished

2 The word "it" in the passage refers to

   (A) function   (B) artifact   (C) calculator   (D) calendar

3 Why does the author mention "Stonehenge" in the passage?

   (A) To illustrate the use of mathematics to build structures

   (B) To provide an example of a notable Mesolithic structure

   (C) To highlight the development of early belief systems

   (D) To demonstrate the significance of rituals in Neolithic times

4 Which of the following can be inferred from paragraph 2 about humans prior to the Mesolithic period?

   (A) They were unable to count higher than ten.

   (B) They inscribed extensive records of numerical data.

   (C) They did not use designated numerical representations.

   (D) They utilized basic mathematics when locating food.

Paragraph 2 is marked with an arrow [➡].

5 According to paragraph 3, all of the following are possible examples of the use of mathematics in the Fertile Crescent EXCEPT

   Ⓐ counting city inhabitants

   Ⓑ regulating local trade

   Ⓒ predicting population growth

   Ⓓ itemizing supplies

Paragraph 3 is marked with an arrow [➡].

6 According to paragraph 4, a primary difference between the Egyptians and earlier civilizations was

   Ⓐ the ability to calculate mathematical equations

   Ⓑ the desire to build impressive monuments

   Ⓒ the utilization of a versatile number system

   Ⓓ the invention of an applied science

Paragraph 4 is marked with an arrow [➡].

7 The word "premise" in the passage is closest in meaning to

   Ⓐ assumption

   Ⓑ contradiction

   Ⓒ concept

   Ⓓ decline

8 Which of the sentences below best expresses the essential information in the highlighted sentence in the passage? *Incorrect* choices change the meaning in important ways or leave out essential information.

   Ⓐ The determination of the shape of the earth by Eratosthenes using geometrical equations led to the development of an enduring system.

   Ⓑ The current method of calculation has its roots in the work of Eratosthenes, who measured important geographical phenomena.

   Ⓒ The exactness of Eratosthenes' equations allowed for the field of geography to be expanded using the constant rules of geometry.

   Ⓓ The reckonings of Eratosthenes, which influenced later geographers, demonstrate the utility of the Greek approach to geometry.

9 Look at the four squares [■] that indicate where the following sentence could be added to the passage.

Due to the limitation of this counting method, people eventually began making marks on bone or wood to keep track of amounts.

Where would the sentence best fit?

Click on a square [■] to add the sentence to the passage.

10 Directions: An introductory sentence for a brief summary of the passage is provided below. Complete the summary by selecting the THREE answer choices that express the most important ideas in the passage. Some sentences do not belong in the summary because they express ideas that are not presented in the passage or are minor ideas in the passage. **This question is worth 2 points.**

Drag your answer choices to the spaces where they belong.
To remove an answer choice, click on it. To review the passage, click on **View Text**.

Early civilizations made significant advances in the field of mathematics.

- ●
- ●
- ●

Answer Choices

(A) The metric system used by the Egyptians increased the utility and diversity of calculations.

(B) Middle Eastern civilizations used their unique numerical system to record important data and study the stars.

(C) The sexagesimal system of the Fertile Crescent has been incorporated into modern time-keeping methods.

(D) Greek philosophy encouraged the study of geometry, resulting in insights into the practical application of science.

(E) The Greek advances in geometry led to the development of a new scientific approach to the study of commerce.

(F) The Egyptians used the mathematical principles of earlier cultures to build enduring structures.

Answer Book p. 64

Social Animals

After Darwin's *On the Origin of Species* was first published in 1859, biologists began to examine the various ways that natural selection influenced the survival of a species. However, a growing number of scientists gradually began to question whether the traditional view of evolution as "survival of the fittest" was sufficient to explain all the factors that shaped the evolution of a species. In particular, if competition was the very basis for the theory of evolution, what could explain the cooperative behavior seen in so many organisms?

It was not until over a century later that biologist E. O. Wilson claimed in his book that altruism was as important as competitive fitness for survival. Therefore, it must also be a product of natural selection. From the standpoint of sociobiology, which is concerned with the social behavior and organization of organisms, cooperation and affection between individuals can result in each contributing more to the gene pool than they otherwise would if they were in direct competition with one another.

➡ All social animals live in groups, and researchers will document the size, factors that limit membership, and causes leading to the formation of the group to glean insight into the animals' behavior. The Arctic tern, for example, long considered a social animal, hides its young in the center of a circular arrangement to ensure maximum protection from mammalian predators. A group will typically have no more than fifty birds. This is because the upper limit of membership is determined by the available resources, which are extremely sparse in the Arctic tundra. It is in the terns' evolutionary interest, though, to live in groups as large as the ecosystem will support because when primary food is unevenly distributed or difficult to find, adventurous individuals may seek out secondary sources. Members who observe their flights or follow them will learn about these alternative food supplies. Therefore, in this view, both avoiding danger and sharing information provide the impetus for the formation of the colony.

➡ Wolves provide another example of animals that cohabitate in large groups, called packs, but do so primarily as a way to successfully trap and kill prey, not to protect themselves from predators. In addition, they have developed territorial behavior, which is another mechanism for survival described and explained through evolution. The members of a wolf pack guard their territory, anywhere from a few square kilometers to a range of several dozen square kilometers, as a way of making sure that they have access to enough prey. They will act aggressively toward coyotes, strange wolves, and domestic dogs if they should wander into their region, although they are more likely to make warning sounds than attack trespassers without provocation. According to evolutionary biology, the development of territoriality in wolves, as well as in other animals, can be attributed to the necessity to protect food supplies.

Once food is acquired, a social animal will share it with other members of the community. Yet, from an evolutionary perspective, it is advantageous to reward those members of the group that

are better able to obtain food so that they continue to perform their roles as hunters or gatherers. Therefore, the most able hunters and gatherers often receive a disproportionate amount of the food to keep them healthy and strong, enhancing their capacity to perform demanding tasks. Over time, these fit members of society tend to take on more prestigious positions than those who are not as fit, and a hierarchy develops within the group. Groups of the common chimpanzee, for 40 instance, give high status to members that have special skills, such as crafting tools or hunting, and this elite group is given priority when it comes to food.

A According to sociobiologists, the development of a social hierarchy in animals, like in humans, can be viewed as a logical step in the evolution of the species. **B** The relationship between humans and other animals is a matter of fierce debate, particularly because, as 45 sociologists will argue, humans have moved beyond the essentials of survival, such as securing food, shelter, and reproductive health. **C** People have evolved a level of consciousness that is a stage beyond even the most complicated animal community. **D**

11 The word "it" in the passage refers to

(A) book   (B) altruism   (C) fitness   (D) survival

12 The word "glean" in the passage is closest in meaning to

(A) offer   (B) show   (C) gather   (D) describe

13 According to paragraph 3, one reason that Arctic terns live in groups is

(A) to supply additional food to hungry chicks
(B) to ensure safety for their young
(C) to defend their territory against predators
(D) to give members the opportunity to become educated

Paragraph 3 is marked with an arrow [➡].

14 Which of the following can be inferred from paragraph 4 about wolves?

(A) They only act violently when fighting for food.
(B) They rate members based on competency in hunting.
(C) They behave belligerently when provisions are low.
(D) They sometimes wander into another pack's domain.

Paragraph 4 is marked with an arrow [➡].

15 Which of the sentences below best expresses the essential information in the highlighted sentence in the passage? *Incorrect* choices change the meaning in important ways or leave out essential information.

(A) Due to some members' submissive quality, those more aggressive and dominant will be compensated with more nourishment.

(B) The theory of evolution states that rewards motivate members of the group to perform better in their jobs as hunters or gatherers.

(C) The best way to safeguard the survival of the group is to have several members who are responsible for getting most of the food.

(D) It makes evolutionary sense that talented predators receive rewards from the group to keep them content enough to persist in their efforts.

16 The word "disproportionate" in the passage is closest in meaning to

(A) impartial

(B) unequal

(C) deliberate

(D) abnormal

17 Why does the author mention "the common chimpanzee" in the passage?

(A) To provide evidence that some animals can be successful predators

(B) To show how some species have evolved to value the construction of tools

(C) To give an example of a species of animals that hunt for their food

(D) To specify a species that endows prestige on highly adept individuals

18 According to the passage, humans cannot be analyzed by sociobiologists in the same way as other animals because

(A) we are no longer preoccupied with the basic elements of survival

(B) we have ceased living in communities that are structured hierarchically

(C) we have become aware of their own existences, thoughts, and feelings

(D) we are unable to be observed by animal behaviorists with precision

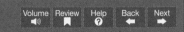
Volume | Review | Help | Back | Next

19 Look at the four squares [■] that indicate where the following sentence could be added to the passage.

This is evidenced by the close genetic relationship between humans and other primates, such as monkeys, that live in hierarchical communities.

Where would the sentence best fit?

Click on a square [■] to add the sentence to the passage.

20 Directions: An introductory sentence for a brief summary of the passage is provided below. Complete the summary by selecting the THREE answer choices that express the most important ideas in the passage. Some sentences do not belong in the summary because they express ideas that are not presented in the passage or are minor ideas in the passage. **This question is worth 2 points.**

Drag your answer choices to the spaces where they belong.
To remove an answer choice, click on it. To review the passage, click on **View Text**.

Using the theory of evolution, scientists can assess the behavior of animals as it facilitates the progression of the species.

- ●
- ●
- ●

Answer Choices

(A) Social hierarchy develops because those members that are better able to contribute provisions are rewarded.

(B) Members of a community that perform exhausting jobs are more likely to procreate than others.

(C) Aggregates of individuals form when it becomes easier to survive as a group than as a solitary creature.

(D) Disproportionate access to energy resources prompts some animals to become versed in different food-gathering strategies.

(E) Territoriality is attributed to animals' need to ward off competitors for the same food supply.

(F) Animals that teach others how to construct important instruments can achieve a greater social standing.

Answer Book p. 65

The Age of Earth

Throughout the medieval period, European scholars attempted to date Earth based on biblical accounts. Those bold enough to propose a much older age based on observable geological processes potentially faced serious consequences, even death. However, the Age of Enlightenment in Europe marked the beginning of considerable scientific inquiry into the issue.

One of the earliest attempts occurred in the eighteenth century when Edmond Halley theorized 5 that the salinity of the ocean could be used to date the planet. Observing that rainwater picks up small pieces of salt from rock and dirt before it eventually reaches the ocean, he concluded that this process was gradually increasing the salinity of the sea as water evaporated from the surface of the ocean. Operating under the assumption that the oceans had initially formed as fresh water, he believed that the age of Earth could then be calculated based on current oceanic salinity and 10 the rate at which it increases. Subsequent researchers applied his method to place the age of the planet at between 50 and 150 million years.

➡ Although influential for a time, the salt theory was eventually discarded because of some intrinsic flaws. First, scientists do not know the original salinity of the oceans, so there is no way to find out how much salt levels have increased, if at all. And contrary to what Halley believed, 15 salt does not remain permanently dissolved in ocean water; instead, some of it combines with other minerals and falls to the sea floor as sediment. Consequently, although the salinity of the ocean fluctuates temporarily, it neither increases nor decreases significantly over time.

➡ In the nineteenth century, physicist Lord Kelvin postulated that the planet could be dated by studying its temperature. His theory assumed that Earth began as molten rock. Based on his 20 observation that upper portions of Earth's crust were cooler than its interior, Kelvin concluded that the planet was becoming colder as heat escaped to the surface and into space. To establish the rate of cooling, he studied the speed at which heat is transmitted from the ground to the atmosphere.

➡ The cooling theory was quickly criticized by other scientists, who pointed out that it relied 25 on faulty assumptions. Kelvin performed his calculations solely based on the conduction of heat through solid rock, but in fact, heat is also transmitted through the planet by the movement of fluids, because portions of Earth's interior are semi-liquid. Kelvin also assumed that Earth was cooling at a constant rate without any heat being added, but this was a controversial view.

Scientists later learned that rocks generate their own heat due to a process known as 30 radioactive decay, making it impossible to accurately measure the rate at which Earth cools. This discovery not only disproved the cooling theory but also led to the development of radiometric dating, which is still used today. The method is viable because radioactive elements gradually break down into stable elements at a fixed rate. Once this rate is determined, geologists can calculate the age of a rock by measuring the amounts of various elements found within it. 35

Thus, applying radiometric dating to old rocks provided a new way of studying Earth's age, and geological materials exceeding 3.5 billion years old were found. However, because rocks have been mixed together over the eons due to processes like weathering and the movement of Earth's tectonic plates, the oldest rocks may be hidden far beneath the surface of the planet.

The solution to this problem was to analyze objects that originated elsewhere in the solar system. Since it is believed that all parts of the solar system formed at approximately the same time, twentieth-century researchers applied radiometric dating to extraterrestrial objects that were not subjected to the same geological processes as terrestrial rocks. **A** This approach was particularly successful with meteorites since they underwent very little change from their formation until they impacted Earth. **B** In the 1950s, researchers estimated that Earth is approximately 4.5 billion years old by dating a meteorite found in Arizona. **C** This figure was confirmed in subsequent years when analyses of dozens of meteorites and moon rocks produced similar results. **D**

Glossary	☒
salinity: the concentration of salt dissolved in waters	

21 The word "considerable" in the passage is closest in meaning to

   (A) thoughtful

   (B) crucial

   (C) substantial

   (D) careful

22 Which of the following can be inferred about scholars in medieval Europe?

   (A) Many of them believed it was impossible to determine the planet's age.

   (B) Some of them believed that Earth was older than what was described in the Bible.

   (C) Few of them accepted that Earth was just over six thousand years old.

   (D) All of them understood how long natural geological processes take.

23 The word "it" in the passage refers to

   (A) rainwater

   (B) salt

   (C) rock

   (D) dirt

Actual Test 1

HACKERS APEX READING for the TOEFL iBT Expert

24 According to paragraph 3, which of the following is NOT a flaw of the salt theory?

 Ⓐ Scientists do not know the initial salt content of the sea.

 Ⓑ The salinity of the oceans does not fluctuate greatly.

 Ⓒ Salt does not stay suspended in seawater indefinitely.

 Ⓓ Many minerals in the sea do not readily bind with salts.

Paragraph 3 is marked with an arrow [➡].

25 According to paragraph 4, what made Kelvin think that Earth was cooling?

 Ⓐ The interior of the planet was warmer than the exterior.

 Ⓑ Surface temperatures were decreasing over time.

 Ⓒ He observed molten lava escaping to the surface.

 Ⓓ He believed atoms were continually losing heat.

Paragraph 4 is marked with an arrow [➡].

26 According to paragraph 5, Kelvin assumed that

 Ⓐ Earth cools at a consistent speed over time

 Ⓑ parts of the interior of the planet are semi-liquid

 Ⓒ the amount of heat in solid rock cannot be calculated

 Ⓓ atoms contain massive amounts of potential energy

Paragraph 5 is marked with an arrow [➡].

27 The word "disproved" in the passage is closest in meaning to

 Ⓐ destroyed

 Ⓑ refuted

 Ⓒ transformed

 Ⓓ corroborated

28 Why does the author mention "weathering and the movement of Earth's tectonic plates"?

 Ⓐ To show that the geological processes on Earth are unique in the solar system

 Ⓑ To provide the basis for using terrestrial rocks in the field of radiometric dating

 Ⓒ To explain why terrestrial rocks are not completely reliable for dating Earth

 Ⓓ To highlight the discovery that led to more precise methods of dating Earth

29 Look at the four squares [■] that indicate where the following sentence could be added to the passage.

Scientists also achieved good results by applying the method to lunar rocks.

Where would the sentence best fit?

Click on a square [■] to add the sentence to the passage.

30 Directions: An introductory sentence for a brief summary of the passage is provided below. Complete the summary by selecting the THREE answer choices that express the most important ideas in the passage. Some sentences do not belong in the summary because they express ideas that are not presented in the passage or are minor ideas in the passage. **This question is worth 2 points.**

Drag your answer choices to the spaces where they belong.
To remove an answer choice, click on it. To review the passage, click on **View Text**.

> **Throughout history, scientists have devised different techniques to measure the age of our planet, with varying degrees of success.**
>
> ●
>
> ●
>
> ●

Answer Choices

(A) While he was subsequently proven wrong, Lord Kelvin claimed that the planet could be dated by calculating the rate at which heat leaves Earth.

(B) In the eighteenth century, Edmond Halley developed a process to establish the age of the planet by studying the increase in the salinity of the oceans, although it was later discredited.

(C) Edmond Halley made the first estimate of the age of the planet by measuring the amount of salt found on the ocean floor.

(D) The cooling theory developed by Kelvin was highly controversial in his own day, but scientists later proved it to be accurate.

(E) Objects of extraterrestrial origin, such as meteors, are particularly useful for radiometric dating because their mineral composition has remained intact.

(F) Modern scientists have applied a process known as radiometric dating to conclude that our planet is approximately 4.5 billion years old.

Answer Book p. 67

Actual Test 1

HACKERS APEX READING for the TOEFL iBT Expert

Army Ants

Formicidae, a taxonomic group of insects commonly referred to as ants, is comprised of over twenty thousand distinct species, making it one of the most varied families of organisms on the planet. The degree of speciation within this family has led to a significant level of genetic diversification. This has allowed the insects to succeed in a variety of ecological niches that include, among others, urban areas, rainforests, deserts, and mountains. A range of specialized 5 adaptations also have allowed ants to thrive in such diverse ecosystems.

➡ Among the earth's many specialized ants are army ants, which have several physical and behavioral characteristics that make them particularly well suited for life in the tropical jungles they inhabit. Army ants are divided into two distinct subfamilies that each includes dozens of varieties. Those that inhabit South America fall under the subfamily Ecitoninae, while their 10 African counterparts are classified as Dorylinae. Although both subfamilies possess distinguishing attributes, the two groups share many traits that have their roots in a common evolutionary heritage. Both subfamilies are, in fact, descended from a single ancestor, and the complex behavioral traits shared by each have remained in an evolutionary stasis for over 100 million years. 15

➡ By the mid-Cretaceous, the key characteristics that distinguish modern varieties of this insect had already been established. For instance, all army ants are nomadic, as they must continually migrate within a region in search of food. Their nomadic lifestyle has resulted in a very unique method for providing shelter. Unlike most ant species, which construct permanent nests, army ants create temporary living shelters known as bivouacs, which are formed by the bodies of worker 20 ants. This mass of living bodies offers protection for the queen, both from potential predators and from the elements. Another common feature is an activity known as swarming, whereby millions of soldier ants move in organized formations in search of prey, which may include other insects, birds, lizards, and even large mammals. The quest for sustenance is the primary focus of both subfamilies of army ants, as their queens are among the most prolific breeders of all ants, 25 producing over four million eggs each month.

➡ Despite sharing these same basic behavioral patterns, each subfamily utilizes its own distinctive strategies when engaging in predation. In Africa, the Dorylinae, also known as driver ants, rely on their mandibles. These are long appendages on the ants' jaws that act as powerful pinchers, which are capable of easily killing smaller prey and removing chunks of flesh from larger 30 animals.

African army ants utilize a swarm front when hunting, a method that involves a concentrated mass of raiders that sweep through an area in order to flush out prey. **A** As there are often over twenty million individuals working in unison in each swarm front, it poses a significant threat to animals of all sizes. **B** Extending behind this front is a fan-shaped network of workers traveling 35 along set trails that eventually merge into a vast column leading back to the bivouac. **C** As the workers travel back and forth carrying food, they are protected by soldiers that form a living shield along the pathways. **D**

Unlike their African counterparts, the Ecitoninae army ants rely on their potent sting to disable and kill their prey. As the South American species are unable to swallow solid material, their venom contains a tissue-dissolving enzyme that breaks down the flesh of their victims into a digestible form. Although these ants possess a formidable set of mandibles, these are not as big as those of the Dorylinae. They are primarily used to dismember small insects and lizards once they have been immobilized.

➡ When hunting, Ecitoninae employ a strategy whereby the colony divides into small foraging parties that travel in several columns to form a tree-like pattern, branching off from the bivouac. A continuous two-way stream of ants travels along these trails, ensuring that a constant supply of food is returned to the bivouac. These species do not pose a hazard to creatures much larger than themselves, and in fact are viewed with favor by many farmers as they eliminate other insects that hamper agricultural activities.

1 The word "diversification" in the passage is closest in meaning to

  (A) dominance

  (B) entity

  (C) variety

  (D) maturity

2 Why does the author mention "urban areas, rainforests, deserts, and mountains" in the passage?

  (A) To highlight factors that limit the adaptability of ants

  (B) To provide a reason for the numerous ant variants

  (C) To identify ecosystems that a species can best adapt to

  (D) To give an example of habitats occupied by an organism

3 The word "their" in the passage refers to

  (A) both subfamilies

  (B) distinguishing attributes

  (C) the two groups

  (D) many traits

4 According to paragraph 2, which of the following is true of army ants?

   Ⓐ They are virtually indistinguishable in their anatomy and physiology.

   Ⓑ They are made up of approximately a dozen species worldwide.

   Ⓒ They originated in Africa before spreading to South America.

   Ⓓ They are extremely well adapted to jungles in tropical areas.

Paragraph 2 is marked with an arrow [➡].

5 According to paragraph 3, both subfamilies of army ant share all of the following traits EXCEPT

   Ⓐ the urge to travel regularly as a group

   Ⓑ the need to build enduring residences

   Ⓒ the use of collective hunting methods

   Ⓓ the production of large numbers of young

Paragraph 3 is marked with an arrow [➡].

6 Which of the following can be inferred from paragraph 4 about the African army ants?

   Ⓐ They present a danger to animals that are larger than them.

   Ⓑ They prefer to travel through locations with established trails.

   Ⓒ They form large colonies that include multiple queens.

   Ⓓ They hunt individually and then share the food with the whole colony.

Paragraph 4 is marked with an arrow [➡].

7 The word "immobilized" in the passage is closest in meaning to

   Ⓐ eliminated   Ⓑ paralyzed   Ⓒ injured   Ⓓ stabilized

8 According to paragraph 7, why do many farmers view the Ecitoninae as beneficial?

   Ⓐ They allow the cultivation of inaccessible areas.

   Ⓑ They are not dangerous to bigger creatures.

   Ⓒ They destroy bugs considered to be pests.

   Ⓓ They are not likely to damage the harvest.

Paragraph 7 is marked with an arrow [➡].

9 Look at the four squares [■] that indicate where the following sentence could be added to the passage.

Even humans may be threatened if they are old, ill, or injured.

Where would the sentence best fit?

Click on a square [■] to add the sentence to the passage.

10 **Directions:** Select the appropriate phrases from the answer choices and match them to the subfamily of army ants with which they are associated. **This question is worth 3 points**.

Drag your answer choices to the spaces where they belong.
To remove an answer choice, click on it. To review the passage, click on **View Text**.

Answer Choices	Ecitoninae
Ⓐ Hunt in a single group with over 20 million individuals	•
Ⓑ Possess a venomous sting	•
Ⓒ Conduct raids on other army ant colonies	•
Ⓓ Depend on powerful jaws to kill prey	**Dorylinae**
Ⓔ Consume vegetation in addition to other creatures	
Ⓕ Produce a substance that dissolves flesh	•
Ⓖ Break up into smaller groups when looking for food	•

Answer Book p. 68

Schizophrenia

Schizophrenia is a psychiatric condition characterized by social and occupational dysfunction, impairments in the perception of reality, and delusions or auditory hallucinations. Diagnosis is primarily based on personal accounts of the patients and of those close to them, in addition to secondary observations made by medical professionals. Approximately eight in every thousand North Americans will develop the disease, which crosses all socioeconomic, ethnic, and racial 5 boundaries, and is the main motivation for admissions to mental hospitals across the country.

➡ During the late nineteenth century, doctors believed that the condition was a physiological ailment related to the improper development of the frontal lobe of the brain, and many attempted to cure their patients with a psychosurgical method known as a lobotomy. This technique, first performed in 1890 by Swiss-born Dr. Gottlieb Burckhardt, involved the separation of the right 10 and left hemispheres of the brain in order to sever the malfunctioning "emotional" side from the healthy "analytical" one. The procedure was conducted by driving a flat metal instrument through the top of the skull. Initially, the crude procedure was met with intense skepticism by the public, but further refinements by a Portuguese neurologist, António Egas Moniz, who won the Nobel Prize for Medicine for his work, showed that it did alleviate many symptoms of schizophrenia. 15

➡ Yet, despite the documented success of the lobotomy in several thousand people, the surgery remained highly controversial because of its known risks. Because such little research could be ethically conducted on the brains of living people, physicians frequently made incorrect assumptions based on experiments performed on the tissues of deceased patients. This, in combination with the delicate nature of the procedure itself, resulted in frequent errors being made during surgeries. 20 Some subjects entered into permanent vegetative states, some could no longer function without assistance, and others even died following the procedure. Many in the medical profession were repulsed by the idea that treatment of a mental disorder required the destruction of healthy neural tissue and advocated the use of pharmaceuticals instead. As such, with the advent of antipsychotic medications, such as chlorpromazine, the practice of psychosurgery rapidly declined. 25

➡ The contemporary pharmacological approach to treating schizophrenia is based on advanced twentieth-century neurological research indicating that the brain must manage several naturally occurring hormones in order to maintain normal functionality. If a neurochemical is present in an abnormal quantity, a patient experiences changes in emotional states, ranging from minor mood swings to intense periods of depression or mania. **A** In schizophrenic brains, the level of 30 dopamine, a hormone known to facilitate the flow of information into the frontal lobe from other areas of the brain by binding to resident chemical receptors, is extremely high. **B** Therefore, the frontal lobe is inundated with data that it cannot process, and memory, attention, and problem-solving skills suffer. **C** Antipsychotic medication acts as a blocking agent, binding to the receptors in place of the dopamine, and provides momentary relief from the symptoms of 35 psychosis. **D** Mental health professionals argue that this should not be considered a cure, but the

administration of these pharmaceuticals has allowed many people who suffer from schizophrenia to live healthy lives outside of hospital facilities.

As more patients learn to manage their symptoms on their own, alternative therapy options that work in conjunction with medical treatment have emerged as a way to help these people integrate fully into the larger society. Counseling sessions boost self-esteem and social functioning by teaching life skills and have been shown to be quite successful. Additionally, nutritionists have discovered that supplementing a schizophrenic's diet with omega-3 fatty acids, naturally found in fish and some vegetables, has helped patients become more aware of their surroundings and better able to synthesize information.

These alternatives emphasize the notion of psychiatric diseases as lifelong conditions that require holistic, informal, and community-oriented treatment. Interestingly, this approach has proven much more successful than medical treatment of the illness by ensuring patient autonomy and better preparing them to endure the symptoms related to schizophrenia.

11 The word "malfunctioning" in the passage is closest in meaning to

(A) unpleasant   (B) unreasonable   (C) incredible   (D) inoperative

12 According to paragraph 2, what did Dr. Burckhardt want to achieve with his psychosurgical method?

(A) To partition the so-called emotional and analytical regions of the brain
(B) To better understand the relationship between the brain's two hemispheres
(C) To allow patients to distinguish between their illusions and physical reality
(D) To prove to other scientists that it could be used to treat various disorders

Paragraph 2 is marked with an arrow [➡].

13 The word "others" in the passage refers to

(A) errors   (B) surgeries   (C) subjects   (D) states

14 Why does the author mention "chlorpromazine" in the passage?

(A) To describe the kind of drugs replaced by psychosurgical methods
(B) To illustrate the great range of pharmaceuticals available to doctors
(C) To give an example of a pharmaceutical used to treat psychosis
(D) To specify a drug proven to be most effective for treating neural tissue

15 According to paragraph 3, what was a main cause for repeated surgical mistakes?

   (A) The brain was too fragile an organ to operate on.

   (B) Doctors were commonly untrained in their discipline.

   (C) Speculation based on tests was often erroneous.

   (D) Experiments were occasionally performed on live patients.

Paragraph 3 is marked with an arrow [➡].

16 In paragraph 4, what does the author imply about antipsychotic medication?

   (A) Its efficacy dwindles after repeated administration.

   (B) Its effects will diminish after cessation of application.

   (C) Its capacity to heal mental illness is quite limited.

   (D) Its strength is directly related to the number of neural receptors.

Paragraph 4 is marked with an arrow [➡].

17 Which of the sentences below best expresses the essential information in the highlighted sentence in the passage? *Incorrect* choices change the meaning in important ways or leave out essential information.

   (A) By increasing the amount of fat in their meals, schizophrenics can improve their overall social integration and brain functionality.

   (B) Giving a dietary supplement to schizophrenic patients has been found to enhance their capacity for cognition and comprehension.

   (C) The substances that are consumed by people with schizophrenia can affect the way they perceive themselves.

   (D) A lack of fish and vegetables in their diet can reduce the tendencies of schizophrenics to cope with new places and facts.

18 The word "autonomy" in the passage is closest in meaning to

   (A) assistance

   (B) confidence

   (C) independence

   (D) emphasis

19 Look at the four squares [■] that indicate where the following sentence could be added to the passage.

This allows the patient to better cope with situations that involve a great deal of auditory or visual input.

Where would the sentence best fit?

Click on a square [■] to add the sentence to the passage.

20 **Directions:** An introductory sentence for a brief summary of the passage is provided below. Complete the summary by selecting the THREE answer choices that express the most important ideas in the passage. Some sentences do not belong in the summary because they express ideas that are not presented in the passage or are minor ideas in the passage. **This question is worth 2 points.**

Drag your answer choices to the spaces where they belong.
To remove an answer choice, click on it. To review the passage, click on **View Text**.

Schizophrenia is a prevalent mental illness that has been treated in a number of ways.

-
-
-

Answer Choices

Ⓐ Medical investigations revealed that the condition is triggered by an imbalance in neurochemicals, which can be helped with the use of antipsychotic medications.

Ⓑ Early studies into the disease determined that it was caused by a dysfunctional part of the brain and could be cured by an invasive surgical procedure.

Ⓒ Many scientists were concerned that a lobotomy could permanently damage a person's brain, so they preferred the utilization of less severe treatments.

Ⓓ As the pharmaceutical industry progressed, new medicines that could specifically address mental illness started to be sold on the market.

Ⓔ An increased emphasis on holistic treatments related to patients' better adaptability to society involves changes to diet and ongoing therapy.

Ⓕ Scientists have fervently debated whether schizophrenia is a curable medical condition or a lifelong affliction that should be treated in a variety of ways.

Answer Book p. 69

The Orion Nebula

The Sun is approximately four and half billion years old and is expected to burn for another four to five billion years before its helium completely fuses into carbon. Once this happens, its gases will disperse and create a planetary nebula, a diffuse collection of interstellar particles. This process, called stellar evolution, affects all stars in the 5 universe; they constantly form, thrive for as long as their chemical compositions will allow, and then disappear. Evidence of stellar evolution can be observed in the Orion Nebula, a greenish-hued cloud located just below the belt in the Orion constellation. For hundreds of years, early astronomers studied this, first with the naked eye and then with primitive telescopes, for clues about the overall structure of the universe. 10

One of the most famous historical works on the subject was written in 1755 by Immanuel Kant. The German-born philosopher suggested that, based on Newton's Law of Gravity, stars form as a nebula cloud slowly rotates, gradually collapsing into a flattened disk due to gravitational pressure. From this disk, a plethora of collections of hot solar gases, or young stars, materialize. The remaining particles merge into planetesimals, or small clumps that eventually accrete enough 15 mass to become protoplanets, all held together by gravity. Therefore, the Orion Nebula was not only a birthplace for stars, but also a nursery for entire solar systems.

➡ Kant's astrophysics work, however, was initially ignored by scientists, who did not lend much credence to the theory, as it was merely philosophical and contained little actual data. Therefore, it was more than forty years before these ideas achieved any acceptance in the field of astronomy, 20 and only after French mathematician Pierre-Simon Laplace applied scientific methodology to Kant's propositions and published his own treatise on stellar formation. Gravitational attraction, he argued, is indeed the driving force behind solar system formation; once a young star forms, cools, and contracts, angular momentum results in a surge in rotational velocity, pushing particles outward while gravitational attraction pulls them toward the center. When the forces finally 25 balance, numerous equatorial rings of gas and dust are left behind and each will coalesce into a planet. This model, combined with Kant's predictions, is now known as the Kant-Laplace nebular hypothesis and was considered the orthodox model for stellar evolution for the next hundred years.

➡ Nevertheless, there were several objections to the hypothesis, namely those stated in the 30 late nineteenth century by British physicist James Clerk Maxwell, whose gravitational calculations invalidated Laplace's treatise. Instead, he argued that if all matter assumed to comprise the known planets was once distributed in a disk-like cloud around the Sun, then the gravitational force would have pulled all of this matter directly toward the Sun, preventing the formation of distinct planets. 35

Actual Test 2

HACKERS APEX READING for the TOEFL iBT Expert

A The debate between Maxwell's supporters and proponents of the Kant-Laplace hypothesis raged until the launch of the Hubble Space Telescope, a sophisticated interstellar observatory, in 1990. **B** The Hubble was designed to record visible, ultraviolet, and infrared light bounced off two mirror instruments attached to the main lens column. **C** Using this information, it draws high-resolution composite images of areas of space more than three light years in width. **D**   40

➡ Hubble's chief scientist, Robert O'Dell, used one such photograph of the Orion Nebula to seek further answers about celestial formation. Initially, his analysis of the morphology of several systems seemed to support the Kant-Laplace hypothesis: the juvenile, or protoplanetary, systems, each with a protostar at its epicenter, presented in disk-like shapes as predicted. However, upon closer examination, the Hubble images revealed the disks to be folded down at their ends into a   45 slightly concave structure. This meant, he argued, that gradual stellar evolution does take place up to the point where the star is surrounded by a series of protoplanetary rings, but instead of relying solely on gravity to somehow bring together particles, planets are formed by catastrophic collisions with other protoplanetary rings within the same region, satisfying the objections to the hypothesis. In the Orion Nebula, with hundreds of systems within reach, cataclysmic planetary   50 formation is more likely to happen. Interestingly, this also heightens the feasibility that a planet that can support life will be formed.

Glossary	☒
planetesimals: solid objects formed in the early solar system	◢

21 The word "this" in the passage refers to

Ⓐ Evidence   Ⓑ cloud   Ⓒ belt   Ⓓ constellation

22 Why does the author mention "Newton's Law of Gravity" in the passage?

Ⓐ To explain the basic theory that Kant used to formulate his proposition
Ⓑ To show the kind of regulations Kant had to comply with in his works
Ⓒ To refute an accepted concept that Kant utilized to argue his case
Ⓓ To provide an example of a work that was disproved by Kant's premise

23 The word "plethora" in the passage is closest in meaning to

Ⓐ absence   Ⓑ precision   Ⓒ abundance   Ⓓ recognition

24 According to paragraph 3, why was Kant's writing largely dismissed by experts?

(A) It contained speculations rather than data.

(B) It was not compatible with other theories.

(C) It did not include scientific terms.

(D) It included improbable information.

Paragraph 3 is marked with an arrow [➡].

25 The Kant-Laplace hypothesis proposed all of the following EXCEPT:

(A) Stars dissipate heat and subsequently spin at their axis.

(B) Gravity pulls excess particles away from the solar center.

(C) Rings form after a stable environment has been achieved.

(D) Dust and gas combine to create planets.

26 In paragraph 4, what do Maxwell's gravitational calculations imply?

(A) Stars do not actually spin as fast as Laplace predicted.

(B) Collisions occur frequently between planetesimals in young solar systems.

(C) The gravity holding protoplanet clumps together is weak.

(D) The Sun's gravitational pull is stronger than the force exerted by planetesimals.

Paragraph 4 is marked with an arrow [➡].

27 The word "feasibility" in the passage is closest in meaning to

(A) procedure   (B) likelihood   (C) appeal   (D) expectation

28 According to paragraph 6, what discovery led Robert O'Dell to question the Kant-Laplace hypothesis?

(A) The edges of the flattened protoplanetary system were bent.

(B) The systems contained more than one protostar at its center.

(C) The probability of impacts was augmented by the proximity of planetesimals.

(D) The ring of protoplanetary material was not present.

Paragraph 6 is marked with an arrow [➡].

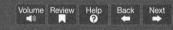

29 Look at the four squares [■] that indicate where the following sentence could be added to the passage.

The telescope also features a broad range of adaptable optical filters to capture important data.

Where would the sentence best fit?

> Click on a square [■] to add the sentence to the passage.

30 **Directions:** An introductory sentence for a brief summary of the passage is provided below. Complete the summary by selecting the THREE answer choices that express the most important ideas in the passage. Some sentences do not belong in the summary because they express ideas that are not presented in the passage or are minor ideas in the passage. **This question is worth 2 points.**

> Drag your answer choices to the spaces where they belong.
> To remove an answer choice, click on it. To review the passage, click on **View Text**.

Observations of the Orion Nebula have provided insight into the process of star and planet formation.

- ●
- ●
- ●

Answer Choices

(A) Earth's closest nebula is more than three light years in width as evidenced by the composite image drawn by the Hubble Telescope.

(B) The pressure caused by gravitational force causes the nebula to cave in and take on a thin, round shape.

(C) A band of materials that slam into each other forms around each new star at the center of a typical solar system.

(D) Collectively, the work of Kant and Laplace led to the once widely accepted nebular hypothesis of stellar evolution.

(E) Observations made with the Hubble Telescope helped clarify certain aspects of stellar formation and also how planets are formed.

(F) The Kant-Laplace hypothesis was challenged by new research, leading to a longstanding debate.

Answer Book p. 71

MEMO

|H|A|C|K|E|R|S|

APEX
READING
for the
TOEFL iBT®   Expert

COPYRIGHT © 2022, by Hackers Language Research Institute

September 28, 2022

All rights reserved. No part of this publication may be reproduced, stored in a retrieval system, or transmitted, in any form or by any means, electronic, mechanical, photocopying, recording, or otherwise, without the prior written permission of the author and the publisher.

Hackers Language Research Institute
23, Gangnam-daero 61-gil, Seocho-gu, Seoul, Korea
Inquiries publishing@hackers.com

ISBN 978-89-6542-511-3 (53740)

Printed in South Korea

1 2 3 4 5 6 7 8 9 10   28 27 26 25 24 23 22

The Most Preferred Education Brand in Korea,
HACKERS BOOK(www.HackersBook.com)
• Free supplementary study materials

No. 1 in Hankyung Business' Most Preferred Brand Rankings 2019, Education Group category

HACKERS

APEX
READING
for the
TOEFL iBT

Expert

HACKERS

APEX
READING
for the
TOEFL iBT® Expert

Answer Book

HACKERS

Example

본문 p.13

1 (C) 2 (D) 3 (C)

기억상실증

모든 기억상실증의 사례는 단기, 중기, 장기 기억 상실의 주요한 세 가지 유형으로 한층 더 나뉜다. 첫 번째를 앓는 사람은 이전의 몇 초 동안 일어난 어떤 사건도 기억하지 못한다. 두 번째는 기억상실증의 발병 전 몇 초에서 며칠 사이에 일어난 사건에 대한 기억 불능을 수반한다. 마지막은 가장 심각한 유형이며 더 오래전의 사건에 대한 기억 불능을 수반한다.

기억상실증의 원인은 머리에의 타격이나 질병의 결과로 인한 뇌 손상을 포함하여 다양하다. 전자의 경우, 뇌진탕과 같은 머리 부상은 단기간의 의식 불명과 머리 타격에 앞서 일어난 사건들에 대한 뒤이은 기억 불능을 초래할 수 있다. 후자의 경우, 뇌종양, 퇴행성 장애, 혹은 뇌졸중과 같은 심각한 질환이 기억 상실을 유발할 수 있다.

기억상실증은 종종 치매와 혼동되는데, 치매는 70세에서 79세 사이 인구의 약 3퍼센트에 영향을 미치며 고령층에서 훨씬 더 흔한 질환이다. 기억 상실과 함께, 치매는 일반적으로 언어, 시각 및 공간 능력, 판단력, 감정 조절 장애를 초래한다. 치매가 노화 과정의 불가피한 일부라는 흔한 오해가 있지만, 그것은 사실 뇌의 신경세포 손상이나 소실에 의해 유발된다.

amnesia 몡기억상실증   dementia 몡치매   immediate 혱단기의
intermediate 혱중기의   preceding 혱이전의   inability 몡불능
onset 몡발병, 시작   entail 동수반하다   concussion 몡뇌진탕
unconsciousness 몡의식 불명   subsequent 혱뒤이은
precede 동앞서 일어나다   degenerative 혱퇴행성의
stroke 몡뇌졸중   in conjunction with ~과 함께
impairment 몡장애   spatial 혱공간의   misperception 몡오해
unavoidable 혱불가피한

1 지문의 단어 "onset"과 의미가 가장 비슷한 것은?

(A) 종료
(B) 악화
(C) 시작
(D) 깨달음

2 지문의 단어 "subsequent"와 의미가 가장 비슷한 것은?

(A) 우세한
(B) 비행을 저지른
(C) 눈에 띄는
(D) 뒤따르는

3 지문의 어구 "In conjunction with"와 의미가 가장 비슷한 것은?

(A) ~ 때문에
(B) ~에 의해
(C) ~과 함께
(D) ~과 반대로

사막 생물

사막은 평균적으로 연 강우량이 250밀리미터 미만이다. [2B]정오에는 최고 섭씨 50도에서 밤에는 최저 섭씨 0도까지 이르러 기온의 일교차가 극심하다. 이는 이 생태계들의 극도로 낮은 습도 때문이다. [2C/2D]낮에는, 많은 양의 태양 복사열이 땅에 흡수되는데, 이는 그것을 분산시킬 수증기가 공기 중에 없기 때문이다. 그러나, 수증기는 또한 단열의 특성도 지니기 때문에, 일단 해가 지면 이 열은 빠르게 소멸한다.

암반의 노출부를 풍화시키고 부서진 입자들을 한 곳에서 다른 곳으로 운반하는 역할을 하는 풍식 작용과 함께, 제한된 습기와 혹독한 기온은 주로 바위나 모래로 뒤덮인 지표면으로 이루어진 사막의 풍경을 형성한다. 따라서, 토양은 최소한으로만 발달되며, 조약돌과 자갈을 포함하는 하성 퇴적물이 저지대 전역에 분산된다. 이러한 복합적인 요인들은 사막에서 어떠한 생물도 고유한 환경적 압박에 대처하기 위한 상당한 형태 및 행동적 적응 없이는 생존하기 매우 어렵게 한다.

사용할 수 있는 수분이 깊은 지하 저수지에 저장되어 있거나 희박한 양으로 불규칙하게 내리기 때문에 물 관리는 생물의 주요 관심사이다. 그러므로, 사막의 식물은 그러한 제한된 원천으로부터 수분을 얻고 유지하기 위한 몇 가지 혁신적인 전략을 발전시켜왔다. 이 식물들 중 일부는 강우가 내릴 때 방대한 양의 강우를 빠르게 얻어서 밀랍질의 외부 조직에 의해 보호되는 중심 구조물에 그것을 저장할 수 있는 넓은 방사형의 뿌리 체계를 발달시켰는데, 단 한 번의 강우가 그것들을 수년 동안 버티게 해줄 수 있다. 다수는 잎 대신 가시를 갖고 있는데, 이 좁고 뾰족한 구조물은 공기 중으로 유실되는 물의 양을 제한하고 동물로부터 그 식물을 보호한다.

[3]먹이사슬을 더 올라가면, 곤충들은 사막 기후에서 번성하는데, 여기에서 특히 개미와 나비의 전체 개체군은 하나 또는 몇 개의 식물만 먹고도 살 수 있다. 예를 들어, 딱정벌레는 부드러운 과일을 먹어 치우고 더 큰 관목에 침입함으로써 식물의 분해에 큰 역할을 한다. 그것들의 두꺼운 외골격은 수분을 가두며, 그것들의 체강은 그렇지 않다면 호흡으로 손실될 여분의 물을 저장한다.

캥거루쥐와 햄스터 같은 몇몇 작은 초식성 설치류 종들은 다른 방식으로 물 부족을 극복해낸다. [4]그것들은 마른 씨앗 소화의 부산물로 물을 생산하고, 신장에 부착된 미세한 관을 통해 그것을 소변에서 혈류로 보내 재순환시킨다. 그런 다음, 그것들은 아늑한 지하 굴로 물러나는데, 그곳에서 그것들은 비강 내 특수 기관을 이용해 호흡 과정 동안 유실될 수 있는 수분을 되찾을 수 있다. 종종, 이 굴은 뜨겁고 건조한 바람이 휩쓸고 지나가며 수분을 흡수하는 것을 막기 위해 모래로 봉쇄된다.

낮 동안 땅속에 숨는 것은 또한 태양에의 노출을 제한하며, 이 야행성 습성은 이 작은 설치류들이 두 번째 주요 관심사인 열을 피하는 데 도움을 준다. 그 대신에, 특정 종의 포유류와 파충류는 최소한의 태양 복사열에 노출되는 해 질 녘 시간에만 활동한다. 다른 종들은 여름 동안 완전히 잠자고 있다가 가을이나 겨울비가 공기를 식힌 다음에만 밖으로 나옴으로써 과열을 피한다. [6]일 년 내내 계속 활동하는 소수는 열을 덜 흡수하거나 빠르게 잃게 해주는 적응 형태를 가지고 있다.

precipitation 몡강우량, 강우   diurnal temperature gradient 일교차
solar radiation 태양 복사열   dissipate 동소멸하다
insulating 혱단열의   weather 동풍화시키다   outcrop 몡노출부
fluvial deposit 하성 퇴적물   compounding 혱복합적인
substantial 혱상당한   morphological 혱형태적인

inherent 형 고유한   irregularly 뷔 불규칙하게
sparse 형 희박한, 드문   retain 동 유지하다   radial 형 방사형의
subsist on ~을 먹고 살다   decomposition 명 분해, 부패
exoskeleton 명 외골격   respiration 명 호흡
herbivorous 형 초식성의   rodent 명 설치류
by-product 명 부산물   microscopic 형 미세한
subterranean 형 지하의   burrow 동 (굴에) 숨다
nocturnal 형 야행성의   evade 동 피하다
alternatively 뷔 그 대신에   dormant 형 잠자는, 휴면의

1 지문의 단어 "dissipates"와 의미가 가장 비슷한 것은?

(A) 희석되다
(B) 축적되다
(C) 사라지다
(D) 상승하다

2 1단락에 따르면, 다음 중 사막의 특징이 아닌 것은?

(A) 밤낮으로 심한 더위
(B) 극심한 기온 변화
(C) 증가된 태양 에너지 흡수
(D) 공기 중의 수증기 부족

3 4단락에 따르면, 곤충 개체군은 왜 사막에서 번성하는가?

(A) 매우 다양한 식물을 섭취할 수 있다.
(B) 숨을 크게 쉬어도 탈수되지 않는다.
(C) 최소한의 자원이 전체 군집을 지탱할 수 있다.
(D) 토착 식물이 특히 그것들에게 취약하다.

4 5단락에 따르면, 작은 설치류는 물 부족에 어떻게 대처하는가?

(A) 상당한 양의 수분을 함유한 씨앗을 섭취한다.
(B) 소화 과정 동안 수분을 생산하고 그것을 재사용한다.
(C) 소변을 만들어낸 직후에 즉시 그것을 마신다.
(D) 효율적인 신장 체계를 이용하여 체내 혈류를 조절한다.

5 지문의 단어 "evade"와 의미가 가장 비슷한 것은?

(A) 강요하다
(B) 피하다
(C) 보존하다
(D) 탐지하다

6 6단락에 따르면, 일 년 내내 활동하는 사막 동물에 관해 사실인 것은?

(A) 시원한 겨울 동안 두꺼운 털을 기른다.
(B) 열 흡수를 제한하거나 열 손실을 촉진하도록 적응했다.
(C) 여름 동안 그늘에 남아 있는다.
(D) 다량의 물을 유지할 수 있는 능력을 발전시켰다.

Reading Practice 2

1 (B)   2 (A)   3 (B)   4 (C)   5 (D)   6 (D)

일본

섬나라로서, 일본은 그것의 역사 상당 부분 동안 그것의 정치 및 문화적 자치를 유지할 수 있게 해온 중요한 이점을 가지고 있다. 이는 그것

의 고립을 긍정적이면서도 결정적인 특징으로 간주하게 된 다소 배타적인 사회의 발전을 가져왔다. 그러나, 외부 세력은 그것의 발전에 상당한 영향을 미쳤는데, 일본 국가의 기본 요소들 중 많은 것들이 중국 본토와 한반도의 문명들에 의해 기여된 종교적, 법적, 문화적 개념의 직접적인 결과로 만들어졌기 때문이다.

불교는 대략 서기 538년부터 710년까지의 야마토 시대 후반에 종종 중국 문화 전파의 통로 역할을 했던 한국의 백제 왕국을 통해 일본에 전해졌다. 이 당시에, 야마토국은 선진적인 야금 및 농업 기술에의 접근 욕구 때문에 백제의 한반도 패권 다툼에 크게 관여했다. 그 결과, 종종 황족의 조언자로서 역할을 했던 한국의 승려들은 매우 존경받았고 많은 권한을 부여받았다. ³서기 594년에 그들의 성공적인 스이코 여제 개종은 국가적인 불교 공인으로 이어졌다. 이는 학업 중에 자주 왕래하는 학자들로 인해 일본과 주변국들 사이 문화 교류 수준의 급격한 증가를 초래했다. 게다가, 일본인들은 처음으로 인도와 페르시아같이 먼 곳에서 온 철학 서적들에 접근하게 되었는데, 이는 이러한 가르침들이 불교의 확산과 함께 실크로드를 따라 전파되었기 때문이다.

같은 기간 동안, 야마토국과 중국 당나라 간의 접촉이 강화되었고 중국 사회의 많은 요소들이 일본인들에 의해 직접 이식되었다. 여기에는 특히 건축, 예술, 서예, 요리법, 의복이 포함되었다. 그러나, 가장 중요한 응용은 정치와 법률에 관한 것이었으며, 야마토 통치자들은 본토 제도의 구조와 용어를 모두 모방하기 위해 의식적인 노력을 기울였다. 서기 603년의 궁정 계급 제도 확립은 왕실의 지배하에 있는 고도로 중앙집권화된 국가를 만들기 위한 공동의 노력의 일환이었다. ⁴ᴺ/⁴ᴰ서기 646년의 다이카 개신은 전제 군주제의 확립과 궁정에 의한 지방 당국의 권력과 특권 축소와 함께 이 과정을 한 단계 더 나아가게 했다. ⁴ᴮ이 칙령들이 제정되기 위해, 한자 체계가 정식으로 채택되었고 많은 학자들이 이 학문을 연구하기 위해 중국으로 보내졌다.

일본은 외국 문화와의 접촉에 대한 대응에 있어 항상 매우 실용적이었는데, 유용한 사상과 관습을 기꺼이 채택하지만 핵심적인 사회적 가치가 영향받지 않도록 하는 방식으로 그것들을 흡수한다는 점에서 그러하다. 이는 장기간에 걸친 대내외 갈등의 시기 이후 17세기와 18세기 동안 외부 접촉으로부터 스스로를 고립시키려 했던 일본의 시도에 의해 분명히 보여진다. 천황으로부터 권력을 장악한 군사 정부인 막부는 일본 사회가 불안정하게 만든다고 여겨지는 중국 사상의 측면을 배척하도록 장려했다. ⁶아시아 전역에 널리 퍼져 있던 후기 철학 학파인 성리학은 당시의 정치 및 사회적 분위기에 적용되도록 학자들에 의해 미묘하게 변형되었다. 특히, 사무라이 규범인 무사도의 두 가지 중요한 개념인 충성과 개인적인 명예에 대한 자격 요건이 강조되었다.

autonomy 명 자치, 자치권   insular 형 배타적인
seclusion 명 고립, 격리   conduit 명 통로, 도관
dissemination 명 전파, 보급   hegemony 명 패권, 주도권
metallurgical 형 야금술의   conversion 명 (종교의) 개종
recognition 명 인정, 승인   calligraphy 명 서예   culinary 형 요리의
adaptation 명 응용, 각색   concerted 형 공동의, 합의된
absolute monarchy 전제 군주제   curtailment 명 축소
prerogative 명 특권   edict 명 칙령, 포고령   enact 동 제정하다
discipline 명 학문   pragmatic 형 실용적인
assimilate 동 흡수하다   shogunate 명 막부(일본의 무사 정권)
destabilize 동 불안정하게 만들다
bushido 명 무사도(일본 사무라이의 도덕 체계)

1 지문의 단어 "seclusion"과 의미가 가장 비슷한 것은?

(A) 확장
(B) 고립

CHAPTER 01 | Vocabulary 3

(C) 혼돈

(D) 평판

2 지문의 단어 "its"가 가리키는 것은?

(A) 야마토국

(B) 백제

(C) 패권

(D) 한반도

3 2단락에 따르면, 다음 중 일본과 주변국들 사이의 문화 교류를 촉진시킨 것은?

(A) 스이코 여제의 황위 계승

(B) 국가에 의한 종교 승인

(C) 백제의 선진적인 기술 전파

(D) 실크로드를 통한 아시아 주변국들과의 접촉

4 3단락에서, 다음 중 정치적 또는 법적 응용으로 언급되지 않은 것은?

(A) 중앙집권화된 정부의 수립

(B) 한자의 정식 채택

(C) 전제 군주제 폐지

(D) 지방 당국의 권력 축소

5 지문의 단어 "pragmatic"과 의미가 가장 비슷한 것은?

(A) 문제 있는

(B) 뛰어난

(C) 능동적인

(D) 실용적인

6 4단락에 따르면, 일본 학자들은 왜 성리학을 변형했는가?

(A) 중국 철학 연구를 장려하기 위해

(B) 황제의 행동 규칙을 확립하기 위해

(C) 그것을 중국의 이념에 확실히 일치하게 하기 위해

(D) 그것을 당대의 문화와 양립할 수 있게 하기 위해

Reading Practice 3　　　　본문 p. 18

1 (B)　　**2** (C)　　**3** (C)　　**4** (C)　　**5** (B)　　**6** (B)

아카데믹 미술

아카데믹 미술은 예술가와 장인을 구별하기 위해 루이 14세의 통치 기간 중에 설립된 프랑스 왕립 회화 및 조각 아카데미의 영향을 받아 제작된 회화와 조각이다. 이탈리아의 원칙을 본으로 삼은 그 기관은 회원 자격에 대해 엄격한 위계 구조를 유지했다. 예비 학생은 검토를 위해 작품을 제출했고, 그 작품이 승인되면 그 학생은 그 기관에서의 지위가 올라가면서 후원자에 의해 후원받았다. 가장 재능 있는 이들은 예비 훈련을 마치자마자 로마 상을 수여받았고, 르네상스 시대의 거장들, 특히 라파엘로의 작품들을 직접 연구할 수 있도록 로마로 보내졌다. 예술가들은 귀족 사회의 일원이나 종교인으로부터 개인 소장품이나 공공시설을 위한 작품을 만들도록 의뢰받으면 프랑스로 돌아왔다.

뛰어난 학술적 집단일 뿐만 아니라 프랑스 문화를 보호하고, 감시하고, 육성하는 수단으로 여겨진 그 아카데미는 빠르게 미술을 독점했는데, 그것의 궁극적인 쇠퇴까지, 소수의 예외를 제외하면 기관 외부의 후원

은 얻을 수 없었다. 그 결과, 회화와 조각을 모두 아우르는 아카데믹 미술은 양식과 주제 표현에서 획일적인 경향을 보인다. ³고전 미술의 신조에 따르면, 미술 창작의 목적은 창작, 비례, 색채, 표현, 구성의 다섯 가지 범주의 완벽의 실현이었다. 따라서, 훌륭한 화가는 이상적인 형태의 세계를 묘사함으로써 창조적이고 독특한 표현으로 이 모든 요소들을 혼합할 수 있었다. 주제상으로는, 우화가 모든 매체의 지배적인 초점이 되었고, 여기서 선과 색채는 종교 신화에 익숙한 관객들에게서 감정적인 반응을 불러일으켰다. 화가의 의도는 느낌, 생각, 감정을 하나의 응집력 있는 표현으로 종합하는 것이었는데, 즉, 각 그림이나 조각은 하나의 완전한 이야기를 전달했다.

일단 이러한 표준적인 주제들을 혁신적인 방식으로 재현할 수 있는 거장으로 간주되면, 졸업생은 자신의 자격을 의심받지 않고 전문 화가로서의 경력을 쌓을 수 있었다. 화가는 또한 파리의 공공 갤러리인 루브르궁의 살롱 카레에서 정기적으로 작품을 전시하는 것에 동의하는 한 아카데미의 회원 자격을 유지했다. 시간이 지남에 따라, 이 전시회들은 파리 살롱이라고 알려진 선풍적인 연 2회의 행사로 바뀌었고, 그것들의 두 달의 진행 동안 무려 50만 명의 관중을 끌어들였다. 그것들은 또한 사회의 엘리트 구성원들이 만나 예술 동향을 논하거나 유망한 젊은 화가들을 발굴할 수 있는 사교 모임이 되었다. 전문 미술 평론 분야는 살롱 작품에 관해 발행된, 이따금씩 신랄한 논평을 포함했던 해설에서 기원했다.

거의 2세기 동안, 살롱은 프랑스 사회와 문화에 명백한 영향력을 미쳤으나, 19세기 중반경, 한 무리의 비주류 화가들이 미술의 구상과 제작에 관한 아카데미의 지배에 대해 진지한 의문을 제기하기 시작했다. ⁶그들 중 다수는 살롱을 혁명가들이 맞서 싸웠던 사회 내 엘리트주의의 상징으로 여겼다. 객관적인 현실을 재현하려고 하기보다는 세상에 대한 주관적인 인상을 그렸기 때문에 현재는 인상주의 화가라고 알려진 이 화가들은 유럽에서 아방가르드 운동의 탄생과 아카데미의 권위의 쇠퇴를 알리는 일련의 독립 전시회를 열었다. 그럼에도 불구하고, 아카데믹 미술은 서구 세계 전역에서 계속해서 교육되고, 감상되며, 구매되고 있다.

---

artisan 圆장인, 기능 보유자　hierarchical structure 위계 구조
prospective 圈예비의, 장래의　benefactor 圆후원자
confer 圄(상·자격을) 수여하다　preliminary 圈예비의, 준비의
commission 圄(미술 작품을) 의뢰하다　aristocracy 圆귀족 사회
preeminent 圈뛰어난, 탁월한　monopoly 圆독점
patronage 圆(화가 등에 대한) 후원　unattainable 圈얻을 수 없는
encompass 圄아우르다, 포함하다　tenet 圆신조, 주의, 원리
actualization 圆실현, 현실화　allegory 圆우화, 풍자
summon 圄불러일으키다　synthesize 圄종합하다, 합성하다
cohesive 圈응집력 있는, 혼합하는　credential 圆자격, 자격 증명서
challenge 圄(정당성 등을) 의심하다　scathing 圈신랄한, 냉혹한
undisputed 圈명백한, 반박의 여지없는　fringe 圆비주류

1 지문의 단어 "conferred"와 의미가 가장 비슷한 것은?

(A) 관련되다

(B) 수여되다

(C) 보장되다

(D) 지명되다

2 지문의 단어 "unattainable"과 의미가 가장 비슷한 것은?

(A) 어찌할 바를 모르는

(B) 반드시

(C) 손이 닿지 않는

(D) 수요가 있는

3 2단락에 따르면, 고전적 원칙에 따른 미술 창작의 동기는

    (A) 독특한 양식의 창작이었다

    (B) 세상의 사실적 묘사였다

    (C) 완벽의 성취였다

    (D) 종교 신화에 대한 비평이었다

4 네 개의 네모[■]는 다음 문장이 삽입될 수 있는 곳을 나타내고 있다.

    그것들은 또한 사회의 엘리트 구성원들이 만나 예술 동향을 논하거나 유망한 젊은 화가들을 발굴할 수 있는 사교 모임이 되었다.

    이 문장은 어디에 들어가는 것이 가장 적절한가?

5 지문의 단어 "their"가 가리키는 것은?

    (A) 전시회들

    (B) 행사

    (C) 관중

    (D) 사람들

6 4단락에 따르면, 많은 비주류 화가들은 살롱을 어떻게 생각하는가?

    (A) 그것이 그 시대에 비해 너무 혁명적이라고 생각했다.

    (B) 그것이 엘리트 문화를 대변한다고 여겼다.

    (C) 그것이 화가들에게 충분히 보상하지 못한다고 생각했다.

    (D) 그것이 예술적 표현을 위한 가장 훌륭한 장소라고 여겼다.

iBT Reading Test 1
본문 p.20

1 (A)   **2** (C)   **3** (C)   **4** (A)
5 (B)   **6** (B)   **7** (D)   **8** (D)
9 (D)   **10** (B), (D), (E)

화성의 먼지 폭풍

화성은 주로 바위와 먼지가 두드러지는 건조한 환경으로 특징지어진다. 지구의 사막 환경에서와 마찬가지로, 화성 표면의 침식을 지배하는 과정은 대부분 '풍화 작용에 의한' 것인데, 이 용어는 "바람과 관련되거나 바람에 의해 야기된" 것을 의미하며, 그리스 바람의 신 아이올로스의 이름에서 유래한다. 지구에서와 마찬가지로, 화성의 바람은 지형을 가로질러 퇴적물을 밀어 모래 언덕을 형성하며, 미세한 입자를 공중으로 들어 올려 안개를 만들거나, 만약 그것들이 충분히 강하면 먼지 폭풍을 일으킬 수 있다. ²화성에서 며칠 또는 몇 주 동안 지속되는 주요 먼지 폭풍은 20세기 초에 망원경을 통해 관측되었으며 드문 사건이라고 잘못 가정되었으나, 이후의 관측과 탐사는 그것들이 실제로는 그 붉은 행성에서 흔히 일어나는 일임을 밝혀냈다.

1971년, NASA는 표면과 대기의 변화를 측정하기 위해서뿐만 아니라 화성의 지형을 측량하기 위해 마리너 9호 우주선을 발사했다. ⁴처음에, 그 측량은 마리너 8호에 계획되었으나, 그것의 발사 실패로 인해, 두 작업이 모두 마리너 9호에 맡겨졌다. 이 초반의 차질은 마리너 9호가 화성에 접근하는 동안 먼지 폭풍이 시작되어 곧 거대한 폭풍으로 발달했을 때 또 다른 문제로 이어졌다. 그 폭풍은 행성 전체를 에워쌌고 화성에서 가장 높은 올림푸스몬스의 정상을 포함한 네 개의 화산의 정상들을 제외하고는 그것의 표면을 완전히 가렸다. 그 폭풍은 먼지구름이 극에서 극으로 뻗어나가며 정말로 전역적이었기 때문에, 과학자들은 그것을 전역 먼지 폭풍이라고 불렀다. 1976년 바이킹 탐사선(바이

킹 1호와 바이킹 2호)의 뒤이은 두 번의 탐사 또한 거대한 먼지 폭풍들을 발견했다. 그러나, 그것들 중 하나는 한쪽 반구에만 영향을 미쳤고, 다른 하나는 두 반구 모두에 영향을 미쳤지만 1971년의 것처럼 행성 전체에 걸친 규모는 아니었다.

이러한 발견들은 화성 먼지 폭풍의 빈도와 규모에 대한 새로운 정보를 주었지만, 그것들의 형성에 대한 정확한 세부 사항은 여전히 불분명했다. 그러나, 그것들이 어떻게 형성되는지를 이해하는 데 있어 상당한 진전이 2001년 화성 전역 조사선의 화성 관측 카메라(MOC)의 도움으로 이루어졌는데, 이것은 협각 카메라 한 개와 광각 카메라 두 개를 갖춘 사진 기기였다. MOC는 전역 먼지 폭풍이 형성되는 바로 그 순간의 생생한 사진을 보냈고, 연구원들은 곧 그 전역 폭풍의 기원이 사실 화성의 남반구에서 쉽게 알아볼 수 있는 충돌구인 헬라스 분지 바로 근처에서 발생한 일련의 외란 현상임을 알아냈다.

천문학자들은 남극의 찬 공기가 적도의 더 따뜻한 공기를 향해 북쪽으로 밀고 나아가면서 지면의 먼지가 이동했고, 그것이 더 따뜻하고 밀도가 낮은 공기에 도달함에 따라 대기 위로 높이 들어 올려졌다고 가설을 세웠다. 몇 주 안에, 두꺼운 먼지층은 불투명한 구름으로 사실상 행성 전체를 덮었다. ⁷결국, MOC의 사진들은 과학자들이 화성의 전역 먼지 폭풍은 국지적으로 시작되며 다수의 작은 외란들이 크기가 커지고 엄청난 속도로 합쳐질 수 있다는 것을 이해하게 해주었다.

과학자들은 지식을 위해 그 폭풍을 계속 연구하지만, 그들은 또한 이 지식의 유용한 내포적 의미에 깊은 관심이 있다. 실제로, 과학 측정은 화성의 바람이 그러한 피해를 일으킬 만큼 극심하지 않으며 실제로는 지구에서 가장 강한 바람보다 훨씬 덜 강하다는 것을 증명했다. 그럼에도, 폭풍과 바람은 몇 가지 실제적인 문제들을 제시하기 때문에, 모든 화성 탐사를 계획하는 과학자들은 항상 그것들의 정기적인 발생에 대비해야 한다.

---

aeolian 형 풍화 작용에 의한   be derived from ~에서 유래하다
sediment 명 퇴적물   minute 형 미세한   persist 동 지속되다
extraordinary 형 드문, 특별한   occurrence 명 (일어나는) 일, 발생
topography 명 지형   setback 명 차질
blossom into ~으로 발달하다   encircle 동 에워싸다, 둘러싸다
obscure 동 가리다   subsequent 형 뒤이은
murky 형 불분명한, 애매한   discern 동 알아내다
disturbance 명 (바람의) 외란   in close proximity to ~의 바로 근처에
displace 동 이동시키다   opaque 형 불투명한
coalesce 동 합쳐지다   for the sake of ~을 위해
implication 명 내포적 의미

1 지문의 단어 "they"가 가리키는 것은?

    (A) 바람

    (B) 퇴적물

    (C) 모래 언덕

    (D) 입자

2 1단락에 따르면, 다음 중 1900년대 초에 있었던 오해는?

    (A) 바람은 화성의 지형 형성에서 주요 요인이 아니다.

    (B) 지구와 화성의 물리적 환경은 공통점이 없다.

    (C) 화성에서 크고 지속적인 먼지 폭풍은 흔하지 않은 일이다.

    (D) 화성의 먼지 폭풍은 지구에서 망원경으로도 볼 수 없다.

3 지문의 단어 "setback"과 의미가 가장 비슷한 것은?

    (A) 업적

    (B) 노력

(C) 지장

(D) 계략

4 2단락에서 추론할 수 있는 것으로, 마리너 9호는

(A) 원래 화성의 지형을 측량하기로 예정되어 있지 않았다

(B) 이전 모델인 마리너 8호보다 덜 정교했다

(C) 먼지 폭풍으로 인해 일부 기술적 오작동을 겪었다

(D) 화성에 접근하는 동안 NASA와의 통신이 끊겼다

5 지문의 단어 "murky"와 의미가 가장 비슷한 것은?

(A) 아주 깨끗한

(B) 불명확한

(C) 결함이 있는

(D) 명백한

6 지문에서 글쓴이는 왜 "Hellas Planitia"를 언급하는가?

(A) 화성의 남반구 전역에서 분화구가 흔하다는 것을 보여주기 위해

(B) 명확한 지리적 랜드마크를 사용하여 발생하는 폭풍의 위치를 식별하기 위해

(C) 먼지의 이동이 충돌로 야기되었을 수 있음을 시사하기 위해

(D) 차가운 극지방 공기가 따뜻한 적도 공기와 만난 지점을 정확히 나타내기 위해

7 4단락에 따르면, MOC의 사진들은 궁극적으로 과학자들이

(A) 화성의 광범위한 먼지 폭풍은 흔하지만 매년 발생하지는 않는다는 것을 이해하게 해주었다

(B) 전역 먼지 폭풍이 화성의 북쪽 지역에서만 발생한다는 것을 이해하게 해주었다

(C) 작은 외란의 대부분이 대규모의 폭풍으로 이어지지 않는다는 것을 이해하게 해주었다

(D) 여러 개의 국지적 발생이 빠르게 결합하여 전역 먼지 폭풍을 형성할 수 있다는 것을 이해하게 해주었다

8 지문의 어구 "for the sake of"와 의미가 가장 비슷한 것은?

(A) ~에 대응하여

(B) ~에 따라

(C) ~에 의해

(D) ~의 목적으로

9 네 개의 네모[■]는 다음 문장이 삽입될 수 있는 곳을 나타내고 있다.

그러나, 그것들 중 하나는 한쪽 반구에만 영향을 미쳤고, 다른 하나는 두 반구 모두에 영향을 미쳤지만 1971년의 것처럼 행성 전체에 걸친 규모는 아니었다.

이 문장은 어디에 들어가는 것이 가장 적절한가?

10 지시: 지문 요약을 위한 도입 문장이 아래에 주어져 있다. 지문의 가장 중요한 내용을 나타내는 보기 3개를 골라 요약을 완성하라. 어떤 문장은 지문에 언급되지 않은 내용이나 사소한 정보를 나타내므로 요약에 포함되지 않는다. 이 문제는 2점이다.

> 망원경을 이용한 관측과 이후의 탐사는 과학자들이 화성 먼지 폭풍에 관해 더 많은 것을 배우는 데 관심을 갖도록 이끌었다.
>
> · (B) 1970년대 동안, NASA는 여러 차례의 화성 탐사를 수행했고 전역적 규모의 것을 포함한 여러 대형 먼지 폭풍을 관측했다.
>
> · (D) 21세기 초에 수행된 탐사들은 먼지 폭풍의 규모와 형성 위치 및 방법에 대해서도 풍부한 정보를 드러냈다.

· (E) 과학자들은 과학적 이유로 먼지 폭풍에 관심이 있을 뿐만 아니라 현재와 미래의 탐사에 관련된 실제적인 관심사에 의해 동기를 부여받는다.

(A) 화성의 먼지 폭풍을 연구하기 위한 첫 번째 탐사는 한 우주선이 발사에 실패하면서 기술적 어려움 때문에 방해받았기 때문에, 다른 우주선이 모든 자료를 수집해야 했다.

(C) 수많은 화성 탐사 후원에도 불구하고, NASA는 실제로 그 행성을 뒤덮고 있는 먼지 폭풍의 결정적인 증거를 수집할 수 없었다.

(F) 첨단 장비에 의한 측정은 과학자들이 화성의 먼지 폭풍이 지구의 것들만큼 심하지 않다는 결론을 내리도록 이끌었다.

iBT Reading Test 2 본문 p. 24

1 (A)	**2** (D)	**3** (A), (D)	**4** (A)
5 (C)	**6** (C)	**7** (D)	**8** (C)
9 (C)	**10** (B), (E), (F)		

유전자 변형 생물

수 세기 동안, 인간은 선택적 교배를 통해 동식물의 유전자 구성을 변형해 왔으며, 이는 옥수수의 단맛과 경주마의 속도 같은 현대 사육된 종들의 바람직한 특성의 강화를 가져왔다. 전통적인 교배 방법으로 유리한 결과를 얻는 것은 많은 생식 주기를 필요로 할 수 있으며, 종종 엄청나게 오랜 시간이 걸리고 힘들다. 그러나, 생명 공학의 최근 발전은 보다 편리한 유전자 변형 수단을 제공한다. 기증자 생물의 바람직한 유전자는 결과로 나타나는 유전자 변형 생물(GMO)이 선택된 형질을 발현할 수 있도록 이식자 생물에 직접 전달될 수 있다.

GMO에 의해 주어지는 잠재적인 환경적 이익은 무시할 수 없다. 해충을 견디게 하기 위해 농작물 종을 변형하는 것은 화학 살충제의 필요성을 줄이거나 완전히 없앤다. 3A예를 들어, 과학자들은 토양에 사는 박테리아인 Bt의 독소 생성 유전자를 옥수수에 효과적으로 전달했다. 농작물에 광범위한 피해를 주고 수확량을 감소시키는 곤충인 유럽의 옥수수들명나방과 같은 해충에 대한 저항력을 보이는 옥수수 품종을 선택적으로 교배하려는 이전의 노력은 적당히 성공적이었을 뿐이었다. 따라서, 농부들은 해로운 해충으로부터 그들의 옥수수를 보호하기 위해 살충제를 뿌려야 했는데, 그것의 환경 파괴 효과는 충분히 입증되어왔다. 그러나, Bt는 옥수수들명나방을 죽이는 독성 단백질을 생성하기 때문에, Bt 유전자를 옥수수로 전달하는 것은 Bt 변형 옥수수가 과도한 화학 살충제의 필요 없이 해충에 대항하는 자체적인 방어 단백질을 생성할 수 있게 해준다. 3DBt 옥수수의 재배는 전 세계 살충제 사용의 급격한 감소를 가져왔는데, 살충제의 사용은 Bt 옥수수가 처음 도입된 1995년 이후 전 세계적으로 매년 5천만 킬로그램씩 감소해왔다.

유전자 변형 식물은 농부들에 의한 해로운 화학물질 사용을 줄일 뿐만 아니라, 화학 처리된 것들보다 농작물에 피해를 주는 곤충에 더 저항력이 있을 수 있으며, 더 적은 식물이 해충에 의해 손실됨에 따라 농작물 수확량이 증가한다. 5세계 인구가 2050년까지 두 배로 증가할 것으로 예측되면서, 식량 생산을 늘리는 방법을 찾는 것은 인류가 직면한 가장 중요한 문제 중 하나가 될 것으로 예상된다. 그리고 해충이 지구상에서 재배되는 모든 식량의 약 50퍼센트의 파괴에 대해 책임이 있기 때문에, GMO 옹호자들은 그 문제를 완화할 수 있는 잠재적인 방법으로 농작물의 유전자 변형을 가리킨다.

그러나, 유전자 변형과 관련된 무수한 이점에도 불구하고, 모두가 그

생명공학 혁명에 매료된 것은 아니다. 사실, 많은 비평가들은 살아 있는 것에 대한 어떠한 유전자 변형에도 맹렬히 반대하며, GMO를 "프랑켄슈타인 음식"이라고 조롱하여 지칭한다. 그들은 인간 건강에 미치는 영향에 관한 장기적인 연구를 위한 충분한 시간이 경과하지 않았기 때문에 GMO가 안전하다고 가정하기에는 너무 이르다고 주장한다. 게다가, 그들은 변형 생물이 농경지 밖으로 퍼져 야생 생물과 번식하여 자연계의 유전적 오염을 초래할 수 있음을 우려한다. **유전자 변형 농작물들이 이미 그것들의 원래 영역을 벗어난 것으로 보고되었기 때문에, 이러한 우려는 근거 없는 것이 아니다.** 그들은 또한 엄격한 GMO 식단을 먹인 동물에서 부정적 영향을 입증한 과학 연구들을 지적하는데, 증상들은 면역 체계 약화, 발육 부진 및 생식 건강 저하를 포함했다.

GMO 반대자들은 그 관행의 안전성에 대한 우려와 함께 이 연구 결과를 자주 광고해 왔지만, GMO 지지자들은 어떠한 과학적 연구도 인간에 대한 나쁜 영향을 입증하지 못했다고 주장한다. [8]사실, 대부분의 농업 전문가들과 연구원들은 GMO에 대해 널리 퍼진 대중적 반대에 좌절감을 표현해 왔는데, 그들은 그것이 비과학적이며 궁극적으로 인간 건강에 해롭다고 생각한다. 이는 반대자들이 유전자 식량 변형에 대한 완전한 금지를 지지하는 반면, 식량 부족은 전 세계적으로 수그러들지 않고 있기 때문이다.

genetic makeup 유전자 구성   selective 웹 선택적인
breeding 웹 교배   domesticated 웹 사육된, 길들여진
favorable 웹 유리한   reproductive 웹 생식의   laborious 웹 힘든
expedient 웹 편리한   genetic modification 유전자 변형
prospective 웹 잠재적인   impart 웹 주다, 전하다
dismiss 웹 무시하다   eliminate 웹 없애다   variety 웹 품종
yields 웹 수확량   insecticide 웹 살충제
document 웹 입증하다, 상세히 기록하다   defensive 웹 방어하는
resistant 웹 저항력이 있는   alleviate 웹 완화하다
myriad 웹 무수한, 수많은   be enamored with ~에 매료되다
derisively 웹 조롱하여   stunted growth 발육 부진
frustration 웹 좌절감   detrimental 웹 해로운
unabated 웹 수그러들지 않는

1 아래 문장 중 지문 속의 음영된 문장의 핵심 정보를 가장 잘 표현한 것은? 오답은 문장의 의미를 크게 바꾸거나 핵심 정보를 생략한다.

(A) 사람들은 오랫동안 특정 바람직한 특성을 발현시키기 위해 사육된 동식물을 선택적으로 교배해왔다.

(B) 재배된 생물에서 특정 형질의 우세는 수 세기에 걸친 자연 선택의 결과이다.

(C) 옥수수의 단맛 강화와 경주마의 속도 증가는 현대 기술을 이용한 유전자 변형의 결과이다.

(D) 오랜 세월 동안, 사람들은 사육할 목적으로 동식물의 유전자 구성을 강화시켜 왔다.

2 지문의 단어 "laborious"와 의미가 가장 비슷한 것은?

(A) 토착의

(B) 외로운

(C) 신속한

(D) 힘든

3 2단락에 따르면, Bt 옥수수의 두 가지 특성은? 두 개의 정답을 고르시오.

(A) 땅속에서 발견된 박테리아의 유전자를 사용하여 변형되었다.

(B) 해충에 저항하는 능력은 수년간의 선택적 교배의 결과이다.

(C) 해로운 박테리아를 죽이는 단백질을 생성할 수 있는 능력이 있다.

(D) 그것의 사용은 전 세계 살충제 사용을 줄이는 데 역할을 해왔다.

4 지문의 단어 "ones"가 가리키는 것은?

(A) 식물

(B) 화학물질

(C) 농부들

(D) 곤충

5 3단락에 따르면, 식량 생산은 왜 심각한 문제가 될 것으로 예상되는가?

(A) 경작 가능한 토지의 비율은 수십 년 후에 50퍼센트만큼 감소할 것으로 예측된다.

(B) 해충은 GMO 사용으로 인한 수확량 증가를 없앨 수 있을 정도로 빠르게 적응할 가능성이 높다.

(C) 세계의 인구수는 21세기 중반까지 현재 규모의 두 배가 될 것으로 예측된다.

(D) 지구 온난화로 인해 해를 끼치는 곤충들이 훨씬 더 많아질 가능성이 있다.

6 지문의 단어 "myriad"와 의미가 가장 비슷한 것은?

(A) 분별 있는

(B) 예측 가능한

(C) 무수한

(D) 무서운

7 4단락과 5단락에서 글쓴이는 왜 과학적 연구들에 관해 논하는가?

(A) GMO가 동물에 부정적 영향을 미친다는 것을 나타내기 위해

(B) GMO가 자연의 유전자 풀을 오염시킨다는 것을 시사하기 위해

(C) GMO의 이점이 입증되었음을 강조하기 위해

(D) GMO의 안정성이 논쟁의 대상이라는 것을 보여주기 위해

8 다음 중 5단락에서 농업 전문가들과 연구원들에 관해 추론할 수 있는 것은?

(A) 그들 중 GMO가 전통적인 농작물보다 낫다고 믿는 사람은 거의 없다.

(B) 그들 중 대부분은 논란이 되는 GMO 식량 농작물을 기르는 것에 반대한다.

(C) 그들 중 대다수는 GMO를 식량 생산에 포함시키는 것에 찬성한다.

(D) 그들 중 일부는 GMO 농작물의 사용을 완전히 금지하는 것을 지지한다.

9 네 개의 네모[■]는 다음 문장이 삽입될 수 있는 곳을 나타내고 있다.

유전자 변형 농작물들이 이미 그것들의 원래 영역을 벗어난 것으로 보고되었기 때문에, 이러한 우려는 근거 없는 것이 아니다.

이 문장은 어디에 들어가는 것이 가장 적절한가?

10 지시: 지문 요약을 위한 도입 문장이 아래에 주어져 있다. 지문의 가장 중요한 내용을 나타내는 보기 3개를 골라 요약을 완성하라. 어떤 문장은 지문에 언급되지 않은 내용이나 사소한 정보를 나타내므로 요약에 포함되지 않는다. 이 문제는 2점이다.

> 유전자 변형 생물은 전통적인 농작물 품종보다 많은 이점을 제공하지만, 일부 사람들은 안전에 대한 우려를 제기해왔다.
>
> · (B) GMO는 농부들이 농작물에 사용하는 해로운 화학물질의 양을 줄이기 때문에 더 건강한 환경에 기여한다.
>
> · (E) 유전자 변형은 식물을 해충 침입에 더 저항력 있게 만듦으로써 농작물 수확량을 증가시킨다.

- (F) 일부 사람들은 유전자 변형 식품이 인간과 환경에 해롭다고 주장하지만, GMO 옹호자들은 그들의 주장에 이의를 제기한다.
- (A) 농작물의 유전자 구조 변형은 식량 생산량 증대를 가져오기 때문에, 그것은 긴급한 전 세계 기아 문제를 해결할 수 있는 가장 효과적인 방안으로 널리 알려져 있다.
- (C) Bt 옥수수가 변형되지 않은 옥수수보다 해충에 훨씬 더 저항력이 있기 때문에, 과학자들은 그것의 재배가 전 세계 농약 사용량을 크게 줄일 것으로 예상한다.
- (D) 유전자 변형 식품의 비판자들은 GMO가 인간 건강에 장기적으로 부정적인 영향을 미친다는 연구 결과를 인용하며 농업 혁명에 대해 열광하지 않는다.

Vocabulary Review

본문 p.28

1 preeminent	2 conduit	3 undisputed
4 unabated	5 subsist	6 dormant

7 (C)	8 (B)	9 (D)	10 (A)
11 (D)	12 (B)	13 (D)	14 (C)

CHAPTER 02
Reference

Example

본문 p.31

1 (D)	2 (C)	3 (C)

Know-Nothing 운동

1840년대에, 미국으로 들어오는 많은 이민자들은 Know-Nothing 운동이라고 알려진 반이민자 운동의 형성을 촉발시켰다. 그것의 구성원들은 그들의 비밀 조직에 대해 이야기하는 것이 허용되지 않았다. 그것의 구성원들이 그들의 조직에 관한 질문을 받을 때마다 보통 "나는 아무것도 모른다"라고 말하곤 했기 때문에 그 집단은 "Know Nothings"라는 별명을 얻었다.

초기 정착민들의 후손들인 미국 태생의 미국인들 중 다수는 그들의 절대적인 수와 아주 적은 임금을 위해 기꺼이 일하려는 그들의 의지 때문에 이민자에 반대했다. 다른 사람들은 더 최근에 도착한 사람들을 그저 신뢰하지 않았는데, 이는 외모, 언어, 관습, 종교 등 그들에 관한 모든 것이 달랐기 때문이다. 많은 반이민자 비밀 조직들이 결성되었고, 본질적으로, 그들의 목적은 그들이 외국의 영향이라고 간주하는 것과는 싸우고 그들이 기성의 미국적 생활 방식이라고 믿는 것은 유지하는 것이었다. Know-Nothing 운동은 이것들 중 가장 성공적인 것이었다.

1850년대까지, Know-Nothing 운동은 많은 주들에서 지지자들을 끌어모았고 43명의 구성원들을 의회에 앉혔다. 국가의 지휘부를 장악하려는 노력의 일환으로, 그 집단은 1856년 대통령 선거를 위한 그것의 후보자로 밀러드 필모어를 선택했다. 그러나, 이 목표는 대부분 노예제도에 대한 논쟁 때문에 달성될 수 없었다. 노예제도를 지지하는 사람들이 민주당 대표자에게 그들의 표를 행사했던 반면, 그것에 반대하는 사람들은 공화당 후보자에게 투표했다. 그 문제에 대해 중립을 지키기를 택한 필모어는 그 선거에서 매우 부진했다. 이 실패 이후, Know-Nothing 운동은 영향력은 감소하기 시작했다.

trigger 图 촉발시키다　descendant 图 후손
sheer 图 절대적인, 순전한　meager 图 아주 적은
uphold 图 유지하다　established 图 기성의, 확립된
candidate 图 후보자　objective 图 목표

1 지문의 단어 "their"가 가리키는 것은?
- (A) 미국 태생의 미국인들
- (B) 후손들
- (C) 초기 정착민들
- (D) 이민자들

2 지문의 단어 "they"가 가리키는 것은?
- (A) 도착한 사람들
- (B) 관습
- (C) 조직들
- (D) 영향

3 지문의 어구 "this objective"가 가리키는 것은?
- (A) 많은 주들에서 지지자 끌어모으기
- (B) 43명의 구성원을 의회에 앉히기
- (C) 그 국가의 지휘부 장악하기
- (D) 선거를 위한 후보자 선택하기

Reading Practice 1

본문 p.32

1 (B)	2 (A)	3 (D)	4 (B)	5 (D)	6 (A), (D)

사막 수문학

지구 표면의 거의 3분의 1은 식물이 거의 없는 노출된 토양의 광범위한 지역으로 덮여 있다. 사막이라고 알려진 이 생태계는 열대 지방과 극지방 사이에 위치한 중위도 지방에 가장 흔하기는 하지만, 지구 어디에서나 찾을 수 있다. 각각 다른 사막의 종류에 따라 기온에 큰 차이가 있다. 그러나, 모든 것의 본질적인 특징은 강우 부족으로, 이 지역들의 대부분은 연간 250밀리미터 미만을 경험한다.

그것들의 건조함에도 불구하고, 사막은 오랫동안 인구 집단의 거주지였으며, 주민들은 그들이 직면하는 가혹한 환경에 대처하기 위해 보통 유목 생활 방식을 택했다. ²그러나, 인접한 지역의 인구가 계속 증가함에 따라, 사막 생태계는 점점 더 농업 용도로 활용되고 있으며, 이는 이용 가능한 한정된 물에 대한 압박을 가중하고 있다. 따라서, 지금까지 이용되지 않고 남아 있는 이 자원의 공급원을 개발하고 활용하는 것뿐만 아니라, 이용 가능한 수원이 활용되는 효율성을 극대화하는 것은 필수가 되었다.

대부분의 건조한 지역에서 가장 중요한 수원은 일시적인 수계로, 이는 사실 돌발 홍수의 결과로 형성된 간헐적인 물줄기일 뿐이다. 비록 사막이 아주 적은 강우를 경험하지만, 비가 내리면 매우 짧은 기간에 걸쳐 연간 총 강우가 발생할 정도로 상당히 많이 내릴 가능성이 높다. 이것은 향후 홍수에 대한 배수로 역할을 계속하게 될 수로의 급속한 침

식을 초래한다. 매년 특정 지리적 위치가 범람할 가능성이 크기 때문에 그것들은 많은 사막 거주자들의 생활에 필수적인 부분이 되지만, 이러한 물줄기들의 산발적 특성은 그것들의 유용성을 상당히 제한한다. **이 단점은 사막 환경에서 물을 장기간 저장하는 것과 관련된 어려움으로 인해 더 악화된다.**

영구적인 강은 특히 많은 인구의 요구와 관련하여 이용 잠재력이 훨씬 더 큰 수원이다. ⁵나일강, 티그리스강, 유프라테스강을 포함하는 이러한 수계는 모두 사막 환경 외부의 원천에 의해 보충된다는 사실이 특징이다. 나일강의 경우, 아프리카 적도 호수 지역의 계절성 비는 수단의 고지대에서 발생하는 장마에 의해 증대되어 일 년 내내 계속되는 흐름을 만들어낸다. 같은 패턴이 티그리스-유프라테스강 수계에도 해당하는데, 그것은 토로스산맥과 자그로스산맥의 녹은 겨울 눈에 의존한다. 사막 공동체에 대한 이 강들의 중요성은 아무리 강조해도 지나치지 않으며, 사실, 알려진 최초 문명들의 다수가 그것들의 강기슭을 따라 생겨났다.

그러나, 이러한 강에 대한 의존은 인간의 거주지를 그것들의 가장자리를 따라 있는 비옥한 땅의 좁은 범위로 제한하는데, 이는 물을 원래의 수로에서 상당히 먼 거리로 운반하는 것이 어려운 일이기 때문이다. 최근, 지표면 아래 깊은 곳에 존재하는 대수층에 대한 관심과 이 수원의 활용을 가능하게 하는 기술과 방법을 개발할 필요성에 대한 인식이 증가하고 있다. 많은 과학자들은 이러한 물의 저장소로의 접근이 인간 생명을 지탱하는 사막의 능력을 크게 증대할 수 있다고 믿는다. ⁶ᴬ/⁶ᴰ물의 상당 부분이 지표면 아래 너무 깊은 곳에 위치해 있거나 높은 수준의 염분을 포함하고 있기 때문에 과거에 사람들은 이것들을 제한적으로 사용해 왔다. 담수화 기술의 발전과 결합된 시추 기술의 개선이 미래에 이 중요한 자원이 사용될 수 있게 해줄 것으로 기대된다.

hydrology 명수문학(물을 연구하는 학문) be devoid of ~이 없다
vegetation 명식물, 초목 aridity 명건조함 nomadic 형유목의
adjacent 형인접한 imperative 형필수적인, 부득이한
untapped 형이용되지 않은 ephemeral 형일시적인
intermittent 형간헐적인 precipitation 명강우, 강우량
erosion 명침식 conduit 명배수로, 도관 deluge 동범람시키다
integral 형필수적인 sporadic 형산발적인 utility 명유용성
perennial 형영구적인, 지속하는 application 명이용, 응용
replenish 동보충하다, 다시 채우다 augment 동증대시키다
fertile 형비옥한 aquifer 명대수층(지하수를 품고 있는 지층)
cache 명저장소, 저장물 desalination 명담수화

1 지문의 단어 "they"가 가리키는 것은?

(A) 사막
(B) 주민들
(C) 유목 생활 방식
(D) 가혹한 환경

2 2단에 따르면, 사막의 수자원에 대한 압박이 가중된 이유는?

(A) 그 생태계와 접한 지역에 점점 더 인구가 많아지고 있다.
(B) 점점 더 많은 사람들이 유목 생활로 전환하고 있다.
(C) 그 지역의 물 사용 효율이 상당히 높아졌다.
(D) 사람이 사용하기에 적합한 공급원의 수가 한정되어 있다.

3 네 개의 네모[■]는 다음 문장이 삽입될 수 있는 곳을 나타내고 있다.

이 단점은 사막 환경에서 물을 장기간 저장하는 것과 관련된 어려움으로 인해 더 악화된다.

이 문장은 어디에 들어가는 것이 가장 적절한가?

4 지문의 단어 "their"가 가리키는 것은?

(A) 토로스산맥과 자그로스산맥
(B) 이 강들
(C) 사막 공동체
(D) 알려진 초기 문명들

5 4단락에 따르면, 영구적인 수계의 본질적인 특징은?

(A) 많은 대형 인간 정착지들로 둘러싸여 있다.
(B) 매년 침수되는 지역으로 제한된다.
(C) 고도가 높은 곳의 계절성 강우로 보충된다.
(D) 건조하지 않은 지역으로부터 수분을 공급받는다.

6 5단락에 따르면, 사람들이 과거에 대수층의 물을 제한적으로 사용한 두 가지 이유는? 두 개의 정답을 고르시오.

(A) 그것의 상당 부분이 깊은 지하에 있다.
(B) 그것의 대부분이 건기에 사라진다.
(C) 그것 중 많은 양이 인공오염을 포함한다.
(D) 그것의 많은 양이 다량의 소금을 함유한다.

Reading Practice 2　　　　본문 p.34

1 (C)　　2 (D)　　3 (A)　　4 (C)　　5 (A)　　6 (A)

여성 참정권 운동

참정권, 즉 시민들이 정부에서 그들을 대표할 후보자에게 투표할 권리는 현대 민주주의에서 일반적으로 모든 성인 시민에게 확대된다. 그러나, 한때 투표권은 훨씬 더 제한되었고, 여성은 투표하는 것이 허용되지 않았다.

영국 역사의 대부분 동안, 투표권은 특정 가치가 있는 토지를 소유한 남성에게만 부여되었고, 여성은 선거에 참여하는 것이 지속적으로 금지되었다. 때때로 여성의 투표할 권리에 대한 문제가 제기되기도 했다. 그러나, 선거 제도에 전면적인 개정을 했음에도 여성에게까지 투표권을 확대하지는 않았던 1832년의 선거법 개정이 있고 나서야 여성 참정권 운동이 상당한 동력을 얻기 시작했다. ¹그 법률 제정에 대응하여, 많은 부유한 여성들은 토지를 소유하고 그에 따라 세금을 내는 사람은 누구나 그 민주적 절차에서 배제되어서는 안 된다고 주장했다.

처음에, 참정권 집단은 본질적으로 지역적이었고, 영국 전역의 시골과 도시의 다양한 지역 사회에서 생겨났다. 1897년, 선도적인 여성 평등권 활동가였던 밀리센트 포셋은 전국 여성 참정권 연합(NUWSS)을 설립했다. 그것은 여러 더 작은 조직들을 모아 영국에서 증가하는 수의 토지 소유 여성들이 참정권을 부여받고자 하는 열망을 표명하는 최초의 공개 토론회를 제공했다.

NUWSS에 소속된 집단들 중 하나는 런던 기반의 여성 참정권 연맹이었는데, 이들은 에멀라인 팽크허스트의 지도하에 이미 지역 공직 선거에서의 여성 투표권을 쟁취했었다. 그러나, 시간이 흐르면서 더 이상의 진전이 없자, 그녀는 점점 더 초조해졌고, 1903년에 여성 사회 정치 연맹(WSPU)이라는 분리 조직을 설립했다. ⁴NUWSS와는 달리, 팽크허스트의 조직은 남성을 배제했고 더 많은 노동 계급 여성을 모집했는데, 그 조직은 혼인 여부나 사회적 지위와 관계없이 모든 여성을 위한 권리를 요구했다. WSPU 구성원들의 전술은 전투적으로, 활동은 그들이 여성 억압의 주체를 상징한다고 여긴 정부 건물과 다른 공공시설

들뿐만 아니라 국회의원들에 대한 고의적인 폭력 행위를 포함했다. 일부 구성원들은 재물을 파괴하고 의회 정문에 자신들을 사슬로 묶었다.

미국에서, 전국 여성 참정권 협회(NAWSA)에 의해 조직된 여성들은 영국의 상대만큼 참정권에 관심이 있었지만, WSPU보다는 훨씬 덜 공격적이었다. [5]수전 B. 앤서니에 의해 주도된 그들의 로비 활동은 또한 그들이 토지 소유를 참정권의 전제조건으로 포함하지 않았다는 사실로 특징지어졌는데, 이는 투표할 권리가 토지 소유자에게만 국한되어서는 안되는 기본적인 개인권으로 여겨졌기 때문이다. 게다가, 앤서니는 빠르게 팽크허스트의 전투적인 행위로부터 거리를 두었는데, 그녀는 헌법 수정과 평화적인 시민 불복종 운동을 옹호했다. 1920년에 수정헌법 제19조가 비준되어 성별과 관계없이 모든 사람에게 투표할 수 있는 권리를 주었을 때, 그것은 적지 않은 부분에서, 앤서니와 그녀의 협력자들의 글, 청원 및 항의 덕분이었다.

반면에, 팽크허스트는 참정권이 없는 모든 영국 여성들이 투표권을 얻기까지 8년 더 투쟁했다. 일부 역사가들은 WSPU의 전투성이 포셋과 그녀의 동시대인들의 앞선 노력을 망쳤다고 생각하며, 다른 이들은 팽크허스트의 행동이 영국에서 보편적인 참정권을 쟁취하는 데 중요했으며, 그것들이 없었다면 어떤 변화도 이행되지 않았을 것이라고 주장한다.

suffrage 몡참정권, 선거권　perpetually 뿐지속적으로, 영원히
sweeping 옝전면적인　electoral system 선거 제도
momentum 몡동력, 탄력, 가속도　exclude 동배제하다
enfranchise 동참정권을 부여하다　tactics 몡전술
militant 옝전투적인, 공격적인　deliberate 옝고의적인
oppression 몡억압　counterpart 몡상대, 대응하는 것
confrontational 옝공격적인　spearhead 동주도하다
prerequisite 몡전제조건　champion 동옹호하다
amendment 몡(헌법의) 수정; 수정 조항
civil disobedience 시민 불복종 운동　ratify 동비준하다
petition 몡청원, 탄원서　collaborator 몡협력자
instrumental 옝중요한, 도움이 되는　implement 동이행하다

1 2단락에 따르면, 많은 부유한 여성들은 1832년의 선거법 개정에 어떻게 반응했는가?

(A) 그 법이 과세에 미치는 영향에 대해 분노했다.
(B) 투표권이 모든 성인 여성으로 확대되어야 한다고 주장했다.
(C) 모든 토지 소유자들이 투표하도록 허용되어야 한다고 주장했다.
(D) 선거 제도의 개정에 만족했다.

2 지문의 단어 "their"가 가리키는 것은?

(A) 다양한 지역 사회
(B) 평등권
(C) 더 작은 조직들
(D) 토지 소유 여성들

3 지문의 단어 "they"가 가리키는 것은?

(A) WSPU 구성원들
(B) 고의적인 행위
(C) 국회의원들
(D) 공공시설들

4 4단락에 따르면, NUWSS와 WSPU의 차이점은 무엇이었는가?

(A) NUWSS는 상당히 더 많은 회원을 보유하고 있었다.
(B) NUWSS는 더 많은 노동 계급 여성들을 모집했다.
(C) WSPU는 조직에 남성들을 허용하지 않았다.

(D) WSPU는 미혼 여성들을 배제했다.

5 5단락에 따르면, 미국의 참정권 운동을 NUWSS과 차별화한 것은?

(A) 참정권을 토지 소유자에게 제한되는 권리로 보지 않았다.
(B) 폭력 행위를 한 사람들을 경멸했다.
(C) 참정권을 얻으려는 여러 다른 집단들과 정치적으로 연계되어 있었다.
(D) 정부 관료들의 존중을 얻기 위한 전략을 사용했다.

6 지문의 단어 "instrumental"과 의미가 가장 비슷한 것은?

(A) 필수적인
(B) 만연한
(C) 연속적인
(D) 극단적인

Reading Practice 3　　　　　본문 p.36

1 (D)　　2 (A)　　3 (D)　　4 (D)　　5 (C)　　6 (B)

산악 기후

대부분의 기상학자들은 열대성 폭풍이나 도시 열섬 현상과 같은 주요한 기후적 영향에 대해 알고 있다. 그러나, 그들은 지역적인 기상 패턴이 국지적인 바람 패턴, 지형적 특징 및 위치와 관련된 더 작은 규모의 현상에 의해 추가로 영향을 받는다는 점 또한 강조한다. 이러한 이유로, 전문가들은 특정 생물군계에 존재하는 포괄적인 특징들을 설명하는 데 도움을 줄 수 있는 보편적인 분류 체계를 개발했다.

한 가지 지역적 범주는 북아메리카의 산악 기후 체계로, 이는 고산 지역과 주변의 골짜기에서 발견되는 일반적인 날씨를 설명한다. 커다란 육지의 존재는 북향과 남향의 경사면 간에 섭씨 28도만큼의 기온 차를 발생시킬 수 있다. 그 결과, 북쪽 면으로 그늘진 지역은 시원하며 습한 가문비나무 숲을 부양하는 경향이 있는 반면, 반대쪽으로 걸어가면 건조한 미기후가 나타나며, 보통 사시나무나 미루나무를 포함한다.

이러한 기온 변화는 여러 요인의 최종 결과이다. [1]이것들 중 첫 번째는 위도로, 그것은 땅이 태양 광선에 노출되는 각도를 나타낸다. 예를 들어, 적도에서는 태양 빛이 지구에 거의 수직으로 내리쬐지만, 북쪽으로 갈수록 그 각도는 점차 완만해진다. 따라서, 북반구에 위치한 모든 산맥은 최대 66.5도의 각도로 빛을 받고 결코 일직선 위로부터 받지 않으며, 북쪽 면은 가려진 쪽이 된다. 이것은 대륙 분수계를 따라 위치해 있는 로키산맥이 경사면의 상대적 위치에 따라 식물 종에 있어 큰 차이를 보이는 매우 다양한 아한대 생태계를 촉진하는 이유를 설명한다.

두 번째 요인은 고도이다. [3A/3B]고도가 높은 지역은 태양 복사열에 의해 영향을 받기 때문에, 태양에 노출된 모든 지표면은 빠르게 가열되지만, 그늘 안에 있는 지표면은 차게 유지된다. [3C]따라서, 태양빛이나 그늘의 존재는 높은 고도에서 공기의 기온 차에 직접적으로 일조한다. 이러한 태양 복사열의 차이는 남아 있는 북향의 빙하가 지구 온난화 추세에서 살아남을 수 있었던 주된 이유 중 하나이며, 그것들은 다른 것들보다 더 느린 속도로 녹는다. 예를 들어, 컬럼비아 대빙원은 캐나다의 재스퍼 국립공원의 높은 고원을 덮는 두꺼운 얼음덩어리로, 그것이 최고봉의 4분의 3에 의해 가려지기 때문에 안정된 빙하로 남아 있다. [4]게다가, 고도가 높아질수록, 기압은 감소하고, 밀도가 낮은 대기는 보온 능력이 낮기 때문에, 300미터 상승할 때마다 대략 1도에서 2도에 상

응하는 기온 저하가 수반된다. 높은 고도에서는 바람이 너 사납고 낮은 지역은 얼음같이 찬 바람으로부터 보호되기 때문에 증가하는 바람의 영향은 이러한 기온 변화를 두드러지게 한다.

바람의 이동은 또한 산악 지역의 습도에도 깊은 영향을 미친다. 캐나다 서부에서는, 우세한 바람이 브리티시컬럼비아주 해안에서 시작되어 대초원 안쪽을 향해 휘몰아친다. 그것들은 로키산맥 위로 밀려나고, 공기가 상승하면서 그것은 냉각되고 응결된다. 구름이 형성되고, 수증기가 서부 경사면에 상당한 양으로 비가 되어 내리는데, 이는 그 국가의 유일한 온대 우림 지역을 지탱할 수 있을 정도다. [6]공기가 동쪽으로 더 밀고 나아갈수록, 그것은 수분이 고갈되어 비그늘 효과를 일으키고, 그로 인해 동쪽 경사면에서는 비가 거의 내리지 않는다. 남은 건조한 공기는 하강하며, 단시간에 섭씨 30도까지 가열된다.

urban heat islands 도시 열섬 현상   overarching 휑 포괄적인
biome 명 생물군계   alpine 휑 고산의   prevailing 휑 일반적인, 우세한
temperature gradient 기온 차   spruce 명 가문비나무
microclimate 명 미기후   latitude 명 위도
perpendicular 휑 수직의, 직각의   facilitate 통 촉진하다
boreal 휑 아한대의   divergence 명 차이   remnant 명 남아 있는
barometric pressure 기압   heat retention 보온
accompanying 휑 수반되는   equivalent to ~에 상응하는
prairie 명 (북미·캐나다의) 대초원   condense 통 응결되다
precipitate 통 비가 되어 내리다   be depleted of ~이 고갈되다
descend 통 하강하다

1 3단락에 따르면, 위도와 관련이 있는 것은?

(A) 지구 궤도의 지름

(B) 누적 일조량 계산

(C) 적도와 산 사이의 거리

(D) 태양을 향한 지표면의 기울기

2 지문의 단어 "it"이 가리키는 것은?

(A) 컬럼비아 대빙원

(B) 높은 고원

(C) 재스퍼 국립공원

(D) 캐나다

3 다음 중 글쓴이가 고도가 높은 지역에 대한 태양 복사열의 영향에 관해 묘사하지 않는 것은?

(A) 지표면이 따뜻해지는 빨라진 속도

(B) 땅을 시원하게 유지하는 그들의 역할

(C) 서로 다른 고도에서의 기온 차

(D) 기압의 증가

4 4단락에 따르면, 높은 고도에서의 밀도가 낮은 대기에 관해 사실인 것은?

(A) 그것의 기압은 변동한다.

(B) 더 빠른 속도로 빙하가 녹게 된다.

(C) 그것은 태양 복사열의 영향을 덜 받는다.

(D) 열을 유지하는 능력이 감소한다.

5 지문의 단어 "They"가 가리키는 것은?

(A) 습도

(B) 산악 지역

(C) 우세한 바람

(D) 대초원

6 5단락에 따르면, 다음 중 캐나다 서부의 비그늘 효과에 관해 사실인 것은?

(A) 구름이 형성되고 동쪽 경사면에 많은 비가 내리게 한다.

(B) 산의 동쪽 면에 더 건조한 공기를 야기한다.

(C) 대초원에서 불어오는 강한 바람에 의해 증폭된다.

(D) 브리티시컬럼비아주 전역에서 발생하는 심각한 가뭄의 원인이다.

---

iBT Reading Test 1 본문 p. 38

1 (A)	2 (C)	3 (C)	4 (C)
5 (A)	6 (B)	7 (B)	8 (C)
9 (B)	10 (A), (C), (D)		

콩의 건강상 이점

[3]선진국에서 의료 서비스 분야가 질병으로 인한 고통을 개선할 수 있었던 정도는 특정 유형의 암과 심장병을 포함한 여러 질병을 근절하는 데 대한 무능력과 그것들이 점점 더 널리 퍼졌다는 사실에 의해 제한되어 왔다. 의료 전문가들은 이러한 질병에 대한 다양한 원인을 인식하고 있으며, 그것들의 발달에 기여하는 유전적, 환경적, 행동적 요인에 대한 광범위한 분석이 수행되어왔다.

많은 관심을 모았던 연구의 한 갈래는 특정 음식과 질병 예방 사이의 관계이다. 그러한 식품 중 하나는 두과에 속하는 콩으로, 그것은 13,000년 이상 동안 아시아 전역에서 광범위하게 재배되어 왔고 많은 아시아 국가들의 주식으로 자리 잡았다. 중국 북부에서 처음 재배된 후, 이 작물은 서기 1세기까지 중국 남부, 한국, 일본, 동남아시아, 인도 전역으로 퍼졌다. 이 농산물의 성공은 부분적으로 그것의 식감에서 기인하는데, 이는 그것을 여러 가지의 요리 스타일에 적합하게 해준다. 그것은 자연적인 상태, 즉 콩 전체나 콩나물의 형태로 섭취되거나 두부, 두유, 가루로 가공될 수 있다.

콩 섭취율이 가장 높은 중국과 일본 같은 국가에서는 동물성 단백질이 더 규칙적으로 섭취되는 북아메리카에서보다 특정 유형의 암 발병률이 현저히 낮다. 콩은 항산화물로 확인된 화합물들을 함유하고 있으며, 이러한 물질들 중 많은 것들을 다른 영양 공급원, 특히 식물성 식품에서 구할 수 있는 반면, 콩은 구조상 에스트로겐과 유사한 이소플라본의 유일한 알려진 공급원이다. 이 밀접한 관계는 이소플라본이 체내의 에스트로겐 수용체에 결합할 수 있게 함으로써 이 호르몬의 신체적 영향을 약화시킨다. 유방암과 전립선암 둘 다 호르몬에 의해 촉발되기 때문에, 이소플라본은 이러한 악성 종양의 증식을 효과적으로 억제한다.

콩으로 만든 식품은 심장병의 중요한 원인 요소들인 콜레스테롤과 혈압을 둘 다 낮추는 것으로 나타났다. 인체에서 생성되는 콜레스테롤은 해로운 저밀도 지질단백질(LDL)과 유익한 고밀도 지질단백질(HDL)의 두 종류가 있다. 그 위험한 종류는 많은 양의 기름진 음식을 먹는 것과 같은 나쁜 식습관의 결과로 흔히 생성된다. 증거는 콩의 섭취와 LDL 수치의 감소 사이에 강한 상관관계가 있음을 시사한다. [7]이것은 콩의 섬유질이 간이 LDL 콜레스테롤을 처리할 때 그것에 의해 만들어지는 담즙산염과 결합하는 방식에서 비롯된다. 그 결합은 노폐물의 제거를 용이하게 하여 간의 용량을 증가시킨다.

이러한 특정 질병들 외에도, 콩의 약효 성분들은 폐경기 동안과 이후에 여성들이 직면하는, 삶의 이 시기에 일어나는 에스트로겐 생성의 급

격한 감소에서 비롯되는 다양한 건강 문제들을 치료하는 데 유용하다. 콩 제품이 주식인 지역의 여성들은 폐경기의 부정적인 신체적 영향을 서양 여성들과 같은 정도로는 받지 않는 것으로 오랫동안 인식되어 왔다. [8]그 이유는 다시 이소플라본의 에스트로겐 성분과 관련이 있는데, 이소플라본은 에스트로겐 수치가 낮은 사람들의 수용체에 충분한 자극을 제공하여 열감, 피로, 우울증과 같은 흔한 증상을 완화시킨다 . 많은 여성들에게, 콩 섭취는 호르몬 대체 요법과 같은 더 극단적인 치료의 대안으로 입증되었으며, 신중하게 조절된 식단이 건강 관리의 중요한 구성 요소라는 것을 증명한다.

ameliorate (동)개선하다   constrain (동)제한하다, 제약하다
prevalent (형)널리 퍼진   a multiplicity of 다양한, 다수의
legume family 두과(콩과)   dietary staple 주식
disseminate (동)퍼지다   an assortment of 여러 가지의
consumption (명)섭취   incidence (명)발병률, 발생률
anticarcinogen (명)항암물질   estrogen receptor 에스트로겐 수용체
dampen (동)약화시키다   malignant growth (암으로 발전하는) 악성 종양
contributor (명)원인   correlation (명)상관관계
facilitate (동)용이하게 하다   medicinal properties 약효 성분들
menopause (명)폐경기   hot flash (피부의) 열감, 안면 홍조

1 지문의 단어 "ameliorate"와 의미가 가장 비슷한 것은?

(A) 완화시키다
(B) 악화시키다
(C) 끝내다
(D) 강조하다

2 지문의 단어 "their"가 가리키는 것은?

(A) 전문가들
(B) 원인
(C) 질병
(D) 요인

3 다음 중 1단락에서 특정 유형의 암과 심장병에 관해 추론할 수 있는 것은?

(A) 여러 선진국에서 의사들에 의해 근절되었다.
(B) 특정 유전적 특성을 가진 사람들에게 한정된다.
(C) 과거보다 최근 몇 년간 더 많은 환자들에게 영향을 미쳤다.
(D) 일단 병의 원인이 확인되면 쉽게 치료된다.

4 지문에서 글쓴이는 왜 "the highest rates of soy consumption"을 언급하는가?

(A) 아시아에서 가장 흔한 단백질 공급원을 명시하기 위해
(B) 전형적인 동양 식단의 우수성을 입증하기 위해
(C) 일부 암에 대한 민감성에서 식단의 역할을 강조하기 위해
(D) 중국과 일본 각각의 유병률을 비교하기 위해

5 아래 문장 중 지문 속의 음영된 문장의 핵심 정보를 가장 잘 표현한 것은? 오답은 문장의 의미를 크게 바꾸거나 핵심 정보를 생략한다.

(A) 비록 콩에 있는 대부분의 항암 화합물이 다른 음식에서 발견되지만, 이소플라본은 콩에만 존재한다.
(B) 비록 이소플라본의 에스트로겐 특성은 보통 채소에서 발견되지 않지만, 암과 싸우는 콩의 요소는 희귀하지 않다.
(C) 비록 이소플라본이 중요하다고 여겨지지만, 암에 효과가 있다는 것이 입증된 다른 많은 영양소들도 콩에서 발견된다.
(D) 암을 예방하는 데 많은 식용 물질이 사용되는 반면, 콩과 같은 채소는 에스트로겐을 모방하는 이소플라본을 함유한다.

6 지문의 단어 "correlation"과 의미가 가장 비슷한 것은?

(A) 적대감
(B) 관련
(C) 구별
(D) 균형

7 4단락에 따르면, 콩은 어떻게 체내의 해로운 콜레스테롤의 양을 감소시키는가?

(A) 콩은 콜레스테롤을 덜 위험한 물질로 변형시킨다.
(B) 콩은 콜레스테롤을 처리하는 기관의 기능을 향상시킨다.
(C) 콩은 특정 부산물을 파괴해서 콜레스테롤의 생성을 방해한다.
(D) 콩은 콜레스테롤을 흡수하고 제거하는 물질을 생성한다.

8 5단락에 따르면, 이소플라본은 왜 폐경기 증상 치료에 효과적인가?

(A) 신체에 의해 만들어지는 에스트로겐의 양을 줄인다.
(B) 에스트로겐이 체내에서 쉽게 순환하도록 해준다.
(C) 에스트로겐 생성의 감소를 보상한다.
(D) 체내에서 에스트로겐의 생성을 촉진한다.

9 네 개의 네모[■]는 다음 문장이 삽입될 수 있는 곳을 나타내고 있다.

그 위험한 종류는 많은 양의 기름진 음식을 먹는 것과 같은 나쁜 식습관의 결과로 흔히 생성된다.

이 문장은 어디에 들어가는 것이 가장 적절한가?

10 지시: 지문 요약을 위한 도입 문장이 아래에 주어져 있다. 지문의 가장 중요한 내용을 나타내는 보기 3개를 골라 요약을 완성하라. 어떤 문장은 지문에 언급되지 않은 내용이나 사소한 정보를 나타내므로 요약에 포함되지 않는다. 이 문제는 2점이다.

콩은 많은 건강상의 이점을 가지고 있는 다목적 영양 공급원이다.
· (A) 에스트로겐과 유사한 이소플라본의 특성은 폐경기의 부정적인 영향을 감소시킨다.
· (C) 이소플라본은 특정 유형의 암을 예방할 수 있는 것으로 나타났다.
· (D) LDL을 처리하는 간의 능력은 콩으로 만든 식품의 특정 측면에 의해 강화된다.

(B) 체내 에스트로겐의 생성은 종종 두부와 콩을 함유한 다른 음식들의 섭취에 의해 촉진된다.
(E) 콩은 그것이 함유하는 많은 종류의 항암물질의 알려진 유일한 공급원이다.
(F) 폐경기 여성의 호르몬 대체는 콩 섭취에 의해 촉진된다.

iBT Reading Test 2   본문 p.42

1 (C)   2 (C)   3 (B)   4 (D)
5 (A)   6 (D)   7 (B)   8 (C)
9 (A)   10 (A), (B), (E)

머스 커닝햄

[2]1950년 이전에, 무용 안무는 연극적 서사를 전달하기 위해 함께 고안된 무대 구성, 음악 반주, 동작으로 꼼꼼하게 대본이 짜인 공연을 강조하는 경향이 있었다. 이 요소들은 서로 끊임없이 접촉하면서 작업하

는 사람들의 집단에 의해 동시에 구성되었다. 내중의 의식에 스며든 고전 발레가 표준적인 무용의 형태였지만, 여러 안무가들이 즉흥적인 기법을 실험하기 시작하면서 무대와 음악에 대한 태도뿐만 아니라 구성 방법도 20세기 초반에 걸쳐 빠르게 발전했다. 마사 그레이엄과 제롬 로빈스를 포함하여 이 새로운 접근 방식을 지지하는 강사들은 학생들이 기본적인 지시에 따라 자유롭게 움직이도록 장려했다. 이 모험적인 시기는, 결국 전통적인 발레의 한계를 버리는 데 열중한 완전한 한 세대의 공연자들을 육성하여 새롭고 혁신적인 작품들을 만들어냈다. 특히 머스 커닝햄은 이 시기에 전성기에 도달한 가장 선구적이고 재능 있는 무용수로 여겨진다.

어린 나이에 춤을 시작한 커닝햄은 마사 그레이엄 무용단을 포함하여 다수의 레퍼토리 극단과 함께 오리건과 캘리포니아 전역의 관객들에게 공연을 하며 자랐다. 그러나, 그는 곧 현대 무용 기법을 그가 독자적으로 창조한 역할에 접목함으로써 고도의 기교를 보이는 주인공으로서 자신을 드러냈다. [4]그의 작품들은 파드되의 존재를 덜 강조했는데, 이는 발레의 표준적인 서사로, 짧은 도입부, 남성과 여성 발레 무용수의 극적인 춤, 공연 초반의 주제를 반복하는 결론으로 구성되어 있다. 사실, 커닝햄은 스토리텔링이라는 개념을 완전히 제거했고 동작 자체에 의해 불러일으켜진 긴장감에 집중하여 많은 비평가들을 격분시켰으나 다른 이들에게는 깊은 인상을 남겼다. 무용에 대한 커닝햄의 접근 방식은 전통적인 예술 형식에서 벗어나 평범한 사물과 행동에 기초한 자유로운 정신의 창조를 수용할 필요성을 요구했던 예술 운동인 다다이즘의 영향을 받았다. 수년 후, 커닝햄은 고양이가 기지개를 켜거나 사람이 연석을 내려가는 것과 같은 일상적인 동작의 관찰이 그의 경력 초기에 영감을 주었다고 설명했다.

다다이즘은 또한 커닝햄의 안무에서 우연성의 이용과 그의 동작과 통합된 청각 및 시각적 분위기 사이의 관계에서도 두드러졌다. 공간에는 고정된 점이 없다는 알베르트 아인슈타인의 선언과 전위 예술 작곡가 존 케이지의 작업에 고무된 커닝햄은 우연성 기법이라고 알려진 방법을 개발했다. [6B]주사위, 카드, 동전 또는 다른 확률 장치를 사용하여, 그는 무작위로 동작의 유형과 반복을 결정했다. [6A]한편, 음악가가 작곡을 위해 초대되었고 무대 디자이너는 시각적인 환경을 만들었는데, 이는 모두 별개로 이루어졌다. 이러한 의미에서, 커닝햄은 전통적인 협업 방식을 피했는데, 그 요소들은 실연 관객들 앞에서의 초연 동안에만 결합되었다. [6C]즉각적인 찬사를 받은 작품은 유지되어 다시 공연되었고, 그렇지 않은 것들은 레퍼토리에서 제외되었다.

그러나, 커닝햄이 그의 무용수들에게 즉흥적인 동작을 하도록 장려했기 때문에 그의 최종 작품들이 완전히 즉흥적이었다고 가정해서는 안 된다. 반대로, 그의 공연의 모든 단계는 신중하게 계획되고 훈련되어 무용수들이 매 순간 그들이 있어야 할 위치를 정확히 알 수 있었다. 그런 식으로, 커닝햄은 표준적인 무용 표기법으로 그것들을 기록할 수 있었고, 그것들은 같은 공연자나 다른 극단에 의해 다시 공연될 수 있었다. 이것은 또한 그의 우연성 기법에 진정한 안무법으로서의 정당성을 부여하는 역할을 했는데, 그것은 모든 안무가들에게 선택의 여지를 주는 동시에 그들이 작품에서 높은 수준을 유지하도록 보장했다.

scripted 형 대본이 짜인   permeate 동 스며들다, 퍼지다
choreographer 명 안무가   improvisational 형 즉흥적인
subscribe to (의견·이론을) 지지하다   venturesome 형 모험적인
foster 동 육성하다   confine 명 한계, 범위
virtuoso 형 고도의 기교를 보이는   incorporate 동 접목하다, 결합하다
de-emphasize 동 덜 강조하다   evoke 동 불러일으키다
infuriate 동 격분시키다   commonplace 형 평범한, 흔한
aural 형 청각의   avant-garde 형 전위 예술의   at random 무작위로
in isolation 별개로, 따로   collaborative 형 협업의

acclaim 명 찬사   impromptu 형 즉흥적인   notation 명 표기법
legitimize 동 정당성을 부여하다

1 지문의 단어 "permeated"와 의미가 가장 비슷한 것은?

(A) 산만하게 했다
(B) 강요했다
(C) 채웠다
(D) 괴롭혔다

2 다음 중 1단락에서 20세기 중반 이전의 안무에 관해 추론할 수 있는 것은?

(A) 학생들의 기술보다 노련한 공연자들의 기술을 부각시켰다.
(B) 강사에 의해 시각적으로 가르쳐진 기본 조합을 기반으로 했다.
(C) 공연 중 즉흥적인 창의성을 강조하지 않았다.
(D) 동시대의 관객들에게 인기를 잃었다.

3 지문의 단어 "infuriating"과 의미가 가장 비슷한 것은?

(A) 관심을 끄는
(B) 격분시키는
(C) 강요하는
(D) 격리시키는

4 2단락에 따르면, 파드되는

(A) 공연의 줄거리를 해결하는 결론이다
(B) 머스 커닝햄에 의해 비판받은 전통적인 형태의 안무이다
(C) 남녀 발레 무용수들 사이에서 불러일으켜진 긴장감이다
(D) 전통적인 발레가 이야기를 전달하는 순서이다

5 2단락에서 글쓴이는 왜 커닝햄의 일상적인 동작 관찰을 언급하는가?

(A) 그의 경력 초기의 영감의 원천을 확인하기 위해
(B) 그의 안무가 당시에 인기가 없었던 이유를 설명하기 위해
(C) 그의 공연이 일반적인 상황을 묘사했다는 것을 시사하기 위해
(D) 그의 스타일이 전통적인 기대에 부합했다는 것을 보여주기 위해

6 3단락에 따르면, 다음 중 우연성 기법의 측면이 아닌 것은?

(A) 공연의 모든 요소가 격리되어 창작된다.
(B) 동작의 선택이 명확한 패턴 없이 일어난다.
(C) 찬사를 받은 작품만 후속 공연을 위해 유지된다.
(D) 음악가들과 디자이너들이 리허설을 참관하도록 초대된다.

7 지문의 단어 "them"이 가리키는 것은?

(A) 작품들
(B) 단계
(C) 공연
(D) 무용수들

8 아래 문장 중 지문 속의 음영된 문장의 핵심 정보를 가장 잘 표현한 것은? 오답은 문장의 의미를 크게 바꾸거나 핵심 정보를 생략한다.

(A) 우연성 기법은 안무가들에게 혁신적인 작품의 장점을 홍보할 수 있는 진정한 기회를 제공한다.
(B) 우연성 기법의 가치는 안무가들이 전형적인 방식으로 새로운 레퍼토리를 개발할 수 있도록 돕는 능력에 있다.
(C) 우연성 기법은 안무가들이 우수한 수준의 창의적인 작품을 제작할 수 있는 도구로 확인되었다.
(D) 우연성 기법은 확립된 기준을 사용하여 우수한 작품을 제작하고자 하는 안무가들의 관심을 받을 만하다.

9 네 개의 네모[■]는 다음 문장이 삽입될 수 있는 곳을 나타내고 있다. 이 요소들은 서로 끊임없이 접촉하면서 작업하는 사람들의 집단에 의해 동시에 구성되었다.

이 문장은 어디에 들어가는 것이 가장 적절한가?

10 지시: 지문 요약을 위한 도입 문장이 아래에 주어져 있다. 지문의 가장 중요한 내용을 나타내는 보기 3개를 골라 요약을 완성하라. 어떤 문장은 지문에 언급되지 않은 내용이나 사소한 정보를 나타내므로 요약에 포함되지 않는다. 이 문제는 2점이다.

> 새로운 형태의 무용에 대한 머스 커닝햄의 실험은 안무 예술에 혁명을 일으켰다.
> · (A) 다다이즘에 영향을 받아, 그는 우연의 요소뿐만 아니라 일상생활에서의 관찰을 안무에 적용했다.
> · (B) 그의 새로운 무작위로 만들어진 안무 스타일은 공연의 세 요소를 분리하고 그것들을 무대에서 다시 합쳤다.
> · (E) 그의 작품들은 춤에서 서술적 주제를 제거하고 즉흥적인 기법에 집중함으로써 파드되의 전통을 무시했다.

(C) 알베르트 아인슈타인과 존 케이지처럼 다양한 사람들의 생각은 커닝햄이 발레에 새로운 접근법을 개발하도록 영감을 주었다.
(D) 커닝햄의 전통적인 안무에 대한 헌신은 그의 작품이 다른 안무가들에 의해 이용되도록 했다.
(F) 그는 음악가와 무대 디자이너를 포함한 다른 분야의 예술가들과 자주 협업했다.

Vocabulary Review

1 confines	2 meager	3 momentum
4 divergence	5 prerequisite	6 prevailing
7 (B)	8 (D)	9 (A) 10 (B)
11 (A)	12 (B)	13 (D) 14 (C)

CHAPTER 03
Sentence Simplification

Example
본문 p.49

1 (A)   2 (B)

구름의 형성

구름은 액체 상태의 물이 기체로 변한 다음 다시 공기 중의 입자에 달라붙는 액체 방울로 바뀌는 순환의 결과로 형성된다. 그 순환은 증발로 시작한다. 바다, 호수 및 강에 있는 물의 일부는 수증기라고 불리는 기체로 변해서 대기로 올라간다.

대기 중의 수증기는 응결을 통해 다시 액체로 전환되는데, 이것은 두 가지 방법으로 일어난다. 첫째로, 공기는 무한한 양의 수증기를 수용할 수 없으며, 그것이 포화 상태가 되면, 여분의 수증기는 다시 액체 형태로 변해야 한다. 둘째로, 대기의 수증기는 때때로 이슬점 이하로 냉

각되어 액체 상태의 물방울로 응결된다. ¹이 과정은 얼음물이 담긴 유리잔에서 볼 수 있는데, 유리잔 안의 온도는 대기의 이슬점보다 더 차갑기 때문에, 유리잔을 둘러싸고 있는 수증기는 액체로 바뀌어 유리잔에 달라붙는다.

공기 중의 물방울들은 먼지나 꽃가루 같은 입자에 달라붙는다. ²입자에 달라붙는 물방울들은 구름으로 뭉치지만, 처음에는 그 물방울들은 무게가 너무 적게 나가서 비로 떨어지는 대신 바람에 떠다니며 공기 중에 계속 떠 있는다. 구름 속의 물방울이 합쳐져서 더 큰 물방울이 되어야만 강수로 내린다.

particle 명 입자   evaporation 명 증발   condensation 명 응결
saturated 형 포화 상태의   dew point 이슬점   cling to ~에 달라붙다
suspended 형 떠 있는   precipitation 명 강수, 비

1 아래 문장 중 지문 속의 음영된 문장의 핵심 정보를 가장 잘 표현한 것은?
   (A) 공기가 유리잔 안의 물보다 따뜻할 때, 주변의 수증기는 유리잔에 물방울로 응결된다.
   (B) 액체가 얼음물이 담긴 유리잔에 달라붙을 때, 유리잔 안의 온도는 이슬점보다 더 차가워진다.
   (C) 날씨가 더울 때, 얼음물이 담긴 유리잔에 담긴 액체 상태의 물은 유리잔에 달라붙어 대기 중의 수증기로 변한다.
   (D) 얼음물이 담긴 유리잔의 외부 온도가 더 차가우면 대기 중에 존재하는 수증기는 물방울로 응결된다.

2 아래 문장 중 지문 속의 음영된 문장의 핵심 정보를 가장 잘 표현한 것은?
   (A) 물방울이 크기와 무게가 증가함에 따라, 그것들은 입자 주위에 덩어리를 형성하기 시작한다.
   (B) 처음에 구름을 형성하는 입자에 부착된 물방울은 비가 될 만큼 충분히 무겁지 않다.
   (C) 물방울이 비를 만들기 위해서는, 그것들은 구름 안에 집중된 입자들을 흡수해야 한다.
   (D) 구름 속의 물방울들은 매우 작기 때문에, 그것들 중 다수가 바람에 의해 빠르게 흩어진다.

Reading Practice 1
본문 p.50

1 (C)   2 (B)   3 (C)   4 (A)   5 (C)   6 (D)

초기 건축 재료

건물 건축은 선사 시대에 기후의 영향을 완화하기 위한 실용적인 수단으로서, 본질적으로 사람과 악천후 사이에 장벽을 만들기 위해 등장했다. 그것은 원래 동굴 같은 천연 구조물 속에서 나뭇가지와 나뭇잎 같은 발견된 사물들로 만들어진 기초적인 거처로 시작했다. 그 최초의 임시 거처들로부터, 인류는 점차 단독으로 서 있는 건축물을 짓는 것으로 발전했고, 이것들은 주택뿐만 아니라 식량 저장과 의식 행사를 위한 건물들도 포함했다. ²그러나, 농경 이전 역사의 상당 기간 동안, 이것들 중 대부분은 임시로 사용되기 위한 것이었고, 따라서 장기적인 정착을 염두에 두고 건축되지 않았다. 그러나, 농경의 출현과 영구적인 정착지의 형성으로, 사람들은 더 체계적이고 조직적인 방식과 더 복잡한 천연 및 인공 재료로 건축물을 세우기 시작했다.

³많은 신석기 시대의 문화들을 연결하는 널리 퍼진 건축 기법은 간단

14 영어 실력을 높여주는 다양한 학습 자료 제공   HackersBook.com

한 건축물을 세우기 위해 보통 굽거나 굽지 않은 점토 형태의 흙과 보통 잔은 묘목인 목재를 다루는 것이었으나, 농농의 신흙심에서부터 북유럽의 목조 롱하우스에 이르는 예시를 포함하는 주거용 건축물에서, 이러한 천연 재료 사용의 보편성은 초기 건축가들에게 이용 가능했던 석기 시대 도구들뿐만 아니라 그것들의 널리 퍼진 이용 가능성에서 기인한다. 이 양식의 전형적인 예시는 어린나무를 잘라서 땅에 박은 다음 섬유로 묶는 초벽 방식이다. 그런 다음 이 단순한 벽은 강도와 내후성을 높이기 위해 점토가 발라졌다.

그러나 문명이 더 선진화되고 도시들이 성장함에 따라 새로운 방식이 등장했는데, 중요한 것은 벽돌의 제조였다. 건축에서 벽돌의 사용은 비옥한 초승달 지대의 초기 문명들로 거슬러 올라갈 수 있으며, 서기 1200년경에는 그 기술이 아프리카, 아시아 및 유럽 전역으로 퍼졌다. 5벽돌은 건축의 발달에 있어 상당한 발전을 의미했는데, 생산하기 쉬우면서도 저렴한, 기능적이고 내구성 뛰어난 재료가 처음으로 이용 가능했으며, 이것이 벽돌을 특히 도시 인구가 많은 지역에 적합하게 만들었기 때문이다. 게다가, 조립식의 직사각형 디자인이 벽돌을 세로로 쌓기 쉽게 만들었기 때문에, 눈에 띌 만한 크기의 건축물들이 나타나기 시작했는데, 예를 들어, 메소포타미아에서 벽돌 쌓기로 만들어진 몇몇 사원들은 높이가 25미터를 넘었다.

청동기 시대에 이르러, 야금술의 발전은 건축가들에게 금속 도구를 제공했고, 차례로 목재와 채석된 돌 이용의 기회를 열어 주었다. 금속 도구로, 삼림 지역의 사람들은 큰 나무를 베어 넘어뜨려 목재를 뼈대로 사용하거나, 통나무집의 경우에는 건물 전체에 사용할 수 있었다. 목재가 드물고 돌이 많은 곳에서는, 일꾼들이 망치와 끌을 이용해 채석장에서 거대한 돌덩어리를 힘들여 잘라냈다. 6A/6B/6C채석된 돌은 이용되기 위해 높은 수준의 기술과 부와 노동력 측면에서 막대한 자원을 필요로 한다는 점에서 다른 천연 재료와 구별되며, 이것들은 보통 잘 발달된 경제를 갖춘 선진 문화에서만 발견된다. 그 결과, 그것은 공공 건축물이나 최고 부유층의 주택 건축에만 거의 독점적으로 사용되었다. 고대 그리스인들은 파르테논 신전과 헤파이스토스 신전을 비롯한 다양한 종교 및 민간 건축물을 짓기 위해 석회암을 광범위하게 사용했다.

moderate 图완화하다   elements 명(폭풍우 등의) 악천후
rudimentary 형기초적인   makeshift 형임시의
pre-agrarian 형농경 이전의   temporarily 분임시로
advent 명출현   permanent 형영구적인   erect 图세우다, 건설하다
Neolithic 형신석기 시대의   sapling 명묘목   edifice 명건축물
universality 명보편성   be attributable to ~에서 기인하다
wattle-and-daub 명(나뭇가지에 흙을 바른) 초벽   plaster 图바르다
weatherproofing 명(비바람을 견디는) 내후성
prefabricated 형조립식의   vertically 분세로로
masonry 명벽돌 쌓기, 석조 건축   metallurgy 명야금술
exploitation 명이용   quarry 图채석하다; 명채석장
fell 图(나무를) 베어 넘어뜨리다   painstakingly 분힘들여

1 지문의 단어 "moderate"와 의미가 가장 비슷한 것은?

(A) 촉발시키다
(B) 보상하다
(C) 완화하다
(D) 보충하다

2 1단락에 따르면, 대다수의 농경 이전 건축물들의 특징은?

(A) 천연 동굴과 비슷한 모양을 하고 있었다.
(B) 제한된 기간 동안 사용되었다.
(C) 공공 의식을 위해 고안되었다.
(D) 물품 저장을 위한 넓은 공간이 있었다.

3 아래 문장 중 지문 속의 음영된 문장의 핵심 정보를 가장 잘 표현한 것은?

(A) 많은 신석기 시대의 문화들은 보통 굽거나 굽지 않은 점토인 흙을 그들의 단순한 건물에 사용했다.
(B) 건축 방법으로서, 신석기 시대 이전에는 흙과 목재의 사용이 널리 퍼지지 않았다.
(C) 신석기 시대에는, 기본적인 건축물을 짓는 흔한 방법은 흙과 목재의 사용이었다.
(D) 대부분의 신석기 시대의 문화는 건축 재료가 제한적이었기 때문에 같은 단순한 건축 기법을 가지고 있었다.

4 지문의 단어 "their"가 가리키는 것은?

(A) 재료
(B) 예시
(C) 진흙집
(D) 목조 롱하우스

5 아래 문장 중 지문 속의 음영된 문장의 핵심 정보를 가장 잘 표현한 것은?

(A) 대도시 지역은 벽돌 생산이 발달하기 시작한 주요 장소였다.
(B) 벽돌 건축은 훨씬 적은 노동력을 필요로 했기 때문에 도시 지역에서 빠르게 발달했다.
(C) 벽돌은 생산하기에 실용적이고 효율적이었기 때문에, 건축의 발전에서 중요한 단계였다.
(D) 비록 벽돌이 내구성 있고 기능적이었음에도 불구하고, 대도시 지역에서 사용하기에는 비용이 막대했다.

6 4단락에 따르면, 다음 중 돌을 사용하기 위해서 요구되지 않는 것은?

(A) 상당한 자금
(B) 뛰어난 숙련도
(C) 많은 노동자들
(D) 국제 교역

Reading Practice 2   본문 p. 52

1 (C)   2 (A)   3 (D)   4 (D)   5 (B)   6 (D)

미국삼나무

광범위한 거대한 미국삼나무 숲은 한때 아시아, 유럽 및 북아메리카의 광대한 영역을 뒤덮었다. 고대의 상당한 분포 구역의 크기에도 불구하고, 그 거대한 나무들의 현대의 모든 표본들은 현재 제한된 지리적 영역, 주로 북부 캘리포니아와 남부 오리건주에 걸친 해안가의 좁은 띠를 차지하고 있다. 미국삼나무의 독특한 생리는 그것이 이 생태학적 틈새에 특히 적합하게 하며, 그것이 그 지역에서 지배적인 형태의 식물로서의 위치를 유지하게 해주었다.

미국삼나무는 유성 생식과 무성 생식으로 둘 다 번식할 수 있는 능력을 포함하여 그것들의 생물학적 성공을 보장하는 여러 진화적 적응 형태들을 발달시켜왔다. 전자의 경우, 씨앗 생산은 빠르면 10살에서 15살 사이에 시작될 수 있고, 각 개체는 매년 많은 양의 씨앗을 생산한다. 비록 연 생산량의 단 20퍼센트만이 번식 능력이 있고 나머지는 빈 껍데기로 이루어져 있어 씨앗의 생육 가능성은 상당히 낮지만, 과학자들은 이 전략이 번식 상의 이점이 될 수 있다고 추측한다. 1그것은 적은 비율

의 먹을 수 있는 씨앗을 찾는 데 필요한 시간에 의해 기세가 꺾인 씨앗 포식자들을 단념시키는 수단으로서 역할을 한다.

[2]유성 생식이 일반적인 것이지만, 물리적 스트레스는 무성 복제 과정을 촉발할 수 있으며, 이는 한 개체 나무의 여러 유전적 복제물을 낳는다. 대개 강풍에 의해 모체가 넘어진 경우에는, 쓰러진 줄기의 길이를 따라 일련의 새로운 생장 가지들이 돋아날 것이다. 그 가지들은 또한 원래 나무의 건강의 급격한 악화에 반응하여 주요 줄기나 밑에 있는 뿌리 체계에서도 나올 수 있다. 각 경우에, 가지들의 상당 비율이 성숙기까지 생존하는데, 이는 주로 그것들이 자라는 놀라운 속도 때문이며, 종종 그것들의 생애 주기의 첫 20년 동안 매년 평균 1미터씩 성장한다.

미국삼나무의 거대한 크기는 생존에 필요한 수분과 영양분이 나무의 전 영역에 확실히 도달하게 하기 위해 정교한 체계를 필요로 한다. 미국삼나무는 광범위한 뿌리 체계를 통해 인체의 혈관계와 비슷한 내부 도관의 네트워크로 지하수를 끌어들이며, 그것은 줄기 위로 물을 운반하기 위해 압력 차를 이용한다. [4]혼자 힘으로는, 중력이 이 방식으로 수분이 운반될 수 있는 거리를 제한하기 때문에, 그 체계가 미국삼나무에 의해 달성되는 극단적인 수직적 성장을 지원할 수 없을 것이다. 그러나, 이 종은 주된 지하 뿌리 체계를 통해 공급되는 물을 증가시키기 위해 독특한 적응 형태를 통합했다. 미국삼나무는 그것의 바늘 잎과, 이 목적을 위해 실제로 줄기를 올라가는 특수한 뿌리를 통해 수분을 직접 흡수하여 안개와 비의 수분을 이용하는 능력을 발전시켰다.

생태계에서 미국삼나무의 성공은 또한 불의 영향에 대한 불침투성으로 인해 촉진된다. 일단 나무가 다 자라면, 나무껍질이 두꺼워지기 시작하며, 결국 8센티미터 깊이가 넘는 크고 튼튼한 보호 껍데기로 발달한다. 산불이 대부분의 숲에서 매년 발생하기 때문에, 이것은 미국삼나무에게 대부분의 다른 식물들에 비해 상당한 이점을 갖는 특성이다. 게다가, 불에 탄 덤불의 검게 그을린 잔해는 토양을 비옥하게 하며 영양소의 중요한 공급원이다. [6]미국삼나무의 생존을 위한 불 의존성에 대한 연구는 과학자들이 산불이 다른 삼림 지역의 전반적인 건강을 유지하는 데 하는 역할을 재검토하게 했다.

representative 명표본, 대표물　　physiology 명생리, 생리 기능
niche 명틈새　　dominant 형지배적인　　adaptation 명적응 형태
asexually 부무성 생식으로　　viability 명생육 가능성
fertile 형번식 능력이 있는　　daunt 동기세를 꺾다
edible 형먹을 수 있는　　norm 명일반적인 것　　trigger 동촉발하다
vegetative 형(식물) 생장의　　maturity 명성숙기, 완전한 발육
necessitate 동필요로 하다　　elaborate 형정교한
conduit 명(액체 등이 통과하는) 도관
be comparable to ~과 비슷하다　　vascular 형혈관의
incorporate 동통합하다　　augment 동증가시키다
imperviousness 명불침투성　　substantial 형크고 튼튼한
charred 형검게 그을린　　undergrowth 명덤불, 관목

1 2단락에 따르면, 미국삼나무에서 씨앗의 낮은 생육 가능성의 잠재적 이점은?
  (A) 동물들이 씨앗을 더 빨리 퍼뜨리기 때문에 번식을 촉진한다.
  (B) 발아하는 어린나무 사이의 경쟁을 낮추는 결과를 가져온다.
  (C) 포식자들이 먹을 수 있는 씨앗을 찾는 데 더 많은 시간을 소요하게 한다.
  (D) 빈 껍데기가 숲 바닥을 영양분으로 비옥하게 해준다.

2 3단락에 따르면, 무성 생식으로 생산된 어린나무의 독특한 특징은?
  (A) 원래 표본의 복제물이다.
  (B) 성숙기에 도달한 후 빠르게 성장한다.

(C) 건강한 나무들에 의해 생산된다.
(D) 모체에 물리적 피해를 입힌다.

3 지문의 단어 "comparable"과 의미가 가장 비슷한 것은?
  (A) 취약한
  (B) 책임 있는
  (C) 관련된
  (D) 유사한

4 아래 문장 중 지문 속의 음영된 문장의 핵심 정보를 가장 잘 표현한 것은?
  (A) 그 체계는 너무 효율적이어서 그것은 혼자 힘으로 미국삼나무 위로 수분을 수직으로 성공적으로 운반할 수 있다.
  (B) 미국삼나무의 키가 극단적으로 커짐에 따라, 그 체계는 수분을 나무 꼭대기까지 운반하기 위해 중력을 극복해야 한다.
  (C) 수분이 미국삼나무의 수직 끝부분에 도달하기 위해 이동해야 하는 거리 때문에, 중력은 그 체계보다 약한 것이 틀림없다.
  (D) 그 체계는 아마도 중력에 의한 한계 때문에 혼자서 미국삼나무의 엄청난 높이까지 물을 옮길 수 없을 것이다.

5 지문의 단어 "it"이 가리키는 것은?
  (A) 미국삼나무
  (B) 수분
  (C) 안개
  (D) 비

6 아래 문장 중 지문 속의 음영된 문장의 핵심 정보를 가장 잘 표현한 것은?
  (A) 화재가 이 종에 미치는 영향을 더 잘 이해해야 할 필요성이 다른 지역에서의 추가적인 연구를 필요로 하게 했다.
  (B) 미국삼나무와 산불 사이의 관계는 다른 종의 성장을 돕기 위해 화염을 사용하려는 계획을 낳았다.
  (C) 미국삼나무가 확실히 번성하도록 해야 할 필요성은 그 지역에 미치는 산불의 영향에 대한 광범위한 연구를 촉발시켰다.
  (D) 미국삼나무의 불 의존성을 연구한 결과로, 과학자들은 다른 곳에서 화재가 어떻게 삼림 건강을 유지하는지 더 자세히 살펴보고 있다.

Reading Practice 3　　　　본문 p. 54

1 (D)　　2 (D)　　3 (A)　　4 (C)　　5 (A)　　6 (C)

바람과 물의 침식

매년 수천만 명의 관광객들이 콜로라도강과 그것의 지류에 의해 콜로라도고원에 깎여진 거대한 수로인 그랜드 캐니언으로 알려진 놀라운 자연의 경이를 방문한다. 지질학자들은 그 고대의 수계가 그 협곡의 1,600미터 깊이와 466킬로미터 길이의 원인이라는 것을 확신하지만, 5에서 20킬로미터에 이르는 그것의 폭은 매년 거의 50만 톤의 퇴적물을 계속해서 운반하는 자연력들의 조합과 관련이 있을 가능성이 더 크다. 지형이 형성되고 만들어지는 이 과정은 침식이라고 알려져 있으며, 그것은 지각이나 지표면으로부터의 물질 제거와 하천, 해양, 빙하 작용과 같은 자연 작용에 의한 그러한 물질의 운반으로 정의된다.

이동하는 공기는 바람이 종종 시속 240킬로미터 이상의 속도로 모래

를 몰고 갈 수 있는 건조하고 사막인 환경에서 가장 중요한 침식 요인이다. ²ᵃ바람에 의한 심식이라고 불리는 이 작용은 초목의 부족에 의해 악화되는데, 그것은 보통 표토를 뿌리 구조에 융합시키고 작은 입자의 제거를 방지한다. 따라서, 느슨하게 형성된 모래 언덕은 모래를 들어 올려 여러 방향으로 수백 킬로미터를 운반할 수 있는 강한 바람의 돌풍에 특히 취약하다. 이 강력한 바람의 힘이 소멸되면, 모래는 땅 위에 퇴적된다. 이는 사막에서 일반적인 표류하는 모래 언덕 현상을 설명하며, 영향을 받은 지역에 주택이나 다른 구조물을 짓는 데 큰 장애가 된다. 이것은 꽤 최근까지 사막 주민들이 유목 생활을 하는 경향이 있었던 이유 중 하나이다.

³바람에 의해 운반되는 부유 입자는 또한 그것들이 충돌하는 지형에 모래를 분사하는데, 예를 들어, 암석 표면을 풍화시키거나, 그렇지 않으면, 표면에 달라붙어 축적을 일으킨다. 이러한 형태의 풍화의 한 예는 이집트에서 볼 수 있는데, 기자의 스핑크스는 기원전 1400년 이전에 이 지역이 버려진 후 어깨까지 모래에 묻혔다. 20세기 초에 고고학자들은 스핑크스를 복원하려고 시도했지만, 그것은 이미 모래 분사로 인해 얼굴과 몸에 상당한 손상을 입은 상태였다.

그러나, 대부분의 해안 지역에서는 물의 이동이 침식의 주요 원인인데, 이는 비를 포함한 다른 대기 조건에 더하여, 해안선의 손실을 야기하는 것이 파도의 작용이기 때문이다. ⁴들어오는 파도는 해안 지형에 영향을 미쳐 큰 바위를 더 작은 입자로 쪼개고, 나가는 파도의 수압은 해변을 따라 자갈들을 끊임없이 휘저어, 그것들이 해변을 따라 앞뒤로 구르면서 매끄러운 표면으로 풍화시킨다. 게다가, 파도는 해안 절벽을 붕괴 지점까지 침식시키는 원인이 된다. 암반이나 다른 고도로 접합된 물질로 구성된 해안선은 물이 퇴적층 사이의 균열로 들어가 큰 암석 덩어리를 부술 수 있기 때문에 특히 취약하다.

파도의 파괴력은 또한 환경 위험으로부터 인간을 보호하기 위해 고안된 방파제를 포함한 해안의 인공 구조물 건설로 인해 더욱 심해진다. ⁶ᴮ예를 들어, 나이지리아의 라고스에서는, 표류하는 모래로 인한 입구의 토사 퇴적을 방지하기 위해 좁은 항구의 준설된 입구 주변 바다에 거대한 석조물과 큰 돌들이 놓여졌다. ⁶ᴬ그러나, 이 장벽은 또한 파도가 해안에 입자를 퇴적시키는 것을 억제하지만, 수압에 의한 흡인을 제한하지는 못한다. ⁶ᴰ따라서, 모래는 해변에서 제거되지만 대체되지는 않는다. 해안선에 3백만 세제곱미터의 수입 모래가 공급되었음에도 불구하고, 심각한 침식은 쇠퇴하는 국가 관광 산업의 중심지인 그 지역의 해변을 계속 황폐화하고 있다.

erosion 몡침식 tributary 몡(강의) 지류 gorge 몡협곡
agent 몡자력력, 요인 fluvial 혱하천의 aeolian 혱바람에 의한
exacerbate 동악화시키다 vegetation 몡초목 dune 몡모래 언덕
vulnerable 혱취약한 dissipate 동소멸되다, 사라지다
deposit 동퇴적시키다 prevalent 혱일반적인, 널리 퍼진
suspended 혱부유하는, 떠다니는 sandblast 동모래를 분사하다
weather 동풍화시키다 wastage 몡손실, 소모
hydraulic pressure 수압 susceptible 혱취약한
compound 동더욱 심하게 하다 breakwater 몡방파제
masonry 몡석조물, 석조 건축 dredge 동(강바닥을) 준설하다, 파내다
silting 몡토사 퇴적 degrade 동황폐화하다, 저하시키다
focal point 중심지, 초점 lapse 동쇠퇴하다

1 네 개의 네모[■]는 다음 문장이 삽입될 수 있는 곳을 나타내고 있다.
이것은 꽤 최근까지 사막 주민들이 유목 생활을 하는 경향이 있었던 이유 중 하나이다.
이 문장은 어디에 들어가는 것이 가장 적절한가?

2 2단락에 따르면, 사막에서 식물의 부재는

(A) 표토의 질을 떨어뜨린다
(B) 풍속 증가를 촉진한다
(C) 암석 입자의 이동을 제한한다
(D) 바람에 의한 침식을 강화한다

3 아래 문장 중 지문 속의 음영된 문장의 핵심 정보를 가장 잘 표현한 것은?

(A) 바람에 날린 모래는 주변 땅을 마모시키거나 그 위에 쌓일 것이다.
(B) 입자들이 바람에 의해 운반될 때, 그것들은 이전에 축적된 표면을 부수고 나아간다.
(C) 바람에 의해 운반된 모래는 암석에 달라붙어 제거될 수 없는 층을 형성한다.
(D) 바람은 암석 외부에 부딪혀 모래가 바위에 달라붙고 공기 중에 흩날리게 한다.

4 아래 문장 중 지문 속의 음영된 문장의 핵심 정보를 가장 잘 표현한 것은?

(A) 해변의 자갈들은 들어오는 파도에 의해 거칠어지고 나가는 파도에 의해 평평해진다.
(B) 해안선의 특징은 방향에 따라 바위를 부수거나 쌓을 수 있는 파도에 따라 변한다.
(C) 들어오는 파도는 바위를 산산조각 내고, 나가는 파도는 더 작은 바위를 매끄럽게 한다.
(D) 파도는 방향과 상관없이 큰 바위를 조약돌로 만들어 해안선의 형태를 바꾼다.

5 지문의 단어 "compounded"와 의미가 가장 비슷한 것은?

(A) 증대되다
(B) 압축되다
(C) 감소되다
(D) 시행되다

6 5단락에 따르면, 다음 중 라고스의 자연 해변 황폐화에 기여한 것이 아닌 것은?

(A) 들어오는 파도에 대한 제한되지 않은 수압의 견인력
(B) 토사 퇴적을 막기 위해 만들어진 인공 차단물
(C) 다른 지역으로부터의 모래 유입
(D) 모래 퇴적의 감소

iBT Reading Test 1   본문 p. 56

1 (D)	2 (A)	3 (A)	4 (B)
5 (D)	6 (C)	7 (B)	8 (B)
9 (B)	10 (A), (C), (E)		

당나라

당나라(서기 618–907년)는 역사가들에 의해 고대 중국 문명의 정점으로 여겨진다. 당나라 황제들의 거의 3세기에 걸친 통치 동안, 성공적인 군사 작전은 그 영토를 동쪽으로는 한국을 향해, 남쪽 및 서쪽으로는 인도차이나나 주변까지 확장했다.

당나라 초기에, 중국의 승려 현장은 당나라의 수도 장안에서 소아시아

의 안티오크까지 8,000킬로미터가 넘게 뻗은 서로 연결된 일련의 길인 실크로드를 탐험했다. [1]그는 카라반으로 대륙을 횡단했고, 주요 경로를 따라 번성하던 불교의 다양한 양식들을 포함하여, 외국 문화에 대한 그의 관찰을 기록하기 위해 여러 주요 중심지에 머물렀다. 현장은 그 후 인도에서 휴식을 취했고, 그곳에서 불교 문헌을 얻었다.

현장의 장안 복귀는 중국에서의 창조적인 문예 부흥의 시작을 알렸는데, 이는 그가 가져온 문헌을 통한 불교에 대한 더 많은 노출에 의해 촉발되었다. 중국 작가들은 그 문서들에 노출됨으로써 이익을 얻었고, 그들은 이전에 5행의 서술 구조로 도교적 주제를 전달했던 '시'라고 불리는 시 형식으로 불교적 이상을 통합했다. 시인들이 그들의 작품에 불교적 이상을 더하기 시작했을 때, 시는 어조가 완화되고 상상력이 풍부해져, 당나라 말기에 절정에 달했다. '시'의 인기는 또한 목판 인쇄의 발명에 의해 높아졌는데, 그것은 대량 보급을 위해 원문을 빠르고 효율적으로 복제할 수 있었다.

예술에 대한 고조된 관심은 중국의 안정화에 도움이 되었다. [5]고종 황제는 총명하고 창의적인 인재를 정부로 영입할 기회를 보았고, 그래서 그는 모든 남자아이들의 재능을 시험하기 위해 개발된 일련의 객관적인 공무원 시험을 치러 최고 득점자들을 궁정직에 채용했다. 이것은 쿠데타와 주요 정치 인사의 암살을 자주 꾀했던 봉건 가문에 소속되지 않은 학자-관료 계급을 만들어 상대적 안정의 긴 시대가 시작되게 했다.

이러한 장기간의 안정의 혜택은 수도 장안에서 가장 우세했다. [8]당나라 황제들은 동서 교역로를 개방하는 정책을 유지했기 때문에, 수도의 주민들 중 다수가 외국인이었다. 일부는 선교사들이었고, 다른 이들은 자신의 압제적인 고향에서 도피하고자 하는 순례자들이었다. 몇몇은 대사로서 그들의 본국을 대표했으며, 중국의 거장에게 배우는 학자들도 있었다. 그러나, 대부분은 많은 시장에서 희귀 식물, 향신료, 약품 및 진기한 상품들을 취급하는 상인들이었다. 실제로, 그들의 번영은 너무나 널리 알려져서 중국에서 사업을 하는 것의 경제적 이점을 전하는 역사적 기록들이 멀리 터키에서까지 발굴되었다.

국운은 절도사의 지위까지 오른 안녹산이 반란을 일으켰을 때까지 계속되었다. 그의 지휘 하의 군인들은 장안으로 이동해 수도를 거의 장악했다. 황실 정부는 성공적으로 장안을 방어하고 쿠데타를 진압했지만, 그 혼란은 봉건 영주들에게 이웃을 공격하여 자신들의 세력을 키울 기회를 제공했다. 약화된 중앙 정부는 더 이상 중국의 광활한 시골 지역의 치안을 제대로 유지할 수 없었고 실크로드를 따라 이동하는 상인들에게 보안을 제공할 충분한 경비 요원을 공급할 수 없었다. 여행의 높은 위험에 낙담하여, 점점 더 적은 수의 상인들이 중국에 들어왔고, 그들의 부재는 당나라를 특징짓던 사상과 지식의 전승을 둔화시켜 번영 시대의 종말을 알렸다.

pinnacle 몡정점   fringe 몡주변, 가장자리
interconnected 휑서로 연결된   flourish 툉번성하다
herald 툉알리다, 예고하다   incorporate 툉통합하다
zenith 몡절정   block printing 목판 인쇄   dissemination 몡보급
pique 툉(관심·흥미를) 고조시키다   instrumental 휑도움이 되는
stabilization 몡안정화, 안정   personnel 몡인재, 인사
usher in ~이 시작되게 하다   unaffiliated 휑소속되지 않은
feudal 휑봉건의, 봉건 제도의   stage 툉(정치 운동 등을) 꾀하다
missionary 몡선교사   pilgrim 몡순례자   oppressive 휑압제적인
bazaar 몡(중동의) 시장   novelty 휑진기한   rebellion 휑반란

1 2단락에 따르면, 현장이 실크로드 탐험 동안 했던 것은?

(A) 주요 경로를 따라 많은 새로운 도시를 세웠다.
(B) 대륙을 횡단하기 위해 수천 마일을 걸었다.
(C) 불교 철학자들과 함께 여러 작품을 공동 작업했다.

(D) 다양한 종교적 전통의 관습을 목격했다.

2 지문의 단어 "heralded"와 의미가 가장 비슷한 것은?

(A) 알렸다
(B) 가정했다
(C) 준비했다
(D) 결정했다

3 아래 문장 중 지문 속의 음영된 문장의 핵심 정보를 가장 잘 표현한 것은? 오답은 문장의 의미를 크게 바꾸거나 핵심 정보를 생략한다.

(A) 새로운 인쇄 기술은 '시'에 대한 높아진 관심을 야기했다.
(B) 새로운 '시' 작품들이 쓰여질 수 있도록 인쇄 기술의 사용이 장려되었다.
(C) 시집의 배포된 사본은 원문 인쇄를 위한 신속한 새로운 과정을 이용해 만들어졌다.
(D) 목판 인쇄는 '시'를 대량 생산하기 위한 방법으로써 발명되었다.

4 지문의 단어 "piqued"와 의미가 가장 비슷한 것은?

(A) 위임받은
(B) 자극받은
(C) 결함 있는
(D) 감소된

5 4단락에 따르면, 고종 황제가 공무원 시험을 시작한 것은

(A) 이미 정부를 위해 일하고 있던 젊은이들을 평가하기 위해서이다
(B) 정부 관료들과 학자들을 구별하기 위해서이다
(C) 어느 소년들이 창작 예술직에 적합한지 알아내기 위해서이다
(D) 황실에 봉사할 수 있는 최고의 직원을 식별하기 위해서이다

6 지문의 단어 "others"가 가리키는 것은?

(A) 황제들
(B) 교역로
(C) 주민들
(D) 선교사들

7 지문에서 글쓴이는 왜 "historical records"를 언급하는가?

(A) 수도가 수준 높은 도심이었다는 주장을 뒷받침하기 위해
(B) 중국이 먼 지역에서 호의적인 평판을 얻었다는 것을 증명하기 위해
(C) 당나라와 타국 간에 무역이 일어났다는 것을 보여주기 위해
(D) 당나라 황제들에 대한 상인의 중요성을 설명하기 위해

8 5단락에 따르면, 수도가 많은 외국인들의 거주지였던 것은

(A) 중국의 교사들이 먼 지역에서 온 많은 학생들을 끌어모았기 때문이다
(B) 정부 관리들이 누구나 무역망을 이용하는 것을 허용했기 때문이다
(C) 독실한 사람들이 종교 교리의 엄격한 시행에 이끌렸기 때문이다
(D) 다른 국가들이 그들의 대표자들을 수용하기 위해 대사관을 설립했기 때문이다

9 네 개의 네모[■]는 다음 문장이 삽입될 수 있는 곳을 나타내고 있다.

황실 정부는 성공적으로 장안을 방어하고 쿠데타를 진압했지만, 그 혼란은 봉건 영주들에게 이웃을 공격하여 자신들의 세력을 키울 기회를 제공했다.

이 문장은 어디에 들어가는 것이 가장 적절한가?

10 지시: 지문 요약을 위한 도입 문장이 아래에 주어져 있다. 지문의 가장 중요한 내용을 나타내는 보기 3개를 골라 요약을 완성하라. 어떤 문장은 지문에 언급되지 않은 내용이나 사소한 정보를 나타내므로 요약에 포함되지 않는다. 이 문제는 2점이다.

> **중국은 당나라의 지도하에 대대적인 문화 부흥을 겪었다.**
> - (A) 불교가 중국에 전해진 후 예술가들은 번성했고 그들의 작품에 더 창의적인 접근법을 채택했다.
> - (C) 공정한 시험 제도의 발전은 유능한 관료제의 탄생으로 이어졌고, 이는 국가의 안정을 증대했다.
> - (E) 장안은 먼 나라에서 온 다양한 사람들을 끌어들이는 부유하고 인구 밀도가 높은 도심으로 발전했다.

(B) 학자들은 외국 문화의 관습에 대해 배우기 위해 정기적으로 실크로드를 따라 종교 유적지들을 방문했다.

(D) 왕실 정부는 중국의 모든 젊은이들의 지적 능력을 측정하기 위해 시험을 시작했다.

(F) 목판 인쇄의 발명은 문학의 전국적인 확산을 용이하게 했다.

iBT Reading Test 2
본문 p.60

1 (C)	2 (D)	3 (B)	4 (C)
5 (D)	6 (A)	7 (D)	8 (A)
9 (C)	10 (B), (C), (D)		

부두 죽음

서아프리카 전통문화와 로마 가톨릭교회에서 채택된 다양한 전통이 혼합된, 부두라고 알려진 아이티의 영적 체계에 따르면, 사람들은 많은 신비한 원인으로 인해 사망할 수 있다. 예를 들어, 죽음의 원인은 그들이 이전에 기분을 상하게 했던 누군가에 의해 그들에게 행해진 악의적인 몸짓이나 사악한 결과를 가져오도록 고안된 여러 알려진 죽음 예고 주술 중 하나일 수 있다. 다시 말해서, 질병과 그에 따른 죽음은 직접적인 신체적 손상의 증거 없이 오로지 주술에 의해서만 시작될 수 있다. 서양 인류학자들은 19세기 중반에 흔히 '부두 죽음'이라고 지칭되는 이 현상을 본격적으로 연구하기 시작했지만, 처음에는 죽음이 정신 신체의 수단을 통해 유발될 수 있다고 믿는 사람이 거의 없었기 때문에 종종 많은 회의감을 가지고 그렇게 했다.

초기 보고서들은 부두 죽음을 정신 작용의 결과로 봤고 암시의 힘이 충분히 강하다면 피해자는 죽을 것이라는 가설을 세웠다. [4]그러나, 이 설명들은 거부되었는데, 이는 그것들이 인간 동기 부여 연구의 지배적인 모델인 제임스-랑게 감정 이론을 따르지 않았기 때문이다. 그 이론은 감정이 특정 상황에 대한 생리학적 반응의 결과임을 시사한다. 예를 들어, 교통사고는 피해자의 심박수와 아드레날린 생산량을 증가시킬 것이다. 이것은 결국 뇌에 의해 감지되고 두려움을 자극한다. 따라서, 그 사고에 대한 신체 반응은 감정의 표현을 야기하고, 이는 부두 죽음의 개념과는 정반대의 관계이다.

그 현상은 생리학자 월터 캐논이 감정이란 실제로는 신체적 변화들의 결과가 아니라 그것들의 원인이라는 것을 시사한 놀라운 주장을 한 20세기 초까지 인류학자들을 계속 혼란스럽게 했다. [6]제1차 세계 대전 중 심각한 정신적 외상으로 사망한 건강한 유럽 군인들의 사례 연구에서 그가 수집한 관찰 데이터를 사용하여, 캐논은 신체가 감지된 위험에 의해 촉발되는 자연스러운 투쟁-도피 반응 메커니즘을 갖고 있다는 것을 깨달았다. 그는 감정이 사람들이 위험으로부터 도망치거나 자신을 방

어하는 데 필요한 근육의 긴장과 향상된 시력 같은 생리적 변화를 담당하는 주체라고 믿었다. 이렇듯, 심각한 정신적 외상으로 인한 죽음의 모든 사례를 포함하도록 그가 확장한 용어인 부두 죽음은 두려움, 불안, 공황에 대한 지연된 생리적 반응이다.

캐논의 연구는 아이티의 영성에 대한 초기 인류학적 연구를 뒷받침했고 광범위한 장애에 대한 통찰력을 제공했다. [8]그러나, 그것은 의사들이 뇌하수체와 부신의 기능을 밝혀내고 투쟁-도피 반응을 일으키는, 호르몬이라고 불리는 여러 화합물을 확인한 20세기 중반까지 가설로 남아 있었다. 신경계가 교감 신경계를 가지고 있다는 것은 이제 알려져 있는데, 이것은 심혈관계와 상호 연결되어 있고 인체의 항상성을 조절한다. 보통, 사람은 환경적 자극에 의해 반응이 유발될 때까지 휴식을 취한다. 이것은 야생에서 곰을 보거나 부모에게 질책을 받는 것을 포함한다. 그런 다음, 이 정보는 뇌의 감각 피질에서 뇌간으로 전달된다. 이러한 신호들은 혈관을 수축시키고 당(에너지)이 체내로 분비되도록 한다. 이 과정에 대한 연구는 완전히 새로운 과학 분야인 내분비학, 즉 호르몬 체계에 대한 연구를 형성했는데, 이는 캐논 이론의 세부 사항을 계속 채워 나가고 있지만, 그것들을 뒤집지는 않는다.

death-knell 형 죽음을 예고하는　hex 명 주술, 마법
malevolent 형 사악한, 악의적인　sorcery 명 주술, 마법
in earnest 본격적으로, 진심으로　skepticism 명 회의감
invoke 동 유발하다　psychosomatic 형 정신 신체의, 심신의
attribute 동 ~의 결과로 보다　comply with ~을 따르다
prevailing 형 지배적인　in opposition to ~에 반대하여
perceived 형 감지된　visual acuity 시력
spirituality 명 영성, 정신성　hypothetical 형 가설의
pituitary gland 뇌하수체　adrenal gland 부신
sympathetic division 교감 신경계　cardiovascular 형 심혈관의
homeostasis 명 항상성　reprimand 동 질책하다, 꾸짖다
sensory cortex 감각 피질　brain stem 뇌간
endocrinology 명 내분비학　overturn 동 뒤집다

1 지문의 어구 "in earnest"와 의미가 가장 비슷한 것은?
(A) 책임감 있게
(B) 자발적으로
(C) 진지하게
(D) 무시하듯

2 지문의 어구 "comply with"와 의미가 가장 비슷한 것은?
(A) ~을 준비하다
(B) ~을 생략하다
(C) ~을 삼가다
(D) ~에 따르다

3 글쓴이는 2단락에서 왜 교통사고를 언급하는가?
(A) 실생활의 경험이 어떻게 가설의 형성으로 이어졌는지 설명하기 위해
(B) 이론적 모델의 기초가 되는 원리를 보여주기 위해
(C) 이 시기 동안 흔히 발생하는 일들을 강조하기 위해
(D) 제임스-랑게 이론의 타당성을 확인하기 위해

4 2단락에 따르면, 부두 죽음에 대한 초기 가설들은 왜 무시되었는가?
(A) 사회의 약한 구성원들만 영향을 받는다고 시사했다.
(B) 과학계의 비주류 인물들에 의해 기록되었다.
(C) 감정에 대한 주요 심리학 이론에 위배되었다.
(D) 과학적 연구 모델 하에서 수행되지 않았다.

5 지문의 단어 "them"이 가리키는 것은?

(A) 인류학자들

(B) 주장

(C) 감정

(D) 변화들

6 3단락에 따르면, 투쟁-도피 반응은

(A) 위협처럼 보이는 것에 대한 인간의 타고난 반응이다

(B) 군인들에 의해 경험되는 전형적인 시련이다

(C) 모든 생리학적 변화에 대한 설명이다

(D) 감정이 표현되는 과정이다

7 아래 문장 중 지문 속의 음영된 문장의 핵심 정보를 가장 잘 표현한 것은? 오답은 문장의 의미를 크게 바꾸거나 핵심 정보를 생략한다.

(A) 비록 연구가 계속 수행되고 있지만, 내분비계에 대한 새로운 연구는 캐논의 추측을 뒷받침한다.

(B) 내분비학에 대한 캐논의 이론은 호르몬 체계에 대한 과도한 현대의 연구에 의해 평가절하되지 않는다.

(C) 추가 연구의 결과인 내분비학은 호르몬 체계의 존재를 강화하는 사실을 밝혀냈다.

(D) 구별되는 연구 분야로서 내분비학의 진화는 캐논의 연구에 정당성을 부여하고 강화한다.

8 4단락에서 20세기 중반 이전의 캐논의 연구에 관해 추론할 수 있는 것은?

(A) 그의 주장을 뒷받침할 물리적 증거가 없었다.

(B) 전문가들은 제임스-랑게 이론이 옳다고 여겼기 때문에 그것을 거부했다.

(C) 의사들에게 구체적인 답을 제공하기에는 너무 일반적이라고 여겨졌다.

(D) 비과학적이라고 여겨지는 종교의 측면을 통합했다.

9 네 개의 네모[■]는 다음 문장이 삽입될 수 있는 곳을 나타내고 있다.

이것은 야생에서 곰을 보거나 부모에게 질책을 받는 것을 포함한다.

이 문장은 어디에 들어가는 것이 가장 적절한가?

10 **지시:** 지문 요약을 위한 도입 문장이 아래에 주어져 있다. 지문의 가장 중요한 내용을 나타내는 보기 3개를 골라 요약을 완성하라. 어떤 문장은 지문에 언급되지 않은 내용이나 사소한 정보를 나타내므로 요약에 포함되지 않는다. 이 문제는 2점이다.

> **부두 죽음은 인간의 감정과 생리를 연구하는 연구자들을 오랫동안 당혹스럽게 했다.**
>
> · (B) 위험에서 도망치거나 자신을 방어하려는 본능적인 욕구를 소개한 잘 연구된 이론은 부두 죽음에 대한 설명을 제공했다.
>
> · (C) 신체가 변동된 정신 상태에 반응할 수 있다는 이론은 감정이 생리적 변화의 결과라는 생각과 일치하지 않았기 때문에 처음에는 거부되었다.
>
> · (D) 특정 생리학적 과정과 그것이 신체에 미치는 영향을 발견함으로써, 과학자들은 이전에 기록된 연구들을 보강했다.

(A) 사망한 군인의 사례는 영적 수단에 의한 죽음 이야기들과 일치하며, 이는 일부 사람들로 하여금 그것들이 서로 연결되어 있다고 믿게 한다.

(E) 아이티에서는, 심각한 질병의 환자들은 주술에 의해 감지할 수 없는 신체적 손상을 입었다고 믿어졌다.

(F) 질병과 부두 죽음 사이의 연관성은 연구자들에게 두 현상에 대한 연구를 계속하도록 자극을 주었다.

Vocabulary Review

본문 p.64

1 edible	2 painstakingly	3 pinnacle
4 hypothetical	5 malevolent	6 precipitation
7 (A)	8 (B)	9 (B)	10 (C)
11 (B)	12 (A)	13 (D)	14 (A)

CHAPTER 04
Fact

Example

본문 p.67

1 (A)　　2 (C)

원양 생태계

외해, 즉 원양 지역은 해안에서 멀리 떨어진 모든 해수를 포함하며 전 세계 바다 총부피의 약 65퍼센트를 차지한다. [1]무엇보다도 복잡한 형태의 식물과 산호초 형성에 적합한 표면의 부재로 인해, 그 지역에는 연안 해역의 생물 밀도와 다양성이 부족하기는 하지만, 그곳에는 매우 다양한 종들이 서식한다. 원양 지역은 뚜렷이 구분되는 층들로 나뉜다.

해수면에서 약 200미터 깊이까지 뻗어 있는 곳은 유광층으로, 그곳이 광합성을 하기에 충분한 태양 복사가 관통할 수 있는 한계를 나타내기 때문에 햇빛층이라고도 알려져 있다. 그 결과, 그 지역은 원양 지역의 모든 수생 생물의 90퍼센트 이상을 포함하고 있으며, 미세한 박테리아에서부터 고래와 상어 같은 거대한 생물에 이르는 매우 다양한 생물들을 부양한다. 바다의 이 부분의 생물학적 잠재력은 비교적 높은 수온과 낮은 수압에 의해 더욱 강화된다.

200미터 깊이에서 시작하는 박광층은 광합성을 지원할 수 없지만, 그곳은 특수한 적응 형태를 발달시킨 다양한 수생 생물들이 차지하고 있다. [2]많은 물고기 거주종들은 광합성을 하는 수생 식물인 식물성 플랑크톤을 먹기 위해 바다의 상층부로 올라간다. 다른 종들은 먹이를 유인하기 위해 생물에 의해 빛이 생성되는 생물 발광과 같은 적응 형태를 통해 구할 수 있는 한정된 영양물을 효율적으로 이용한다.

pelagic 휑 원양의　open ocean 외해(육지와 인접하지 않은 넓은 바다)
vegetation 圀 식물　stratum 圀 층　euphotic zone 유광층
photosynthesis 圀 광합성　microscopic 휑 미세한
potential 圀 잠재력　disphotic zone 박광층
phytoplankton 圀 식물성 플랑크톤　sustenance 圀 영양물
bioluminescence 圀 생물 발광

1 1단락에 따르면, 외해의 생명 부양 능력을 제한하는 것은?

(A) 발전된 형태의 해양 식물의 부재

(B) 감소된 수생 동물의 종류

(C) 지리적 영역의 적당한 범위

(D) 보다 적합한 수생 서식지의 근접성

2 3단락에 따르면, 다음 중 박광층에서 이용되는 섭식 방법은?

(A) 포식자들은 식물성 플랑크톤을 잡기 위해 빛을 사용한다.

(B) 깊은 곳에 사는 생물들은 유광층의 먹이를 유인한다.

(C) 물고기는 광합성 식물을 섭취함으로써 영양분을 얻는다.

(D) 식물성 플랑크톤은 미세한 박테리아를 먹기 위해 상층부로 올라간다.

Reading Practice 1

1 (D)   2 (A)   3 (C)   4 (D)   5 (A)   6 (A)

배음 창법

화음 창법 또는 목 노래 창법이라고도 알려진 배음 창법은 가창자가 두 개의 다른 음조를 동시에 낼 수 있는 매우 전문적인 발성 기법이다. 많은 다양한 스타일이 있지만, 가장 일반적인 방법은 밑에 있는 하나의 음을 내고, 그 위에 특정 배음, 즉 "배음"의 선택적 보강을 통해 선율이 얹어지는 것을 수반하며, 가장 잘 알려진 형태는 중앙아시아에서 온 것이다.

특히, 남부 시베리아에 있는 러시아 공화국 투바 사람들의 전통 민속 음악은 그것의 아름다움과 독특한 특징들 때문에 과학자들과 음악가들 모두에 의한 많은 정밀 조사의 초점이 되어왔다. 역사 대부분 동안 지리적 및 정치적으로 다른 문명들로부터 고립되어 있던 투바 사람들은 자연 세계와의 강력한 관계를 중심으로 한 독특한 문화유산을 발전시켜 왔다. 투바 사람들은 '흐미'라고 알려진 그들의 창법이 지저귀는 새들, 산을 가로지르는 바람, 강바닥의 바위 위로 흐르는 물에 해당하는 특유의 음색과 함께 자연에서 발견되는 소리에 의해 영감을 얻는다고 주장한다. 많은 사람들은 이 자연에서 발생된 소리들이 듣는 사람들에게 긍정적이거나 부정적인 영향을 줄 수 있다고 느낀다. 흐미와 자연 세계 사이의 인식된 연관성은 아이가 모국어를 말하는 능력을 발달시키는 것과 거의 같은 방식으로, 그것이 형식적으로 학습되기보다는 직관적으로 습득되어야 하는 능력이라는 널리 받아들여진 신념을 낳았다. 표준화된 교육 체계의 부족은 이 창법을 배우기 원하는 외부인들에게 그것을 어렵게 만들었다.

그러나, 국제적인 관심의 증가는 흐미가 불리는 방식에 대한 통찰을 제공해온 여러 연구 프로젝트로 이어졌다. 과학자들은 소리의 근본적인 측면을 조사하는 것으로 시작했다. 소리 에너지는 공기와 같은 전도성 매체를 통해 파동으로 이동하며 여러 변수에 따라 특정 주파수로 진동한다. 소리가 인간의 목소리에 의해 생성될 때, 가장 중요한 요소는 후두에 의해 음색들이 만들어지는 방법과 성대에 의해 그것들이 변하는 방식이다. 성도에 의해 생성되는 음은 더 높은 주파수의 음계를 통해 진동하는 일련의 배음뿐만 아니라 기본 음조도 포함한다.

전통적인 형태의 창법에서, 배음은 실제 음에 대해 보조적인 기능을 가지고 있으며 주로 음색을 더하기 위해 사용된다. 그러나, 그것들은 의도적으로 조작되지 않으며, 대신 구성의 한 측면이라기보다는 개인의 목소리의 고유한 특징으로 여겨진다. 대조적으로, 배음은 투바 창법의 가장 중요한 요소이며, 그것을 조작하는 능력은 그 기술을 익히기 위한 기본적인 요건이다. 흐미에서, 그 과정은 긴 시간 동안 유지되는 웅웅거리는 하나의 음을 발성하는 것으로 시작한다. 성도를 사용하여, 가창자는 음형대라고 알려진 모음 소리를 낸 다음 그 소리를 여러 개의

음형대들과 합친다.

최상의 결과를 얻기 위해서, 흐미 가창자들은 성대의 움직임을 고도로 통제해야 하는데, 이는 이것의 빠른 개방에 의해 배음의 주파수가 증폭되고, 그것들의 폐쇄를 지연시킴으로써 확장되기 때문이다. 이 독특한 물리적 절차는 가창자가 특정 배음을 선택하여 강화하거나 약화시킬 수 있게 하여, 원래의 기본 음조와 동시에 만들어지는 배음 선율의 발성을 용이하게 한다.

overtone 똉배음   simultaneously 튄동시에
underlying 휑밑에 있는   reinforcement 똉보강
harmonic 똉배음   scrutiny 똉정밀 조사
corresponding to ~에 해당하는   traverse 뙝가로지르다
perceived 휑인식된   acquire 뙝습득하다
intuitively 튄직관적으로   standardized 휑표준화된
fundamental 휑근본적인, 기본의   conductive 휑전도성의
medium 똉매체   oscillate 뙝진동하다   frequency 똉주파수
variable 똉변수   larynx 똉후두   vocal folds 성대
vocal tract 성도   auxiliary 휑보조적인   timbre 똉음색
deliberately 튄의도적으로   manipulate 뙝조작하다
inherent 휑고유한, 타고난   formant 똉음형대(음의 주파수 대역)

1 지문의 단어 "simultaneously"와 의미가 가장 비슷한 것은?

(A) 결과적으로

(B) 그 후

(C) 그에 따라

(D) 동시에

2 지문의 단어 "its"가 가리키는 것은?

(A) 전통 민속 음악

(B) 투바

(C) 러시아 공화국

(D) 정밀 조사

3 네 개의 네모[■]는 다음 문장이 삽입될 수 있는 곳을 나타내고 있다.

많은 사람들은 이 자연에서 발생된 소리들이 듣는 사람들에게 긍정적이거나 부정적인 영향을 줄 수 있다고 느낀다.

이 문장은 어디에 들어가는 것이 가장 적절한가?

4 2단락에 따르면, 투바 사람들이 흐미에 관해 믿는 것은?

(A) 자연환경의 야외에서 수행되어야 한다.

(B) 자연에서 발견되지 않는 소리를 사용해야 한다.

(C) 지리적으로 고립된 다른 문화들과 공유되어야 한다.

(D) 학습보다는 직관을 통해 습득되어야 한다.

5 3단락에 따르면, 성대의 기능은 무엇인가?

(A) 다른 기관에 의해 생성되는 소리를 바꾼다.

(B) 소리를 내는 데 필요한 기본 음조를 만든다.

(C) 배음을 한 음계 위로 변동시킨다.

(D) 배음의 주파수를 높인다.

6 4단락에 따르면, 전통적인 가창자들은

(A) 음의 배음을 의도적으로 통제하지 않는다

(B) 음색을 증가시키기 위해 배음을 조작한다

(C) 작곡가에 의해 명시된 음색을 재생한다

(D) 배음에 영향을 주기 위해 그들의 음역을 이용한다

CHAPTER 04 | Fact 21

1 (D)　2 (C)　3 (C)　4 (C)　5 (A)　6 (B)

물거미

물거미는 유럽 본토와 북아시아가 원산지인 작은 거미류로, 여기에서 그것은 민물 서식지의 수생 식물 사이에서 발견될 수 있다. [2]이 거미들은 거미류 중에서 독특한데, 이는 물속에서 호흡하는 데 필요한 생물학적 기관이 없음에도 불구하고 대부분의 일생을 물속에서 보내는 그것들의 성향 때문이다. 이러한 조건에서 살아남기 위해, 이 거미류는 잠수종, 즉 공기 방울을 만드는데, 여기에서 그것의 이름이 유래되었다. 이 거미들은 온도 및 오염 수준 같은 물의 조건에 따라, 수면으로 돌아갈 필요 없이 평균 크기의 공기 방울 속에서 약 24시간을 버틸 수 있다.

비록 수중 호흡 기관은 없지만, 이 종은 복부의 폐를 통해 호흡하는데, 이는 언제든 오직 하반신만이 산소에 대한 접근을 필요로 한다는 것을 의미한다. [3]이 부분은 복부가 물 밖으로 밀려날 때 공기를 옭아매어 거미가 물속을 이동할 때 얇은 공기막을 유지하는 미세한 털들로 덮여 있다. 공기 저장고를 만들기 전에, 거미는 먼저 수중 식물과 같은 적절한 위치를 찾아야만 한다. 이 시점에, 그것은 이용 가능한 산소의 양이 불충분하며, 포식자들로부터 거의 방어할 수 없는 수면으로의 빈번하고 위험한 이동을 견뎌야 한다. 이상적인 위치가 선택되면, 그것은 굵고 가는 거미줄이 겹친 혼합물을 구성하여 공기 저장고를 만들기 시작한다.

공기 방울의 크기와 구조는 각 거미의 성별에 따라 달라진다. 일반적으로 수컷이 암컷보다 작지만, 이 종에서는 그 반대이기 때문에, 이 거미들은 거미류 치고는 이례적인 성적 크기 이형성을 특징으로 한다. 결과적으로, 수컷은 그것들의 더 큰 몸에 공간을 제공하기 위해 더 큰 구조물을 만들어야 하는 반면, 암컷은 비교적 작은 공기 방울을 만든다.

첫 번째로, 공기 방울은 거미가 방해받지 않고 드나들 수 있도록 밑면이 열린 작은 공기주머니 주위에 거미줄을 이용하여 단단한 초승달 모양으로 조립된다. 공기 방울은 외부 압력보다 높은 내부 압력을 유지함으로써 기능하는데, 이는 주변 물의 힘에도 불구하고 그것이 남아 있게 해준다. [5]그런 다음, 거미는 흙 조각을 실 사이의 좁은 공간을 막는 데 사용해서, 공기 방울과 수생 식물 사이에 두꺼운 닻줄을 붙인다. 이러한 방식으로, 그것은 공기 방울이 물살에 의해 씻겨나가는 것을 막기 위해 사용된 식물로의 연결을 강화한다. 다음으로, 수면과 공기 방울 사이의 반복적인 이동을 통해 공기로 저장고를 점차 부풀린다. 공기 방울이 공기로 팽창하면서, 그것은 사실상 외부 아가미가 된다.

공기 저장고가 충분히 커지면, 거미는 물속에서 사냥을 시작한다. 대부분의 시간 동안, 그것은 산소나 에너지를 거의 소모하지 않으면서, 그것의 복부를 공기 방울 내부에 위치하고 정지 상태로 참을성 있게 기다린다. 성별 간의 차이는 사냥에서 더 드러난다. [6A/6D]암컷은 공기 방울 가까이에서 사냥하는 반면, 수컷은 더 멀리 사냥하고 적극적으로 먹이를 쫓는다. [6C]먹이가 포획된 후, 그것은 공기 방울 안으로 끌려 들어가 삼켜지기 전에 제압된다. 어떤 경우에는, 먹이가 너무 커서 거미는 먹이를 잡아먹기 전에 공기 방울을 확장하는 데 약간의 노력을 기울여야 한다. 이러한 방식으로, 이 종은 그것의 서식지가 육지 포식자들로부터 보호해주기 때문에 물속에서 약 2년 동안 생존할 수 있다.

arachnid 📙거미류　　propensity 📙성향, 경향
diving bell 잠수종(종 모양의 잠수 기구)　　apparatus 📙기관, 장치
abdomen 📙복부, 배　　ensnare 📗옭아매다, (덫으로) 잡다
amalgamation 📙혼합물, 융합　　overlapping 📘겹친
silk thread (비단 같은) 거미줄　　atypical 📘이례적인, 전형적이 아닌

sexual size dimorphism 성적 크기 이형성　　diminutive 📘작은
comparatively 📙비교적　　accommodate 📗공간을 제공하다
crescent 📘초승달 모양의　　unimpeded 📘방해받지 않고
affix 📗붙이다　　inflate 📗부풀리다　　gill 📙아가미
stasis 📙정지 상태　　subdue 📗제압하다, 진압하다　　ingest 📗삼키다

1 지문의 단어 "propensity"와 의미가 가장 비슷한 것은?

　(A) 능력
　(B) 무능력
　(C) 꺼림
　(D) 경향

2 1단락에 따르면, 물거미는 다른 거미 종들과 어떻게 다른가?

　(A) 물거미는 물속에서 호흡하는 데 사용되는 아가미가 있다.
　(B) 물거미는 수영으로 강한 다리 근육을 얻는다.
　(C) 물거미는 수중 서식지에서 살아남을 수 있는 능력이 있다.
　(D) 물거미는 민물 종을 사냥할 수 있다.

3 다음 중 2단락에서 물거미의 신체적 특징으로 언급된 것은?

　(A) 높은 압력의 서식지에서 호흡하기 위한 폐를 진화시켰다.
　(B) 저장고에서 물을 밀어내기 위해 특수한 실을 만들었다.
　(C) 대기에서 공기를 포착하기 위한 털을 발달시켰다.
　(D) 폐에서 공기 저장고를 배출시켰다.

4 지문의 단어 "their"가 가리키는 것은?

　(A) 암컷
　(B) 공기 방울
　(C) 수컷
　(D) 구조물

5 4단락에 따르면, 수생 식물은 물거미에 의해 어떻게 이용되는가?

　(A) 물속에서 공기 방울의 움직임을 제한한다.
　(B) 포식자들이 공기 방울을 손상시키는 것을 막는다.
　(C) 공기 방울이 마르는 것을 방지한다.
　(D) 공기 방울을 위한 산소의 원천을 제공한다.

6 5단락에 따르면, 다음 중 물거미의 사냥 습관에 관해 사실이 아닌 것은?

　(A) 그것들의 성별에 따라 다른 사냥 습관을 보인다.
　(B) 그것들의 공기 방울 밖에 있는 먹이를 먹을 수 있다.
　(C) 그것들은 먹기 전에 먹이를 공기 방울 속으로 끌어당긴다.
　(D) 그것들 중 일부는 먹이를 찾으러 가기 위해 공기 방울을 떠난다.

Reading Practice 3 　　　　　　　본문 p. 72

1 (D)　2 (A)　3 (B)　4 (A)　5 (C)　6 (B)

석유

석유는 일반적으로 원시 해양 환경에 방대한 양으로 서식했던 단세포 플랑크톤 식물의 잔해이며 장기간의 열 및 압축 에너지에 노출되어 온 고대 유기 물질의 산물이다. 그 결과, 수백만 년 전에 거대한 수역에 덮여 있던 지역들은 세계 석유 매장량의 대부분을 포함하고 있다. 이것들 중 가장 중요한 것은 아라비아–이란 퇴적 분지이며, 알려진 액체 석유

매장량의 3분의 2 이상이 이 지역에 위치해 있다.

처음에는 광원으로 사용되었지만, 지난 100년 동안 산업화된 국가들은 경제의 모든 측면에서 주요 에너지 형태로 석유 제품에 의존하게 되었다. [3]이러한 전환은 대체로 자동차의 출현에서 기인할 수 있는데, 그 기술을 위한 신뢰할 수 있는 연료를 개발할 필요성이 그 자원의 개발 및 상업화를 위한 재정적 자극을 제공했기 때문이다. 그러나, 개발도상국의 급속한 산업화와 함께 이 에너지 자원에 대한 의존은 기존 매장량의 급격한 고갈을 초래했다. 그 결과, 현재 추출 방법의 효율성을 높이고 접근성이 낮은 매장물의 회수를 촉진하기 위한 기술 개발에 대한 광범위한 연구가 있어왔다.

생산된 석유의 대부분은 기존의 시추 방법으로 접근할 수 있는 거대한 지하 유층에서 추출된다. 이 유전들은 보통 많은 양의 천연가스를 포함하기 때문에, 극도의 압력 하에서 존재하며, 일단 유정이 뚫리면, 석유가 지표면으로 쉽게 올라간다. 1차 회수라고 알려진 이 단계의 과정은 생산자에게 가장 비용 효율적이며 특정 지역에서 전체 생산량의 약 20퍼센트를 차지한다. [4]그럼에도 불구하고, 지하 공간 내부의 압력이 일정 수준까지 떨어지면, 반드시 2차 회수 방법이 이용되어야 한다. 더 최근의 방법들은 매장물에 다시 압력을 가하기 위한 이산화탄소 주입을 수반하지만, 이것들은 전통적으로 펌프 시스템의 사용을 포함한다.

기존의 방법은 또한 해수면 아래에 위치한 것들처럼 접근성이 낮은 매장물을 이용하기 위해 성공적으로 적용되어 왔다. 이를 달성하기 위해서는, 해양 시추 플랫폼이 활용되어야 하는데, 심해 시추를 가능하게 하기 위한 부유식 플랫폼이 현재 설계되고 있기는 하지만, 이것들은 일반적으로 대륙붕에 부착된 고정식 플랫폼으로 구성된다. 그 구조물은 초기 건설과 지속적인 유지 보수 측면에서 엄청나게 비싸지만, 이 기술은 몇몇 북유럽 국가들이 지구상에서 가장 큰 것으로 입증된 북해 매장량을 활용하는 것을 가능하게 했다. 요구되는 막대한 자금 때문에, 해양 석유 시추는 가격이 수익성이 있는 수준까지 상승했을 때만 사용된다.

석유의 가격이 상승함에 따라, 연구자들은 기존의 석유 공급에 대한 대안 개발에 집중하기 시작했다. 모래, 물, 반고체 원유 형태의 역청이 포함된 오일샌드로부터 석유 제품을 생산할 가능성에 상당한 관심이 보여져 왔다. [6]역청은 점도가 매우 높아 기존의 시추 방법으로는 제거가 불가능하며, 이는 그것이 광물을 채굴할 때 사용되는 것과 유사한 과정으로 추출되어야 한다는 것을 의미한다. **일단 이것이 완료되면, 역청은 전문 정제소에서 합성 석유로 가공될 수 있다.** 그러나, 현재의 기술을 이용하면, 그 공정은 많은 양의 온실가스와 폐기물을 생산하기 때문에, 엄청나게 비용이 많이 들고 환경에 상당한 부정적 영향을 미친다.

primeval 형원시의　　thermal 형열의　　compressive 형압축의
reserves 명(석유 등의) 매장량　　sedimentary basin 퇴적 분지
transition 명전환　　be attributed to ~에서 기인하다
developing nation 개발도상국　　depletion 명고갈
consequentially 부그 결과　　extraction 명추출
recovery 명회수, 재생　　deposit 명매장물
conventional 형기존의, 전통적인　　drilling 명(지하자원을 위한) 시추
account for (비율을) 차지하다　　subterranean 형지하의
injection 명주입　　repressurize 동다시 압력을 가하다
continental shelf 대륙붕　　alternative 명대안
considerable 형상당한　　bitumen 명역청, 아스팔트
viscosity 명점도　　prohibitively 부엄청나게, 엄두를 못 낼 만큼

1 아래 문장 중 지문 속의 음영된 문장의 핵심 정보를 가장 잘 표현한 것은?

(A) 수반되는 높은 온도와 압력 때문에 석유 발생에는 많은 양의 살아 있는 유기체가 필요하다.

(B) 단세포 수생생물 종들은 광대한 석유 매장량의 형성에 필요한 방대한 양의 에너지를 생성했다.

(C) 선사시대의 바다는 석유를 생산하기 위해 필요한 지질학적 조건을 갖춘 지역의 위치를 결정했다.

(D) 오래 전에 죽은 바다 생물의 잔해에 장기간 가해진 열과 압력은 석유 발생의 원인이다.

2 지문의 단어 "these"가 가리키는 것은?

(A) 지역들

(B) 수역

(C) 년

(D) 석유 매장량

3 2단락에 따르면, 석유가 주요 연료 자원이 된 이유는?

(A) 농경 사회의 산업 확대

(B) 새로운 교통수단의 광범위한 사용

(C) 믿을 만한 광원의 필요성

(D) 개발도상국들의 급격한 경제 성장

4 3단락에 따르면, 2차 회수 방법의 사용을 필요하게 만드는 것은?

(A) 공간 압력의 손실

(B) 유해 가스의 존재

(C) 전체 생산량의 감소

(D) 석유의 부피 증가

5 네 개의 네모[■]는 다음 문장이 삽입될 수 있는 곳을 나타내고 있다.

일단 이것이 완료되면, 역청은 전문 정제소에서 합성 석유로 가공될 수 있다.

이 문장은 어디에 들어가는 것이 가장 적절한가?

6 5단락에 따르면, 역청의 높은 점도의 결과는?

(A) 유층으로의 시추가 완료되면 석유가 더 쉽게 흐르도록 해준다.

(B) 역청 추출을 위한 전통적인 시추 기술 사용을 배제한다.

(C) 역청의 제거가 상당한 해수 오염을 초래하게 한다.

(D) 주요 에너지원으로서 비효율적인 질낮은 석유를 초래한다.

iBT Reading Test 1　　본문 p. 74

1 (A)　　2 (B)　　3 (C)　　4 (C)
5 (C)　　6 (D)　　7 (B)　　8 (A)
9 (A)　　10 (C), (D), (F)

뇌의 좌우 기능 분화

뇌의 좌우 기능 분화, 즉 뇌의 좌우 반구 사이의 비대칭은 신경과학 연구의 중요한 영역이며 흔한 오해의 대상이다. 만약 사람들이 그들이 오른손잡이인지 왼손잡이인지 질문받는다면, 대부분은 "오른손잡이"라고 답할 것이다. 이것은 인간의 약 90퍼센트가 특정 작업들에서 오른손을 사용하기 때문이다. 그리고 뇌의 왼쪽이 신체의 오른쪽을 통제하고 정보를 받기 때문에, 똑같이 일반적인 가정은 대부분의 사람들이 좌뇌 우위적이라는 것이다.

[3]그러나, 사실, 사람들이 많은 일상적 작업을 수행할 때 어느 한쪽 또는

다른 쪽에 대한 선호도를 나타내지 않기 때문에, 그러한 엄격한 이분법을 제시하는 것은 과장된 말이다. 수많은 연구들은 인간 및 다른 영장류에서 작업의 유형이 뇌의 한쪽 또는 다른 쪽의 우위를 결정한다는 것을 보여주었다. ²예를 들어, 도구를 사용하는 것과 같이 더 많은 손재주를 요구하는 복잡한 작업들은 대부분의 사람들에게서 강한 좌뇌 우위 성향을 보인다. 그러나 물건을 집는 것과 같이 단순한 작업들은 전체 인구에서 어느 한쪽이나 다른 쪽에 대한 선호도를 보이지 않는다.

인간의 양쪽 뇌와 하등 생물들의 그것들을 구분하는 특징은 두 반구가 그것들 사이의 분리된 곳을 가로지르는 일련의 신경 다발로 연결되어 있다는 것이다. 이 "다리들"은 뇌의 한쪽에 의해 수신된 정보를 다른 쪽과 공유하게 해주며, 그것들 중 가장 중요한 것은 뇌량이다. 우리는 뇌량이 언어 처리에서의 그것의 역할로 인해 양쪽 뇌의 의사소통을 돕는 것을 알고 있는데, 언어 처리는 두 가지 주요 언어 영역이 모두 좌뇌에 위치하기 때문에 전통적으로 좌뇌의 노력으로 여겨져 왔다. ⁵그러나, 언어가 하나의 반구로부터의 두뇌 활동 이상을 수반한다는 사실은 외과 의사들이 발작을 완화하기 위해 뇌전증 환자들의 뇌량을 절제하는 이따금의 관행을 시작한 후에 발견되었다. 보통, 이 시술은 뇌 기능에 심각한 부작용이 없었다. 그러나, 일부 환자들의 경우, 수술 후 그들의 언어 능력이 부정적인 영향을 받았으며, 이는 언어 기능에 있어 양쪽 반구 모두 최소한 얼마간의 역할을 한다는 것을 시사한다.

대부분의 사람들이 뇌량이 절제된 후에도 정상적인 뇌 기능을 유지할 수 있다는 사실은 양쪽이 얼마나 독립적으로 기능할 수 있는지 보여주지만, 두 반구는 이전에 가정된 것보다 더 많이 상호 작용한다. 뇌 영상 기술의 발전은 연구자들로 하여금 자극이 뇌를 활성화시키는 곳을 정확히 볼 수 있게 해준다. ⁶ᴮ뇌파도(EEG)를 사용함으로써, 과학자들은 뇌의 특정 부위가 활성화될 때 빛나는 것을 볼 수 있다. ⁶ᴬ/⁶ᶜ그들은 많은 작업들이 동시의 활동이나 뇌의 두 반구 사이를 빠르게 전환하는 형태로 반구들 사이의 간여를 필요로 한다는 것을 발견했다.

예를 들어, 말하기는 뇌의 각 반구를 사용한다. **한쪽은 정확한 문장 구성을 책임지는 반면에, 다른 쪽은 적절한 강세와 억양을 담당한다.** 마찬가지로, 수학에서는, 비록 우뇌가 일련의 물체들의 양을 추정하는 것과 같은 작업에 이용되고, 좌뇌가 일반적으로 수를 세거나 자료를 암기하는 것을 담당하지만, 여러 범주의 작업들이 함께 수행되어야 하는 복잡한 문제를 풀 때는 양쪽 모두가 사용된다. 교대로든지 합동으로든지, 양쪽은 다중 작업하기 위해 효율적으로 작업량을 나눌 수 있다. 이것은 정밀한 정신 활동의 도전에 직면했을 때 뇌가 압도되는 것을 방지한다.

lateralization 휑 (뇌의) 좌우 기능 분화　　asymmetry 휑 비대칭, 불균형
hemisphere 휑 (뇌의) 반구　　assumption 휑 가정, 추정
dichotomy 휑 이분법　　overstatement 휑 과장된 말
primate 휑 영장류　　dexterity 휑 손재주　　priority 휑 우위
favorability 휑 선호도　　bilateral 휑 양쪽의　　nerve bundle 신경 다발
corpus callosum 뇌량　　endeavor 휑 노력
sever 휑 절제하다, 절단하다　　epilepsy 휑 뇌전증, 간질
seizure 휑 발작　　linguistic 휑 언어의
electroencephalogram 휑 뇌파도, 뇌전도　　simultaneous 휑 동시의
in alternation 교대로, 번갈아　　in unison 합동으로
multitask 휑 다중 작업하다　　rigorous 휑 정밀한

1　지문의 단어 "dexterity"와 의미가 가장 비슷한 것은?

　(A) 민첩
　(B) 자신감
　(C) 결단력
　(D) 힘

2　2단락에 따르면, 다음 중 대부분의 사람들에 관해 사실인 것은?

　(A) 작업에 관계없이 오른손을 더 자주 사용한다.
　(B) 복잡한 작업을 수행할 때 좌뇌가 우위적인 경향이 있다.
　(C) 왼손잡이로 키워진다면 우뇌가 우위적일 가능성이 높다.
　(D) 왼손 또는 오른손 사용 사이에서 전혀 선호도를 보이지 않는다.

3　2단락에서, 글쓴이는 오른손잡이와 왼손잡이에 대해 어떤 점을 지적하는가?

　(A) 인간과 다른 영장류 개체군에서 각각의 비율이 동등하다.
　(B) 둘 중 하나에 대한 선호는 유전적 근거가 있다.
　(C) 그들 사이의 구분은 일반적으로 과장되어 있다.
　(D) 한쪽의 다른 쪽보다 우세함은 90퍼센트의 사람들에게서 일어난다.

4　지문의 단어 "them"이 가리키는 것은?

　(A) 양쪽 뇌
　(B) 하등 생물들
　(C) 두 반구
　(D) 신경 다발

5　3단락에 따르면, 다음 중 언어가 양쪽 뇌의 참여를 수반한다는 이해를 가져온 것은?

　(A) 뇌량의 발견
　(B) 뇌전증 발작이 뇌 기능에 미치는 영향
　(C) 간헐적인 외과 수술의 결과
　(D) 뇌 영상 기술의 발전

6　4단락에 따르면, 다음 중 뇌 영상 장치가 밝혀내지 않은 것은?

　(A) 뇌의 반구들이 협력하는 정도
　(B) 서로 다른 작업에 사용되는 뇌의 특정 부분들
　(C) 뇌의 왼쪽과 오른쪽이 상호 작용하는 방식
　(D) 뇌의 각 반구에 똑같이 영향을 미치는 자극의 종류

7　5단락에서 글쓴이는 왜 말하기와 수학을 논하는가?

　(A) 뇌의 양쪽이 독립적으로 작동할 수 있다는 것을 보여주기 위해
　(B) 뇌의 양쪽 반구의 참여를 필요로 하는 작업을 강조하기 위해
　(C) 뇌 영상 기술이 작동하는 방법에 대한 몇 가지 예를 들기 위해
　(D) 뇌파도가 사용되는 주요 연구 분야를 소개하기 위해

8　지문의 단어 "rigorous"와 의미가 가장 비슷한 것은?

　(A) 힘든
　(B) 결과로서 일어나는
　(C) 보람 있는
　(D) 초급의

9　네 개의 네모[■]는 다음 문장이 삽입될 수 있는 곳을 나타내고 있다.
한쪽은 정확한 문장 구성을 책임지는 반면에, 다른 쪽은 적절한 강세와 억양을 담당한다.
이 문장은 어디에 들어가는 것이 가장 적절한가?

10　지시: 지문 요약을 위한 도입 문장이 아래에 주어져 있다. 지문의 가장 중요한 내용을 나타내는 보기 3개를 골라 요약을 완성하라. 어떤 문장은 지문에 언급되지 않은 내용이나 사소한 정보를 나타내므로 요약에 포함되지 않는다. 이 문제는 2점이다.

> 뇌의 좌우 기능 분화는 일반적으로 대중이 오해하는 현상이다.

- (C) 양쪽 뇌의 중요한 측면은 한 반구에서 다른 반구로 정보를 전달할 수 있는 신경 경로의 네트워크이다.
- (D) 뇌의 왼쪽과 오른쪽은 단독으로 기능할 수 있지만, 그것들은 이전에 여겨진 것보다 실제로 더 많이 함께 기능한다.
- (F) 대부분의 사람들에게 우위적인 손이 있는 경향은 사실이지만, 잘 쓰는 손은 오른손잡이나 왼손잡이와 같은 단순 구분에는 맞지 않는다.

(A) 세계의 대다수 사람들은 좌뇌가 우위적이고, 그 결과 그들은 오른손잡이가 된다.

(B) 연구는 뇌량이 절제된 경우에도 언어 능력이 저하되지 않는다는 것을 결정적으로 입증됐다.

(E) 양쪽 반구의 협력 없이는 사람들이 복잡한 말하기와 수학을 처리할 수 있을 가능성이 낮다.

iBT Reading Test 2 본문 p. 78

1 (A)	2 (C)	3 (B)	4 (B)
5 (B)	6 (B)	7 (D)	8 (B)
9 (A)	10 (C), (E), (F)		

토네이도

토네이도 피해 측면에서 1974년 봄은 미국 역사상 가장 파괴적인 것 중 하나였다. 4월의 이틀 동안, 148개의 개별적인 토네이도가 미국 중서부 지역을 휩쓸어, 수많은 사상자와 30억 달러 이상의 피해를 입었다. 비록 이러한 규모의 발생은 드물고, 최근의 연구는 그것들이 반복적인 500년 주기와 관련이 있다고 시사하고 있지만, 토네이도는 지구의 많은 지역에서 정기적으로 발생한다.

지방 및 국가 정부는 이러한 폭풍들이 피해를 입은 지역사회에 미치는 영향을 완화하기 위한 수단을 마련하기 위해 공동의 노력을 기울여 왔다. ³인명 피해가 확실히 제한되도록 하는 최신의 방법은 위협받는 지역의 주민들에게 다가오는 토네이도에 대한 예보를 제공하는 것이라고 오랫동안 언급되어 왔다. 결과적으로, 관련 연구는 토네이도의 강도를 정확하게 측정하는 방법을 개발하는 것뿐만 아니라 토네이도 형성의 지표와 완전히 발달된 폭풍의 특성을 분류하는 데 중점을 두었다.

흔히 "토네이도 앨리"라고 불리는 미국 내륙의 거대한 저지대는 결합하여 그 지역을 기상 이변의 비할 데 없는 발생지로 만드는 수많은 지질학적 및 기후적 특징들을 포함한다. 특히 중요한 것은 육지 고도에 변화가 없다는 것인데, 그것이 북쪽에서 오는 차고 건조한 공기와 남쪽에서 오는 따뜻하고 습한 공기의 쉬운 통과를 촉진하기 때문이다. 두 개의 뚜렷한 기단의 충돌은 토네이도의 생성으로 이어지는 공기의 지속적인 순환에 필요한 에너지를 제공하는 열의 전달을 초래한다. 한랭 전선과 온난 전선이 만나면서, 대기 중의 공기가 회전하기 시작하며, 이는 수평축을 따라 지면에 평행하게 움직이는 확장된 원기둥을 형성한다. 만약 그것이 충분히 강한 상승 기류를 만난다면, 바람의 회전이 수직축을 형성하도록 바뀔 수 있다. 결과적으로, 토네이도의 전제 조건인 회전하는 공기 기둥이 형성될 수 있는 더 높은 고도로 많은 양의 공기가 강제로 유입될 수 있다.

토네이도가 발달하면, 그것은 몇 가지 구별되는 물리적 특징을 갖게 되며, 가장 중요한 것은 토네이도가 거의 항상 격렬하다는 것이다. 북반구에서는 토네이도가 반시계 방향으로 회전하는 반면, 남반구에서

는 시계 방향으로 회전한다. 이 원형의 이동 패턴은 허리케인 같은 이유형의 다른 폭풍에서도 발견된다. 토네이도 내의 풍속은 위치에 따라 달라지는데, 주변부의 바람은 초당 최대 160미터에 이르고 중심부의 수직 상승 기류는 초당 80미터까지 이른다. 기후학자들에 의해 응결 깔때기라고 불리는 토네이도의 독특한 모양은 사실 모구름에서 아래로 뻗어나가는 점점 가늘어지는 기둥 형태의 물방울과 퇴적물의 혼합물이다. ⁶가늘어진 형태는 폭풍이 거세질 때 덜 뚜렷해지며, 그 현상의 가장 강력한 예는 넓은 원기둥을 닮아 있다.

비록 그러한 시각적 지표가 서로 다른 토네이도의 상대적인 강도에 대한 대략적인 지침을 제공하지만, 과학자들은 그것들의 강도를 정확하게 판단하기 위해 후지타 등급에 의존한다. ⁸후지타 시스템은 직접 풍속을 측정하지는 않지만 건물이나 교량 같은 건축물에 토네이도가 입히는 피해를 근거로 풍속을 추정한다. 후지타 등급에서, 토네이도 등급은 점진적인 연속을 따르는데, F1이 가장 약하고 F5가 가장 강하다. 극소수만이 F5로서 분류되기 위해 필요한 격렬함의 수준에 도달하는데, 이 폭풍들은 거의 상상할 수 없는 파괴를 할 수 있기 때문에 이는 다행스러운 것이다. 시속 418킬로미터 이상의 풍속으로, 그것들은 자동차와 다른 거대한 물체들을 들어 올려 100미터가 넘는 거리를 던질 수 있다.

ravage ⑧휩쓸다, 파괴하다 casualties ⑲사상자, 인명 피해
magnitude ⑲규모 recurring ⑱반복적인 concerted ⑱공동의
alleviate ⑧완화하다 advance notice 예보, 사전 통고
indicator ⑲지표 colloquially ⑨흔히 ~이라고 불리는
unparalleled ⑱비할 데 없는, 유례없는
breeding ground 발생지, 번식지 facilitate ⑧촉진하다
horizontal ⑱수평의 updraft ⑲상승 기류 vertical ⑱수직의
prerequisite ⑲전제 조건 distinguishing ⑱구별되는, 특징적인
cyclonic ⑱격렬한 counterclockwise ⑨반시계 방향으로
clockwise ⑨시계 방향으로 peripheral ⑱주변부의
tapered ⑱점점 가늘어지는 pronounced ⑱뚜렷한, 두드러진
inflict upon ~에 피해를 입히다 graduated ⑱점진적인

1 글쓴이는 왜 "a recurring 500-year cycle"을 언급하는가?
(A) 특정 악천후의 드문 빈도를 강조하기 위해
(B) 일종의 폭풍으로 인한 파괴를 강조하기 위해
(C) 토네이도가 예측하기 어렵지 않다는 것을 암시하기 위해
(D) 기후학 분야의 최근 발전을 설명하기 위해

2 지문의 단어 "concerted"와 의미가 가장 비슷한 것은?
(A) 준비된
(B) 구조화된
(C) 통일된
(D) 변경된

3 2단락에 따르면, 토네이도로 인한 인명 피해를 제한하는 가장 효과적인 방법은?
(A) 다가오는 토네이도 인근 지역 주민들을 대피시키는 것
(B) 사람들에게 접근하는 토네이도에 대한 예보를 제공하는 것
(C) 토네이도를 일으킬 수 있는 폭풍의 강도를 정확하게 측정하는 것
(D) 가능한 한 많은 지역사회에 자동 경고 시스템을 설치하는 것

4 아래 문장 중 지문 속의 음영된 문장의 핵심 정보를 가장 잘 표현한 것은? 오답은 문장의 의미를 크게 바꾸거나 핵심 정보를 생략한다.
(A) 토네이도는 엄청난 양의 에너지를 발생시켜 종종 별개의 기단이

충돌하여 기온의 급격한 상승을 초래한다.

(B) 기단 간에 열이 교환됨에 따라, 결과로 생성되는 에너지는 토네이도 발달을 촉진하는 방식으로 공기를 회전시킨다.

(C) 일단 토네이도가 형성되면, 바람의 원형 운동은 강도를 얻기 위해 에너지를 전달해야 하는 고온과 저온 기류를 초래한다.

(D) 토네이도는 많은 양의 에너지를 필요로 하지만, 그것들은 또한 많은 양의 공기 이동에서 발생하는 열에 의존한다.

5 지문의 단어 "it"이 가리키는 것은?

(A) 대기
(B) 원기둥
(C) 지면
(D) 축

6 4단락에 따르면, 응결 깔때기의 점점 가늘어지는 기둥의 특징은 무엇인가?

(A) 가장 강한 바람은 그것의 가장 아래쪽에 있다.
(B) 폭풍이 강해짐에 따라 그 모양이 변한다.
(C) 원기둥에서 퇴적물과 물방울을 배출한다.
(D) 토네이도의 회전 방향은 그것의 크기에 따라 달라진다.

7 지문의 단어 "graduated"와 의미가 가장 비슷한 것은?

(A) 모범적인
(B) 진보한
(C) 제한적인
(D) 점진적인

8 5단락에 따르면, 토네이도의 강도는

(A) 서로 다른 폭풍의 강도를 비교해서 결정된다
(B) 결과로 나타나는 파괴로부터 공기 속도를 추론해서 결정된다
(C) 직접 회전 속도를 측정해서 결정된다
(D) 토네이도의 물리적 형태를 조사해서 결정된다

9 네 개의 네모[■]는 다음 문장이 삽입될 수 있는 곳을 나타내고 있다.

이 원형의 이동 패턴은 허리케인 같은 이 유형의 다른 폭풍에서도 발견된다.

이 문장은 어디에 들어가는 것이 가장 적절한가?

10 지시: 지문 요약을 위한 도입 문장이 아래에 주어져 있다. 지문의 가장 중요한 내용을 나타내는 보기 3개를 골라 요약을 완성하라. 어떤 문장은 지문에 언급되지 않은 내용이나 사소한 정보를 나타내므로 요약에 포함되지 않는다. 이 문제는 2점이다.

> 토네이도의 파괴적인 잠재력은 이 기상 이변 현상에 대한 광범위한 연구로 이어졌다.
>
> · (C) 토네이도는 지형과 기후가 한랭 전선과 온난 전선 사이의 특정 상호작용에 도움이 되는 지역에서 형성된다.
> · (E) 토네이도는 관찰자가 쉽게 식별할 수 있도록 하는 많은 물리적 및 행동적 특성을 가지고 있다.
> · (F) 토네이도의 강도는 그것들이 일으키는 건축적 손상을 기준으로 토네이도를 분류함으로써 간접적으로 결정된다.

(A) 최근 몇 년간 미국 내륙에서 발생하는 토네이도의 수가 크게 증가했다.
(B) 토네이도에 의해 발생되는 파괴는 광범위한 경고 시스템을 개발한 지역에서 덜 심각하다.
(D) 토네이도는 그것들의 형성이 일관된 일정을 따르기 때문에 예측하기 쉽다.

Vocabulary Review
본문 p.82

1 overstatement 2 auxiliary 3 unimpeded
4 diminutive 5 subterranean 6 counterclockwise
7 (C) 8 (D) 9 (A) 10 (D)
11 (B) 12 (C) 13 (A) 14 (C)

CHAPTER 05
Negative Fact

Example
본문 p.85

1 (D) 2 (C)

수생 식충 식물

모든 식물은 자가 영양성인데, 이는 그것들이 자신의 양분을 생산할 수 있다는 것을 의미한다. 가장 흔한 방법은 햇빛을 흡수하여 그것의 청색과 적색의 전자기 스펙트럼을 에너지로 변환하는 녹색 광합성 색소인 엽록소를 이용하는 광합성이다. 이 과정은 햇빛, 물, 이산화탄소를 필요로 하지만, 대부분의 사람들은 이것들이 식물이 필요로 하는 것의 전부라고 잘못 생각하는데, 그러나, 그것은 또한 특정한 일군의 비타민과 영양소를 필요로 하며, 만약 식물이 토양이나 비를 통해 그것들을 얻을 수 없다면, 그것은 다른 수단을 통해 그것들을 찾으려고 할 수 있다.

[1C]일부 영양소, 특히 질소에 대한 접근이 줄어든 경우, 식물은 곤충이나 다른 작은 생물체를 소화하고 그것들의 부드러운 몸에서 영양분을 흡수해서 그것들을 얻어야 할 수도 있다. [1A/1B]이 식물들은 보통 습지의 습한 환경에서 자라며, 일부는 물속에서 일부는 육지에서 자라고, 그것들은 먹이를 유인하고, 포획하고, 섭취한다는 점에서 육식성 또는 식충성이다.

수중 식충 식물은 일반적으로 호수와 개울의 가장자리를 따라 있는 얕은 물에서 발견된다. 예를 들어, 통발은 연약한 잎을 따라 위치한 곱슬하지만 뻣뻣한 털이 줄기에 있어 특수한 여닫이 덮개를 숨기는 복잡한 방법으로 수생 곤충을 잡는다. 생물체에 의해 건드려지면, 그 털들은 그 식물에게 그것의 존재를 알리는 방아쇠 역할을 한다. [2B]다락문처럼 출입문이 열리고 물이 빈 주머니로 세차게 흘러들며, 그것의 힘은 희생물을 관다발 구조 안으로 넣은 다음 출입문을 찰칵 닫아 곤충을 안에 가둔다. [2A/2D]이 동작은 100분의 1초도 채 안 되는 시간에 일어나며 뚜렷한 펑 소리를 낸다. 갇힌 먹이는 결국 죽고, 박테리아에 의해 분해되며, 화합물은 주머니의 벽에 있는 세포에 의해 흡수된다.

carnivorous 형식충의, 육식성의 autotrophic 형자가 영양성의
photosynthesis 명광합성 chlorophyll 명엽록소
pigment 명색소 electromagnetic 형전자기의
erroneously 부잘못, 틀리게 attain 통얻다
insectivorous 형식충성의, 곤충을 먹는 bladder 명주머니
vascular 형관다발의

1 2단락에 따르면, 다음 중 식충 식물에 관해 사실이 아닌 것은?

(A) 높은 습도가 특징인 지역에서 자란다

(B) 육지와 물 모두에서 발견될 수 있다
(C) 곤충과 작은 동물들에서 질소를 얻는다
(D) 양분을 얻기 위해 다른 생물체들과 협력한다

2 다음 중 통발에 관해 언급되지 않은 것은?

(A) 먹이를 포획할 때 독특한 소리를 낸다.
(B) 곤충을 함정으로 몰아넣기 위해 물을 사용한다.
(C) 곤충을 유인하기 위해 연약한 잎을 사용한다.
(D) 단 1초도 안 되는 순간에 먹이를 덫으로 잡는다.

Reading Practice 1 　　　　본문 p.86

1 (A)　　2 (C)　　3 (D)　　4 (C)　　5 (D)　　6 (D)

조류 비행의 진화

조류의 기원에 대한 지배적인 과학 이론은 그것들이 공룡에서 진화했다는 것이며, 이를 뒷받침하는 강력한 해부학적 및 고생물학적 증거가 있다. ²가장 주목할 만한 점은, 화석 기록이 일부 수각류, 즉 두 발로 직립 보행했던 작은 공룡들의 다양한 무리가 특정 육식성 공룡과 조류 사이의 형태학적 중간 단계에 해당함을 분명히 한다는 것이다. 종종 "최초의 새"라고 불리는 '시조새'는 이빨과 긴 꼬리 같은 공룡의 특징을 유지하면서도 날개와 큰 깃털을 포함한 조류 같은 특징을 지닌 동물 중 하나였다.

얼핏 보기에, 조류와 그것들의 조상이 비행을 위해 특별히 깃털을 발달시킨 것이 분명해 보이겠지만, 논리적으로는 둘 사이에는 필연적인 상관관계가 없는데, 결국 박쥐는 훌륭한 비행사이지만 깃털이 없고, 타조는 깃털이 있지만 날 수 없기 때문이다. 어떤 경우이든, 깃털은 생존 상의 이점을 제공했고 궁극적으로 상승력을 발생시키고 동력 비행에서 안정성과 기동성을 만드는 데 유용해졌다. 그러나 그것들은 조류가 그렇게 능숙한 비행사가 되게 한 광범위한 해부학적 변화의 일부에 불과했다. ⁴ᴬ그것들의 몸을 하늘 높이 유지하기에 충분한 추진력을 만들어내기 위해, 조류는 강한 가슴 근육을 발달시켜야 했다. ⁴ᴮ차례로, 더 큰 근육을 지탱하기 위해 가슴뼈가 더 크고 튼튼해지는 것이 필요했다. 비행 최적화를 위한 다른 골격계 변형은 매우 유연한 위시본, 짧아진 허벅지 뼈, 아래 팔의 길어진 뼈, 변형된 손목뼈를 포함했다. ⁴ᴰ전체적으로, 뼈가 가늘어지고 속이 비어 가벼워졌지만 힘을 잃지는 않았다.

지속적인 동력 비행은 높은 신진대사를 필요로 하는 에너지 집약적 활동이기 때문에 생리학적 변화도 마찬가지로 중요했다. 현대의 척추동물에서 그 정도로 높은 신진대사율은 포유류와 조류 같은 온혈 동물에 국한된다. 과학자들은 공룡이 냉혈 동물이었는지 온혈 동물이었는지 논쟁하지만, 그들이 일반적으로 동의하는 바는 조류의 조상이 비행을 시작하기 전에 이미 온혈 동물이 되었거나 내온성이 비행 능력과 함께 생겨났다는 것이다. 온혈 동물로서, 최초의 조류는 근육이 회복되도록 반복적으로 멈출 필요 없이 상당한 기간 동안 날개를 퍼덕일 만큼 충분히 높은 신진대사율을 가지고 있었다. **이 향상된 지구력은 비행에 필요한 유산소 호흡을 제공하는 매우 높은 비율의 붉은 근육 섬유의 발달 덕분이었다.**

그럼에도 불구하고, 이러한 신체 변화 및 특징들은 조류가 정확히 어떻게 처음 날기 시작했는지 설명하지 못한다. 이 능력의 기원에 대한 의견은 전통적으로 두 대립되는 집단에서 나왔다. 첫 번째는 나무에 사는, 조류 같은 동물이 나무에서 혹은 사이를 뛰어다니면서 시작된 점진

적인 행동적 발달을 겪었다고 주장한다. 시간이 지남에 따라, 이 원시 동물은 활공하고 조종하며 날개를 퍼덕이는 법을 배웠고, 궁극적으로 완전히 날개로 비행하는 법을 배웠다. 다른 파는 조류의 조상이 땅에서 두 발로 살았으며, 종종 먹이가 도망치기 전에 잡기 위해 달리거나 뛰어오르는 능력을 이용했다고 주장한다. 예를 들어, 뛰어오르는 것은 키가 더 큰 동물, 또는 나뭇가지에 있거나 큰 바위 위에 앉은 먹이를 공격할 때 이 포식자들에게 유익했을 것이다.

조류가 어떻게 날 수 있는 능력을 발달시켰는지에 관계없이, 변화는 처음에는 점진적으로 유지되었다. ⁶ᴬ/⁶ᴮ/⁶ᶜ'시조새'는 거의 확실히 새처럼 날 수 있었으나 강력한 비행사는 아니었고, 수중 다이빙 새인 '헤스페로르니스'와 키가 2미터가 넘었고 매우 빠르게 달릴 수 있었던 조류 육지 포식자인 '디아트리마'는 여전히 날지 못했다. 그러나 백악기 후기에 더 많은 종들이 진화함에 따라 조류 비행은 상당히 다양해졌다. 조류는 훌륭한 비행사가 되어 지구 각지로 퍼졌고, 그것들의 비행 기술을 연마하고 오늘날 그것들이 차지하고 있는 각각의 특정 생태적 지위에서 생존 기회를 최대화하기 위해 그것들을 수정했다.

anatomical ⑧해부학적인　　paleontological ⑧고생물학적인
theropod ⑨수각류(두 발로 보행한 육식공룡)
Archaeopteryx ⑨시조새　　assume ⑧(특징을) 지니다, 띠다
inevitable ⑧필연적인, 불가피한　　correlation ⑨상관 관계
maneuverability ⑨기동성, 조종성　　aloft ⑨하늘 높이
wishbone ⑨위시본(조류의 목과 가슴 사이의 V자형 뼈)
elongated ⑧길어진　　alteration ⑨변화, 개조
metabolism ⑨신진대사　　endotherm ⑨온열 동물, 정온 동물
ectotherm ⑨냉혈 동물, 변온 동물　　commence ⑧시작하다
primordial ⑧원시적인　　exploit ⑧이용하다　　disperse ⑧퍼지다
hone ⑧(기술을) 연마하다　　niche ⑨생태적 지위, 틈새

1 지문의 단어 "assumed"와 의미가 가장 비슷한 것은?

(A) 획득했다
(B) 모방했다
(C) 복제했다
(D) 생산했다

2 1단락에 따르면, 다음 중 화석 기록이 일부 수각류에 관해 나타내는 것은?

(A) 꼬리와 이빨을 잃은 최초의 공룡들이었다.
(B) 그것들의 행동은 공룡보다 조류와 더 비슷했다.
(C) 그것들의 신체 구조는 조류와 공룡의 신체 구조 중간에 있었다.
(D) 깃털을 발달시킨 마지막 공룡들 중 하나였다.

3 지문의 단어 "they"가 가리키는 것은?

(A) 박쥐
(B) 비행사
(C) 타조
(D) 깃털

4 다음 중 2단락에서 조류의 비행에 기여한 해부학적 변화로 언급되지 않은 것은?

(A) 가슴 근육이 더 튼튼해졌다.
(B) 가슴뼈가 커졌다.
(C) 아래 팔이 짧아졌다.
(D) 뼈가 가늘어지고 속이 비게 되었다.

5 네 개의 네모[■]는 다음 문장이 삽입될 수 있는 곳을 나타내고 있다.

이 향상된 지구력은 비행에 필요한 유산소 호흡을 제공하는 매우 높은 비율의 붉은 근육 섬유의 발달 덕분이었다.

이 문장은 어디에 들어가는 것이 가장 적절한가?

6 5단락에 따르면, 다음 중 디아트리마에 관해 사실이 아닌 것은?

(A) 일반적인 사람보다 키가 컸다.
(B) 육지에서 빠르게 움직일 수 있었다.
(C) 결코 날 수 있는 능력을 발달시키지 못했다.
(D) 주로 수생동물을 사냥했다.

Reading Practice 2
본문 p. 88

1 (B) 2 (C) 3 (B) 4 (C) 5 (D) 6 (A)

이란의 유목

고대 이란에서, 농경은 지리적 제약에 의해 방해받았다. 이란고원은 대규모 농경 정착지에 필요한 주요 강과 다른 천연 수원이 부족했다. 국가의 대부분이 경작될 수 없고 방목에만 적합했기 때문에, 유목은 이란의 초기 역사에서 유일하게 지속되는 농경 관행이 되었다.

유목은 그것을 하는 사람들에게 많은 경제적 이득을 주었다. 강우량이 충분한 곳에서 유목민들은 일정 기간 정착할 수 있었지만, 대부분의 메마른 지형에서는 초목이 드문드문 분포되어 있었기 때문에, 하나의 목초지는 그들의 가축 떼를 오래 부양할 수 없었다. 가축 떼는 유목민들에게 고기와 유제품뿐만 아니라 다양한 직물 생산을 위한 양모와 가죽을 제공했기 때문에 매우 중요했다. 이 상품들은 수메르로부터 곡물 등 다른 상품들과 거래되었다. 필수적인 상품과 재료의 생산자로서, 유목민들은 이란의 영구적인 정착지 발전에 중요한 역할을 했다. ²그들의 정착 공동체들과의 교류는 유목민과 정착민 사이에서 이란 역사 전반에 걸쳐 일관되게 유지된 경제적 상호 의존성을 만들어냈다.

어느 시점(아마 약 2700년 전)에, 페르시아 제국의 사람들은 그들이 지역의 수원 없이 땅을 경작할 수 있게 해주는 기술적 돌파구를 마련했다. 이것은 더 높은 고도의 지점에서 더 낮은 고도의 지점에 있는 배출구로 물을 돌리기 위해 운하를 사용한 관개 및 물관리 시스템인 "카나트"였다. 카나트 시스템은 많은 수직 통로를 포함했는데, 그것들은 간격을 두고 배치되어 지하 통로에 연결되었다. ³땅의 자연적인 경사로 인해 중력이 물을 언덕 아래로 운반할 수 있었기 때문에 펌프는 필요하지 않았다.

카나트 시스템은 영구적이거나 반영구적인 농경 공동체를 형성하는 것을 더 쉽게 만들었지만, 유목민들은 계속해서 이란 정치 문제 뒤에서 주요 원동력이 되었다. 그들은 부족 연합을 통해 이란의 역사와 문화에 흔적을 남겼으며, 그것들 중 일부는 자율적이고 고도로 조직적이었다. ⁵ᴮ강한 지도자들을 가진 부족들은 전통적인 이란 정치에서 상당한 영향력을 미쳤으며, 그들의 세력은 많은 기병대를 양성하고 유지하는 능력에 달려 있었다. ⁵ᴬ/⁵ᶜ유목민들의 기술은 쉽게 군사 활동으로 전환되었고, 가장 성공적인 부족들은 경쟁 부족들을 정복함으로써 그 땅의 필수적인 수자원들을 포함하여 넓은 영토를 장악할 수 있었다. 정착 공동체들은 유목민 부족들의 세력에 필적할 수 없었는데, 이는 대체로 그들의 적은 수와 군사 작전 참여를 꺼리는 것 때문이었다.

19세기 말, 이란의 많은 부분은 강력한 유목민 부족들의 지배하에 있었다. 그러나, 20세기의 첫 4분의 1이 지난 후, 유목민들은 내부 및 외부 세력으로부터 점점 더 많은 압력을 받게 되었다. ⁶ᴮ/⁶ᶜ많은 유목민들

이 영구적인 정착지로 이끌렸고, 이란 민족의식의 고양은 국가적 단결과 정착 공동체를 선호하는 이란 지도부의 파벌들을 만들었다. ⁶ᴰ이 집단들은 유목민 부족들을 안정성에 대한 위협으로 간주했고, 각 가정에 토지에 대한 권리를 부여하여 유목민들의 생활 방식을 억압하려고 했다. 게다가, 현대적인 기계화된 군사 기술의 출현은 강력한 중앙집권적 정부가 유목민들에게 그것의 의지를 행사하는 것을 가능하게 했고, 세력을 중앙집권화하고 정착 문명을 확립하려는 이러한 노력은 압도적으로 성공적이었다. 그 결과, 전통적으로 이란 인구를 구성했던 유목민 대다수는 20세기 후반에 인구의 5퍼센트 미만으로 줄어들었다.

nomadic 휑유목의 pastoralism 몡목축 hamper 통방해하다
constraint 몡제약, 제한 settlement 몡정착지
grazing 몡방목, 목축 sparse 휑드문드문한
pasture 몡목초지, 초원 herd 몡(가축의) 떼, 무리
permanent 휑영구적인 sedentary 휑정착하는
interdependence 몡상호 의존성 migrant 휑유목하는, 이주하는
breakthrough 몡돌파구 divert 통(방향을) 돌리다
at intervals 간격을 두고 cavalry 몡기병대
reluctance 몡꺼리는 것 faction 몡파벌, 분파
stability 몡안정성 overwhelmingly 뿐압도적으로

1 지문의 단어 "hampered"와 의미가 가장 비슷한 것은?

(A) 촉진되다
(B) 방해받다
(C) 확대되다
(D) 영감받다

2 2단락에 따르면, 다음 중 이란의 대부분의 역사에서 계속 유지되었던 것은?

(A) 지역민들은 수메르의 곡물과 같은 외국 상품에 크게 의존했다.
(B) 다양한 주변국의 상인들은 이란의 지역 시장을 방문했다.
(C) 유목민들과 정착 공동체들은 상업을 위해 서로 의존했다.
(D) 유목민과 정착민은 경제적 목표가 상충하는 경향이 있었다.

3 3단락에 따르면, 카나트에서의 펌프 사용은 왜 불필요했는가?

(A) 물이 쉽게 자연 운하로 돌려졌다.
(B) 중력이 물을 언덕 아래로 움직였다.
(C) 수직 통로가 손으로 접근할 수 있을 정도로 얕았다.
(D) 녹은 눈과 계절성 비로 통로가 가득 찼다.

4 지문의 단어 "their"가 가리키는 것은?

(A) 넓은 영토
(B) 수자원들
(C) 정착 공동체들
(D) 유목민 부족들

5 4단락에서, 다음 중 유목민들이 사회에 영향을 미친 방법으로 언급되지 않은 것은?

(A) 군사력으로 경쟁 부족들을 압도한 것
(B) 상당한 규모의 기병을 보유함으로써 정치적 영향력을 행사한 것
(C) 중요한 수자원을 장악한 것
(D) 우수한 농경 기술을 개발한 것

6 다음 중 5단락에서 유목민 부족의 세력과 영향력 쇠퇴의 이유로 언급되지 않은 것은?

(A) 국제 지도자들은 이란인들이 정착 공동체를 형성하도록 압력을 가했다.

(B) 유목민들은 영구적인 공동체에 정착했다.
(C) 이란 지도자들은 정착 공동체를 선호하는 민족주의 정책을 추진했다.
(D) 각 가정에 토지에 대한 권리가 부여되었다.

Reading Practice 3
본문 p. 90

1 (D)　　2 (B)　　3 (C)　　4 (A)　　5 (C)　　6 (D)

공기에 대한 역사적 관점

오늘날, 화학자들은 공기를 기체의 혼합물로 생각하지만, 17세기에는 소수의 과학자만이 공기를 액체 및 고체와 유사한 측정 가능한 실체로 보기 시작했다. 어쨌든, 물이나 바위를 관찰하는 것은 간단한 문제였지만, 기체는 실험 가능한 범주 밖에 있는 것으로 여겨졌다. ²개념적으로, 반 헬몬트의 기체와 공기의 구분은 기념비적인 발전이었지만, 그것은 기체를 조작하는 것은 불가능하다는 많은 화학자들의 믿음으로 인해 완화되었다.

그럼에도 불구하고, 공기에 대한 이해의 초기 진척은 17세기에 존 메이오에 의해 일어났으며, 그는 불꽃뿐만 아니라 식물과 동물도 밀폐된 컵 아래에 갇히면 결국 죽는다는 것을 밝혀냈다. 그는 호흡과 연소에 의해 공기의 양이 감소한다고 결론지었고, 두 과정 모두 공기에서 동일한 입자들을 빼앗았다고 추론했다. ³메이오의 실험은 그로 하여금 생명과 연소에 필요한 공기의 공통 요소가 있다고 믿게 했다. 메이오는 산소와 이산화탄소를 발견하기 직전이었던 것으로 보인다. 그러나, 그의 연구는 거의 한 세기 동안 크게 무시당했고, 그 기간 동안 필적할 만한 어떠한 진전도 이루어지지 않았다.

실험 기구와 관련하여, 1700년대 초반에 화학에서의 중요한 혁신은 스티븐 헤일스에 의해 제공되었다. ⁴ᴮ/⁴ᴰ헤일스에게 측정이란 자연 세계를 이해하는 근본적인 도구였고, 그는 다른 과학자들에게 공기를 양적으로 간주할 것을 권고했다. 헤일스는 특히 다양한 물질이 연소할 때 방출되는 공기의 양을 밝혀내는 데 관심이 있었다. ⁴ᶜ이 측정을 수행하기 위해 그는 기체 채취용 수조라고 불리는 기구를 개발했다. 그것은 연소된 물질의 배출물을 플라스크 안으로 옮겨 물을 대체하도록 기체가 유리관을 통해 물통 안에 잠긴 뒤집힌 플라스크에 전달되는 체계였다. 따라서, 물질 속에 갇힌 공기의 양은 방출되어 측정될 수 있었다.

헤일스의 장치는 18세기에 있었던 실험들의 물결에 영감을 주었으며, 기체 수용이라는 두 번째 편리한 용도가 있음이 발견되었다. ⁶ᴬ집단적으로 기체 화학자들로 알려진 한 무리의 과학자들은 비슷한 장치들을 이용하여 다양한 "공기들"을 분리해 설명하기 시작했다. 메이오의 "니트로 공기 입자"(산소), 조지프 블랙의 "고정된 공기"(이산화탄소), 헨리 캐번디시의 "인화성 공기"(수소)는 모두 "유일한 공기"라는 공기에 대한 관점에서 "공기들" 중 하나라는 관점으로의 개념적 변화를 나타냈다. 캐번디시는 전기 스파크가 있는 데서 수소와 산소를 혼합하여 수증기를 만들 수 있었는데, 이는 공기와 물이 둘 다 고대부터 추정되어온 것처럼 근본적인 원소가 아님을 분명히 입증했다.

⁶ᴮ기체 화학자들의 유산은 후세에 잊히지 않았다. 그들의 방법과 기구는 여전히 실험실에서 사용되며 교육 및 실험 화학의 주요 요소가 되었다. 그러나, 그들의 모든 업적에도 불구하고, 이 영국인들은 물질의 기체 상태를 완전히 파악할 수 없었고, 이러한 무능력함은 그들이 여전히 널리 받아들여지고 있던 플로지스톤설 내에서 수행했다는 사실 때문이었다. 플로지스톤설에 따르면, 불 같은 근본적인 요소가 연소를 통

해 모든 가연성 물질로부터 방출되었다. 따라서 기체 화학자들은 일부 금속은 연소될 때 무게가 줄어들기보다는 증가한다는 사실을 깨닫고 혼란스러워했다. ⁶ᶜ산화가 완전히 설명되지 않았음에도 불구하고, 18세기 전반에 걸쳐 플로지스톤은 지배적인 이론으로 남아 있었다. 화학 혁명으로 알려진 시대를 열 중대한 도약을 하는 것은 프랑스 화학자 앙투안 라부아지에에게 남겨졌다.

perspective 명 관점　　measurable 형 측정 가능한
entity 명 실체, 존재　　monumental 형 기념비적인, 엄청난
breakthrough 명 (과학적) 발전　　temper 동 완화하다
manipulate 동 조작하다　　expire 동 소멸하다, 죽다
respiration 명 호흡　　combustion 명 연소　　deprive 동 빼앗다
constituent 명 요소, 성분　　on the verge of ~의 직전에
comparable 형 필적할 만한　　furnish 동 제공하다
quantitatively 부 양적으로　　pneumatic 형 기체의
inverted 형 뒤집힌　　submerge 동 물에 잠기게 하다
discharge 명 배출물　　application 명 용도　　posterity 명 후세, 후대
staple 명 주요 요소　　oxidation 명 산화　　momentous 형 중대한
usher in ~을 열다, 시작하게 하다

1　지문의 단어 "monumental"과 의미가 가장 비슷한 것은?
　(A) 독창적인
　(B) 상대적인
　(C) 논란의 여지가 있는
　(D) 중요한

2　1단락에서, 다음 중 글쓴이가 화학자들이 공기를 측정 가능하다고 간주하지 않은 이유로 언급한 것은?
　(A) 반 헬몬트의 결론에 회의적이었다.
　(B) 기체가 통제될 수 있다고 믿지 않았다.
　(C) 실험적인 방법은 무시되었다.
　(D) 화학은 단지 미신으로 여겨졌다.

3　2단락에 따르면, 메이오의 실험은
　(A) 연소가 공기로부터의 입자 방출에 의해 야기된다는 발견으로 이어졌다
　(B) 산소와 이산화탄소가 공기의 기본적인 구성 요소라는 발견으로 이어졌다
　(C) 유기체와 불꽃 모두 공기 없이 존속할 수 없다는 발견으로 이어졌다
　(D) 식물과 동물 모두 공기를 빼앗겼을 때 빠르게 죽는다는 발견으로 이어졌다

4　다음 중 3단락에서 헤일스의 과학적 견해와 실험과 관련하여 언급되지 않은 것은?
　(A) 다른 과학자들의 결론을 반박하려고 노력했다.
　(B) 자연을 측정되어야 하는 것으로 여겼다.
　(C) 그 실험을 수행하기 위한 기구를 만들었다.
　(D) 다른 과학자들이 공기를 양적 방식으로 관찰하도록 독려했다.

5　아래 문장 중 지문 속의 음영된 문장의 핵심 정보를 가장 잘 표현한 것은?
　(A) 기체 상태의 물질에 대한 그들의 업적 때문에, 이 영국인들은 널리 지지를 받고 있는 이론을 넘어설 수 없었다.
　(B) 이 영국인들은 비록 성공적이었지만, 당시 널리 받아들여졌던 플로지스톤설에 기체를 통합하는 데 실패했다.
　(C) 그들의 업적에도 불구하고, 이 영국인들은 플로지스톤설에 의해 제한을 받았기 때문에 기체를 완전히 이해할 수 없었다.

(D) 그들의 업적에도 불구하고, 이 영국인들은 플로지스톤을 믿었기 때문에 물질의 기체 상태를 이해하는 데 거의 기여하지 못했다.

6 4단락과 5단락에 따르면, 다음 중 기체 화학자들에 관해 사실이 아닌 것은?

(A) 기체를 분리하기 위해 기구를 사용했다.
(B) 화학에 오래 지속되는 영향을 미쳤다.
(C) 금속의 산화를 설명할 수 없었다.
(D) 그들은 실험에서 협력했다.

iBT Reading Test 1 본문 p. 92

1 (C)   2 (B)   3 (A)   4 (A)
5 (D)   6 (B)   7 (B)   8 (B)
9 (B)   10 (C), (D), (E)

이누이트족 예술

이누이트족은 캐나다와 알래스카의 북극 지역에 거주하는 문화적으로 동질적인 토착민들을 묘사하기 위해 사용되는 포괄적인 용어이다. 1700년대 후반은 이 사람들의 문화사에 중대한 변화를 나타냈다. ³ᴰ이는 유럽의 모피 무역상들이 이누이트족과의 수익성 높은 흰여우 모피 무역에서 이익을 얻기 위해 북쪽으로 이동하기 시작한 최초의 시기였는데, 그들의 원시적인 경제는 수백 년 동안 포획, 포경, 사냥에 집중되어 있었다.

³ᴮ그러나, 흰여우 남획이 결국 무역의 붕괴로 이어지자, 이누이트족은 경제적 어려움과 대규모 기아에 직면했다. ³ᶜ캐나다 대법원의 판결이 조약에 의해 교육 및 의료 서비스를 보장받는 캐나다의 다른 토착민들과 동등한 권리와 특권을 이누이트족에게 부여하기 전까지 이 심각한 상황은 지속되었다. 안타깝게도, 그것은 그들에게 새로운 수입원을 제공하지 못했고, 그들이 전통적인 유목 생활 방식에서 영구적인 마을로 빠르게 전환함에 따라, 원로들은 공동체를 부양할 새로운 방법을 모색했다.

유명한 토론토 예술가 제임스 휴스턴이 일부 북부 정착지들을 방문하여 마을 사람들에 의해 만들어진 부적과 도구에 관심을 가졌을 때 한 가지 선택지가 자신을 드러냈다. 이누이트족은 상품으로서의 예술의 개념을 가지고 있지 않았다. ⁴그들의 조각과 에칭은 장식용으로 소규모로 제작되었고, 휴스턴은 그 작품들에 깊은 인상을 받았으며 그것들이 고유한 미적 가치를 지니고 있다고 믿었다. 그는 이것들 중 몇 개를 그의 미술관으로 가져와 전시했고 비평가들의 호평을 받았다.

⁵ᶜ처음에는, 그 작품들은 조잡했으며 상아, 돌, 드물게는 나무 등 북극에서 구할 수 있는 재료를 활용했다. ⁵ᴮ가장 중요한 것은, 이 작품들이 유목민들의 나머지 개인 물건들과 함께 이곳저곳으로 쉽게 운반될 수 있을 만큼 충분히 작았다는 점이다. **휴대할 수 있는 물건들을 소유하는 것은 더 적은 소지품들이 남겨진다는 것을 의미하기 때문에 이것은 편리할 뿐만 아니라 낭비를 줄였다.** ⁵ᴬ대부분의 예술은 칼의 손잡이 같은 실용적인 물건들을 장식하기 위해 행해졌지만, 영국인들에 의해 그들에게 소개된 카드 게임의 진행을 쉽게 하기 위해 간단하게 디자인된 크리비지 점수판도 있었다. 몇몇 작품들은 친척이나 신뢰할 수 있는 거래 상대자에게 주는 기념품으로서 제작되었고, 이것들은 소중한 소유물이었다.

특히, 이 후자 범주의 물품들은 매우 시장성이 높은 것으로 드러났는데, 이는 주로 그것들이 고래, 북극곰, 물개, 자녀와 함께 있는 엄마 같은 "원시적인" 주제를 다뤘고, 많은 소비자들이 이것이 이누이트족의 생활 방식을 대표한다고 인식했기 때문이다. 따라서, 젊은 남녀들은 포획이나 다른 전통적인 생존 수단을 추구하는 대신 전업 장인이 되기 위해 그들의 조각 기술을 연마했다. 많은 이들이 그들의 관행을 표준화하고 신진 예술가들에게 훈련 기회를 제공하기 위해 이누이트족 예술 길드를 설립하는 것을 도왔다. 1970년대 중반까지, 모든 마을 사람들이 이 작은 상아와 돌 조각품을 생산하면서 전국의 미술관에서 기념품 가게에 이르기까지 다양한 판매처와 거래 제휴를 구축했다.

⁸이누이트 예술이 순수 예술이라는 개념을 둘러싸고 논란이 있는데, 이는 그 용어가 보통 상업적 이익이 아닌 다른 목적으로 그 작업이 이루어진다는 의미를 전달하기 때문이다. 그럼에도 불구하고, 그 작품들이 그들의 심미적 특성을 기반으로 전 세계의 광범위한 팬들을 끌어모으기 때문에, 그 주장은 이론적일 뿐이다. 그것들은 또한 외부인들로 하여금 서구식 생활방식으로 엄청난 전환을 겪고 있는 사람들과의 연결 고리를 느낄 수 있도록 하면서, 매우 감정적이고 표현력이 뛰어나다는 찬사를 받고 있다.

homogenous 휑동질적인   indigenous 휑토착의
lucrative 휑수익성 높은   rudimentary 휑기본의   whaling 몡포경
dire 휑심각한, 비참한   linger 동지속되다   treaty 몡조약
transition 동전환하다; 몡전환   nomadic 휑유목의
permanent 휑영구적인   elders 몡원로들, 어른들   amulet 몡부적
commodity 몡상품   intrinsic 휑고유한   aesthetic 휑미적인
acclaim 몡호평, 갈채   crude 휑조잡한, 대충 만든
token 몡기념품, 증표   possessions 몡소유물, 소지품
hone 동(기술을) 연마하다   craftspeople 몡장인
up-and-coming 휑신진의

1 지문의 단어 "dire"와 의미가 가장 비슷한 것은?

(A) 관련 없는
(B) 혐오스러운
(C) 심각한
(D) 무모한

2 지문의 단어 "it"이 가리키는 것은?

(A) 상황
(B) 판결
(C) 교육
(D) 의료 서비스

3 1단락과 2단락에 따르면, 다음 중 이누이트족 문화의 주요한 변화에 기여한 요소가 아닌 것은?

(A) 지역 마을의 이누이트족 공동체로의 전환
(B) 전통적인 경제의 몰락
(C) 이누이트족에게 다양한 권리를 제공하기로 한 법적 결정
(D) 이누이트족의 외국 무역상에 대한 노출

4 3단락에 따르면, 제임스 휴스턴은 왜 이누이트족의 공예품에 깊은 인상을 받았는가?

(A) 그것들이 예술적 가치를 가지고 있다고 믿었다.
(B) 그것들이 중요한 영적 도구라고 생각했다.
(C) 그것들의 판매로 이익을 얻기를 기대했다.
(D) 그것들이 장식용으로 쓰일 수 있다고 생각했다.

5 다음 중 4단락에서 초기 이누이트족 예술 작품의 특징으로 언급되지

않은 것은?

  (A) 일반적으로 다른 물품들을 장식하기 위해 만들어졌다.
  (B) 사람들이 움직이기 쉽게 설계되었다.
  (C) 주로 천연 재료로 만들어졌다.
  (D) 다양한 이누이트족 게임에 사용하기 위해 고안되었다.

6 지문의 단어 "honed"와 의미가 가장 비슷한 것은?

  (A) 문서화했다
  (B) 향상시켰다
  (C) 전파했다
  (D) 전시했다

7 글쓴이는 왜 "fine art galleries"와 "souvenir shops"를 언급하는가?

  (A) 장인들이 자신의 기술 홍보에 쏟은 헌신을 보여주기 위해
  (B) 이누이트족 예술가들이 이용할 수 있는 경제적 기회의 범위를 강조하기 위해
  (C) 토착의 장인들을 고용하는 사업체의 예를 들기 위해
  (D) 이누이트족 예술품을 구매하는 소비자의 좁은 범위를 설명하기 위해

8 6단락에 따르면, 일부 비평가들은 왜 이누이트족 예술을 예술로 분류하는 데 의문을 제기하는가?

  (A) 장인들이 제도적인 환경에서 훈련을 받지 않는다.
  (B) 작품들이 주로 경제적인 상품으로서 생산된다.
  (C) 창작자들이 새로운 아이디어를 도입할 동기가 부족하다.
  (D) 그 주제가 구식이다.

9 네 개의 네모[■]는 다음 문장이 삽입될 수 있는 곳을 나타내고 있다.

  휴대할 수 있는 물건들을 소유하는 것은 더 적은 소지품들이 남겨진다는 것을 의미했기 때문에 이것은 편리할 뿐만 아니라 낭비를 줄였다.

  이 문장은 어디에 들어가는 것이 가장 적절한가?

10 **지시:** 지문 요약을 위한 도입 문장이 아래에 주어져 있다. 지문의 가장 중요한 내용을 나타내는 보기 3개를 골라 요약을 완성하라. 어떤 문장은 지문에 언급되지 않은 내용이나 사소한 정보를 나타내므로 요약에 포함되지 않는다. **이 문제는 2점이다.**

  > 이누이트족은 문화 및 경제 위기에 대응하여 전통 예술을 기반으로 한 산업을 발전시켰다.
  >
  > · (C) 이누이트족 예술의 상품화는 일부 사람들로 하여금 그것을 과소평가하게 했으나, 그것의 예술적 가치는 널리 인정받았다.
  > · (D) 공예품의 시장성은 이누이트족이 그것들의 창작에 집중하고 그것들의 판매처를 찾도록 장려했다.
  > · (E) 예술에 대한 문화적 이해 없이, 장식 작품은 원래 캐나다 북부 고유의 재료를 활용하여 만들어졌다.

  (A) 소비자들은 원시적인 주제가 전통적인 북극 공동체의 상징이라고 생각했기 때문에 선호했다.
  (B) 새로운 법은 다른 토착 캐나다인들과 마찬가지로 이누이트족에게 기본적인 권리를 부여했다.
  (F) 공예품을 판매하는 발상은 자신의 조각품을 미술관에 소개한 유명 이누이트 예술가의 성공에서 영감을 받았다.

1 (B)	2 (A)	3 (A)	4 (B)
5 (C)	6 (D)	7 (C)	8 (A)
9 (D)	10 (B), (C), (D)		

태양 에너지

석유, 석탄, 천연가스와 같이 인간에 의해 흔히 사용되는 연료원은 유한하며, 그것들이 고갈되고 있는 속도는 실용적인 대체 연료원에 대한 탐색이 필요하게 만들었다. 다양한 선택지가 고려되었지만, 태양 에너지는 세계의 현재와 미래의 에너지 수요를 충족시키기에 가장 유망하다는 것이 널리 인식되고 있다.

절대 변하지 않기 때문에 태양 상수라고 알려진 지구를 둘러싼 대기 주변에 도달하는 복사 에너지는 제곱미터당 평균 1,400와트이다. ²간섭으로 인해, 지표면에 도달하는 양은 훨씬 적으며 서로 다른 지리적 위치 사이에 큰 차이가 있다. 그렇기는 하지만, 그 총량은 여전히 전기를 생산하는 모든 전통적인 방식의 총 생산량보다 기하급수적으로 더 크다. 그 자원의 잠재력에 대한 광범위한 인식은 그것의 막대한 재생 가능 에너지의 효과적인 이용을 용이하게 하는 다양한 기술의 개발로 이어졌다.

태양 복사 에너지를 이용하는 가장 간단한 방법은 그것을 물을 가열하는 데 이용하는 것으로, 1세기 이상 동안 많은 국가들에서 사용되어 온 기술이다. ³미국에서, 그 방법은 사실 지금보다 20세기 초에 더 널리 퍼져 있었다. 이것은 석탄의 높은 비용과 땔감에 접근할 수 없는 것이 이 연료들을 도시 거주자들에게 매력적이지 않게 했기 때문이었다. 1920년대까지, 상당수의 개인 주택들은 에너지 요금을 줄이기 위해 간단한 태양광 온수기를 설치했다. 그 기술은 미국에서 광범위한 천연가스 매장층이 발견되면서 대부분 폐기되었고, 그것은 훨씬 더 편리한 합리적 가격의 대안을 제공했다. 그러나, 1970년대 이후 연료비가 계속 상승함에 따라, 이 태양광 에너지 장치에 대한 관심이 다시 높아지고 있다.

태양열이 태양 에너지의 성공적이고 실용적인 사용의 한 예이기는 하지만, 그것이 보통 하나의 구조물이나 장소로 고립된 소규모적 시도에만 적절하다는 점에서 그것의 유용성은 다소 제한적이다. 따라서, 과학자들은 태양 에너지를 더 전체적으로 적용 가능한 전기로 변환하는 방법을 개발하기 시작했다.

화력 발전소는 이 목표를 달성하기 위한 첫 번째 시도를 대표하며, 그것들은 다양한 형태를 취하지만, 모두 동일한 근본 기술을 기반으로 한다. ⁴ᴰ태양 에너지를 포착하기 위해, 태양 광선이 물이 담긴 파이프나 보일러에 집중되도록 포물선 모양의 대형 거울들이 배치된다. ⁴ᴬ/⁴ᶜ물이 가열되면, 그것은 결국 증기로 변환되어 터빈을 돌리기에 충분한 압력을 생성하며, 이는 전기의 생산으로 이어진다. 이는 낮에만 가능하며, 결과적으로 대부분의 발전기는 혼합형으로, 이는 그것들이 낮에는 태양 에너지를, 밤에는 전통적인 연료를 사용한다는 것을 의미한다. 서로 다른 발전소들 사이에 큰 차이가 있지만, 이것들은 일반적으로 석유, 석탄, 가스를 포함한다. ⁵이 기술의 기반 시설 요구 사항은 그것을 대량 에너지 생산에 가장 적합하게 하며, 그것은 기존의 여러 전력망에 성공적으로 포함되었다.

더 최근의 기술은 대규모 전력 생산에 응용할 수 있고 국지적인 전력원으로서의 역할을 할 수 있기 때문에 태양열과 화력 전기의 장점을 모두 통합했다. 처음에 인공위성을 위해 개발된 광전지는 태양 복사 에너지를 전기로 직접 변환한다. 태양 빛이 전지를 비추면, 전자는 수많은 실

리콘 전지판 사이에서 전달되어 전류를 발생시키는 양전하와 음전하를 생성하며, 이는 즉시 사용되거나 향후 사용을 위해 저장될 수 있다. 이러한 방법은 화력 발전보다 훨씬 효율적이지만, 기술의 높은 비용과 복잡성이 그것의 이용을 제한해 왔다.

finite 휑유한한   deplete 홍고갈시키다
necessitate 홍~을 필요하게 만들다   viable 휑실용적인, 실행 가능한
alternative 휑대체의, 대안의; 휑대안   periphery 휑주변
solar constant 태양 상수   interference 휑간섭, 전파 방해
exponentially 휜기하급수적으로   harness 홍이용하다
radiation 휑복사 에너지   prevalent 휑널리 퍼진, 일반적인
discard 홍폐기하다, 버리다   reasonably 휜합리적으로
apparatus 휑장치   utility 휑유용성, 효용성
congruent 휑적절한, 알맞은   endeavor 휑시도, 노력
applicable 휑적용 가능한   underlying 휑근본적인, 기초가 되는
parabolic 휑포물선 모양의   incorporate 홍통합하다
photovoltaic cell 광전지

1 지문의 단어 "finite"와 의미가 가장 비슷한 것은?

(A) 확장된
(B) 한정된
(C) 완료된
(D) 수정된

2 다음 중 2단락에서 태양 복사 에너지에 관해 추론할 수 있는 것은?

(A) 대기에 도달하는 그것의 많은 양은 지표면에 전달되지 않는다.
(B) 그것의 일부는 다시 우주로 반사되지만, 대부분은 결국 표면에 도달한다.
(C) 서로 다른 지리적 위치 사이의 양 차이는 미미하다.
(D) 그것의 대부분은 대기 중에 에너지를 가두는 입자에 의해 흡수된다.

3 3단락에 따르면, 미국에서 태양 복사 에너지로 물을 가열하는 것은

(A) 현재보다 과거에 더 흔했다
(B) 화석 연료를 사용하는 것보다 더 비쌌다
(C) 도시보다 시골 지역에서 더 인기가 있었다
(D) 전통적인 가열 방법보다 더 진보되었다

4 5단락에 따르면, 다음 중 화력 발전소가 태양 에너지를 전기로 변환하는 과정에서의 단계가 아닌 것은?

(A) 터빈이 회전한다.
(B) 화석연료가 변환된다.
(C) 물이 증기로 변한다.
(D) 태양 광선이 조준된다.

5 5단락에 따르면, 화력 발전소는

(A) 햇빛이 비치는 시간 동안에만 기능한다
(B) 현재의 전력 시스템에서 사용되지 않는다
(C) 많은 양의 전기를 생산한다
(D) 일반 발전기만큼 효율적이지 않다

6 지문의 단어 "incorporated"와 의미가 가장 비슷한 것은?

(A) 제정했다
(B) 강화했다
(C) 뒤집었다
(D) 통합했다

7 지문에서 글쓴이는 왜 "satellites"를 언급하는가?

(A) 기술의 이점을 입증하기 위해
(B) 기술의 가능한 용도를 제안하기 위해
(C) 기술의 기원을 설명하기 위해
(D) 기술의 한계를 지적하기 위해

8 아래 문장 중 지문 속의 음영된 문장의 핵심 정보를 가장 잘 표현한 것은? 오답은 문장의 의미를 크게 바꾸거나 핵심 정보를 생략한다.

(A) 당장 또는 나중에 사용할 수 있는 전기는 실리콘 전지판에 부딪히는 태양 빛에 의해 야기되는 화학 반응에 의해 발생된다.
(B) 태양 빛에서 태양 전지판으로의 전자 전달은 강력한 전류의 생성으로 이어진다.
(C) 태양 전지판에 저장된 에너지가 태양 빛과 직접 접촉할 때 전하가 생성된다.
(D) 전기의 장기적인 저장은 실리콘 태양 전지판이 널리 활용되기 전에 극복되어야 하는 장애물이다.

9 네 개의 네모[■]는 다음 문장이 삽입될 수 있는 곳을 나타내고 있다.

서로 다른 발전소들 사이에 큰 차이가 있지만, 이것들은 일반적으로 석유, 석탄, 가스를 포함한다.

이 문장은 어디에 들어가는 것이 가장 적절한가?

10 지시: 지문 요약을 위한 도입 문장이 아래에 주어져 있다. 지문의 가장 중요한 내용을 나타내는 보기 3개를 골라 요약을 완성하라. 어떤 문장은 지문에 언급되지 않은 내용이나 사소한 정보를 나타내므로 요약에 포함되지 않는다. 이 문제는 2점이다.

> 태양 에너지를 사용하기 위해 많은 서로 다른 기술들이 만들어졌다.
> · (B) 태양 복사 에너지의 전기로의 직접 변환은 비싼 많은 구성 요소를 필요로 하는 복잡한 기술을 수반한다.
> · (C) 물을 가열하기 위해 태양의 열에너지를 이용하는 것은 가장 오래된 방법일 뿐만 아니라 가장 간단한 방법이다.
> · (D) 태양열은 물을 증기로 변환하는 데 사용될 수 있으며, 이것은 그다음 전기를 생산하는 데 사용된다.

(A) 지구 표면에 도달하는 태양 에너지의 불변의 특성은 새로운 발전 방법의 개발을 촉진했다.
(E) 위성 기술은 대규모 태양 에너지 발전기 발명에 큰 기여를 했다.
(F) 미래의 모든 태양 에너지 방법은 태양으로부터 받는 복사 에너지를 보충하기 위해 화석 연료에 의존할 가능성이 크다.

Vocabulary Review 본문 p.100

1 commence	2 endeavor	3 acclaim
4 nomadic	5 periphery	6 reasonably
7 (C)	8 (A)	9 (C)	10 (B)
11 (A)	12 (C)	13 (D)	14 (B)

Example　　　　　　본문 p. 103

1 (C)　　2 (B)

나바호어 암호병

미군에게, 제2차 세계대전 동안 통신은 당혹스러운 문제가 되었다. 일본의 암호 해독자들은 극비의 군사 암호를 그것들이 고안되는 즉시 신속하게 해독하는 데 자신들이 놀랍도록 능숙하다는 것을 입증하고 있었다. [1]많은 일본 암호 해독자들은 미국에서 교육받았고, 그곳에서 그들은 영어를 말하는 것을 배워 속어와 비속어를 포함한 미국 구어체 표현에 익숙해졌다. 그 결과, 미국의 전투 계획은 종종 실행 가능해지기 전에, 거의 즉시 적에게 알려지게 되었고, 가능한 해결책이 없는 것처럼 보였다.

1942년, 제1차 세계대전 참전 용사인 필립 존스턴은 나바호어를 기반으로 한 군사 암호를 만들 계획을 세웠다. 이 언어에 유창했던 존스턴은 이 언어가 사용되는 억양에 따라 의미가 달라지는 많은 단어들을 포함하고 있었기 때문에 그것을 택했다. [2]그 결과, 그것을 말하면서 자라지 않은 대부분의 사람들은 그 언어를 사실상 이해할 수 없다. 암호병으로 알려진 나바호어 원어민의 이용은 큰 성공으로 입증되었다. 암호를 나바호어에 기반함으로써, 미군은 군인들 간의 대화가 적에게 이해되지 않을 것이라고 확신할 수 있었다. 암호병의 효과는 태평양 작전에서의 중요한 전환점이었던 이오지마 전투에서의 역할로 입증된다. 전투 중 안전한 통신을 제공하기 위해 스스로를 큰 개인적 위험에 빠뜨린 여섯 명의 나바호어 암호병이 없었다면, 미군은 패배에 직면했을 것이라고 일반적으로 받아들여진다.

bewildering 형당혹스러운　　cryptographer 명암호 해독자, 암호 전문가
adept at ~에 능숙한　　colloquialism 명구어체 표현
slang terms 속어, 은어　　profanity 명비속어, 욕설
operational 형실행 가능한　　inflection 명억양, 어조
incomprehensible 형이해할 수 없는　　exchange 명대화
effectiveness 명효과, 효율성　　turning point 전환점

1 다음 중 1단락에서 제2차 세계대전 초기의 미국 암호에 관해 추론할 수 있는 것은?

　(A) 일본 군인들에 의해 만들어졌다.
　(B) 주로 전투 계획을 전달하기 위해 사용되었다.
　(C) 속어와 비속어를 포함했다.
　(D) 먼 거리로는 전송될 수 없었다.

2 2단락에서 글쓴이가 암시하는 것으로, 필립 존스턴은

　(A) 여섯 명의 나바호어 암호병 중 한 명이었다
　(B) 어렸을 때 나바호어를 말한 경험이 있다
　(C) 이오지마 전투에서 암호를 해독했다
　(D) 제1차 세계대전에서 암호병으로 복무했다

침팬지

침팬지는 호모 사피엔스와 가장 가까운 유인원 종이다. 1970년대에 영국인 연구자 제인 구달에 의해 획기적인 연구가 발표된 이래로, 그것들의 주목할 만한 수준의 지능뿐만 아니라, 그것들의 비교적 유사한 생리학적 구조는 동물들의 행동을 그것들의 자연 서식지에서 연구해온 동물 생태학자들의 관심을 사로잡았다. [2]탄자니아의 곰베 국립공원에서 침팬지 집단 속에서 살면서, 구달은 이전에 한 번도 기록된 적이 없는 행동을 관찰했다. 그렇지 않으면 초식성일 그것들의 식단에서 단백질을 모으기 위한 노력으로, 암컷 침팬지는 풍부한 흰개미 둥지를 이용하는데, 이는 제작된 도구를 필요로 하는 기술이다. 그녀의 연구는 인간이 도구를 만드는 유일한 동물이라는 견고한 신념과 정면으로 충돌했는데, 이는 먹이를 찾고, 은신처를 짓고, 영역을 방어하기 위해 그저 손에 넣을 수 있는 물건만 이용하는 영장류를 호모 사피엔스와 구분하는 행동 특성이었다.

구달의 기록에 따르면, 곰베 침팬지는 흰개미를 "낚시하러" 가기 위해 의식적으로 재료를 모으고 필요에 맞게 그것을 만들어낸다. 먼저, 그것들은 긴 가지를 찾아 그것의 나무껍질과 잎을 깎아 매끈한 막대기를 만든다. 그것들은 가장 많은 곤충을 내어줄 지하 공간을 찾아 햇볕에 말라 단단해진 흙더미에 구멍을 뚫을 것이다. [3]그런 다음, 그것들은 노출된 흰개미를 수확하기 위해 두 번째 도구를 이용하는데, 그것은 종종 그것들의 입으로 잡아 뜯기고 송곳니에 의해 한쪽 끝이 갈라진 긴 풀잎이다. 그 도구의 붓처럼 생긴 끝이 영양가 높은 벌레들로 덮이면, 그것들은 즉시 먹어 치워진다. 침팬지들이 서식 곤충이 풍부한 둥지를 찾고 항상 올바른 도구를 손에 들고 도착하기 때문에 이 모든 과정은 선견지명을 보여준다. 그것들은 심지어 도구를 만들기 위해 특정 식물 종을 선호하는데, 이를 얻기 위해 그것들은 자주 먼 거리를 여행해야 한다.

새로운 도구를 제작하기 위해서, 침팬지들은 그것들의 목표와 관련된 모든 조건을 정신적으로 개념화하고 이 목표를 달성하기 위해 재료를 얻어내야 한다. 만일 특정 재료가 의도한 대로 기능하지 않으면, 그것들은 다른 재료를 선택하고 다시 시도할 수 있다. 그것들의 창의적이고 유연한 사고력은 그것들이 A 계획이 실패했을 때 B 계획으로 넘어갈 수 있도록 해준다. [4]코트디부아르의 타이 숲에 사는 침팬지의 경우가 그러하다. 그것들은 영양을 제공하는 속 알맹이에 닿기 위해 돌을 이용하여 단단한 겉껍질을 부수어 열고, 종종 그것들이 견과류를 여는 데 효과적으로 기능하는 것을 찾을 때까지 돌을 하나하나 시험해 본다.

영민한 지능에도 불구하고, 침팬지는 도구를 구할 때 부모 및 다른 공동체 구성원의 행동을 모방하며 점진적인 형태의 학습에 의해 크게 영향을 받는다. 새끼들이 어미로부터 피드백을 받으면서 부적절하거나 비효율적인 응용을 교정함에 따라, 능숙함은 시간이 지나며 강화된다. 나이 든 침팬지들은 최고의 원료를 제공하는 나무를 가리키거나 좋은 암석 표본을 가지고 돌아와 어린 침팬지들에게 그것들의 매력적인 자질을 가르칠 수 있다. 이러한 사회적 상호작용은 침팬지 문화화의 기초이며, 심지어 새끼들보다 훨씬 더 경험이 많은 4, 5세 된 침팬지들도 그들의 멘토들에게 지속적으로 도움을 받는다.

구달의 발견 및 그녀의 동료들의 발견에 자극을 받아, 현대의 연구자들은 이전에 문서화되지 않은 침팬지의 도구 사용을 포착하기 위한 노력으로 적외선 동작 감지 비디오카메라를 도입했다. [6]자료가 계속 축적됨에 따라, 과학자들은 이 유인원의 능력에 대한 과거의 가정들을 재검

토해야 할 것으로 보이며, 그것은 분명히 한때 전문가들이 생각했던 것보다 훨씬 더 정교하다.

physiological 혤생리학적의   ethologist 몡동물 생태학자
breakthrough 혤획기적인   herbivorous 혤초식성의
capitalize on ~을 이용하다   termite 몡흰개미
entrenched 혤견고한   forage 동먹이를 찾다
fashion 동(재료를 써서) 만들다   subterranean 혤지하의
fray 동갈라지게 하다   canine teeth 송곳니   utensil 몡도구, 기구
nutritious 혤영양가 높은   foresight 몡선견지명, 예지력
fabricate 동제작하다   implement 몡도구; 동도입하다
kernel 몡(견과류 등의) 알맹이   quick-witted 혤영민한
procure 동구하다   adroitness 몡능숙함, 노련함
inappropriate 혤부적절한   ineffectual 혤비효율적인
enculturation 몡문화화, 적응   spur 동자극하다, 격려하다
infrared 혤적외선의   assumption 몡가정
sophisticated 혤정교한

1 지문의 단어 "capitalize"와 의미가 가장 비슷한 것은?
(A) 파괴하다
(B) 이용하다
(C) 입증하다
(D) 급증하다

2 1단락에 따르면, 다음 중 제인 구달에 관해 사실인 것은?
(A) 야생에서 침팬지들 사이에서 살았던 최초의 사람이었다.
(B) 침팬지의 도구 사용에 대한 증거를 기록한 최초의 사람이었다.
(C) 과학 현장 연구를 위해 곰베 국립공원에 들어간 최초의 사람이었다.
(D) 그녀는 침팬지의 식단에 대해 연구한 최초의 사람이었다.

3 2단락에 따르면, 침팬지가 긴 풀잎을 이용하는 것은
(A) 둥지에서 흰개미를 얻기 위해서이다
(B) 흰개미 흙더미에 구멍을 내기 위해서이다
(C) 먹이를 먹기 위한 이를 갈기 위해서이다
(D) 흰개미가 있는 곳을 찾기 위해서이다

4 3단락에서 추론할 수 있는 것으로, 타이 숲에 사는 침팬지들은
(A) 서로 다른 도구의 효율성을 비교할 수 있다
(B) 제대로 기능하도록 돌의 모양을 만들 것이다
(C) 겉껍질에서 제거하기 쉬운 알맹이를 선호한다
(D) 영양가 높은 먹이의 부족으로 고통받는다

5 지문의 단어 "their"가 가리키는 것은?
(A) 나이 든 침팬지들
(B) 나무
(C) 암석 표본
(D) 어린 침팬지들

6 글쓴이가 암시하는 것으로, 현대 연구자들이 도입한 특수 카메라는
(A) 침팬지의 기술에 관한 이야기의 대부분이 과장된 것임을 밝힐 것이다
(B) 침팬지의 도구 사용에 대한 이전 연구와 일치하는 데이터를 생성할 것이다
(C) 침팬지의 능력에 대한 과학적 견해를 혁신적으로 바꿀 것이다
(D) 과학자들이 항상 침팬지의 행동을 추적할 수 있도록 할 것이다

Reading Practice 2
본문 p. 106

1 (A)   2 (B)   3 (A)   4 (D)   5 (B)   6 (B)

엠파이어 스테이트 빌딩

1,454피트의 높이로 선, 엠파이어 스테이트 빌딩은 1931년 5월 1일 세계에서 가장 높은 건물로 개장했다. 그것은 뉴욕시의 아이콘이 되었고 불가능한 것을 성취하려는 인류의 도전의 상징이 되었다.

²1889년에 파리에서 에펠탑이 984피트 높이로 지어졌을 때, 전 세계의 건축가들은 더 높은 것을 짓도록 도발되었다. 20세기 초까지, 1909년에 메트로폴리탄 라이프 타워가 700피트까지 올라갔고, 1913년에 792피트의 울워스 빌딩이 그 뒤를 빠르게 따르면서, 고층 건물 경쟁은 계속되었다. 1929년에 맨해튼 은행 빌딩은 927피트 및 71층에 도달함으로써 이 높이를 넘어섰다. 이러한 다른 건축물들을 능가하기로 결심한 크라이슬러사의 설립자 월터 크라이슬러는 크라이슬러 빌딩을 건설하기 시작했으며, 그는 건축이 완료될 때까지 그것의 높이를 비밀로 유지했다. 제너럴 모터스의 전 부사장 존 제이콥 라스콥은 경쟁에 참여하여 그의 이전 경쟁자를 능가하기로 결심했고, 그는 약 1,600만 달러에 34번가와 5번가에 있는 부동산을 구입했다.

엠파이어 스테이트 빌딩의 부지를 확보한 후, 라스콥은 그의 새로운 고층 빌딩을 위해 건축회사 슈레브, 램 앤 하몬을 고용했고, 그것을 기술적으로 가능한 한 최대한 높게 만들 것을 요청했다. ³램은 공기 순환 시스템, 우편 활송 장치, 화장실, 복도를 포함하는 공유 공간의 내부 피라미드를 만들어 간단하면서 논리적인 디자인을 고안했다. 그는 이 중심부의 둘레를 28피트 깊이의 사무실 공간으로 둘러싸, 건물의 모든 사무실이 창문 가까이에 있도록 했다. 그 건물은 80층 높이로 설계되었지만, 크라이슬러 빌딩이 더 높도록 재설계되었기 때문에 엠파이어 스테이트 빌딩은 85층까지 올려졌다.

라스콥은 크라이슬러가 마지막 순간에 그의 건물 높이를 더 높이기 위해 속임수를 쓸까 봐 여전히 걱정스러웠다. 따라서, 그는 당시 항공 여행에 일반적으로 사용되었던 비행선이라고 하는 팽창식 비행선을 위한 도킹 스테이션을 추가하기로 결정했다. 이 거대한 비행선들이 엠파이어 스테이트 빌딩의 꼭대기에 정박하고 나면, 승객들이 내려서 엘리베이터를 타고 지상층까지 내려갈 것이라는 계획이었다. ⁵비록 이것은 착륙하는 비행선을 고정할 대규모 지상 승무원들에 대한 필요성 때문에 불가능한 것으로 판명되었지만, 도킹 스테이션의 포함은 엠파이어 스테이트 빌딩에 그것이 세계에서 가장 높은 건물이 되기 위해 필요한 추가적인 높이를 주었다. 그것은 1972년 세계 무역 센터가 개장할 때까지 이 차별성을 유지했다.

엠파이어 스테이트 빌딩이 수년간 누려온 랜드마크로서의 위상은 그것의 거대한 규모뿐만 아니라 아름다운 외관의 결과였다. 그것은 많은 사람들에게 아르 데코 양식의 상징이 되는 표현물로 여겨지는데, 그것은 1920년대와 1930년대에 유행했던, 대담한 기하학적 형태와 뚜렷한 선을 강조하는 설계 양식이다. 건물의 기본 형태는 매우 대칭적이며 상당히 뾰족해지는데, 꼭대기 층들이 바닥 층들보다 훨씬 더 좁다. 이것은 단형 후퇴의 사용을 통해 달성되었는데, 이는 건물이 높아짐에 따라 그것의 측면을 축소시키는 계단형 후퇴이다. ⁶건축가들은 엠파이어 스테이트 빌딩에 그것의 독특한 외관을 제공하는 매우 눈에 띄는 일련의 직사각형 블록들을 만들기 위해 단형 후퇴의 사용을 받아들이기는 했지만, 이것들은 원래 뉴욕시의 구역 규제에 대한 대응으로 그 건물의 설계에 포함되었다. 그 규제의 목적은 엠파이어 스테이트 빌딩을 에워싼 더 작은 건물들에 햇빛이 도달하는 것을 보장하는 것이었다.

taunt 图 도발하다, 조롱하다   eclipse 图 (경쟁 상대를) 능가하다
perimeter 图 둘레   pull a trick 속임수를 쓰다
inflatable 图 팽창식의   dirigible 图 비행선
disembark 图 (비행기·배에서) 내리다   inclusion 图 포함
distinction 图 차별성   immense 图 거대한
well-defined 图 뚜렷한, 명확한   taper 图 뾰족해지다
incorporate 图 포함하다   regulation 图 규제, 규정

1 지문의 단어 "eclipse"와 의미가 가장 비슷한 것은?

(A) 능가하다
(B) 감명을 주다
(C) 약화시키다
(D) 모방하다

2 글쓴이가 암시하는 것으로, 파리의 에펠탑은

(A) 미국 건축에 도전하기 위해 지어졌다
(B) 완공과 동시에 세계에서 가장 높은 건축물이 되었다
(C) 미국 건축가들에 의해 설계되었다
(D) 산업혁명에 대한 기념물로 세워졌다

3 3단락에 따르면, 엠파이어 스테이트 빌딩의 내부 피라미드는

(A) 모든 세입자에 의해 공유되는 시설을 포함한다
(B) 사무실 직원들에게 창문으로의 접근 기회를 제공한다
(C) 유지 보수 작업자를 제외한 모든 사람에게 출입 금지이다
(D) 주거 공간으로 둘러쌓여 있다

4 지문의 단어 "his"가 가리키는 것은?

(A) 하몬
(B) 램
(C) 라스콥
(D) 크라이슬러

5 4단락에서 추론할 수 있는 것으로, 비행선은

(A) 항공 교통 관제소의 감독 없이는 착륙할 수 없었다
(B) 엠파이어 스테이트 빌딩에 착륙할 수 없었다
(C) 1972년 이후 세계 무역 센터의 꼭대기에 착륙했다
(D) 착륙을 도울 지상 승무원을 태웠다

6 5단락에 따르면, 엠파이어 스테이트 빌딩의 설계에 포함된 단형 후퇴는

(A) 직사각형 요소의 선을 부드럽게 했다
(B) 정부 기관에 의해 명령받았다
(C) 처음에 건축가들에 의해 거부되었다
(D) 인근 건축물의 가시성을 낮췄다

Reading Practice 3
본문 p. 108

1 (B)   **2** (B)   **3** (C)   **4** (D)   **5** (D)   **6** (C)

체온 조절

열 관리는 특정 생물군계에서 생물이 생존할 수 있을지를 결정하는 핵심 요소 중 하나이다. 체온 조절이라고도 알려진 그것은 주변 온도가 크게 변동할 때도 특정 범위 내에서 체온을 유지하는 능력이다. 이를

달성하기 위해 생물에 의해 이용되는 방법은 그것들이 변온(냉혈)인지 항온(온혈)인지에 따라 달라지며, 후자는 전자보다 훨씬 더 효과적으로 체온을 조절할 수 있다. [1]포유류와 조류같은 항온 동물은 그것들이 다양한 종류의 기후대에서 서식하게 해주는 여러 가지의 발달된 조절 방법을 활용한다.

항온 동물이 가지는 주요한 장점 중 하나는 외부 조건에 상관없이 그것들의 체온을 유지하기 위해 신진대사 과정을 이용하는 능력이다. 열 항상성이라고 알려진 이 과정은 지방과 당의 에너지로의 변환에서 기인한 다음, 체내에서 열을 발생시키는 데 사용된다. [3]이것은 각 세포 내에 있는 다수의 미토콘드리아의 존재에 의해 가능해지는데, 이것은 흔히 "세포 발전소"라고 불리는 막으로 둘러싸인 조직이다. 항온 동물의 미토콘드리아는 또한 최대 8배 많은 열을 낼 수 있는 훨씬 더 효율적인 에너지 변환기라는 점에서 변온 동물에서 발견되는 미토콘드리아와 크게 다르다.

세포 수준에서 생성된 열 에너지는 순환계를 통해 분배되는데, 이것은 따뜻한 혈액을 손발까지 운반함으로써 몸 전체 온도의 상대적 균일성을 보장한다. 이 과정은 온도 조절 장치와 같은 기능을 하는 뇌의 구성 요소인 시상하부에 의해 제어된다. 열 변화에 대응하여, 그것은 피부 속 혈관의 지름을 조절하는 신경 자극을 내보내며, 이것들의 수축 또는 팽창이 혈액이 몸 전체에 흐르는 속도를 결정한다.

단열은 열을 유지하기 위해 항온 동물에 의해 이용되는 또 다른 방법이며, 털 및 깃털과 같은 외피뿐만 아니라 피하 지방을 포함한다. 내부 단열 체계는 생물에 의해 의식적으로 조작될 수는 없지만, 털과 깃털 모두 털 세움이라고 알려진 방법을 통해 영향을 받을 수 있다. 이것은 개별적인 털이나 깃털의 각도를 바꿈으로써 단열의 강도를 조절하는 특수 근육 사용을 수반한다. 물에서 건조한 육지로의 지속적인 전환이 체온의 급격한 변동을 가져오기 때문에, 그 기능은 추운 생태계의 수생 조류에게 특히 중요하다. 이것은 그것을 보상할 방법이 없는 생물의 건강에 부정적으로 영향을 미칠 수 있다.

반대로, 따뜻한 기후대에 사는 항온 동물들은 그것들이 과열되지 않도록 하는 똑같이 효과적인 방법을 가지고 있다. 가장 효율적이고 흔한 접근 방식은 증발, 즉, 물의 수증기 변환을 통한 열의 발산을 이용하는 것이다. 이것이 달성되는 한 가지 방법은 수분을 분비하는 피부 내부에 위치한 특수 세포군인 땀샘의 이용을 통한 것이다. [5]이 샘을 가지고 있지 않거나 제한된 수만 있는 동물들은 대개 타액 생성의 현저한 증가를 경험하며, 그것은 그런 다음 헐떡거림이라고 불리는 독특한 호흡법을 통해 흩어져 사라지게 된다.

증발은 체온을 낮추기 위해 항온 동물들에 의해 이용되는 가장 일반적인 방법이지만, 그것만이 유일한 것은 아니다. 자연 선택의 과정은 코끼리 귀의 부채질부터 특정 설치류의 긴 꼬리를 통한 열의 발산에 이르기까지 각각의 종들에게 그것들의 서식지에 특별히 맞춤화된 독특한 적응 형태를 부여했다.

thermoregulation 图 체온 조절   biome 图 생물군계
ambient 图 주변의   fluctuate 图 변동하다
ectothermic 图 변온의, 변온 동물의
endothermic 图 항온의, 항온 동물의   metabolic 图 신진대사의
homeostasis 图 항상성   circulatory system 순환계
uniformity 图 균일성, 균일   extremities 图 손발
hypothalamus 图 시상하부   thermostat 图 온도 조절 장치
diameter 图 직경, 지름   constriction 图 수축   dilation 图 팽창
piloerection 图 털 세움, 입모   dwell 图 살다, 거주하다
sweat gland 땀샘   secrete 图 분비하다
dissipate 图 흩어져 사라지게 하다   evaporation 图 증발
adaptation 图 적응 형태, 적응

1 다음 중 1단락에서 변온 동물에 관해 추론할 수 있는 것은?

(A) 자신의 체온을 조작할 수 없다.
(B) 그것들의 지리적 범위는 제한되어 있다.
(C) 기후 변동에 영향을 받지 않는다.
(D) 그것들의 혈액 온도는 절대 변하지 않는다.

2 아래 문장 중 지문 속의 음영된 문장의 핵심 정보를 가장 잘 표현한 것은?

(A) 신진대사 과정은 항온 동물 특유의 절차를 이용한 체온 유지를 통해 설명된다.
(B) 신진대사 과정은 환경적 변동에도 불구하고 열 안정성을 보장함으로써 온혈 동물에게 도움이 된다.
(C) 온혈 종에서 체온의 항구성은 내부의 신진대사 과정보다는 주변 환경에서 비롯된다.
(D) 항온 동물이 체온을 유지하기 위해 사용하는 신진대사 과정은 외부 조건에 의해 영향을 받을 수 있다.

3 2단락에 따르면, 열 항상성은

(A) 특정 영양분의 섭취에 달려 있다
(B) 충분한 열의 발생에 달려 있다
(C) 세포 조직의 존재에 달려 있다
(D) 에너지에서 음식으로의 전환에 달려 있다

4 네 개의 네모[■]는 다음 문장이 삽입될 수 있는 곳을 나타내고 있다.

이것은 그것을 보상할 방법이 없는 생물의 건강에 부정적으로 영향을 미칠 수 있다.

이 문장은 어디에 들어가는 것이 가장 적절한가?

5 5단락에서 글쓴이가 암시하는 것으로, 헐떡거림은

(A) 단일 기능을 가진 피부 세포가 활성화될 때 발생한다
(B) 체온이 상승함에 따라 호흡 문제를 일으킨다
(C) 입 속 타액의 양을 증가시킨다
(D) 물이 액체에서 수증기로 변하는 결과를 낳는다

6 6단락에서 글쓴이는 왜 코끼리의 귀와 설치류의 꼬리를 언급하는가?

(A) 특정 냉각 방법이 다른 것들보다 좋다는 것을 제시하기 위해
(B) 특정 생물군계에서 증발이 효과적이지 않은 이유를 입증하기 위해
(C) 체온 조절과 관련된 독특한 특징의 예를 제시하기 위해
(D) 항온 동물의 유전적 다양성을 설명하기 위해

---

iBT Reading Test 1
본문 p.110

1 (A)   2 (C)   3 (B)   4 (D)
5 (B)   6 (C)   7 (D)   8 (A)
9 (B)   10 (B), (E), (F)

스페인의 잉카 제국 기록

스페인 탐험가 프란시스코 피사로가 고향의 동료 탐험가들이 "금이 풍부하"이라고 묘사했던 (오늘날 페루라고 알려진) '피루'에 대한 이야기를 들은 후, 그는 남아메리카의 태평양 해안을 따라 항해하기 위해 새로운 탐험대를 조직했다. [2A/2B/2D]이 귀한 땅을 찾으려는 그의 첫 번째

시도는 악천후, 식량 부족, 원주민과의 충돌로 인해 방해받아, 배는 목적지에 도달하지 못했다. 그러나, 이후의 작전은 성공적이었으며 결국 1532년에 페루 정복으로 이어졌다. 그 당시, 페루는 안데스산맥을 포함한 그 대륙의 태평양 해안 지역을 지배했던 잉카 제국의 중심지였다. 스페인의 정복은 한때 강력했던 이 사회의 존재에 대해 서구 세계에 가르쳐 주는 것을 도왔지만, 그것은 또한 정복 이전, 도중, 이후에 실제로 일어난 일에 대한 혼동을 일으키기도 했다.

최초의 기록은 정복자들 스스로에 의해 작성되었다. [3A]그들은, 잉카 제국이 문자를 개발한 적이 없기 때문에 이중 언어 구사 능력을 결코 알 수 없을, 스페인어 훈련을 받은 통역사들을 활용하여 현지인들과 면담을 진행했다. [3C]문제를 더 복잡하게 만든 것은, 원주민의 이야기들이 서로 상당히 달랐다는 것이다. 그 차이가 너무 커서 초기 스페인 기록자들은 50개가 넘는 버전의 잉카 구전 역사를 기록했다. [3D]그리고 다양한 설명들이 일치했을 때는, 그 사실들은 신화, 종교 및 선전의 관점에 의해 왜곡되었다. 스페인인들이 기록한 공식적인 이야기는 잉카 제국이 그 지역 전역으로 퍼졌고 문화가 없는 원시인들에게 문명화된 삶을 가져다주었으며, 잉카 제국의 확장은 신들에게 영감을 받았다는 것을 나타낸다.

이 이야기는 자기들의 페루 침략에 대한 스페인인들의 설명과 기이할 정도로 비슷했는데, 그것에서 그들은 가톨릭교로 개종시키려는 희망을 가지고 야만적인 사회를 정복하는 것에 대한 명분으로서 신의 섭리를 인용했다. 사실, 대부분의 스페인 "역사가들"은 인류학적 정확성에 의해 동기 부여가 되지 않았으며, 그들의 목표는 그것이 스페인 국왕이든, 성직자이든, 행정관이든, 그들의 독자를 기쁘게 하는 것이었다. 이는 페드로 피사로가 그의 사촌인 프란시스코의 정복, 잉카 황제 아타우알파의 생포와 처형, 그리고 스페인 제국의 확장을 찬양한 '페루의 발견과 정복'에 반영되어 있다. 페드로는 잉카의 춤에 대한 설명과 같은 잉카의 풍습에 대한 세부 사항을 포함했지만, 전반적으로 그는 원주민들을 아주 존중하는 방식으로는 표현하지는 않았다. 현지인들에 대한 그의 사촌의 태도에 대해서도 비슷한 평가가 내려질 수 있다. 스페인의 카를로스 1세 국왕에게 보낸 편지에서, 프란시스코는 페루의 수도 쿠스코를 너무나 훌륭하여 동시대 유럽의 어떤 지방 자치 도시와도 비견될만한 도시라고 직접 칭찬했지만, 이 언급은 이기적인 것이었다. 그는 이 귀한 영토를 획득한 공로를 인정받으려 했으며 잉카 제국의 이전 업적을 강조할 의도는 없었다.

잉카 제국의 기록을 더욱 복잡하게 만든 것은 메스티소의 후기 기록들이다. 메스티소는 스페인인과 잉카인 양쪽 혈통으로, 일반적으로 스페인인 아버지와 원주민 어머니 사이에서 태어났다. 그러한 교혼은 흔한 관행이 되었고 혼혈 자손의 급증으로 이어졌다. [7]보통, 메스티소 기록자들은 그들의 스페인의 전통에 대해 공감을 보였지만, 그들을 차별화한 것은 잉카인 관점에 대한 그들의 감정 이입이었다. 예를 들어, 1570년에 한 선교사의 메스티소 조수에 의해 쓰인 '페루 정복에 관한 잉카인의 기록'은 스페인인들에 의한 현지인 학대를 묘사했다. [8]그 글은 1916년까지 스페인 정부에 의해 출판 금지되었고, 전문의 영어 번역은 2005년이 되어서야 등장했다.

---

hamper (동) 방해하다   inclement weather (명) 악천후   rations (명) 식량
skirmish (명) 충돌, 접전   subsequent (형) 이후의
subjugation (명) 정복, 정벌   enlighten (동) 가르치다, 계몽하다
conquistador (명) (스페인의) 정복자   competence (명) 능력
bilingualism (명) 이중 언어 구사   substantially (부) 상당히
chronicler (명) 기록자, 연대기 작가   concur (동) 일치하다
skewed (형) 왜곡된, 편향된   propaganda (명) (정치적 목적의) 선전
eerily (부) 기이할 정도로   divine providence 신의 섭리
justification (명) 명분, 정당화   subdue (동) 정복하다, 굴복시키다

barbaric 웹 야만적인   anthropological 웹 인류학적인
municipality 몡 지방 자치 도시   self-serving 웹 이기적인
mestizo 몡 메스티소(스페인인과 아메리카 원주민의 혼혈)
parentage 몡 혈통   intermarriage 몡 (다른 인종 간의) 교혼, 결혼
proliferation 몡 급증, 확산   progeny 몡 자손
empathy 몡 감정 이입, 공감   suppress 통 출판 금지하다

1 지문의 단어 "it"이 가리키는 것은?

(A) 정복
(B) 서구 세계
(C) 존재
(D) 사회

2 1단락에 따르면, 피사로의 첫 번째 임무 실패에 원인이 되지 않은 것은?

(A) 현지인들과의 갈등
(B) 불충분한 식량 공급
(C) 원시적인 범선
(D) 불리한 기후 조건

3 다음 중 2단락에서 스페인인들의 기록의 문제로서 언급되지 않은 것은?

(A) 잉카인들은 문자가 없었다.
(B) 스페인인들은 이중 언어 통역사를 구할 수 없었다.
(C) 원주민들은 서로 다른 설명을 내놓았다.
(D) 구전 역사를 통해 제시된 세부 사항들은 왜곡되었다.

4 지문의 단어 "subduing"과 의미가 가장 비슷한 것은?

(A) 무시하는
(B) 모집하는
(C) 놀라게 하는
(D) 억압하는

5 3단락에서 글쓴이는 왜 페드로 피사로의 작품에 대한 논의를 포함하는가?

(A) 일부 스페인 작가들이 객관성을 유지하는 능력을 입증하기 위해
(B) 정확한 정보가 스페인 기록자들의 목표가 아니었음을 보여주기 위해
(C) 피사로 가족의 동기가 얼마나 이기적이었는지 지적하기 위해
(D) 잉카 제국이 스페인인들을 불신했음을 시사하기 위해

6 지문의 단어 "progeny"와 의미가 가장 비슷한 것은?

(A) 조상
(B) 영재
(C) 자손
(D) 유산

7 4단락에 따르면, 메스티소 기록자들의 독특한 점은 무엇이었는가?

(A) 스페인인들에 대한 묘사에 있어 적대적이었다.
(B) 가톨릭 신학을 채택한 최초의 남아메리카인들이었다.
(C) 잉카의 후손들과 광범위한 면담을 실시했다.
(D) 잉카인의 관점에 대한 공감을 보여주었다.

8 다음 중 '페루 정복에 관한 잉카인의 기록'에 관해 추론할 수 있는 것은?

(A) 그것의 내용은 페루의 스페인 통치자들에 의해 바람직하지 않다고 여겨졌다.

(B) 18세기에 처음으로 스페인어로 번역되었다.
(C) 그것의 어조는 원주민 반란에 대한 강한 반대를 전달했다.
(D) 2005년 이후 서구 세계에 널리 보급되었다.

9 네 개의 네모[■]는 다음 문장이 삽입될 수 있는 곳을 나타내고 있다.

현지인들에 대한 그의 사촌의 태도에 대해서도 비슷한 평가가 내려질 수 있다.

이 문장은 어디에 들어가는 것이 가장 적절한가?

10 지시: 지문 요약을 위한 도입 문장이 아래에 주어져 있다. 지문의 가장 중요한 내용을 나타내는 보기 3개를 골라 요약을 완성하라. 어떤 문장은 지문에 언급되지 않은 내용이나 사소한 정보를 나타내므로 요약에 포함되지 않는다. 이 문제는 2점이다.

> 스페인의 페루 정복 전후 기간에 관한 역사 기록은 불확실성에 싸여 있다.
> · (B) 스페인인들의 혼혈 자손인 메스티소는 페루 역사의 다른 모습을 묘사하기 시작했다.
> · (E) 잉카 제국의 세력 확장 이야기와 마찬가지로, 스페인인들의 역사는 미개한 민족 정복을 묘사한다.
> · (F) 정복한 스페인인들은 역사적 설명을 기록하기 시작했고, 이것들은 모호함과 왜곡으로 특징지어졌다.

(A) 스페인인들에 대한 잉카인의 기록은 그들을 세련된 문화가 없는 원시인으로 묘사했다.
(C) 스페인의 침략 이전에, 잉카인의 기록은 그들이 또 다른 강력한 안데스 부족에 의해 정복당했다는 것을 암시한다.
(D) 페드로 피사로의 이야기는 다른 역사가들이 결코 갖지 못했던 잉카 문명에 대한 감상을 보여준다.

---

iBT Reading Test 2   본문 p.114

1 (D)	**2** (B)	**3** (C)	**4** (A)
5 (B)	**6** (C)	**7** (A)	**8** (D)
9 (D)	**10** (A), (B), (F)		

엘니뇨와 남방 진동

몇 년에 한 번씩, 대기와 해양 사이의 복잡한 상호 작용은 동태평양에서 평균보다 더 따뜻한 수온을 만들어낸다. 이 간헐적인 해양 온난화는 한 세기도 더 전에 에콰도르와 페루 연안에서 남아메리카 어부들에 의해 발견되었고, 그것이 일반적으로 크리스마스쯤에 일어나는 것처럼 보였기 때문에 그들은 그것을 스페인어로 "남자아이"를 의미하고 아기 예수를 가리키는 '엘니뇨'라고 이름 지었다. ¹그것이 특히 그 산업의 구성원들에게 눈에 띄는 이유는 그것이 그렇지 않으면 수익성이 있을 멸치 수확을 심각하게 방해한다는 사실 때문이다. 비록 그 현상의 전반적인 원인은 아직까지 부분적으로만 이해되지만, 몇 가지 주요 요인이 엘니뇨를 대표하는 것으로 확인되었다.

엘니뇨 현상은 서태평양에서 유난히 넓은 따뜻한 표층수의 축적에서 비롯된다. 엄청난 양의 따뜻한 물이 동쪽에서 서쪽으로 부는 우세한 열대 바람 즉, 무역풍으로 인해 점차 서쪽에 집중되는데, 이는 엘니뇨가 없는 상태에서 지구의 자전으로 인해 계속해서 그 방향으로 분다. ³무역풍이 해수면을 가로질러 휩쓸고 가면서, 태양 복사에 의해 자연적으로 가열된 최상층의 물은 말 그대로 바다를 가로질러 밀려 나가 서쪽의 해수면이 동쪽보다 더 높아지게 된다. 수개월에 걸쳐, 이 차이는 수

천 킬로미터 넓이의 지역을 덮는 바닷물의 약 0.5미터로 커진다. 바람이 약해지면, 필연적으로 그렇듯이, 그것들은 더 이상 계속해서 따뜻한 물 덩어리를 서쪽으로 밀어낼 수 없어 그 광대한 저수지는 다시 남아메리카의 서해안으로 후퇴하여 엘니뇨 현상을 촉발시킨다. **다시 말해, 동태평양의 바닷물은 상당히 따뜻해진다.**

온도 차의 결과로 엘니뇨 동안 지구 대기압의 정상 패턴의 반전이 발생한다는 것 또한 명백하다. [5]일반적으로, 기압은 동태평양에서 더 높고 서태평양에서 더 낮지만, 이러한 대기압 패턴은 대략 3년에서 8년마다 바뀌는 경향이 있으며, 이 시소 패턴을 '남방 진동'이라고 한다. 기압의 변화는 엘니뇨와 매우 밀접하게 연관되어 있어서 두 개는 종종 엔소(ENSO)라는 약자로 결합된다. 기상학자들에 따르면, 대기압의 변화는 따뜻한 바닷물 덩어리의 동쪽 이동 때문이며, 이것은 열대 지방의 강한 태양 광선과 함께 작용하여 주변 공기를 상승시킨다.

최근 수십 년 동안, 열대 지방의 폭발적 화산 활동이 엘니뇨 현상의 발생 가능성을 크게 높일 수 있다는 일부 증거가 나타났다. 이 이론은 이전에는 휴화산으로 추정되었던 멕시코의 엘치촌 화산이 예기치 않게 폭발하고 불과 몇 달 후인 1982년 겨울에 처음 등장했다. 엘니뇨가 그 역사적 폭발 이후에 발생했기 때문에, 기후학자들은 화산에 의해 다량의 이산화황과 미세먼지가 대기 중으로 방출될 때 발생하는 냉각 효과가 무역풍의 방향을 바꾸어 엘니뇨를 유발할 수 있다고 이론화했다.

비록 정확히 무엇이 엘니뇨를 발생시키는지에 대한 포괄적인 그림은 아직 밝혀지지 않았지만, 과학자들은 일단 그것이 시작되면 그 현상이 어떻게 진화하는지 잘 이해하고 있으며, 이 지식은 최대 6개월에서 9개월 전에 앞서 그것을 합리적인 정확도로 예측하는 데 도움이 되기 때문에 훨씬 더 실용적인 가치가 있을 수 있다. 엘니뇨는 계절에 맞지 않는 가뭄과 같은 파괴적인 결과를 초래할 수 있기 때문에, 사전 경보는 영향을 받은 지역 사회가 비정상적인 기상 패턴이 발생하기 훨씬 전에 대비하는 데 도움을 줄 수 있다.

Southern Oscillation 남방 진동   noticeable 혱눈에 띄는, 뚜렷한
hamper 동방해하다   profitable 혱수익성 있는
anchovy 몡멸치, 안초비   representative 혱대표하는
accumulation 몡축적   exceptionally 閏유난히
prevailing 혱우세한   trade winds 무역풍
discrepancy 몡차이, 불일치   inevitably 閏필연적으로
barometric pressure 기압   temperature gradient 온도 차
inextricably 閏밀접하게, 불가분하게   acronym 몡약자, 약어
attributable to ~ 때문인   in conjunction with ~과 함께
particulate matter 미세먼지   comprehensive 혱포괄적인
be on the horizon 곧 밝혀지다, 닥치다   devastating 혱파괴적인
unseasonal 혱계절에 맞지 않는   aberrant 혱비정상적인, 이변의

1 다음 중 1단락에서 바닷물의 주기적인 온난화에 관해 추론할 수 있는 것은?

   (A) 이전에는 매우 드물었기 때문에 한 세기 이상 주목받지 못했다.

   (B) 일부 남아메리카 국가의 어부들에 의해 크게 의존되고 있다.

   (C) 전 세계 해류의 흐름에 지대한 영향을 미친다.

   (D) 일부 지역에서 평소보다 훨씬 적은 특정 물고기의 수를 야기한다.

2 지문의 단어 "discrepancy"와 의미가 가장 비슷한 것은?

   (A) 위반

   (B) 불일치

   (C) 애매함

   (D) 빈도

3 2단락에 따르면, 다음 중 무역풍의 정상적인 이동의 결과는?

   (A) 해수면의 물은 식는다.

   (B) 서태평양의 따뜻한 물은 동쪽으로 밀려간다.

   (C) 서태평양의 해수면이 상승한다.

   (D) 최상층의 물은 더 요동치게 된다.

4 지문의 어구 "attributable to"와 의미가 가장 비슷한 것은?

   (A) ~에 의해 야기되는

   (B) ~을 동반하는

   (C) ~에 연결된

   (D) ~에 포함된

5 3단락에 따르면, 다음 중 남방 진동에 관해 사실인 것은?

   (A) 매년 예측 가능한 패턴으로 발생한다.

   (B) 동쪽과 서쪽 사이에서 저기압 지역을 역전시킨다.

   (C) 그것과 엘니뇨의 연관성은 대부분의 연구자들에 의해 의심받고 있다.

   (D) 그것의 원인은 해수 온도와는 무관하다.

6 글쓴이는 왜 멕시코의 엘치촌 화산을 언급하는가?

   (A) 기후학자들이 예측하지 못했던 역사적 폭발을 지적하기 위해

   (B) 이론에 대한 제한적인 증거가 있음을 암시하기 위해

   (C) 현상에 대한 한 가지 설명을 제공하기 위해

   (D) 화산 폭발이 무역풍에 직접적으로 영향을 미치는 방법을 보여주기 위해

7 아래 문장 중 지문 속의 음영된 문장의 핵심 정보를 가장 잘 표현한 것은? 오답은 문장의 의미를 크게 바꾸거나 핵심 정보를 생략한다.

   (A) 연구자들은 무엇이 엘니뇨를 발생시키는지 완전히 이해하지는 못하지만, 이 이상 기후 현상이 어떻게 발달하는지 알고 있으며, 이는 엘니뇨의 발생을 미리 예측하게 해주기 때문에 유용하다.

   (B) 엘니뇨의 정확한 원인은 미스터리로 남아 있지만, 과학자들은 일단 엘니뇨 현상이 시작되면 정확한 지속 기간을 예측할 수 있을 정도로 그 과정을 잘 이해하고 있다.

   (C) 일반적으로 6개월에서 9개월 동안 지속되는 엘니뇨는 아직 전문가들에 의해 완전히 이해되지는 않지만, 그들은 엘니뇨 현상을 더 정확하게 예측하게 해주는 유용한 발견을 했다.

   (D) 기후학자들은 엘니뇨 현상이 완전히 발달하기 약 6개월에서 9개월 전에 초기 징후를 알아볼 수 있지만, 아직까지 그 현상의 근본적인 원인을 밝혀내지 못하고 있다.

8 지문의 단어 "they"가 가리키는 것은?

   (A) 결과

   (B) 가뭄

   (C) 지역 사회

   (D) 패턴

9 네 개의 네모[■]는 다음 문장이 삽입될 수 있는 곳을 나타내고 있다.
다시 말해, 동태평양의 바닷물은 상당히 따뜻해진다.
이 문장은 어디에 들어가는 것이 가장 적절한가?

10 지시: 지문 요약을 위한 도입 문장이 아래에 주어져 있다. 지문의 가장 중요한 내용을 나타내는 보기 3개를 골라 요약을 완성하라. 어떤 문장은 지문에 언급되지 않은 내용이나 사소한 정보를 나타내므로 요약에 포함되지 않는다. **이 문제는 2점이다.**

과학자들은 엘니뇨의 근본 원인을 완전히 이해하지 못하지만, 그것에 기여할 수 있는 몇 가지 현상을 발견했다.

- (A) 따뜻한 물은 우세한 무역풍에 의해 태평양을 가로질러 서쪽으로 밀려갔다가 바람이 약해지면 동쪽으로 다시 흐른다.
- (B) 최근 몇 년 동안 수행된 연구는 열대 지방의 화산 활동과 이후의 엘니뇨 현상 발생 사이에 관계가 있음을 나타낸다.
- (F) 현상의 근본 원인을 밝혀냄으로써, 과학자들은 엘니뇨 현상이 언제 발생할지 예측하는 방법을 배웠고, 이는 영향을 받은 지역사회가 대비하도록 도왔다.

(C) 태평양에서의 기압 패턴 변화는 서부 열대 지방에 광범위한 따뜻한 해수벽이 축적되게 한다.
(D) 엘니뇨 발생 직전의 1982년 멕시코 대형 화산 폭발은 화산 활동이 엘니뇨와 연관되어 있음을 결정적으로 보여주었다.
(E) 엘니뇨 효과로 인한 기상 패턴의 변화는 남아메리카 서부 해안의 풍부한 어류 수확에 부분적으로 책임이 있다.

Vocabulary Review

본문 p.118

1 skirmishes	2 incomprehensible	3 aberrant
4 skewed	5 dilation	6 barbaric
7 (C)	8 (B)	9 (D)	10 (C)
11 (A)	12 (B)	13 (A)	14 (C)

CHAPTER 07
Rhetorical Purpose

Example

본문 p.121

1 (C)   2 (A)

신생대 제4기 기후 변화

약 2백만 년 전에 시작되어 현재까지 이어지는 신생대 제4기 동안, 지구는 빙하기와 간빙기의 반복적인 주기를 겪었다. 가장 최근의 것이 약 만 년 전에 끝난 빙하기 동안, 거대한 빙상이 온대 지역 대부분을 뒤덮는다. 빙하기는 온도가 상승하기 시작하고 빙상이 극지방으로 후퇴하기 전까지 일반적으로 7만 년에서 9만 년 동안 지속된다. 그것들의 거대한 크기 때문에, 이러한 빙상의 움직임은 근본적으로 지형을 바꾸는데, 예를 들어, 북아메리카의 오대호는 이 과정의 결과로 형성되었다. 간빙기는 일반적으로 만 년 동안만 지속되는데, 이는 현재의 간빙기가 금세 끝날 가능성이 높다는 것을 의미한다.

과학자들 사이에서 가장 널리 받아들여지고 있는 이 현상에 대한 설명은 태양 주위를 도는 지구 궤도의 주기적 변동과 관련이 있다. 지구의 공전 궤도는 10만 년마다 타원형에서 원형으로 그리고 다시 반대로 교체된다. 그것이 타원형일 때, 지구는 일 년 중 대부분 동안 평소보다 태양으로부터 훨씬 더 멀리 떨어져 있다. 또 다른 요인은 지구 축의 기울

기가 4만 천 년에 걸쳐 변한다는 것이다. 기울기가 클수록 겨울 동안 북반구 및 남반구가 받는 태양 복사는 줄어든다. 1920년에, 세르비아의 수학자 밀루틴 밀란코비치는 과거 빙하기의 시작은 지구의 궤도가 타원형이고 자전축의 기울기가 가장 뚜렷했던 시점과 일치한다고 주장했다.

Quaternary Period 신생대 제4기   glacial 혱빙하기의
interglacial 혱간빙기의   temperate zone 온대 지역
recede 통후퇴하다, 물러나다   fundamentally 튀근본적으로
variance 뎽변동   alternate 통교체되다   onset 뎽시작
correspond with ~과 일치하다

1 지문에서 글쓴이는 왜 "the Great Lakes of North America"를 언급하는가?
   (A) 지질학적 과정의 비정상적인 결과에 대한 설명을 제공하기 위해
   (B) 빙상이 후퇴해온 정도를 강조하기 위해
   (C) 빙상이 지표면에 미치는 영향을 설명하기 위해
   (D) 온도 변화가 큰 수역에 어떻게 영향을 미칠 수 있는지 보여주기 위해

2 2단락에서 글쓴이의 주된 목적은?
   (A) 장기적인 기후 패턴을 설명하는 이론을 제시하기
   (B) 다양한 요인이 지구의 기후에 영향을 미칠 수 있음을 입증하기
   (C) 날씨 패턴에 대한 설명에 반대하는 주장을 제시하기
   (D) 빙하기의 원인에 관한 계속되는 논쟁을 설명하기

Reading Practice 1

본문 p.122

1 (B)	2 (C)	3 (D)	4 (A)	5 (D)	6 (A)

MBTI

많은 북아메리카 중학교에서, 학생들은 캐서린 쿡 브릭스와 이사벨 브릭스 마이어스의 모녀 심리학자 팀에 의해 1940년대에 처음 개발된 표준화 검사인 마이어스-브릭스 유형 지표(MBTI)를 볼 기회가 주어진다. [1]MBTI는 독특한데, 다른 표준화 시험과는 달리 지능이나 수학 실력과 같은 특성을 측정하는 것이 아니라, 대신 선호를 평가하기 위해 고안된 일련의 질문에 대한 응답에 기반하여 기질을 확인하는 데 도움을 준다. 예를 들어, 한 질문은 응답자들에게 강한 사회적 상호작용에 의해 활력을 얻는지 또는 지치는지 밝히도록 요구할 수 있는데, 그에 대한 대답은 그들이 외향적인 또는 내향적인 성향을 보이는지 보여준다.

이러한 질문들을 개발하는 데 사용된 표준은 전적으로 스위스의 정신과 의사이자 분석 심리학의 창시자인 칼 융의 연구에서 비롯되었다. [2]인간의 정신을 연구하는 융의 접근 방식은 꿈, 종교, 신화와 같이 비과학적인 지식의 원천에 대한 탐구에 중점을 두었다. 종종 급진적이어서 지크문트 프로이트를 포함한 동시대 사람들에게는 거의 받아들여지지 않았던 그의 저술은, 인지란 모든 무의식 및 의식적 경험의 총합이라고 제시했다. 그는 또한 성격 발달에 관한 여러 이론을 제시했는데, 이는 그것이 사고의 두 영역 사이의 균형과 상호 작용과 관련이 있기 때문이다.

융에 따르면, 성격이 무의식에 의해 영향을 받는 한 가지 방식은 '콤플렉스'를 통한 것으로, 그것은 어린 시절의 일반적인 사건들과 대단히 충격적인 사건들 둘 다와 관련된 감정과 도덕을 포함한다. 그는 콤플

렉스를 그렇지 않으면 기이하거나 설명하기 어려운 행동으로 자신을 드러내는 마음속 매듭 같은 것으로 묘사했다. 융이 '아니마'(남성)와 '아니무스'(여성)라고 부른 그의 핵심 콤플렉스는 성별과 관련된 사전에 형성된 개념들의 묶음으로, 그것은 가령 한 남성이 여성을 향해 비합리적으로 행동하게 만든다. 융의 결론은 만약 그 남성이 성인기의 여성에 대한 개념과 상관없이 어린 시절 내내 여성에 대한 부정적인 표상으로 가득 차 있었다면, 여성에 대한 그의 버릇은 무의식적인 거부감이나 불편함을 나타낼 수 있다는 것이었다.

이러한 콤플렉스들을 더 분석하기 위해, 융은 단어 연상 검사를 이용했는데, MBTI와 마찬가지로 피실험자에게 무작위의 단어를 주고 가장 먼저 마음에 떠오르는 것을 즉시 응답하도록 했다. 그 응답들로, 융은 의식적인 행동을 자극하는 기저의 콤플렉스의 개요를 밝히기 위해 그의 환자들의 정신 지도를 만들었다. 수백 건의 사례를 검토한 후, 융은 환자들의 성격에 이러한 콤플렉스로 특징지어지는 분명한 패턴이 있다는 것을 알아챘다. 그는 이러한 사고방식과 그것들의 전형적인 표상을 원형이라고 불렀다. 흥미롭게도, MBTI는 응답들을 전반적인 기질 묘사에 이용되는 감정, 직관, 사고, 느낌의 네 가지 인지 기능의 범주로 배치함으로써 그것의 평가에 이러한 원형들을 통합한다. 결과적으로, 각 응답자는 제한된 수의 성격 유형 중 하나로 분류된다.

이 검사의 회의론자들은 단지 포러 효과로 인해 응답자들이 그것이 정확하다고 인식하기 때문에 정확할 뿐이라고 주장한다. 6그것은 사람들이 자신에게 맞춤화되어 있는 것 같지만, 실제로는 모호하고 광범위한 사람들에게 적용할 수 있는 성격 묘사에 타당성을 부여한다는 관찰이다. 한편, 많은 직업 상담사, 직원 훈련자, 그리고 리더십 코치들은 그것을 특정 개인에게 어떤 직업과 생활 방식이 가장 적합할 것인지 이해하는 데 필수적인 도구로서 간주한다.

standardized 형 표준화된   temperament 명 기질
assess 동 평가하다   extroverted 형 외향적인
introverted 형 내향적인   be derived from ~에서 비롯되다, 유래하다
exclusively 부 전적으로   contemporary 명 동시대 사람
cognition 명 인지, 인식   realm 명 영역
traumatic 형 대단히 충격적인   manifest 동 드러내다
preconceived 형 사전에 형성된   irrational 형 비합리적인
be inundated with ~으로 가득 차다   representation 명 표상
mannerism 명 (독특한) 버릇   psyche 명 정신, 마음
underlying 형 기저의, 근본적인   archetype 명 원형, 전형
skeptic 명 회의론자   tailored 형 (특정 대상에) 맞춤화된
applicable 형 적용할 수 있는

1 1단락에 따르면, 마이어스-브릭스 유형 지표의 특이한 점은 무엇인가?

(A) 모녀에 의해 개발되었다.
(B) 성격과 관련된 특성을 조사한다.
(C) 인간의 인지에 관한 정보를 제공한다.
(D) 사회적 상호작용을 측정하기 위해 고안되었다.

2 다음 중 2단락에서 융의 동시대 사람들에 관해 추론할 수 있는 것은?

(A) 융이 의도적으로 자료를 조작했다고 믿었다.
(B) 무의식의 중요성을 인식하지 못했다.
(C) 인간의 정신 이해에서 비과학적인 도구에 가치를 두지 않았다.
(D) 꿈이 인간의 경험과 관련이 없다고 생각했다.

3 지문의 단어 "manifests"와 의미가 가장 비슷한 것은?

(A) 대체하다

(B) 구별하다
(C) 흡수하다
(D) 드러내다

4 글쓴이는 왜 "negative representations of women"을 언급하는가?

(A) 남성 피실험자의 여성에 대한 비논리적인 행동을 설명하기 위해
(B) 여성이 비합리적으로 행동하는 이유를 제시하기 위해
(C) 성 편견을 뒷받침할 증거를 제공하기 위해
(D) 남성이 여성을 이해할 수 없는 이유를 제시하기 위해

5 글쓴이는 왜 "Forer effect"를 언급하는가?

(A) MBTI 대안의 예시를 제공하기 위해
(B) MBTI의 일반적인 사용에 의문을 제기하기 위해
(C) MBTI가 정확하다는 주장을 뒷받침하기 위해
(D) MBTI의 비판에 대한 근거를 제시하기 위해

6 5단락에서, 다음 중 일부 성격 묘사에 관해 언급된 것은?

(A) 변별성이 부족하고 많은 사람들에게 적용될 수 있다.
(B) 유능한 전문가들에 의해 제공되는 한 정확하다.
(C) 특정 개인에게 맞춤화될 만큼 충분히 개별적이다.
(D) 응답자들이 그것들이 신뢰할 만하다고 생각하지 않기 때문에 반드시 실패한다.

Reading Practice 2   본문 p. 124

1 (D)   2 (B)   3 (C)   4 (D)   5 (A)   6 (C)

에칭

유명 화가 렘브란트 판 레인(1606-1669)은 성경 장면의 놀라운 시각적 묘사로 가장 잘 알려져 있다. 그의 기술은 특히 그의 동시대 사람들이 필적할 수 없는 힘과 에너지로 종교적이고 우화적인 주제를 묘사하는 데 특히 적합했다. 캔버스에 유화 물감을 사용하여, 그는 일생 동안 600점 이상을 창작했으며, 그중 다수가 고전 명작으로 여겨진다.

게다가, 그는 중세 시대에 금속 세공품을 장식하기 위해 금 세공인들에 의해 개발된 화학적 판화법인 에칭을 최초로 실험한 예술가 중 한 명이었다. 이는 렘브란트로 하여금 그 공정에 관련된 많은 복잡한 단계를 완료하기 위해 고급 제지 기술을 개발할 뿐만 아니라, 야금술을 배우고 화학에 대한 실무 지식을 익히도록 했다. 먼저, 화가는 그림이 새겨진 금속판인 에칭을 만들어야 한다. 이를 위해, 동판은 보통 산의 부식 효과를 견딜 수 있는 밀랍, 역청 및 수지의 혼합물과 같은 물질로 칠해진다. 1C그런 다음, 화가는 에칭 그라운드라고 불리는 칠에 날카로운 도구를 사용하여 그림을 새기고, 금속을 공기 중에 노출시킨다. 1B완성 즉시, 그 판은 질산에 담가지는데, 이는 노출된 동에 반응하여 움푹 패인 선의 패턴을 형성한다. 1A그런 다음 동판은 남은 칠을 제거하기 위해 문질러지고, 새겨진 그림을 보이는 깨끗한 금속판을 남긴다.

이것이 완료되면, 화가는 (보통 나무껍질, 짚, 옥수수 수염뿌리 펄프와 같은 현지 자원으로 만들어진) 종이 한 장을 적시고, (보통 검은색 또는 파란색) 잉크로 판을 칠한다. 2움푹 패인 선은 금속의 매끄러운 표면보다 더 많은 잉크를 담을 수 있기 때문에, 판이 종이에 눌러지면 그림이 전사된 잉크의 나머지 부분보다 더 어둡게 보여서, 화가의 원래 새긴 그림의 좌우대칭의 자국을 만들어낸다.

렘브란트와 동시대 사람들은 에칭을 만드는 데 두 가지 주요 이점이 있다는 것을 곧 깨달았는데, '음각'이라고 알려진 판화 제작 방식이 그것들이 잉크를 흡수할 수 있는 한 많은 종류의 표면에 적용 가능하다는 것과 이 방법으로 창작된 예술 작품이 복제 가능하다는 것이었다. 전자는 예술가들이 작품을 표현하는 새로운 방법을 시도하도록 장려했고, 결과적으로 장식 예술에 대한 관심을 증가시켰다. 예를 들어, 직물은 더 상세한 이미지로 인쇄될 수 있어, 음각 직물에 대한 수요 증가로 이어졌다. [5]그러나, 후자는 다음 세기에 걸친 그 방법의 유럽 전역 확산의 핵심 요인이었기 때문에 어쩌면 더 중요했다. 재사용 가능한 새겨진 판은 예술가들에게 작품을 복제하고 하나의 작품으로 더 많은 부를 얻을 수 있는 도구를 제공했다. 게다가, 그것은 더 많은 이용 가능한 작품을 제작함으로써 개인 및 공공 미술 소장품의 성장을 촉진했다.

오늘날에도 그러한 것과 같이, 음각은 19세기와 20세기 동안 예술가들에게 계속해서 영감을 주었다. 1800년대 초, 스페인 왕실의 궁정 화가인 고야는 인쇄물에 색조 효과를 주기 위해 내산성 분말 수지로 그린 볼록한 선으로 음각을 보완하는 '애쿼틴트'라고 불리는 에칭의 변형을 완성했다. 그의 작품은 차례로, 특히 파블로 피카소와 그의 친구이자 라이벌인 앙리 마티스와 같은 이후 세대를 위한 토대를 닦아주었다. 특히, 피카소는 애쿼틴트 음각을 사용하여 아방가르드 미술 운동인 큐비즘에 기여했다.

allegorical 혱 우화적인, 비유적인   contemporary 혱 동시대 사람
metallurgical 혱 야금술의   copperplate 혱 동판, 구리판
compound 혱 혼합물   bitumen 혱 역청, 아스팔트
resin 혱 수지, 송진   corrosive 혱 부식하는   recessed 혱 움푹 패인
incised 혱 새긴, 조각한   mirror-image 혱 좌우대칭의
impression 혱 자국   intaglio 혱 음각
reproducible 혱 복제할 수 있는   arguably 분 어쩌면, 거의 틀림없이
proliferation 혱 확산   reap 동 얻다, 거두다   facilitate 동 촉진하다
variant 혱 변형   supplement 동 보완하다
acid-resistant 혱 내산성의, 산을 견디는   tonal 혱 색조의
pave the way for ~을 위한 토대를 닦다

1   2단락에 따르면, 에칭을 만들기 위해 필요하지 않은 것은?

(A) 금속판에서 여분의 물질을 제거하기

(B) 화학 용액에 동판을 담그기

(C) 금속 표면에 그림을 새기기

(D) 산의 영향에 취약한 칠 바르기

2   에칭에서, 그림은 왜 전사된 잉크의 나머지 부분보다 어두운가?

(A) 금속의 압력이 잉크를 종이 깊숙이 주입한다.

(B) 움푹 패인 선은 매끄러운 금속보다 더 많은 양의 잉크를 담고 있다.

(C) 대비를 만들기 위해 두 가지 다른 색조의 잉크가 사용된다.

(D) 종이의 습기가 일부 잉크를 번지게 한다.

3   3단락에서 글쓴이의 주된 목적은

(A) 그림을 제작하는 대안적인 방법을 제안하는 것이다

(B) 에칭 기술의 심각한 결점을 지적하는 것이다

(C) 복잡한 준비 과정의 최종 결과를 보여주는 것이다

(D) 현지 출처의 재료 사용에 대한 선호를 설명하는 것이다

4   지문의 단어 "they"가 가리키는 것은?

(A) 동시대 사람들

(B) 이점

(C) 에칭

(D) 표면

5   4단락에 따르면, 음각은 왜 유럽 전역에 퍼졌는가?

(A) 예술가들이 그들의 작품을 여러 개 복제할 수 있게 해주었다.

(B) 많은 다른 화가들에 의한 실험을 촉진했다.

(C) 섬유 디자인과 패션에 대한 관심을 높였다.

(D) 다른 에칭 화가들에 의해 쉽게 모방될 수 있는 작품들을 만들어냈다.

6   글쓴이는 지문에서 왜 "Goya"를 언급하는가?

(A) 에칭이 스페인으로 퍼졌다는 증거를 제시하기 위해

(B) 에칭이 피카소 이후 예술가들에게 영향을 미친 한 가지 방법을 설명하기 위해

(C) 음각의 영향을 받은 예술가의 예를 제시하기 위해

(D) 에칭이 19세기에 가장 큰 인기를 얻었다는 것을 시사하기 위해

Reading Practice 3   본문 p.126

1 (B)   2 (B)   3 (B)   4 (D)   5 (A)   6 (C)

루이 파스퇴르

루이 파스퇴르는 현대 역학에 질병의 세균 이론을 도입한 것뿐만 아니라 면역학 및 미생물학을 포함한 수많은 과학 분야의 기반을 마련하는 데 기여한 역사상 가장 영향력 있는 과학자 중 하나로 자주 언급된다. 그는 또한 전 세계 수백만 명의 생명을 구한 의학적 혁신에 단독으로 이바지했다.

파스퇴르는 처음에 주류 산업에서 흔한 문제인 젖산 형성으로 인한 맥주와 포도주의 신맛을 해결하기 위해 알코올 발효를 연구하려고 했다. 당시, 알코올에 효모 세포가 존재한다는 것은 알려져 있었으나, 이는 당시의 지배적인 과학 모델인 자연 발생설에서 기인한 것이었다. 이 이론에 따르면, 혼합물의 모든 유기 분자는 발효 과정 동안 일어나는 화학 반응의 부산물이다. 그러나, 파스퇴르는 실제로는 효모가 발효의 촉매이며 다른 미생물들이 이 과정에 부정적인 영향을 미칠 수 있다고 의심했다. 현미경을 사용하여, 그는 발효가 성공했을 때 건강한 효모 세포만 존재한다는 것을 확인했다. 그러나, 신맛이 나는 알코올에는 작은 막대기 모양의 미생물도 포함되어 있었다. 파스퇴르는 이 미생물들이 젖산 형성의 원인이라고 믿었다. 그 가설을 입증하기 위해서는 더 많은 증거가 필요했다. 그의 발상을 시험하기 위해, 그는 모든 미생물 제거하기 위해 포도즙을 가열하여 살균한 다음 효모 세포를 첨가하여 발효를 시작했다. 파스퇴르의 실험은 오염되지 않은 알코올을 생산했다.

이 과정의 성공은 외부 미생물, 즉 세균의 유입이 전염병과 같은 질병의 원인일 수 있다는 것을 암시했기 때문에 인간 건강 전문가들에게 큰 시사점을 가졌다. [3]파스퇴르의 연구에 영감을 받아, 몇몇 유럽 의사들은 수술 전에 수술 도구를 체계적으로 살균하기 시작했는데, 이는 수술 후 사망률을 극적으로 감소시킨 관행이었다. 그러나 많은 사람들은 여전히 전 세계적인 유행병의 규모로 사망을 초래하고 있던 콜레라, 디프테리아, 매독과 같은 더 큰 질병에 미생물이 원인이 될 수 있다는 것을 인정하기를 주저했다.

결정적인 증거를 찾기 위해, 파스퇴르는 프랑스에서 양과 소를 병들게 하는 것으로 의심되는 미생물인 탄저균을 연구하기 시작했다. 그는 무균 배양액에 감염된 양의 혈액 한 방울을 첨가하여 탄저균을 분리했고,

탄저균이 증식할 시간을 준 뒤, 혼합물 한 방울이 새로운 배양액에 첨가되었다. 이러한 희석 과정은 원래 혈액에서 탄저균 외에는 아무것도 남지 않을 때까지 반복된 다음, 그 결과로 나온 물질이 건강한 양에게 실험되었고, 그것은 주사를 맞자 병에 걸렸다. [4]최종 배양액은 원래의 것만큼 강력하게 유지되었으며, 탄저균이 의심할 여지 없이 질병의 원인이며, 한 마리의 양에서 다른 양으로 전염되는 그것들의 능력은 세균 전염 이론을 입증했다.

그러나, 그 균이 공기로 운반되는 포자를 통해 쉽게 전달되는 들판에서 기원했기 때문에 탄저병에 대한 노출을 제한하는 것은 어려운 일임이 드러났다. 이것은 파스퇴르가 다른 방향을 검토하도록 장려했는데, 에드워드 제너의 천연두 백신에 의해 제공된 선례를 따라, 파스퇴르는 질병의 확산을 막기보다는 동물들에게 질병에 대한 면역을 제공할 수 있는 치료법 개발에 관심을 돌렸다. 파스퇴르는 탄저병 백신을 개발하기 위해 다양한 기술을 실험했고, 마침내 열처리된 석탄산의 혈청을 생산했다. 이 방법은 성공적인 것으로 판명되었으며, 결국 미생물 병원체에 의해 야기된 질병의 치료에 대한 과학적 탐구의 새로운 영역을 열었다. 그것은 또한 파스퇴르에게 전문가와 대중의 찬사를 가져다주었고, 일부는 심지어 그를 인류의 가장 위대한 은인 중 한 명으로 칭송하기도 했다.

immunology 명 면역학   epidemiology 명 역학
single-handedly 부 단독으로   breakthrough 명 혁신
fermentation 명 발효   lactic acid 젖산
be attributed to ~에서 기인하다
spontaneous generation 자연 발생설   prevailing 형 지배적인, 우세한
by-product 명 부산물   catalyst 명 촉매
microorganism 명 미생물   microbe 명 미생물, 세균
sterilize 통 살균하다   implication 명 영향   malady 명 질병
mortality rates 사망률   hesitant 형 주저하는   syphilis 명 매독
anthrax 명 탄저병, 탄저균   sterile 형 무균의   culture 명 배양액, 배양
dilution 명 희석   potent 형 강력한   immunity 명 면역
carbolic acid 석탄산   accolade 명 찬사   hail 통 칭송하다

1 지문에서 글쓴이는 왜 "spontaneous generation"를 언급하는가?

(A) 과거에 알코올이 어떻게 생산되었는지 설명하기 위해
(B) 파스퇴르가 틀렸음을 입증한 설명을 제시하기 위해
(C) 파스퇴르의 실험에 영감을 준 생각을 명시하기 위해
(D) 젖산이 처음에 어떻게 발견되었는지를 나타내기 위해

2 네 개의 네모[■]는 다음 문장이 삽입될 수 있는 곳을 나타내고 있다.
그 가설을 입증하기 위해서는 더 많은 증거가 필요했다.
이 문장은 어디에 들어가는 것이 가장 적절한가?

3 다음 중 3단락에서 수술 도구에 관해 추론할 수 있는 것은?

(A) 파스퇴르의 초기 실험 이전에는 아직 발명되지 않았다.
(B) 파스퇴르 시대 이전에는 일반적으로 살균되지 않았다.
(C) 파스퇴르의 연구가 공개된 후 재설계되었다.
(D) 유럽 병원에서 대부분의 사망자를 발생시켰다.

4 4단락에 따르면, 파스퇴르가 실험으로 탄저균에 관해 알게 된 것은?

(A) 프랑스의 양과 소의 질병과 관련이 없다는 것
(B) 특정 인간 사회에서 질병의 원인이었다는 것
(C) 백신에 의해 효과적으로 대응되지 않는다는 것
(D) 특정 동물에서 발생하는 질병의 원인이 된다는 것

5 지문에서 글쓴이는 왜 "Edward Jenner's smallpox vaccine"을 언급하는가?

(A) 파스퇴르가 그의 연구의 기초를 둔 치료 모델을 보여주기 위해
(B) 1800년대 전염성 연구 현황에 대한 배경 정보를 제공하기 위해
(C) 파스퇴르 시대에 흔했던 전염병 치료법을 설명하기 위해
(D) 파스퇴르의 실험이 어떻게 다른 과학자에게 동기를 부여했는지 보여주기 위해

6 지문의 단어 "accolades"와 의미가 가장 비슷한 것은?

(A) 통지
(B) 안내
(C) 존경
(D) 제안

iBT Reading Test 1 본문 p. 128

1 (B)	2 (D)	3 (B)	4 (D)
5 (D)	6 (A)	7 (B)	8 (B)
9 (B)	10 (B), (C), (D)		

아일랜드의 켈트족 구전

켈트족의 철기 시대와 기원후 첫 4세기 전반에 걸쳐, 아일랜드의 역사는 글로 기록되지 않았다. 켈트인들은 자신들의 이야기를 기억해서 구두로 전달했기 때문에 글을 쓸 필요를 느끼지 못했다. 또한 현실적인 문제도 있었다. 그들이 가진 유일한 문자 체계는 오검 문자였는데, 이것은 다양한 길이와 수의 선으로 글자를 표현하는 매우 번거로운 체계였다. [2]이것은 왜 현존하는 비문들이 전적으로 이름과 족보만을 위한 것인지 설명할 수 있다. 묘비와 토지를 표시하기 위해 비문을 사용하는 것은 합리적이었겠지만, 역사적 사건이나 문학적 산문을 기록하는 데 그것들을 사용하는 것은 헛된 일이었을 것이다.

[3]우리가 초기 아일랜드에 관해 가지고 있는 대부분의 역사적 지식은 켈트인들에 대한 정보를 간접적으로 받았을 로마 작가들에게서 나온 것이다. 역사적 사건들이 보통 그것들이 실제로 발생한 지 한참 뒤에 기록되었기 때문에, 그러한 초기 기록들이 얼마나 믿을 만한지는 논란의 여지가 있는 문제다. 그러나, 서기 500년부터, 일부 켈트인들은 기독교로 개종했고 유럽으로 유학을 갔다. 돌아와서, 그들은 라틴어로 경전을 작성했다. 그 결과, 6세기부터 문서 자원의 수가 증가했다. 예를 들어, 서기 800년경의 아름다운 삽화가 있는 기독교 필사본인 '켈즈의 서'는 초기 아일랜드 문학의 가장 뛰어난 예 중 하나이다. 마침내, 글로 쓰인 역사가 나타나기 시작했지만, 초기에는 읽고 쓰는 능력은 주로 종교 단체들에 한정되어 있었다.

6세기 이전의 이러한 읽고 쓰는 능력의 상대적인 부재를 문화적 교양의 부족과 연관 짓는 것은 솔깃할 수도 있다. 그러나, 그러한 견해는 어느 특정 계급에 국한되지 않았던 기술인 켈트족 구전의 웅변술을 과소평가한다. 교육받은 엘리트들이 들려주는 이야기들은 분명히 평민들에 의해 경청되고 반복되었다. [4]웅변의 솜씨 측면에서, 켈트인들은 그들의 동시대인인 갈리아인들과 대등한 수준이었는데, 이들은 당시의 로마 연대기 작가들에 의해 그들이 군사적 영광만큼이나 웅변술에서의 탁월함을 강조한 민족으로 묘사되었다. 마찬가지로, 켈트인들은 구전 시, 연설, 노래를 인류의 업적 중 가장 강력한 것으로 여겼다.

암기와 웅변은 철기 시대 동안 켈트족의 전통 유지에 필수적이었는데,

그것들이 켈트인들이 그들의 집단적 지혜를 다음 세대에 전달할 수 있는 유일한 수단이었기 때문이다. 명확성과 사실의 정확성은 전달의 주된 목표가 아니었다. 구전 역사는 때때로 저명한 인물들의 특정한 자질을 과장하는 서정시 이야기인 찬송 시의 형태를 취하기도 했다. 과거의 지도자들은 종종 관대함과 백성의 복지에 대한 관심으로 칭송을 받았고, 전사들은 그들의 영웅적인 용기와 무기를 다루는 솜씨로 찬사를 받았다.

대부분의 경우, 구전은 지배 계급의 관심사를 홍보하기 위한 교육 선전으로 사용되었다. 따라서 시인들이 청중을 사로잡기 위해 생동감 있고 생생한 세부 사항을 사용했다는 것은 이해할 만하다. 게다가, 웅변은 노래로 불리기 위한 운율 형식으로 구성되었다. 켈트인들은 역사적 정보를 전달하는 매개체로서 운문의 이점을 아주 잘 알고 있었다. [8]운율적인 패턴으로 불려진 운문은 켈트족 젊은이들의 기억 속에 쉽게 박혔고, 시인은 문어에 전문가가 되지 않아도 된다는 장점도 있었다. 따라서, 시인들은 지식의 도관 역할을 했고 미래 세대들의 교육에 중심이 되었다. 지식의 총체가 다음 세대에 전파되고 소멸로부터 보호될 것을 보장한 것은 다름 아닌 구어였다.

transmit 동전달하다　cumbersome 형번거로운, 성가신
extant 형현존하는　exclusively 부전적으로
genealogy 명족보, 가계도　futile 형헛된, 소용없는
literacy 명읽고 쓰는 능력　sophistication 명교양
eloquence 명웅변술　oratory 명웅변
be on par with ~와 대등하다　contemporary 명동시대인
imperative 형필수적인　vehicle 명수단, 매개체
panegyric 명찬송 시, 찬사　lyrical 형서정시의
discourse 명이야기, 담화　extol 동칭송하다, 극찬하다
metrical 형운율의　vessel 명도관, 관　corpus 명총체
disseminate 동전파하다　safeguard 동보호하다
dissipation 명소멸, 소실

1 지문의 단어 "cumbersome"과 의미가 가장 비슷한 것은?

(A) 이례적인
(B) 불편한
(C) 무관한
(D) 실질적인

2 1단락에 따르면, 다음 중 오검 문자에 관해 사실인 것은?

(A) 유럽 본토에서 아일랜드로 전달되었다.
(B) 주로 산문이나 역사적 사건을 기록하는 데 사용되었다.
(C) 켈트족의 철기 시대에 처음 개발되었다.
(D) 주로 이름과 족보를 나타내는 데 사용되었다.

3 2단락에서 아일랜드에 대한 초기 역사 기록에 관해 추론할 수 있는 것은?

(A) 아일랜드 역사 분야의 대부분의 학자들에 의해 신뢰할 수 없다고 여겨진다.
(B) 대개 아일랜드에서의 직접적인 경험이 없는 사람들에 의해 써졌다.
(C) 일반적으로 유럽 수도원의 종교 성직자들에 의해 편찬되었다.
(D) '켈즈의 서'에 영감이 되었다고 여겨진다.

4 3단락에 따르면, 다음 중 켈트인들과 갈리아인들의 공통점은?

(A) 군사적 기량으로 유명했다.
(B) 대부분 문맹이었다.
(C) 사회적 계층을 초월한 구전이 있었다.

(D) 웅변을 중시했다

5 지문에서 글쓴이는 왜 "panegyrics"를 언급하는가?

(A) 집단적 지식이 전달된 주요 수단을 밝히기 위해
(B) 철기 시대 동안 켈트족의 구전 역사에서 일어난 변화를 강조하기 위해
(C) 켈트인들이 주로 명확하고 정확한 이야기에 관심이 있었다는 것을 반박하기 위해
(D) 구전 역사가 반드시 말 그대로 받아들여질 의도는 없었다는 것을 보여주기 위해

6 지문의 단어 "extolled"와 의미가 가장 비슷한 것은?

(A) 칭송받다
(B) 보상받다
(C) 모방되다
(D) 비교되다

7 지문의 단어 "disseminated"와 의미가 가장 비슷한 것은?

(A) 제공되다
(B) 퍼지다
(C) 방출되다
(D) 허가되다

8 5단락에 따르면, 노래로 불려진 운문에서 운율적인 패턴을 사용하는 것의 장점은 무엇이었는가?

(A) 운문이 청중들에게 생생한 세부 사항을 더 잘 전달할 수 있게 했다.
(B) 젊은이들이 들은 것을 쉽게 기억하게 했다.
(C) 전통 노래의 문자 형태로의 전환을 용이하게 했다.
(D) 시인들이 과거 사건들의 연대기를 창조적으로 상세히 기술하게 해주었다.

9 네 개의 네모[■]는 다음 문장이 삽입될 수 있는 곳을 나타내고 있다.

교육받은 엘리트들이 들려주는 이야기들은 분명히 평민들에 의해 경청되고 반복되었다.

이 문장은 어디에 들어가는 것이 가장 적절한가?

10 **지시**: 지문 요약을 위한 도입 문장이 아래에 주어져 있다. 지문의 가장 중요한 내용을 나타내는 보기 3개를 골라 요약을 완성하라. 어떤 문장은 지문에 언급되지 않은 내용이나 사소한 정보를 나타내므로 요약에 포함되지 않는다. **이 문제는 2점이다.**

> 그들의 초기 역사 동안, 아일랜드 켈트인들은 문자 전통보다 구전을 강조했다.
> · (B) 켈트족은 구두 의사소통을 문명의 가장 중요한 측면 중 하나로 여겼다.
> · (C) 구전 역사의 주된 기능은 주요 인물들을 칭찬하고 교육적인 선전을 하는 것이기 때문에 사실의 정확성은 부차적으로 중요했다.
> · (D) 비록 문자 전통이 6세기 이전에 잘 발달하지 못했지만, 켈트인들은 정교한 구전 전통을 가지고 있었다.

(A) 오검 문자는 작성에 상당한 공간이 필요했기 때문에 주요 작문에는 적합하지 않았다.
(E) 찬송 시는 주목할 만한 인물에 대한 과장된 찬사가 특징이다.
(F) 젊은이들을 교육시키는 역할을 했기 때문에, 서정시 운문에 능숙한 시인들은 켈트 사회에서 가장 높은 계급을 차지했다.

1 (A), (C) 2 (C) 3 (B) 4 (B)
5 (D) 6 (D) 7 (B) 8 (D)
9 (D) 10 (A), (B), (F)

과잉 착취와 동물 멸종

저명한 생물학자 E. O. 윌슨에 따르면, 만약 그것들이 사라지고 있는 현재의 속도가 유지된다면, 지구상의 모든 생물 종의 절반이 21세기 말까지 멸종될 것이다. [1A/1C]생물은 서식지를 파괴하는 자연재해와 종간 경쟁과 같은 자연적 요인에 의해 때때로 사라지지만, 개체군에서 너무 많은 개체들이 포획되어 그것이 더 이상 자신을 지탱할 수 없게 하는 인간에 의한 과잉 착취는 많은 생물들을 멸종되거나 멸종 위기에 처하게 했다.

선사시대 이래로, 사냥과 낚시는 영양분의 필수적인 원천을 제공함으로써 인류에게 깊이 혜택을 주었다. [4]안타깝게도, 그것들은 이전에 번성했던 몇몇 종들의 멸종이나 멸종 위기에 기여했다. 예를 들어, 여행비둘기는 예전에는 개체가 너무 많아서 한때 그것들의 한 무리가 3일 동안 지속적인 흐름으로 하늘 위로 날아가는 것이 목격되기도 했던 북아메리카 새였다. 그러나, 그 종은 19세기에 값싼 고기 공급원으로 점점 더 인기를 끌었고, 수요 증가는 그 새들의 대규모 상업적 사냥을 부추겼다. 그 결과, 마지막 여행비둘기는 1914년에 신시내티 동물원에서 죽었다.

식량을 위해 동물을 포획하는 것 외에도, 인간은 특정 동물의 특정 신체 부위를 그것들의 알려진 약효 때문에 목표로 삼아왔다. 지속 불가능한 채집은 일부 의학적으로 가치 있는 종의 급격한 개체수 감소를 초래했다. 한 가지 예는 상하이에서 홍콩까지 중국 앞바다에 널리 퍼져 있던 거대한 물고기인 황순어이다. 특수 낚시 장비의 도움으로, 어부들은 그것의 부레를 위해 이 물고기를 집중적으로 잡았는데, 그 기관은 일반적인 자양 강장제로 매우 가치 있으며 심장 및 폐 질환을 치료한다고 여겨진다. 수요가 많은 그것의 부레의 시장 가치가 현재 금의 그것보다 높기 때문에, 이 종의 암컷은 번식력이 매우 높아 매년 수백만 개의 알을 낳음에도 불구하고 황순어는 희귀해졌다.

외래종 애완동물에 대한 욕구는 인간이 특정 종을 착취해온 또 다른 수단이며, 식량이나 약을 위해 사냥당하는 동물과 마찬가지로 포획된 표본에 대한 시장의 수요는 그것들의 가격을 상승시키고 더 많은 밀렵을 부추긴다. 일부 외래종 애완동물은 가두어 사육되지만, 다수는 그들의 자연 서식지에서 직접 채집된다. 1994년에 로티뱀목거북의 발견 이후, 그것은 특이하게 긴 목 때문에 외래종 애완동물 주인들 사이에서 대단히 인기를 끌었고, 매년 많은 그 거북들이 포획되어 판매된다. 그 결과, 그 거북은 멸종 위기에 처해 있다. 작은 섬 하나에 오직 세 개의 개체군만이 존재하며, 이러한 유일성은 그것을 더 탐나게 하는 결과를 낳았다. 이러한 수요 증가로 인해, 그 거북들은 여전히 해외에서 판매되기 위해 채집되고 섬 밖으로 옮겨진다. 취미용으로 멸종 위기에 처한 거북을 거래하는 것을 중단시키기 위한 보호법이 제정되었지만, 이 거북과 관련된 거래는 밀렵꾼들이 저항하기에는 너무 수익성이 높은 것으로 입증되었다.

최근 역사에서 인구가 폭발적으로 증가하고 기술이 발전함에 따라, 동물 종의 과잉 착취는 기하급수적으로 증가했고 현재 종 멸종의 주요 원인이 되고 있다. 만약 인간이 종의 영구적인 손실에 대해 걱정한다면, 그들은 더 지속 가능한 방식으로 동물 종을 포함한 천연자원을 이용하기 위해 현재의 행동을 조정해야 할 것이다. [7A/7C/7D]개선된 천연자원 관리에 더하여, 필요한 변화에는 침입종에 대한 더 많은 통제와 기후

변화에 대처하기 위한 보다 적극적인 조치가 포함된다.

overexploitation 명 과잉 착취, 과잉 이용   extinct 형 멸종된
interspecies 형 종간의   sustenance 명 영양분
prolific 형 번성한, 풍부한   populous 형 개체가 많은, 인구가 많은
purported 형 ~이라고 알려진   medicinal properties 약효
unsustainable 형 지속 불가능한   precipitous 형 급격한, 갑작스러운
swim bladder (물고기의) 부레   health tonic 자양 강장제
sought-after 형 수요가 많은   fertile 형 번식력이 높은
avenue 명 수단, 방법   exploit 동 착취하다
specimen 명 (동식물의) 표본   poaching 명 밀렵
in captivity 가두어, 감금하여   exclusivity 명 유일성, 배타성
coveted 형 탐내는   transaction 명 거래   lucrative 형 수익성이 높은
exponentially 부 기하급수적으로   sustainable 형 지속 가능한

1 지문에 따르면, 종 멸종의 원인이 되는 두 가지 자연적 요인은? 두 개의 정답을 고르시오.

(A) 자연재해로 인한 서식지 손실
(B) 기상 패턴의 변화
(C) 종간의 경쟁
(D) 번식에 관한 문제

2 지문의 단어 "sustenance"와 의미가 가장 비슷한 것은?

(A) 편안함
(B) 기초
(C) 영양분
(D) 위험

3 지문의 단어 "they"가 가리키는 것은?

(A) 선사시대
(B) 사냥과 낚시
(C) 인류
(D) 필수적인 원천

4 다음 중 2단락에서 종의 멸종에 관해 추론할 수 있는 것은?

(A) 선사시대에는 인간의 활동으로 인한 멸종이 흔했다.
(B) 엄청난 개체 수는 멸종에 대한 효과적인 보호 장치가 아니다.
(C) 인간에 의한 멸종을 피하기 위해서는 높은 번식률이 필요하다.
(D) 매우 번식력이 높은 종들은 단기간에 멸종할 가능성이 적다.

5 지문의 단어 "precipitous"와 의미가 가장 비슷한 것은?

(A) 명백한
(B) 점진적인
(C) 무작위의
(D) 급격한

6 아래 문장 중 지문 속의 음영된 문장의 핵심 정보를 가장 잘 표현한 것은? 오답은 문장의 의미를 크게 바꾸거나 핵심 정보를 생략한다.

(A) 그것의 희귀성의 결과로, 황순어는 매년 수백만 개의 알을 방출함으로써 생존하도록 진화했다.
(B) 황순어의 부레는 그 물고기가 거의 멸종 위기에 처해 있음에도 불구하고 매우 높은 가격을 요구한다.
(C) 비록 황순어는 매우 번식력이 높지만, 그것은 야생에서 너무 드물게 되어 현재 금보다 더 희귀하다.
(D) 번식 잠재력이 높음에도 불구하고, 황순어는 그것의 귀중한 부레에 대한 높은 수요 때문에 멸종 위기에 처해 있다.

7 다음 중 5단락에서 인간 행동에 필요한 조정으로 언급되지 않은 것은?

(A) 침입종에 대한 더 실질적인 제한

(B) 종 착취에 대한 더 심각한 법적 처벌

(C) 더 나은 자원 관리

(D) 기후 변화에 맞서기 위한 더 강력한 조치

8 5단락에서 글쓴이의 주된 목적은?

(A) 문제에 관한 몇 가지 일반적인 오해를 강조하기

(B) 과잉 착취와 멸종 간의 관계 연결하기

(C) 더 효과적인 자원 관리의 필요성을 강조하기

(D) 독자들에게 문제의 심각성을 이해하도록 촉구하기

9 네 개의 네모[■]는 다음 문장이 삽입될 수 있는 곳을 나타내고 있다.

이러한 수요 증가로 인해, 그 거북들은 여전히 해외에서 판매되기 위해 채집되고 섬 밖으로 옮겨진다.

이 문장은 어디에 들어가는 것이 가장 적절한가?

10 지시: 지문 요약을 위한 도입 문장이 아래에 주어져 있다. 지문의 가장 중요한 내용을 나타내는 보기 3개를 골라 요약을 완성하라. 어떤 문장은 지문에 언급되지 않은 내용이나 사소한 정보를 나타내므로 요약에 포함되지 않는다. **이 문제는 2점이다.**

> **동물 멸종의 주요 원인은 인간에 의한 과잉 착취이다.**
> · (A) 희귀한 외래종 애완동물에 대한 수요는 로티뱀목거북과 같은 일부 종의 지속 불가능한 채집으로 이어졌다.
> · (B) 특정 동물들은 특정 신체 부위의 인식된 의학적 가치를 위해 집중적으로 채집되기 때문에 멸종 위기에 처해 있다.
> · (F) 과도한 사냥과 낚시는 일부 종들을 멸종시켰고 다른 생물들의 개체 수를 크게 감소시켰다.

(C) 취미 목적의 사냥의 인기가 많은 동물들이 멸종 위기에 처하게 될 정도로 높아졌다.

(D) 황순어의 부레는 건강상의 이점 때문에 인간에게 매우 귀하게 여겨진다.

(E) 불법 애완동물 거래가 주요 환경 문제가 되었기 때문에, 입법자들은 외래종 애완동물의 유통을 금지하는 법안을 제정했다.

Vocabulary Review
본문 p. 136

1 irrational   2 immunity   3 tailored
4 contemporaries   5 sustainable   6 captivity
7 (A)   8 (A)   9 (B)   10 (C)
11 (A)   12 (B)   13 (D)   14 (A)

CHAPTER 08
Sentence Insertion

Example
본문 p. 139

1 (B)   2 (C)

쟁기 사회

농경 정착 사회 발달 이전, 대부분의 인구 집단들은 사냥꾼, 채집가, 양치기로 구성되어 있었다. 그러한 집단들은 그들의 식량 공급원이 제한되어 있었기 때문에 당연히 비교적 작아야 했다. 게다가, 그렇게 하지 않으면 자원의 필연적인 고갈이 있었을 것이기 때문에 그들은 이곳저곳을 옮겨 다닐 수밖에 없었다. 어느 시점에 농경 사회들이 나타났고, 그것들은 파종을 위한 토양을 갈기 위한 충분한 수단뿐만 아니라 식물 경작에 대한 지식에 의존했다. 이용된 최초의 도구들은 뾰족한 막대기로, 원시 농부들이 땅을 찌르고 긁어내는 데 사용했지만, 이것들은 점차 토양을 가는 데 사용할 수 있는 날을 가진 더 나은 도구인 괭이로 변형되었다.

농경 정착지와 관련된 주요한 획기적 발전은 쟁기의 발명이었는데, 그것은 씨를 뿌리거나 심기 위한 여러 줄의 긴 고랑을 만들기 위해 비옥한 땅에서 끌릴 수 있었다. 두 사람이 함께 밭을 가로질러 쟁기를 끌 수 있었지만, 비록 쟁기 사용이 이전의 방법들에 비해 큰 장점이었음에도 불구하고, 그것은 엄청난 양의 물리적인 힘을 필요로 했다. 게다가, 그것은 고된 일이었기 때문에, 혁신적인 농부들은 그들의 노동을 줄이기 위해 짐을 끄는 동물에 의지했다. 소가 끄는 쟁기는 한 사람이 더 적은 시간에 비교적 광활한 땅을 경작할 수 있게 해주었다. 그럼에도 불구하고, 쟁기와 이 다루기 힘든 짐승들을 통제하는 데 필요한 물리적인 힘은 상당했다.

따라서, 쟁기의 발명으로, 경제적 생산성의 측면에서 밭을 가는 데 있어서의 여성의 노동이 덜 가치 있어짐에 따라, 밭을 가는 일은 남성의 책임이 되었다. 그전에는 여성들이 토양을 개간하는 책임을 분담했지만, 이 임무에서 해방되어 다른 활동에 전념할 수 있는 시간이 생겼고, 따라서 쟁기는 성 역할을 바꾸는 데 영향을 미쳤다.

sedentary ⓗ정착의   implement ⓝ도구   hoe ⓝ괭이
till ⓥ갈다, 경작하다   breakthrough ⓝ획기적 발전   plow ⓝ쟁기
tremendous ⓗ엄청난   arduous ⓗ고된   unwieldy ⓗ다루기 힘든
influential ⓗ영향을 미치는

1 1단락에서 네 개의 네모[■]는 다음 문장이 삽입될 수 있는 곳을 나타내고 있다.

게다가, 그렇게 하지 않으면 자원의 필연적인 고갈이 있었을 것이기 때문에 그들은 이곳저곳을 옮겨 다닐 수밖에 없었다.

이 문장은 어디에 들어가는 것이 가장 적절한가?

2 2단락에서 네 개의 네모[■]는 다음 문장이 삽입될 수 있는 곳을 나타내고 있다.

소가 끄는 쟁기는 한 사람이 더 적은 시간에 비교적 광활한 땅을 경작할 수 있게 해주었다.

이 문장은 어디에 들어가는 것이 가장 적절한가?

Reading Practice 1
본문 p. 140

1 (A)   2 (B)   3 (D)   4 (D)   5 (B)   6 (D)

포유류 이동 습관

생물학에서, 주기적으로 한 장소에서 다른 장소로 이동하는 습관은 보통 비행 및 수생 동물과 관련이 있다. 그러나, 수많은 포유류 종들도 자원 및 짝의 변동하는 이용 가능성에 대응하여 이동에 참여한다. 이것

의 세 가지 두드러진 예는 북방물개, 북아메리카의 가지뿔영양, 아프리카코끼리이다.

북태평양 지역에서 발견되는 바다사자류의 가장 큰 종인 북방물개는 번식을 목적으로 이동한다. 수륙 양생의 종으로서, 북방물개는 먼 거리를 헤엄칠 수 있다는 점에서 이동성 육상 포유류에 비해 상당한 이점을 가진다. 그 결과, 북방물개의 이동은 3,000마일까지 연장될 수 있다. 매년, 그 물개들은 짝을 만나기 위해 베링해의 프리빌로프 제도에 있는 번식지로 돌아온다. 수컷 물개는 5월에 번식지에 먼저 도착하고, 암컷은 약간 더 늦게 도착한다. 11월 말경에, 새끼 물개들이 젖을 뗀 후, 물개들은 겨울을 나기 위해 남쪽 방향으로 퍼진다.

수컷들은 일반적으로 베링해와 태평양 상부에서 겨울을 보내는 반면, 암컷들은 헤엄쳐 캘리포니아주의 남단까지 간다. ²ᴬ철저한 연구 끝에, 과학자들은 이 이동 범위의 차이에 대한 이유가 종들의 크기 차이에서 기인한다고 믿는데, 수컷들은 암컷들보다 40퍼센트까지 더 길고 370퍼센트까지 더 무겁게 자랄 수 있다. ²ᶜ/²ᴰ상당히 더 작은 암컷들은 태평양 상부의 혹독하게 추운 겨울을 견디지 못하며 겨울에는 더 따뜻한 지역으로 수천 마일을 이동해야 한다. 그러나, 물개의 이동은 인간 활동에 의해 방해받을 위험에 처해 있다. 예를 들어, 과도한 어업은 그것들의 이동을 방해할 수 있는데, 충분한 먹이를 얻을 수 없는 암컷은 번식지로 돌아가는 여정을 완수할 충분한 기력이 없기 때문이다.

북아메리카의 가지뿔영양은 단 3일 만에 짧은 이동을 마친다. 와이오밍주 그랜드 티턴 국립공원의 가지뿔영양 무리들은 그린 리버 분지의 온화한 기후에 도달하기 위해 남쪽으로 100마일 이상 이동한다. 그것들의 길은 단편적인 사유지와 공유지에 걸쳐 있으며, 각각에는 사람이 만든 장애물이 줄지어 있다. ⁴시속 55마일로 달릴 수 있는 능력에도 불구하고, 가지뿔영양은 장애물을 쉽게 뛰어넘을 수 없다. 결과적으로, 농경 및 보안용 울타리가 심각한 장애물을 생성하고, 가지뿔영양은 울타리를 통과하거나 그 아래를 비집고 지나가도록 시도해야만 하며, 이 행동은 그것들을 포식에 매우 취약하게 한다. 이러한 어려움을 인식하여, 비영리 및 정부 기관은 힘을 합쳐 가지뿔영양 친화적인 지역을 조성했다. 가지뿔영양이 고속도로를 안전하게 건널 수 있도록 잔디 고가도로가 건설되었다. 도로를 원활하게 건널 수 있음에 따라, 여러 지역의 가지뿔영양은 차량 충돌로 인한 죽음을 거의 겪지 않았다.

다른 포유류 종들과 비교할 때, 아프리카코끼리의 이동은 잘 알려져 있지 않다. 이 동물들은 매우 예측하기 어렵고, 그것들의 서로 다른 이동 패턴은 환경 보호론자들에게 도전이 된다. 게다가, 다른 이동성 포유류와 달리, 코끼리는 특정 지역에서 번식해야 하는 생물학적 의무에 의해 이끌리는 것처럼 보이지 않으며, 그것들의 이동은 먹이 자원의 위치에 의해서도 촉진되지 않는다. 대신에, 짐바브웨의 황게국립공원에서 수행된 연구는 일부 코끼리들이 가뭄 동안 수원을 찾아가기 위해 60마일 이상 이동했음을 발견했다. ⁶안타깝게도, 이러한 이동은 보호 공원을 빠져나가, 코끼리들이 밀렵 위험이 높은 지역으로 건너갈 때 그것들을 위험에 빠뜨린다.

periodically (부)주기적으로   availability (명)이용 가능성, 가용성
procreation (명)번식, 생식   amphibious (형)수륙 양생의
rookery (명)(물개·펭귄의) 번식지   wean (동)젖을 떼다
exhaustive (형)철저한   disparity (명)차이, 격차
fragmented (형)단편적인   impediment (명)장애물, 방해
vulnerable (형)취약한   predation (명)(동물의) 포식
disparate (형)서로 다른, 이질적인   imperative (명)의무, 명령
poaching (명)밀렵, 불법 포획

1   지문의 단어 "exhaustive"와 의미가 가장 비슷한 것은?

(A) 철저한
(B) 정확한
(C) 최고의
(D) 눈에 띄는

2   3단락에 따르면, 다음 중 북방물개 수컷과 암컷의 차이가 아닌 것은?

(A) 수컷은 암컷보다 상당히 더 크다.
(B) 암컷은 번식지에 가장 먼저 도착한다.
(C) 수컷은 더 추운 지역에서 겨울을 보낸다.
(D) 암컷은 겨울에 더 먼 거리를 이동한다.

3   네 개의 네모[■]는 다음 문장이 삽입될 수 있는 곳을 나타내고 있다.
도로를 원활하게 건널 수 있음에 따라, 여러 지역의 가지뿔영양은 차량 충돌로 인한 죽음을 거의 겪지 않았다.
이 문장은 어디에 들어가는 것이 가장 적절한가?

4   4단락에 따르면, 가지뿔영양의 이동을 제한하는 제약은?

(A) 그것들은 눈 속을 달릴 수 없다.
(B) 그것들은 집단으로만 이동할 수 있다.
(C) 그것들은 이동 경로를 식별할 수 없다.
(D) 그것들은 장애물을 지나가는 데 어려움을 느낀다.

5   아래 문장 중 지문 속의 음영된 문장의 핵심 정보를 가장 잘 표현한 것은?

(A) 먹이의 위치는 코끼리의 이동의 주된 이유이다.
(B) 코끼리는 그것들의 이동에 있어 번식이나 먹이 공급원에 의해 동기가 부여되지 않는다.
(C) 다른 것들과 비교했을 때, 코끼리는 생물학적 필요성에 의해 이끌리지 않는다.
(D) 다른 종들의 이동 습관은 코끼리와 쉽게 비교될 수 있다.

6   5단락에 따르면, 코끼리의 이동은 왜 보호 활동에 지장을 주는가?

(A) 한 국가 내에 머물고 싶어하지 않는다.
(B) 환경 보호론자들에게 알려지지 않은 지역으로 이동한다.
(C) 그것들의 섭식 습관은 예측할 수 없는 시기에 일어난다.
(D) 그것들의 경로는 안전한 구역 밖으로 끌어낸다.

Reading Practice 2   본문 p. 142

1 (D)   2 (A)   3 (B)   4 (C)   5 (C)   6 (D)

아틀란티스

유토피아는 보통 평화와 평등을 향한 인간의 열망을 표현하는 완벽한 공동체로 정의된다. 유토피아에 관한 가장 유명한 이야기들 중 하나는 소크라테스식 대화 '티마이우스'와 '크리티아스'에서 나오는데, 이 대화에서 플라톤은, 엄청난 자연재해 속에서 바다에 의해 삼켜진, 아틀란티스라는 섬에 대해 이야기한다. ¹그의 글에서, 플라톤은 다리, 신전, 경마장을 포함하는 기반 시설뿐만 아니라 상아, 금, 은으로 지어진 황궁을 지녔던 선진 문명인 과거의 아틀란티스 제국의 상실을 탄식한다.

플라톤의 아틀란티스 이야기는 그의 철학 작품들에 포함되어 있으며 고안된 이론들을 뒷받침하기 위한 것이기 때문에, 그 작가가 실제 역

사를 전달하려고 의도했다고 믿는 학자는 거의 없다. 그러나, 아틀란티스 신화가 실제 과거 사건에 대한 기억에 의해 영감을 받았을 가능성은 남아 있다.

잘 알려진 한 가지 가설은 아틀란티스의 파괴가 기원전 1650년경 청동기 시대에 지중해에서 폭발한 테라 화산을 기반으로 한다는 것이다. 이 자연재해는 트로이 전쟁 이전 에게해 지역에서 일어난 가장 중요한 사건이었을 것이고, 플라톤은 그것이 초래한 파괴에 대해 분명히 알고 있었을 것이다. 일부 고고학자들은 이 대격동적 지질학적 사건이 그리스 크레타섬을 중심으로 한 강력한 항해 문화 공동체인 미노아 문명의 몰락을 촉발했다고 믿는다. 이 폭발은 그 섬에 약 10센티미터의 화산재를 떨어뜨려 모든 토착 식물을 질식시켰고, 결과적으로 동물과 인간 집단에 공통으로 대규모 기아를 초래했다. 동시에, 화산 폭발이 산토리니 칼데라의 붕괴를 일으켰을 때 발생된 일련의 해일이 크레타 해안을 황폐화했다. [4]미노아 해군의 요새와 상업 항들이 유실되었다. 그들의 식량 생산 능력이 심각하게 감소하고 항해 생계가 사실상 파괴되면서 미노아인들은 생존을 위해 고군분투했고 그들의 문명은 200년 후에 결국 사라졌다.

다른 이들은 남부 스페인의 해안 지역이 플라톤의 작품에서 묘사된 아틀란티스라고 추측한다. 이 가설은 대개 침몰한 도시처럼 보이는 것을 보여주는 위성 사진을 기반으로 하는데, 일부 학자들은 그것이 고대 도시 타르테소스라고 믿는다. 고대 그리스 및 이집트 문헌에 따르면, 타르테소스 사람들은 지중해 서쪽 끝에서 온 부유한 귀금속 무역상들이었으며, 이 묘사는 플라톤의 아틀란티스에 대한 묘사와 일치한다. 그러나, 이 이론의 한 가지 문제는 타르테소스는 섬이 아니었고, 플라톤의 아틀란티스는 섬이었다는 점이다. **이것은 타르테소스 이론에 대한 상당한 회의로 이어졌다.** 그럼에도 불구하고, 그 이론의 지지자들은 그의 대화에서 이집트의 역사 문헌을 자주 사용했던 플라톤이 "해안"을 의미하는 상형 문자를 "섬"을 의미하는 것과 혼동했다고 말하며 그 모순을 설명하는데, 이는 다른 그리스어 작품에서 꽤 흔한 실수였다.

세 번째 주장은 플라톤이 아틀란티스의 바다에 대해 이야기했을 때, 그가 실은 현재 대서양으로 알려진 바다를 지칭했다는 것이다. 그의 설명에서, 플라톤은 지중해가 대서양으로 흘러 들어가는 헤라클레스의 기둥 너머의 광대한 바다에 아틀란티스가 위치했다고 언급한다. 따라서, 이 불운한 유토피아 도시는 지중해 밖에 위치했었을 수도 있다. [6B]이 이론의 지지자들은 그 전설이 거석 무덤을 남긴 아일랜드의 신석기 문화 공동체에 대한 역사적 설명을 포함한다고 제시한다. [6A/6C]게다가, 아일랜드는 (대략 300마일의 길이와 200마일의 너비라는) 아틀란티스의 지리적 묘사에 들어맞는 세계에서 유일한 섬이며, 그것의 지형은 마지막 빙하기 말기의 기후 변화와 관련된 자연재해로 인해 완전히 바뀌었다.

lament 통탄식하다   infrastructure 명기반 시설
embed 통포함시키다, 끼워 넣다   invented 형고안된
hypothesis 명가설   cataclysmic 형대격동의
seafaring 형항해의   indigenous 형토착의
devastate 통황폐화하다, 파괴하다   postulate 통추측하다
contradiction 명모순   hieroglyphic 명(이집트의) 상형 문자
doomed 형불운한, 운이 다한   megalithic 형거석의

1 1단락에 따르면, 플라톤의 대화는 아틀란티스 제국을

   (A) 부유한 사람들의 집단으로 묘사한다

   (B) 계급 없는 공동체로 묘사한다

   (C) 평화로운 사회로 묘사한다

   (D) 고도로 발달된 문명으로 묘사한다

2 지문의 단어 "embedded"와 의미가 가장 비슷한 것은?

   (A) 통합되다

   (B) 발견되다

   (C) 고립되다

   (D) 암시되다

3 지문에서 글쓴이는 왜 "Trojan War"를 언급하는가?

   (A) 플라톤이 아틀란티스의 근거로 트로이 전쟁을 사용했을 수도 있었음을 시사하기 위해

   (B) 테라 화산의 폭발이 고대 그리스 세계에서 얼마나 중요했는지 강조하기 위해

   (C) 지질학적 재해 이후에 주요 무력 충돌이 발생했다는 주장을 뒷받침하기 위해

   (D) 플라톤의 대화에서 등장할 수 있는 또 다른 역사적 사건의 예를 제시하기 위해

4 다음 중 3단락에서 미노아인들에 관해 추론할 수 있는 것은?

   (A) 화산섬에 살았다.

   (B) 농경 기술이 없었다.

   (C) 많은 배를 이용했다.

   (D) 음식을 위해 동물에 의존했다.

5 네 개의 네모[■]는 다음 문장이 삽입될 수 있는 곳을 나타내고 있다.

이것은 타르테소스 이론에 대한 상당한 회의로 이어졌다.

이 문장은 어디에 들어가는 것이 가장 적절한가?

6 다음 중 아일랜드가 아틀란티스의 위치일 수 있다는 이론을 뒷받침하는 데 사용되는 증거가 아닌 것은?

   (A) 그것의 크기는 플라톤이 묘사한 섬과 비슷하다.

   (B) 그것은 대형 석조 건축물을 짓는 사회의 본거지였다.

   (C) 그것은 파괴적인 자연 현상에 의해 변형되었다.

   (D) 그것의 주민들은 헤라클레스 신을 숭배했다.

Reading Practice 3   본문 p.144

1 (A)   2 (D)   3 (C)   4 (C)   5 (A)   6 (B)

지구공학

지난 100년 동안, 평균 지표면 온도는 섭씨 0.6도 상승했다. 지구의 기후는 과거에 비슷한 변화를 겪어왔지만, 인간 활동이 가장 최근의 지구 기온 상승의 원인이라는 것을 보여주는 연구 결과가 늘고 있다. [1]이 개념은 산업화된 사회가 이산화탄소, 메탄 및 아산화질소 같은 기체의 배출을 크게 증가시킨 기간 동안 기온의 상승이 일어났다는 사실에 의해 강화된다. 이 물질들은 대기에 갇힌 기체가 우주로의 열 방출을 막는 온실 효과의 주요 원인으로 널리 여겨진다.

지구 온난화의 결과는 광범위한 추측의 대상이 되었으며, 일부 장기적 예측은 해수면의 급격한 상승, 해류의 변화, 강수량의 변동을 보여준다. 이러한 예측은 서식지 변화로 인해 발생할 수 있는 광범위한 사막화와 대량 멸종에 대한 우려로 이어졌다. 지구 온난화의 부정적인 영향이 먼 미래에 국한되지 않는다는 공감대도 커지고 있다. 많은 기후학자들은 그것이 허리케인, 태풍, 토네이도와 같은 기상 이변의 최근의 발생률 증가에 책임이 있다고 주장한다. 그 결과, 과학자들은 지구 온난

화에 대처하기 위한 대안적인 방법을 모색하기 시작했는데, 이것들 중 가장 두드러진 것은 지구공학이며, 이것은 지구의 물리적 특성을 변경하기 위한 인간 기술의 사용이다.

1990년, 영국의 물리학자 존 래텀은 기온 상승 문제에 대한 가장 간단한 해결책은 지구의 반사 능력, 즉, 알베도를 상승시키는 것이라고 주장했다. 비록 많은 요인들이 지구의 빛을 반사하는 능력에 기여하지만, 낮은 고도의 층적운은 항상 특히 중요하게 여겨져 왔다. 래텀의 제안은 현재 있는 구름에 소금 입자를 방출하는 방식으로 바닷물을 원자화하는 특수 장치를 사용하여 이를 활용할 것이다. ⁴이것은 물방울이 주변에 형성될 수 있는 핵을 제공함으로써 구름의 전체 범위의 부피를 증가시키는 동시에 현재 있는 구름의 밀도를 증가시킴으로써 알베도를 상승시키는 이중 효과를 가질 것이다. 그 계획은 다수의 장치들이 바람에 의해 동력을 공급받고 인공위성에 의해 조종되며 지속적으로 대양을 횡단할 여러 자동화 선박에 부착될 것을 요구한다. 재생 가능 에너지원이 사용될 것이기 때문에, 그것들은 장기간 작동할 수 있을 것이다. 지지자들은 이 계획이 환경에 미치는 영향이 적고 쉽게 되돌릴 수 있다는 사실을 강조하지만, 일부 전문가들은 그것이 의도한 효과를 가져올지에 대해 우려를 표해왔다.

지구에 도달하는 태양 복사의 양을 제한하는 더 최근의 방법은 더 많은 논란의 여지가 있는 것으로 드러났는데, 그것이 다년 간 지속될 지구 대기의 변화를 가져올 것이기 때문이다. 과학자들은 대기 중 특정 입자의 증가된 수준이 지구 기온의 하강을 초래한다는 것을 오랫동안 인식해 왔는데, 이것은 대규모 화산 폭발 이후의 기후 연구에 의해 확인된 사실이다. 이 자료를 바탕으로, 노벨상을 수상한 화학자 폴 크루첸은 성층권에 황 입자를 주입함으로써 지구의 알베도를 상승시킬 수 있다고 제안했다. 비록 이 발상의 효과에 대한 논란은 거의 없지만, 그것의 안전성에 대한 심각한 우려가 있다. 부정적인 결과가 있을 경우 그 효과가 역전되는 데 수 년이 걸릴 뿐만 아니라, 황 입자가 지표면으로 되돌아와 잠재적인 건강 위험을 초래할 가능성이 높다. 결과적으로, 그 계획은 기후 조건이 급격히 악화되는 상황에 대처하는 데 가장 적합한 최후의 수단으로 제시되었다.

geoengineering 똉지구공학　bolster 똉강화하다, 지지하다
conjecture 똉추측　fluctuation 똉변동　precipitation 똉강수량
desertification 똉사막화　consensus 똉공감대, 의견 일치
prevalence 똉발생률　alternative 똉대안적인
prominent 똉두드러진　property 똉특성
stratocumulus cloud 층적운　atomize 똉원자화하다
nucleus 똉핵　apparatus 똉장치, 기구
proponent 똉지지자, 옹호자　reversible 똉되돌릴 수 있는
last resort 최후의 수단　deteriorate 똉악화되다

1 1단락에 따르면, 최근의 지구 평균 기온 상승이 인간의 활동에서 기인하는 것은

　(A) 선진국들이 특정 대기 오염물질의 생성을 확대했기 때문이다
　(B) 현대의 공장들이 태양 에너지를 흡수하는 기체를 생성하기 때문이다
　(C) 부유한 국가들이 유해 물질에 의존하는 제품을 만들기 때문이다
　(D) 많은 산업들이 그것들이 생산하는 상품의 양을 증가시켰기 때문이다

2 지문의 단어 "conjecture"과 의미가 가장 비슷한 것은?

　(A) 결과
　(B) 서약
　(C) 전제조건
　(D) 추측

3 네 개의 네모[■]는 다음 문장이 삽입될 수 있는 곳을 나타내고 있다.

재생 가능 에너지원이 사용될 것이기 때문에, 그것들은 장기간 작동할 수 있을 것이다.

이 문장은 어디에 들어가는 것이 가장 적절한가?

4 3단락에 따르면, 래텀에 의해 발명된 장치는 지구의 온도를 어떻게 낮출 것인가?

　(A) 물방울의 수를 증가시켜, 더 많은 강수를 가져올 것이다.
　(B) 바다의 물을 구름으로 끌어올려, 더 찬 공기의 흐름을 가져올 것이다.
　(C) 구름 속으로 물질을 몰아 넣어, 그것의 밀도와 부피를 증가시킬 것이다.
　(D) 대양을 횡단하여, 특정 기상 시스템의 영향을 줄일 것이다.

5 지문의 단어 "it"이 가리키는 것은?

　(A) 방법
　(B) 양
　(C) 복사
　(D) 지구

6 글쓴이는 왜 "a duration of multiple years"를 언급하는가?

　(A) 제안된 조치의 효과를 설명하기 위해
　(B) 프로젝트가 많은 이들에 의해 적합하지 않다고 여겨지는 이유를 설명하기 위해
　(C) 지구 온난화에 대한 장기적인 해결책의 필요성을 강조하기 위해
　(D) 태양 복사가 지구에 도달하는 정도를 나타내기 위해

iBT Reading Test 1　　　　　　본문 p. 146

1 (D)	**2** (B)	**3** (D)	**4** (D)
5 (A)	**6** (C)	**7** (D)	**8** (D)
9 (B)	**10** (B), (D), (F)		

도자기

도자기는 그것의 이용에 능숙해진 문화 사회들에 깊은 영향을 미친 비교적 단순한 기술의 한 예이다. 도자기 물레 발명 이전에는, 제작 방법은 완성품을 만들기 위해 손으로 형태를 빚은 점토의 고리와 공의 사용이 수반되었다. ¹ᴬ/¹ᴮ/¹ᶜ그것의 독특한 특성과 광범위한 사용 가능성으로 인해, 점토는 초기 항아리의 제작에 사용된 주된 재료였는데, 그 물질은 젖으면 형태를 바꿀 수 있고, 건조하면 굳어지며, 강한 열을 가하면 콘크리트처럼 단단해지기 때문이다.

저장, 운송, 조리를 위한 내구성 있고 실용적인 구운 점토 그릇을 제작하는 데 필요한 전문 기술과 지식이 습득되자, 사회 구조는 그것의 많은 근본적인 특징들을 바꾸는 방식으로 변형되었다. 초기 문명사회들이 기술적 및 경제적으로 더 발전함에 따라, 더 많은 노력과 자원이 그릇의 장식에 투입되었고, 이 물건들은 예술적이면서도 기능적인 역할을 하게 되었다.

도자기의 널리 퍼진 사용의 알려진 최초의 예는 일본의 조몬 시대로, 고고학자들이 발굴한 파편들의 연대는 1만 년에서 1만 5천 년 사이로 추정된다. ⁴ᴮ조몬이라는 이름은 일본어로 "끈 무늬"를 의미하며, 이 신석기 문화의 사람들이 그들의 도자기를 장식했던 방식에서 따온 것이다. ⁴ᶜ조몬 도자기는 식물 섬유와 으깨진 조개껍데기를 포함한 다양한

재료로 형성되었다. ⁴ᴬ대부분의 신석기 도자기가 그러하듯, 그릇들은 여성들에 의해 제작되었고, 물레의 도움 없이 만들어졌다.

⁵광범위한 연구는 초기 사회에 도자기의 중요성에 대한 많은 통찰을 제공했으며, 초기 사회에 대한 도자기의 가장 중요한 공헌은 도자기 그릇이 음식을 끓이거나 찌는 것을 가능하게 했다는 것으로, 이는 한 집단이 채식 위주의 영양 공급원에 더 의존적인 식단에 적응할 수 있으려면 필수적인 것이다. 이러한 식단의 변화와 그에 대응하여 발달한 원시적인 형태의 농업은 인류가 유목 생활 양식에서 반 정착 생활 양식으로 전환함에 따라 신석기 시대 동안 인구의 급격한 증가로 이어졌다.

그러나, 도자기의 유용성은 원시 문화에만 국한되지 않았고, 그것은 흔히 비옥한 초승달 지대라고 불리는 곳에서 생겨난 복잡한 사회, 문화, 정치 체계의 성장에 크게 공헌했다. 도시화 과정이 일어나기 위해서는, 공동체의 식량 비축물을 먹어 치울 수 있는 설치류 및 다른 해충으로부터 그것을 보호하는 방식으로 방대한 양의 식량을 저장할 수 있어야 했다. 이것은 많은 도시에서 문제였으며 큰 인구 증가에 장애물로 작용했다. 규격화된 그릇을 대량으로 생산할 수 있게 해준 도자기 물레의 발명으로 안전한 식품 저장이 가능해졌고, 그 기술을 활용하기 위해 필요한 전문 기술은 새로운 장인 계급으로 이어졌다. 결국, 특정 지역들은 주요 경제 활동으로서 도자기에 집중하기 시작했고, 그 결과 점토 그릇 자체가 중요한 무역품이 되었다.

도자기 생산이 점점 상업화되면서, 초점은 사치품 시장을 겨냥한 독특한 장식품의 제작으로 옮겨졌다. 이것은 도자기가 창조적 표현의 매개체로서만 기능할 수 있는 가능성에 대한 인식 증가를 가져왔고, 이는 그리스 문화의 성장과 함께 정점에 달한 경향이었다. ⁸단순히 실용적인 용도로 쓰이기보다, 그리스 꽃병들은 종종 정교하게 장식되어 부유한 가정에서 예술 작품의 역할을 했다.

application 뗑이용, 응용; (열·힘 등을) 가함   availability 뗑사용 가능성
predominant 혱주된, 두드러진   malleable 혱형태를 바꿀 수 있는
expertise 뗑전문 기술   utilitarian 혱실용적인   adornment 뗑장식
nomadic 혱유목의   semi-sedentary 혱반 정착의
utility 뗑유용성, 효용성   urbanization 뗑도시화   reserve 뗑비축물
provisions 뗑식량   commercialize 통상업화하다
vehicle 뗑매개체, 수단   elaborately 뭐정교하게
affluent 혱부유한

1 1단락에 따르면, 다음 중 점토의 특성이 아닌 것은?

(A) 습기는 그것을 유연하게 만든다.
(B) 고온은 그것을 내구성이 있게 만든다.
(C) 건조는 그것을 단단하게 만든다.
(D) 유약을 바르는 것은 그것을 열에 강해지게 만든다.

2 지문의 단어 "utilitarian"과 의미가 가장 비슷한 것은?

(A) 영향력이 있는
(B) 실용적인
(C) 적절한
(D) 논란의 여지가 있는

3 지문의 단어 "its"가 가리키는 것은?

(A) 전문 기술
(B) 지식
(C) 그릇
(D) 사회

4 3단락에 따르면, 다음 중 조몬 도자기에 관해 사실이 아닌 것은?

(A) 전형적으로 여성에 의해 제작되었다.
(B) 그것의 이름은 그것의 밧줄 같은 디자인에서 유래되었다.
(C) 다양한 천연 재료로 만들어졌다.
(D) 그것의 제작은 물레의 사용으로 보조되었다.

5 4단락에 따르면, 도자기는 어떻게 신석기 사회에 영향을 미쳤는가?

(A) 다른 종류의 음식 섭취를 촉진했다.
(B) 재배 활동의 효율성에 기여했다.
(C) 인구 과잉의 해로운 영향을 감소시켰다.
(D) 집단들이 식량을 찾아 더 멀리 여행할 수 있도록 했다.

6 지문에서 글쓴이는 왜 "rodents and other pests"를 언급하는가?

(A) 도시들에 매우 많은 양의 음식이 필요했다는 것을 보여주기 위해
(B) 높은 인구 밀도와 관련된 문제를 시사하기 위해
(C) 초기 도시 형성에서 도자기가 한 역할을 설명하기 위해
(D) 중동에서 사용된 점토 항아리의 단점을 입증하기 위해

7 아래 문장 중 지문 속의 음영된 문장의 핵심 정보를 가장 잘 표현한 것은? 오답은 문장의 의미를 크게 바꾸거나 핵심 정보를 생략한다.

(A) 안전한 음식 그릇의 필요성은 필요한 기술을 만들기 위해 도예가들이 함께 일하는 것을 필요로 했다.
(B) 도자기 산업의 전문화는 도자기 물레와 같은 더 안전한 기술의 발달로 이어졌다.
(C) 특정 지식을 가진 장인들이 도자기 물레의 사용에 더 능숙해짐에 따라, 도자기의 질은 비약적으로 향상되었다.
(D) 도자기 물레의 발명은 음식의 안전한 보관을 가능하게 했고, 새로운 범주의 장인들이 그것의 사용에 숙달됨으로써 등장했다.

8 다음 중 6단락에서 그리스의 장식 도자기에 관해 추론할 수 있는 것은?

(A) 그리스의 주요 상업 수출품 중 하나였다.
(B) 보통 저장 용기로 사용되었다.
(C) 대부분의 가정에서 발견되었다.
(D) 모든 가정에서 살 수 있는 가격은 아니었다.

9 네 개의 네모[■]는 다음 문장이 삽입될 수 있는 곳을 나타내고 있다.

이것은 많은 도시에서 문제였으며 큰 인구 증가에 장애물로 작용했다.

이 문장은 어디에 들어가는 것이 가장 적절한가?

10 **지시:** 지문 요약을 위한 도입 문장이 아래에 주어져 있다. 지문의 가장 중요한 내용을 나타내는 보기 3개를 골라 요약을 완성하라. 어떤 문장은 지문에 언급되지 않은 내용이나 사소한 정보를 나타내므로 요약에 포함되지 않는다. **이 문제는 2점이다.**

> **도자기는 인류 문명의 발전에 중요한 역할을 해왔다.**
> · (B) 도자기 물레의 등장과 함께, 장인들은 경제 성장에 기여하는 제품들을 생산하기 시작했다.
> · (D) 식량 저장에 적합한 그릇의 사용 가능성은 고대 도시의 성장에 기여했다.
> · (F) 도예가들이 더 정교한 디자인을 실험하면서, 도자기는 예술적인 매체가 되었다.

(A) 도자기의 예술적 잠재력은 고전 세계에서 이용되었고, 이것은 새로운 표현 방식의 창조로 이어졌다.
(C) 도자기의 초기 예는 영구적인 농경 공동체 설립에서 그것의 중요성을 보여준다.
(E) 유목민 부족들은 부패하기 쉬운 음식을 운반하기 위해 점토 그릇에 의존했다.

1 (C)	**2** (C)	**3** (B)	**4** (D)
5 (B)	**6** (B)	**7** (A)	**8** (A)
9 (C)	**10** (B), (E), (F)		

숙주-기생충 체계

곤충 외부 기생충은 숙주의 철분이 풍부한 헤모글로빈이나 신체 분비물을 섭취하면서 동물의 외부에서 살아가는 것들이다. 그것들은 육식성 모기와 혼동되어서는 안 되는데, 이 생물들은 비록 다른 것들의 피를 먹고 살지만, 실제로 그것들의 먹이에서 살지는 않기 때문이다. 진정한 외부 기생충은 숙주에 주요 서식지를 만들고, 이 틈새 환경에 고도로 적응되어 있으며, 종종 그들이 사는 동물과 동시에 진화한다. 대부분은 과학자들은 숙주-기생충 체계라고 부르는 복잡한 관계인 공진화의 결과로 강한 발톱, 흡입하는 입 기관, 기능하는 날개의 상실과 같은 형태상의 변형을 발달시켰다.

널리 분포된 날아다니는 포유류인 박쥐는 이러한 공진화적 상호작용 형태의 좋은 예를 제공하는데, 그것들이 대부분이 외부 기생충인 수많은 기생 생물종과 관련되어 있기 때문이다. 박쥐에서 외부 기생충의 발달을 촉진하는 여러 주요한 원인이 되는 요인들이 있는데, 그것들 모두는 숙주-기생충 체계를 이해하는 데 중요하다. 그것들은 크기가 상당히 다양하고 거의 1,000여 개에 달하는 별개의 종으로 분리될 수 있지만, 모든 박쥐는 그것들을 유리한 숙주 및 질병 전파자로 만드는 사회적 행동을 보인다. 4B예를 들어, 그것들은 수백에서 백만 마리의 개체에 이르는 크기의 군집에서 생활하며, 성공적인 먹이 찾기를 용이하게 하기 위해 다른 구성원과 가까이 있는 것을 선호한다. 군집 당 많은 박쥐의 수는 외부 기생충에게 적합성 장점을 제공하는데, 특히, 외부 기생충은 박쥐의 형태상 또는 행동적 변화에 대처하기 위해 진화하는 동안 먹이로 삼을 여러 숙주를 가진다. 4A/4C외부 기생충의 발달은 기온이 안정적이고 습도가 높은 동굴, 지하 배수로, 혹은 버려진 건물과 같은 고립된 구조에서 동성의 다른 박쥐들과 함께 공동으로 둥지를 트는 것을 좋아하는 박쥐의 선호에 의해 추가로 촉진된다. 이러한 모든 요인들은 한 숙주에서 다른 숙주로의 체외 기생충의 높은 전파율에 기여한다.

여러 종의 박쥐에 서식하는 박쥐파리는 박쥐 숙주에서 번성하는 외부 기생충 생물의 전형적인 예가 된다. 5이 날개 없는 곤충은 변형된 신체 부분, 뒷경절, 박쥐의 털에 달라붙는 데 사용되는 강한 털과 함께 고도로 특화되어 있다. 특히, 그것들의 입 기관은 피부를 뚫고 피를 빨 수 있도록 적응되어 있다. 박쥐파리의 번식기는 봄과 여름에 몇 달 동안 지속되며, 박쥐 둥지의 번데기 껍질 속에서의 변태는 30일이 걸리며, 그 결과 7월에 많은 곤충들이 출현하게 된다.

파리를 퇴치하기 위해, 박쥐들은 여름 동안 긴 털 손질 기간에 참여하는데, 그때 그것들은 털을 깨끗이 하고 유지하는 데 여러 방법을 사용한다. 6이 활동이 짝짓기 행동과 관련이 있음을 시사하는 일부 증거에도 불구하고, 박쥐가 주로 동성의 구성원들과 둥지를 튼다는 사실은 그것이 친족의 몸에서 외부 기생충을 제거할 목적으로 행해질 가능성이 더 높으며, 증진된 번식적 성과는 간접적인 결과라는 것을 시사한다. 어린 박쥐는 깨어 있는 시간의 대부분을 자신의 털을 손질하는 데 보내지만, 나이가 들면서 그것들의 노력을 군집의 다른 구성원들의 털을 손질하는 데 전환한다. 7특정 군집에서 외부 기생충이 더 많을수록 박쥐는 이에 대응하여, 가령, 파리 개체수가 편안한 수준으로 줄어들 때까지 자신과 다른 개체들의 털을 손질하는 데 더 오랜 시간을 소비한다.

그러나, 공진화는 박쥐파리가 털 손질에 의한 지속적인 제거 위협에 대처하기 위한 고유한 전략을 개발할 수 있게 했다. 많은 수가 각 숙주에

달라붙으며 숙주들이 짝짓기 활동하는 동안 수컷 박쥐에서 암컷 박쥐로 바꿀 수 있다. 이것은 하나의 특정 숙주를 다 소모하는 것을 피할 뿐만 아니라 그들이 한 종류의 털 손질에의 노출을 줄이기 위해 성별 특정적인 둥지를 번갈아 가며 살 수 있게 해주어, 그것들의 장기적인 생존 가능성을 향상시킨다.

ectoparasite 명 외부 기생충   subsist 동 살아가다
secretion 명 분비물   carnivorous 형 육식성의
niche 명 (시장의) 틈새   concurrently 부 동시에
morphological 형 형태상의   modification 명 변형
coevolution 명 공진화(복수 생물체의 동시 진화)
causative 형 원인이 되는   in close proximity to ~과 가까이
predilection 명 선호, 좋아함   roost 동 (새가) 둥지를 틀다; 명 둥지
communally 부 공동으로   culvert 명 지하 배수로
transmission 명 전파   exemplify 동 전형적인 예가 되다
bristle 명 (짧고 뻣뻣한) 털   metamorphosis 명 변태, 탈바꿈
puparium 명 번데기 껍질   grooming 명 (동물의) 털 손질

1 지문에서 글쓴이는 왜 "mosquitoes"를 언급하는가?

(A) 외부 기생충이 섭취하는 생물 종류를 설명하기 위해
(B) 외부 기생충의 예를 들기 위해
(C) 곤충 외부 기생충의 특성을 확인하기 위해
(D) 두 가지 유형의 외부 기생충을 구별하기 위해

2 지문의 단어 "concurrently"와 의미가 가장 비슷한 것은?

(A) 애매하게
(B) 비례하여
(C) 동시에
(D) 무심코

3 지문의 단어 "predilection"과 의미가 가장 비슷한 것은?

(A) 약점
(B) 선호
(C) 매력
(D) 사려 깊음

4 2단락에 따르면, 다음 중 박쥐를 외부 기생충에 적합한 숙주로 만드는 특성이 아닌 것은?

(A) 그것들은 성별에 특정한 큰 집단에서 함께 잠을 잔다.
(B) 그것들은 먹이를 찾기 위해 많은 수로 모인다.
(C) 그것들이 선호하는 휴식 장소는 습하다.
(D) 그것들의 신체는 온도 변화에 빠르게 적응한다.

5 다음 중 3단락에서 박쥐파리에 관해 추론할 수 있는 것은?

(A) 약 1년 동안 산다.
(B) 날 수 없다.
(C) 여름보다 봄에 더 흔하다.
(D) 박쥐가 아닌 포유류에서 산다.

6 전문가들은 왜 털 손질이 짝짓기 행동의 한 측면이라는 생각을 거부하는가?

(A) 그 습관은 여름 짝짓기 기간 후에 시작된다.
(B) 박쥐는 동성의 다른 박쥐를 손질하는 경향이 있다.
(C) 박쥐는 같은 나이의 가족을 손질하는 경향이 있다.
(D) 그 행위는 번식을 향상시키는 것으로 나타나지 않았다.

7 4단락에 따르면, 박쥐가 털 손질에 쏟는 시간을 결정하는 것은?

(A) 외부 기생충 개체군의 크기
(B) 군집 구성원이 깨어 있는 시간
(C) 상호적인 털 손질을 기꺼이 하는 박쥐들의 근접
(D) 군집에 기생하는 외부 기생충의 유형

8 지문의 단어 "them"이 가리키는 것은?

(A) 박쥐파리
(B) 전략
(C) 숙주
(D) 활동

9 네 개의 네모[■]는 다음 문장이 삽입될 수 있는 곳을 나타내고 있다.

특히, 그것들의 입 기관은 피부를 뚫고 피를 빨 수 있도록 적응되어 있다.

이 문장은 어디에 들어가는 것이 가장 적절한가?

10 **지시:** 지문 요약을 위한 도입 문장이 아래에 주어져 있다. 지문의 가장 중요한 내용을 나타내는 보기 3개를 골라 요약을 완성하라. 어떤 문장은 지문에 언급되지 않은 내용이나 사소한 정보를 나타내므로 요약에 포함되지 않는다. **이 문제는 2점이다.**

> **박쥐와 기생 생물 사이의 상호작용은 숙주-기생충 체계의 전형적인 예가 된다.**
> · (B) 박쥐는 자기 몸에 있는 외부 기생충의 수를 줄이는 자기 손질 방법을 개발했고, 필요에 따라 이 작업을 수행할 것이다.
> · (E) 작은 기생 생물들은 박쥐 숙주가 자신을 방어하기 위해 하는 모든 변화에 대처하기 위해 계속해서 그것들의 행동을 수정한다.
> · (F) 박쥐는 다양한 사회적 행동을 보이기 때문에 동시에 진화하는 기생 생물 종에게 훌륭한 숙주가 되어준다.

(A) 박쥐는 무리를 지어 잠을 자고 먹이를 찾으며, 이는 성별 특정적인 외부 기생충 개체군이 번성할 좋은 기회를 제공한다.
(C) 외부 기생충은 박쥐가 둥지로 사용하는 동일한 외딴 환경에서 번성하기 때문에 박쥐 개체군에서도 번성한다.
(D) 적응된 형태를 가진 곤충은 숙주의 노폐물을 섭취함으로써 박쥐의 피부와 털에서 산다.

Vocabulary Review
본문 p. 154

1 sedentary   2 reversible   3 resort
4 expertise   5 unwieldy   6 devastated
7 (A)   8 (B)   9 (A)   10 (D)
11 (B)   12 (C)   13 (D)   14 (A)

CHAPTER 09
Summary

Example
본문 p. 157

1 (A), (C), (E)

수메르 설형 문자

수메르는 메소포타미아에서 기록된 최초의 문명으로, 기원전 4000년경에 설립되었고 현대의 이라크 남부 지역에 위치했다. 그 사회는 기원전 3000년 이전의 어느 시점에 아무런 전신 없이 출현한 글자 체계인 수메르 설형 문자로 기록되었다. 설형 문자 표시는 대규모 무역 거래와 기타 중요한 정보를 기록하기 위해 점토판에 새겨졌다.

시간이 지남에 따라, 수메르의 그림 문자는 정확하고 실용적이 되었다. 이것은 이전에 구두로 낭독되었던 법률이 보존되기 위해 점토에 기록되어 수메르 도시들 전역에 확산되었기 때문에 유익했다. 게다가, 세금으로 수집된 음식 및 다른 자원들에 대한 설명은 관료적인 목적을 위해 기록되었다. 이 기록 체계는 탈세를 줄이고 모두가 정확한 액수의 세금을 납부하고 있는지 확인하기 위해 모든 가구의 납부 세금이 면밀히 확인되었기 때문에 그 문명 사회의 부를 강화했다.

글쓰기를 통해, 각 후대의 학자들과 더불어, 메소포타미아의 축적된 지식이 활용되며 쌓일 수 있었다. 이것은 농부와 도공과 같은 핵심 노동자들이 필수적인 정보를 잊어버리거나 특화된 기술을 잃지 않았기 때문에 낭비를 방지했다. 한 가지 예는 수메르 농부의 연감으로, 상세한 농업 설명이 담긴 작은 점토판이다. 이 선들은 밭을 관개하는 방법, 사용하기에 가장 좋은 도구, 그리고 씨앗 심기에 최적의 깊이를 설명한다.

설형 문자의 창조는 수메르인과 인류 전체의 문화를 발전시키는 데 결정적인 역할을 했다. 문자 언어의 발달은 인류 지식의 한계를 확장시켰고, 여러 세대에 걸쳐 정보가 안정적으로 공유되게 해주었다. 글이 없었다면, 인류 역사 전체가 달라졌을 것이다. 게다가, 점토의 사용은 고대 메소포타미아 왕국에서 수백만 개의 문서들이 살아남게 해주었고, 이는 역사가들에게 고대 사회에 대한 풍부한 정보를 제공했다.

cuneiform 명 설형 문자   precursor 명 전신, 선행물
transaction 명 거래   pictogram 명 그림 문자
transcribe 동 기록하다, 필기하다   bureaucratic 형 관료적인, 절차적인
bolster 동 강화하다   contribution 명 납부 세금, 기부금
tax avoidance 탈세   wastage 명 낭비

1 **지시:** 지문 요약을 위한 도입 문장이 아래에 주어져 있다. 지문의 가장 중요한 내용을 나타내는 보기 3개를 골라 요약을 완성하라.

설형 문자의 발명은 수메르인들이 지식을 저장하고 전승함으로써 이익을 얻는 기록 보관 사회가 되도록 했다.

(A) 세금 및 법적 목적을 위한 설형 문자의 사용은 수메르 사회에 이점을 제공했다.
(B) 설형 문자는 학자들에게 수메르 가정의 일상 활동에 대한 통찰력을 제공한다.
(C) 문자 정보의 공유는 숙련된 근로자들이 여러 세대에 걸쳐 주요 기술을 전달하게 해주었다.
(D) 점토는 메소포타미아의 도시들에서 다양한 관료적 및 교육적 이유로 채택되었다.
(E) 설형 문자는 수메르 문화와 인류 문화의 발전에 중요한 역할을 했다.
(F) 설형 문자는 구두로 보존되지 않은 지식을 기록할 수 있었기 때문에 유용했다.

Reading Practice 1
본문 p. 158

1 (D)   2 (C)   3 (D)   4 (C)   5 (A), (B), (E)

이탈리아 르네상스 건축

이탈리아 르네상스 시대의 사고하는 남녀들은 고대 그리스-로마 시대의 유적에 매료되었는데, 그들은 중세 시대부터 자신들의 시대가 시작될 때까지 예술과 인문학이 상당한 쇠퇴를 겪었다고 생각했기 때문이었다. 따라서, 이러한 학문들을 그것들의 본래의 영광으로 회복하기 위해 창작자들은 고대인들의 작품을 열정적으로 모방했으며, 그것들의 우수성에 필적하거나 그것을 능가하기 위해 노력했고, 그 결과 이탈리아는 문화의 부흥을 경험했다.

따라서, 이 시기의 건축 양식은 기둥, 아치 및 돔을 포함한 고전 로마의 요소들과 르네상스 예술가들에 의해 발전된 이것들의 변형들의 통합이었다. 가장 중요한 고려사항은 'symmetra' 즉 대칭의 개념으로, 어떤 건축물이든 기하학적으로 균형을 이루어야 한다는 것인데, 그것은 인문주의 운동에 의해 강조되었던 것처럼 완벽한 동등함의 개념의 반영이었다. 게다가, 건축물의 구성 요소들은 모든 것이 서로 조화를 이루어야 한다는 것을 요구하는 'disposito' 즉 배열로 건축되어야 했다. 높고 뾰족한 피라미드 지붕을 가진 교회는 이러한 기본적인 규칙에 따라 양쪽에 하나씩 수학적으로 비례하는 두 개의 작은 첨탑으로 균형이 맞춰지곤 했다.

그러나, 건축가들은 자신의 혁신도 추가했으며, 이 시대의 첫 번째 위대한 건축가인 필리포 브루넬레스키는 피렌체의 산 로렌초와 산토 스피리토의 교회에서 새로운 건축 양식을 만들었다. 교황의 지시에 따라, 그는 또한 피렌체 대성당에 거대한 돔을 지을 혁신적인 설계도 제시했다. 비록 이것이 실제로 실현되지는 않았지만, 그것의 대담한 디자인은 많은 다른 건축가들로 하여금 비슷한 위업을 시도하게 했다. 가장 중요한 것은, 그의 작품들이 그것들이 등장한 도시의 두드러진 특징이었을 뿐만 아니라, 그것들의 청사진은 유명한 건축 이론가인 레온 바티스타 알베르티의 글에서 묘사되고 분석되었기 때문에 후속 프로젝트의 견본 역할을 했다.

알베르티와 다른 영향력 있는 작가들의 작품 보급은 그 분야에 관심 있는 증가하는 수의 예술가들에게 건축 이론에 더 쉽게 접근할 수 있게 했기 때문에 그 학문에 엄청난 영향을 미쳤다. ³인쇄 문화의 발전을 가능케 한 획기적인 발명품인 가동 활자 인쇄기의 도입에 힘입어 건축 원리에 대한 지식은 빠르게 확산되었다. 그러나, 아마도 가장 중요한 책은 안드레아 팔라디오에 의해 저술된 네 권으로, 그는 고전 로마 건축의 알려진 모든 측면을 개괄했으며 그 요소들의 동시대의 건축물으로의 할당을 설명했다. 그것은 신진 건축가들의 훈련을 보완하고 전문 예술가들에게 영감을 주기 위해 의도된 노력이었다.

그러한 문학의 확산은 또한 시민들이 예술의 후원자가 되도록 동기를 부여하는 데 도움을 주는 필수적인 도구였으며, 이는 어떤 형태의 예술이든 지속적인 성공에의 열쇠였다. ⁴대부분의 르네상스 시대의 건축물들은 부유한 은행가나 영향력 있는 상인 같은 개인적인 자금 공급원으로 명확히 출처를 확인할 수 있으며, 다수는 여전히 이 후원자들의 이름을 가지고 있다. 예를 들어, 피렌체의 중심부에 위치한 궁전인 메디치궁전은 영향력 있는 메디치 가문에 의해 기부된 돈으로 지어졌는데, 많은 저명한 예술가들에 대한 그들의 아낌없는 후원은 피렌체를 유럽의 뛰어난 건축 중심지로 변화시켰다. 그것은 또한 이러한 건축물들을 장식하거나 그것들의 내부에 있는 방의 초점이 될 작품들을 제작한 도나텔로와 미켈란젤로 같은 일부 유명 예술가들이 피렌체에 거주하도록 장려했다.

1 아래 문장 중 지문 속의 음영된 문장의 핵심 정보를 가장 잘 표현한 것은?

(A) 고전 로마 건축은 르네상스 양식을 정의하는 다양한 요소들을 포함했다.

(B) 르네상스의 접근 방식은 고전 로마 건축의 모든 측면을 통합했다.

(C) 고전 로마 건축의 측면에 대한 모방은 르네상스 양식으로 이어졌다.

(D) 고전 로마 디자인의 요소들과 이것들에 대한 변형들이 르네상스 건축의 본질을 좌우했다.

2 네 개의 네모[■]는 다음 문장이 삽입될 수 있는 곳을 나타내고 있다.

비록 이것이 실제로 실현되지는 않았지만, 그것의 대담한 디자인은 많은 다른 건축가들로 하여금 비슷한 위업을 시도하게 했다.

이 문장은 어디에 들어가는 것이 가장 적절한가?

3 4단락에 따르면, 가동 활자 인쇄기 발전의 결과는 무엇이었는가?

(A) 인쇄된 건축 서적의 질이 극적으로 상승했다.

(B) 건축 학교와 학생들의 수가 급격히 증가했다.

(C) 고대 건축 기술은 새로운 것으로 대체되었다.

(D) 건축 기준에 대한 이해가 빠르게 확산되었다.

4 5단락에 따르면, 다음 중 르네상스 시대의 많은 건축물들에 관해 사실인 것은?

(A) 피렌체의 건축물을 본떠서 만들어졌다.

(B) 공공의 자금으로 비용이 지불되었다.

(C) 자금을 대준 사람들의 이름을 따서 명명되었다.

(D) 그것들은 도나텔로와 미켈란젤로에 의해 설계되었다.

5 지시: 지문 요약을 위한 도입 문장이 아래에 주어져 있다. 지문의 가장 중요한 내용을 나타내는 보기 3개를 골라 요약을 완성하라.

고전 그리스 로마 건축 요소의 재발견은 르네상스 이탈리아의 건축 분야에 활기를 불어넣었다.

(A) 예술가들을 지원하기 위해서 개인 후원자들의 자금이 필요했고, 궁극적으로 이러한 종류의 후원들은 훌륭한 건축 작품들이 세워지도록 하는 원인이 되었다.

(B) 학문의 진흥은 중요한 발상을 문서화하고 예술가들에게 영감을 주려고 의도되었던 문학의 확산에 의해 도움을 받았다.

(C) 초보자이든 전문가이든, 사실상 르네상스의 모든 건축가들은 팔라디오의 작품을 통해 고전 로마 양식을 배웠다.

(D) 형식적인 훈련과 옛 건축물을 조사하는 실제 경험의 결합은 유명한 건축가가 되기 위해 필요한 기술을 제공했다.

(E) 균형과 조화와 같은 고전 로마 건축 요소들이 강조되었지만, 건축가들은 혁신적인 요소들도 포함했다.

(F) 더 많은 인쇄된 책들이 사용 가능해짐에 따라, 건축가들은 양식의 다양성에 대해 배웠고 고전 로마 양식을 거부하기 시작했다.

1 (B)   2 (B)   3 (A)   4 (C)   5 (B), (C), (D)

야생아

세계의 신화는 길을 잃거나 버려진 다음 야생에서 동물들에 의해 길러지고 몇 년 후에 발견된 아이들에 대한 수십 개의 이야기를 포함한다. 아마도 이것들 중 가장 유명한 것은 아마도 늑대에 의해 길러졌다고 하는 신화에 나오는 로마의 건국자인 로물루스와 레무스에 관한 것이다. 야생아에 대한 그러한 허구적인 이야기는 대개 그들이 평균 또는 평균 이상의 인간 지능, 키워준 동물 부모로부터 배운 뛰어난 기술, 그리고 야생에서 살아남기 위한 특별한 능력을 가진 것으로 묘사한다. 이것은 그들의 문명사회로의 재통합을 비교적 쉽게 만든다.

그러나, 실제로는, 보고된 대부분의 야생아 사례들은 동물 보호자를 포함하지 않으나, 아동이 의도적으로 다른 인간들로부터 격리된 상황을 포함한다. [1]일단 구조되면, 이 아이들은 사회에 적응하려고 할 때 거의 극복할 수 없는 장애물에 직면하게 되며, 그들을 사회로 복귀시키기 위한 많은 노력에도 불구하고, 그들에게 기본적인 사회적 기술을 가르치려고 시도할 때 과학자들은 흔히 성공적이지 못하다.

사회학자들은 개인이 문화의 확립된 규범에 대한 지식을 습득하는 수단을 문화화라고 한다. 아이가 더 넓은 사회의 틀 안에서 허용되는 것과 허용되지 않는 것뿐만 아니라 특정한 맥락 안에서 적절한 행동을 배우는 것은 문화화를 통해서이다. 다른 공동체 구성원들과의 지속적인 의사소통에서 파생된 문화화 없이 길러진 야생아는 결코 공유된 관념 인식이나 기대되는 상호 작용의 형태에 대한 이해를 발달시키지 못한다. 게다가, 그들은 화장실을 사용하는 것이나 직립 보행하는 것과 같은 간단한 일을 수행하는 방법을 이해하지 못할 수도 있다.

과학자들은 또한 사회화가 없는 환경에서 길러진 아이들이 심리사회적 왜소증으로 알려진 문제로 고통받는 경향이 있다는 것을 알아냈다. 그 질환은 영양부족이 아닌 극심한 정서적 스트레스에 의해 발생하며, 비정상적으로 낮은 체중, 미성숙한 골격, 작은 키로 특징지어진다. 그 질환은 점진적으로 진행되지만, 만약 그 아이들이 잘 양육하고 보살피는 가정에 있게 된다면 때때로 역전될 수 있다. 그럼에도 불구하고, 이 아이들의 대부분은 새로운 환경에 호의적으로 반응하지 못하며 일반적으로 어린 나이에 사망한다.

하지만, 야생아를 치료하는 데 있어 극복해야 할 가장 어려운 장애물은, 대부분의 경우, 그 어린 소년 소녀들이 언어에 노출된 적이 없거나 말하는 법을 배우기를 단념했다는 것이다. 이러한 상황에서, 연구자들은 아이들의 일반적인 지능 수준과 상관없이, 그들이 문법이나 문장 구조를 이해하지 못하는 것으로 보인다는 점에 주목했다. 이것은 1970년 방임하는 부모로부터 구조되어 캘리포니아 로스앤젤레스에 있는 어린이 병원에 입원한 13세 소녀 지니의 경우도 마찬가지였다. 비록 그녀는 화장실 사용법을 빠르게 배웠고 그녀의 사회적 기술은 즉시 향상되었지만, 그녀는 수년간의 교육 후에도 완전한 문장으로 말하는 것을 해낼 수 없었다. 그녀는 대상을 가리키며 치료사가 하는 말을 반복하면서 어휘를 익혔지만, 그녀는 "애플소스 사다 상점" 같은 문장으로 동사와 명사를 겨우 활용할 수 있었다.

전반적으로, 야생아가 문법에 어려움을 겪는 것처럼 보이기 때문에, 일부 연구자들은 사람들이 그들의 잠재력을 완전히 잃기 전에 언어적으로 의사소통하는 방법을 배워야 하는 결정적인 기간이 있음을 시사했다. [4]이론 언어학자 놈 촘스키는 이것이 언어 습득 장치(LAD)라고 불리는 뇌의 한 부분과 관련이 있는데, 그것은 언어 학습에 도움을 주지

만 언어 구조를 판단하기 위해서는 외부 원천에서의 데이터 입력이 필요하다고 제시했다. 따라서 언어는 내재적이면서도 학습되며, 숙달하기 위해서는 부모-자녀 관계를 필요로 한다. 이러한 사회적 상호작용이 없다면, 야생아는 인생에서 나중에 성취할 수 없는 인간 발달의 중요한 단계를 놓친다.

reintegration 몡재통합, 재융화   insurmountable 혱극복할 수 없는
rehabilitate 통사회로 복귀시키다   norms 몡규범
enculturation 몡문화화, 문화 적응   permissible 혱허용되는
devoid of ~이 없는   dwarfism 몡왜소증
abnormally 閉비정상적으로   immature 혱미성숙한
diminutive 혱작은   progressive 혱점진적으로 진행되는
favorably 閉호의적으로   syntax 몡문장 구조, 구문법
negligent 혱방임하는, 방치하는

1   2단락에 따르면, 다음 중 대부분의 야생아들에 관해 사실인 것은?

   (A) 그들의 사회적 기술은 종종 빠르게 향상된다.

   (B) 사회에 적응하는 데 극심한 어려움을 겪는다.

   (C) 그들의 사회 복귀는 결코 성공적이지 않다.

   (D) 일반적으로 동물들과 정서적 유대감을 발달시킨다.

2   지문의 단어 "diminutive"와 의미가 가장 비슷한 것은?

   (A) 모호한

   (B) 작은

   (C) 특이한

   (D) 안정적인

3   지문에서 글쓴이는 왜 "Genie"를 언급하는가?

   (A) 언어를 숙달하지 못한 야생아의 예시를 제공하기 위해

   (B) 야생아가 명사와 동사를 학습한 상황을 설명하기 위해

   (C) 모든 야생아들이 사회에 통합될 수는 없음을 시사하기 위해

   (D) 치료사들이 말을 못 하는 야생아를 가르치는 방법을 설명하기 위해

4   다음 중 6단락에서 인간의 뇌에 관해 추론할 수 있는 것은?

   (A) 자연스럽게 어휘를 이해할 수 있다.

   (B) 새로운 정보를 쉽게 통합할 수 있다.

   (C) 언어를 배우려면 외부 자극이 필요하다.

   (D) 어떤 나이에도 언어를 습득할 수 있다.

5   **지시**: 지문 요약을 위한 도입 문장이 아래에 주어져 있다. 지문의 가장 중요한 내용을 나타내는 보기 3개를 골라 요약을 완성하라.

   야생아에 대한 허구적인 이야기들은 그들이 직면하는 어려움을 정확하게 묘사하지 않는다.

   (A) 그들은 언어 의사소통 기술을 습득하고 숙달하는 데 필요한 유전적 능력을 가지고 있지 않다.

   (B) 잘 보살피는 환경이 차단된 사람들은 키가 작고 저하된 지능을 보이며 사회에 동화될 때 어려움을 겪는 경향이 있다.

   (C) 야생아는 정상적인 행동 패턴을 배우지 못하기 때문에 공유된 사회적 틀이 부족하다.

   (D) 그들의 언어 습득 과정은 불완전하며, 그들은 흔히 적절한 문법을 사용하여 완전한 문장을 표현할 수 없다.

   (E) 많은 야생아는 사회 내에서 문화화된 사람들의 평균 수명에 도달하기 전에 사망한다.

   (F) 다른 사람들과 지속적인 상호작용 없이 자란 아이들은 사회적 및 반사회적 행동의 차이를 인식하지 못한다.

1 (B)　**2** (D)　**3** (D)　**4** (D)　**5** (A), (B), (E)

초신성 폭발의 단계

별은 별의 소멸이라고 불리는 일련의 변화를 겪으며, 이러한 소멸 중 적은 비율은 별이 빠르고 강렬한 연소를 겪는 엄청난 초신성을 발생시킬 것이다. 초신성으로 발전하기 위해서는, 별은 특정한 질량을 얻어야 한다. 이는 1930년 수브라마니안 찬드라세카르에 의해 발견되었으며, 그는 활동 중인 별의 최대 질량이 태양 질량의 1.4배임을 밝혀냈다.

[1]별의 질량이 찬드라세카르 한계를 초과하면 별은 더 이상 자신을 지탱할 충분한 에너지를 생산할 수 없게 된다. 태양보다 작은 별들은 더 낮은 중력 때문에 핵융합을 시작하는 데 필요한 열을 발생시킬 수 없다. 따라서, 이는 대개 태양보다 큰 별에서 발생하는데, 이는 이것들이 핵융합이 더 빠른 속도로 일어나게 촉진하는 더 뜨거운 핵 온도를 특징으로 하기 때문이다. 이것은 전체적인 크기를 증가시키고, 천천히 타는 작은 별들에 비해 상대적으로 짧은 수명을 갖게 한다. 찬드라세카르 한계를 넘어가면, 그 구조는 붕괴하기 시작하고, 초신성이 일어난다.

천문학자 루돌프 민코프스키는 초신성을 I형과 II형이라는 두 형태로 분류했다. [3]I형 초신성은 그것들의 핵에 있는 수소를 소진한 활동을 중단한 별에서 발달한다. 일반적으로, 이것은 그것의 핵의 열을 우주로 빼앗기면서 별이 천천히 비활동성 백색왜성으로 변하게 하는 점진적인 과정이다. 그러나, 쌍성계라고 알려진 것에서 소멸하는 두 별이 서로 인접해 있는 경우 초신성이 발생할 수 있다. I형 초신성이 발생하려면, 그 별들은 한 별이 나머지 별로부터 물질을 끌어당길 수 있을 정도로 충분히 가까워야 한다. 백색왜성이 찬드라세카르 한계를 넘어설 만큼 충분한 물질을 축적하면, 그것은 불안정하게 되고, 이로 인해 I형 초신성이 나타난다.

II형 초신성에서는, I형 초신성과는 달리, 내부 핵융합 과정은 핵의 수소 연료가 소진된 후에도 여전히 활동한다. 이것이 일어나면, 핵 수축은 헬륨 원자가 탄소로 변환하도록 하는 극도로 높은 온도를 만들어내고, 이는 추가적인 에너지를 소모하여, 에너지를 보존하기 위해 가장 바깥쪽 층을 팽창시킨다. 이 팽창을 통해, 별은 적색거성이 된다. [4]그런 다음, II형 초신성은 핵에서 철과 니켈 같은 무거운 원소를 생성하는데, 이것은 더 큰 에너지를 필요로 하고 전체 질량을 증가시킨다. 핵융합이 추가적인 무게를 지탱할 수 있는 충분한 에너지를 더 이상 만들어 낼 수 없기 때문에, 적색거성은 찬드라세카 한계를 넘어 초신성 폭발로 스스로 붕괴한다.

이 폭발의 주요 결과 중 하나는 방출된 물질로 구성된 엄청난 먼지와 가스 구름인 성운의 생성이다. 수천 년에 걸쳐, 밀도가 높은 성운은 그 자체의 중력 때문에 물질을 축적할 것이며, 그 결과 행성, 별, 그리고 폭발한 별로부터의 물질로 일부 이루어진 다른 우주 물체들의 형성을 야기할 것이다. 동시에, 핵은 초신성에서부터 냉각되어 밀도가 높고 차가운 중성자별을 형성한다. 이것들은 핵융합을 수행할 능력이 없기 때문에 열이나 에너지를 발생시킬 수 없다는 점에서 백색왜성과 비슷하다. 그러나, 중성자별은 초신성 폭발 동안의 핵의 압축 때문에 백색왜성보다 밀도가 훨씬 높다. 천문학자들은 우리 은하에 약 1억 개의 중성자별이 있다고 추정하는데, 이는 초신성 발생의 정도가 높다는 것을 나타낸다.

supernova 명초신성　combustion 명연소
predominantly 부대개, 대부분　transpire 동발생하다, 일어나다
disintegrate 동붕괴하다, 해체되다　white dwarf 백색왜성
sap 동빼앗다, 약화시키다　adjacent 형인접한
accrue 동축적하다, 누적하다　red giant 적색거성　nebula 명성운

expel 동방출하다　amass 동축적하다　neutron star 중성자별
postulate 동추정하다　occurrence 명발생, 발생하는 것

1　2단락에 따르면, 찬드라세카르 한계는 무엇인가?

(A) 핵융합이 발생할 수 있는 최고 온도이다.
(B) 별이 유지할 수 있는 최대 질량이다.
(C) 별이 초신성으로 발전하는 마지막 단계이다.
(D) 별이 원소를 생성하게 될 수 있는 최대 크기이다.

2　지문의 단어 "accrues"와 의미가 가장 비슷한 것은?

(A) 포함하다
(B) 소진하다
(C) 촉진하다
(D) 축적하다

3　3단락에 따르면, 백색왜성은

(A) 핵융합 과정에서 헬륨 원자의 생성을 통해 생성된다
(B) 핵 속 열의 점진적인 축적을 통해 생성된다
(C) 쌍성계에서 별의 느린 분리를 통해 생성된다
(D) 핵에 있는 수소의 궁극적인 고갈을 통해 생성된다

4　4단락에 따르면, II형 초신성의 한 가지 특징은?

(A) 외부 층의 수소 부족
(B) 핵의 헬륨 원자 부족
(C) 내부 핵융합의 중단
(D) 핵에서의 무거운 원소 발달

5　지시: 지문 요약을 위한 도입 문장이 아래에 주어져 있다. 지문의 가장 중요한 내용을 나타내는 보기 3개를 골라 요약을 완성하라.

비록 모든 별들이 어떤 한 가지 방식의 별의 소멸을 경험하지만, 별들은 초신성 폭발을 발생시키기 위해 특정한 요구 조건을 달성해야 한다.

(A) 초신성은 별이 자신의 질량을 지탱할 수 있는 충분한 에너지를 생산할 수 있는 능력을 상실할 때 발생한다.
(B) 두 개의 주요 초신성 유형은 구조적 붕괴 시점에 핵융합을 수행할 수 있는 능력으로 구분된다.
(C) 초신성은 별이 적색거성으로 알려진 생애주기 단계에 도달했을 때 발생할 수 있다.
(D) 중성자별은 현재 우리 은하에서 확인 가능한 별의 대부분을 차지한다.
(E) 초신성은 성운을 형성하기 때문에 새로운 별과 다른 천체의 발달에 기여한다.
(F) 소멸하는 두 별이 서로 가까이 있을 때, 그것들은 물질을 공유할 수 있으며, 이는 초신성을 발생시킨다.

iBT Reading Test 1

본문 p. 164

1 (B)　**2** (B)　**3** (A)　**4** (A)
5 (D)　**6** (A)　**7** (C)　**8** (C)
9 (D)　**10** (B), (C), (E)

빙하 작용과 빙하기

1836년 스위스 알프스에서, 루이 아가시는 부근의 암석과 전혀 닮지 않은 바위를 발견했다. 이 바위들 중 일부는 심하게 긁혀 있었고, 마치

그것들은 그곳에 좌초된 것처럼 계곡 벽 위에 높이 위치해 있었다. 아가시는 이질적인 암석 지형이 과거의 빙하 작용에 의해 가장 잘 설명될 수 있다고 결론지었다. 그는 북극에서 유럽 알프스에 이르는 전 지역이 한때 빙상으로 덮여 있었다고 주장했는데, 그는 이것이 장기간의 추운 기온, 즉 빙하기 때문에 가능하게 된 현상이라고 주장했다. ²나중에, 아가시는 미국 내 다양한 지역에서 유사한 퇴적물과 지형을 발견했다. 이것은 빙하 작용이 유럽에 국한되었던 것이 아니라, 광범위하게 퍼져 아마도 심지어 북반구 전체로 확장되었을 것이라고 그에게 확신시켰다.

아가시의 급진적인 생각은 처음에 상당한 반대에 부딪혔다. 어쨌든, 그 당시의 지배적인 견해는 지구가 생성 이래 서서히 냉각되어 왔다는 것이었다. 그러나 곧 다른 과학자들은 빙하 표류에 의해 퇴적된 여러 개의 뚜렷한 퇴적층을 발견했다. 만약 여러 층이 있다면, 실제로는 오랜 기간에 걸쳐 여러 빙하기가 있었음이 분명했다. 19세기 후반 북아메리카와 유럽의 빙퇴토에 대한 철저한 연구와 비교는 빙하의 전진과 후퇴의 4대 주요 시기가 있었다는 것을 인정하게 했다. 20세기의 후속 연구는 이 빙하기들의 정확한 연대를 알아내기 위해 방사성 탄소 연대 측정법을 이용했으며, 그것들의 마지막은 플라이스토세 말기쯤인 대략 1만 년 전에 끝났다.

지질학자들은 빙하 작용들 사이의 휴지기를 간빙기라고 불렀다. 빙하 작용 동안에는 얼음이 팽창했고, 간빙기 동안에는 후퇴했다. ⁵지질학자들은 빙하의 표류층 사이에서 잘 발달된 토양과 따뜻한 기후에서만 자랄 수 있었던 식물의 잔해를 발견했다. 이 발견들은 그 사이의 기간 동안 기후가 급격하게 변했다는 결정적인 증거를 제공했다. 지속적인 냉각이나 단 한 번의 빙하기가 있었다는 것은 더 이상 받아들이기가 불가능했다. ⁶그러나, 빙하기와 과거의 기후에 대한 과학적 이해는 여전히 불완전했고, 해양 퇴적물에서 얻은 증거들은 빙하기와 관련된 또 다른 사고의 혁명을 일으켰다.

해저층은 주로 방해석으로 만들어진 껍질을 가진 작은 단세포 생물인 무수한 유공충을 포함한 비교적 흐트러지지 않은 퇴적층들로 구성되어 있다. ⁸이 미소동물상은 물에서 산소를 흡수하며, 껍질에 존재하는 다양한 형태의 산소의 동위원소 농도를 측정하기 위해 실험될 수 있다. 바닷물이 증발할 때, 무거운 산소-18은 대기로 덜 쉽게 이동한다. 결과적으로, 땅에 떨어져서 눈과 얼음을 형성하는 물은 산소-16이 많다. 과거 빙하기 동안, 이 가벼운 산소의 대부분이 지표면의 빙상에 갇혀 있었을 때, 바닷물의 산소-18의 수준은 비교적 더 높았고, 더 높은 비율의 무거운 산소를 함유한 유공충은 따라서 빙하기를 나타낸다.

이 심해 핵 견본들과 동위원소 비교는 과학자들이 빙하기를 바라보는 방식에 혁명을 일으켰다. 유럽과 북아메리카에서 구분된 4개의 고전적 빙하기 대신, 해양의 동위원소 분석은 플라이스토세 동안 16개 이상의 주요 빙하 작용 사건을 밝혀냈다. 지구는 기본적으로 얼음 증가와 얼음 축소의 지속적인 순환으로 특징지어지는 빙하 환경이며 가끔 지난 만 년 동안의 것과 같은 비정상적으로 따뜻한 시기를 겪기도 한다. 고위도의 고산 지대에서부터 열대 지방에 이르기까지 지구 각지는 빙하 작용의 영향을 받는다. 빙하기는 식물의 분포와 지구에서 발견되는 생명체의 종류까지도 좌우한다. 예를 들어, 과학자들은 화석 기록을 통해 동물의 멸종이 빙하기의 결과로 일어났다는 것을 알고 있다.

glaciation 圓빙하 작용   boulder 圓바위
bear no resemblance to ~을 전혀 닮지 않다, 차이가 나다
strand 圖(배 등을) 좌초시키다   heterogeneous 圐이질적인
deposit 圓퇴적물; 圖퇴적시키다   radical 圐급진적인
prevailing 圐지배적인   sediment layer 퇴적층   glacial till 빙퇴토
retreat 圓후퇴; 圖후퇴하다   subsequent 圐후속의
radiocarbon dating 방사성 탄소 연대 측정법
interglacial 圓간빙기; 圐간빙기의   intervening 圐사이의

undisturbed 圐흐트러지지 않은   innumerable 圐무수한
foraminifera 圓유공충   calcite 圓방해석
microfauna 圓미소동물상   isotopic concentration 동위원소 농도
comparatively 图비교적   be indicative of ~을 나타내다

1 아래 문장 중 지문 속의 음영된 문장의 핵심 정보를 가장 잘 표현한 것은? 오답은 문장의 의미를 크게 바꾸거나 핵심 정보를 생략한다.

(A) 아가시에 따르면, 극도로 추운 기온은 북극에서 유럽 알프스에 이르는 다양한 곳에서 빙상이 형성되도록 했다.

(B) 아가시는 빙하기가 한때 북극에서 유럽 알프스까지의 전 지역을 뒤덮었던 빙상의 형성을 가져왔다고 주장했다.

(C) 아가시는 북극과 유럽 알프스 사이의 빙상이 빙하기 이후에도 오래 살아남았다고 주장했다.

(D) 아가시는 장기간의 추운 기온의 결과로 생긴 큰 빙상이 과거에만 형성될 수 있었을 것이라고 주장했다.

2 1단락에 따르면, 과거의 빙하 작용이 광범위했다고 아가시를 확신시켰던 것은?

(A) 계곡 벽의 언덕 위에 좌초된 많은 바위들
(B) 미국의 많은 다른 지역에서의 유사한 지질 현상들의 존재
(C) 유럽과 미국에서 활동 중인 빙하의 존재
(D) 북극에서 알프스산맥까지 뻗어 있는 거대한 빙상

3 지문의 단어 "prevailing"과 의미가 가장 비슷한 것은?

(A) 지배적인
(B) 철저한
(C) 정확한
(D) 설득력 있는

4 지문에서 글쓴이는 왜 "glacial till"을 논하는가?

(A) 여러 빙하기가 일어났다는 추가 증거를 제공하기 위해
(B) 아가시의 생각을 수정하게 된 발견을 확인하기 위해
(C) 19세기에 과학 지식이 얼마나 많이 변했는지 강조하기 위해
(D) 지구가 생성 이후 서서히 냉각되지 않았음을 확인하기 위해

5 3단락에 따르면, 지질학자들에 의해 발견된 잘 발달된 토양과 식물에 관해 사실인 것은?

(A) 번갈아 일어난 따뜻한 기간과 추운 기간이 동일했다는 주장을 반박했다.
(B) 지질학자들이 지구의 기후에 대해 항상 믿어온 것을 검증했다.
(C) 빙하 작용이 북쪽에서 시작되어 남쪽으로 퍼졌다는 이론이 틀렸음을 입증했다.
(D) 빙하 작용 사이에 극적인 기후 변화가 일어났다는 것을 확인했다.

6 다음 중 3단락에서 해저에 관해 추론할 수 있는 것은?

(A) 그것의 퇴적물은 육지의 그것보다 빙하 작용에 대한 더 넓은 이해를 제공한다.
(B) 그것의 화학 성분은 기후 변화 기간에도 비교적 안정적이다.
(C) 그것의 화학 조성은 주로 방해석 퇴적물에 의해 결정된다.
(D) 그것의 퇴적층은 대륙의 그것보다 훨씬 더 자주 흐트러진다.

7 지문의 단어 "comparatively"와 의미가 가장 비슷한 것은?

(A) 잇따라서
(B) 고의로
(C) 비교적
(D) 확실히

8 4단락에 따르면, 과학자들은 과거의 해양 조건에 대해 알기 위해 유공충 껍질을

(A) 껍질에 있는 산소의 양을 평균 대기 산소 수준과 비교함으로써 활용한다

(B) 시간이 지남에 따라 껍질에 의해 흡수된 방해석의 총량을 계산함으로써 활용한다

(C) 껍질이 포함하는 산소 동위원소의 상대적인 양을 측정함으로써 활용한다

(D) 껍질들을 세고 빙하 작용이 다른 생물에 미치는 영향을 추정함으로써 활용한다

9 네 개의 네모[■]는 다음 문장이 삽입될 수 있는 곳을 나타내고 있다.

예를 들어, 과학자들은 화석 기록을 통해 동물의 멸종이 빙하기의 결과로 일어났다는 것을 알고 있다.

이 문장은 어디에 들어가는 것이 가장 적절한가?

10 지시: 지문 요약을 위한 도입 문장이 아래에 주어져 있다. 지문의 가장 중요한 내용을 나타내는 보기 3개를 골라 요약을 완성하라. 어떤 문장은 지문에 언급되지 않은 내용이나 사소한 정보를 나타내므로 요약에 포함되지 않는다. **이 문제는 2점이다.**

> 빙하기의 최초 발견 이후, 추가적인 연구가 새로운 이해로 이어졌다.
> · (B) 대륙의 연구는 주요 기후 변화로 특징지어지는 네 번의 빙하기가 있었다는 증거를 발견했다.
> · (C) 심해 핵 견본들과 산소 동위원소 분석을 포함한 연구들은 과학자들이 빙하기 동안 빙하 작용에 대한 보다 포괄적인 이해를 발전시키는 데 도움을 주었다.
> · (E) 해저에서 채취한 유공충은 여러 차례의 빙하기 가능성에 대한 증거를 제공했다.

(A) 루이 아가시는 과거의 빙하기의 존재를 확신했지만, 그 이론은 그의 동시대인들에 의해 받아들여지지 않았다.

(D) 루이 아가시의 지질학적 관측은 빙하기 가설로 이어졌고, 이후 여러 빙하기들을 수용하기 위해 수정되었다.

(F) 간빙기 층에서 채취한 토양과 식물 화석은 유럽과 북아메리카가 먼 과거에 유사한 식물군을 가지고 있었다는 것을 나타낸다.

iBT Reading Test 2
본문 p. 168

1 (D)	2 (A)	3 (A)	4 (A)
5 (B)	6 (B)	7 (A)	8 (D)
9 (D)	10 (A), (C), (E)		

초월주의

1836년 9월 8일 미국 초월주의 클럽의 첫 회의가 매사추세츠주 보스턴에서 열렸다. 그 단체는 당시의 사회 상태에 좌절했던 젊은 지식인들로 이루어져 있었으며, 그것은 정치적 행동주의를 위한 조직적인 토대를 제공했다. 그것의 핵심 신념들 중에는 인간이 확립된 종교 교리의 개입 없이 자연적인 직관을 통해 영적 깨달음을 성취하거나 물질주의적인 세상과 감각 및 논리의 한계를 초월할 수 있다는 개념이 있었다. 당시 급진적이었던 그 클럽은 권위에 도전하고 개인주의를 선호하는 초월주의라고 불린 새로운 철학적 이상을 낳았다.

한 가지 중요한 초월주의적 이상은 당대의 가장 영향력 있는 작가들 중 한 명인 랠프 월도 에머슨의 수필에서 언급되었다. ²그는 초월주의의 주요 주제를 "자연의 신비한 통일성"이라고 표현했는데, 이는 환경은 그 안에 사는 사람들을 포함하여, 별개 요소의 합이 아닌 하나의 완전한 전체로서 간주되어야 한다는 것을 의미한다. 미국 대륙의 광활한 미개척 지역에서 영감을 받아, 에머슨은 사람들에게 문명과 야생 사이의 미묘한 균형을 고려하고 인간의 손에 의한 훼손으로부터 환경을 보호하도록 장려했다. 그에 더해, 에머슨은 불공정하거나 시민에게 자연에 대한 권력을 부여하는 법률에 대한 도덕적 항의의 형태로서 조용한 시민 불복종 활동을 장려했다. 이러한 근본 원칙은 마하트마 간디와 마틴 루터 킹 주니어 같은 이후의 평화 운동가들에게 깊은 영향을 미쳤다.

초월주의에서 자라난 두 번째 개념은 2차 대각성 운동으로 나타났는데, 이는 자신의 종교적 신념을 통합함으로써 에머슨의 작품을 확장한 클럽 회원들의 작품으로 시작된 영적 부흥의 시기이다. ⁴그들의 글에서 그들은 자연환경 보호가 전체론적 세계를 유지하는 데 필수적일 뿐만 아니라, 성경에 명시된 의무라는 생각을 강조했다. 인간을 지상의 관리자로 여기는 이러한 관념을 홍보하고자, 뉴잉글랜드주와 애팔래치아 산맥 전역에 전도사들이 빠르게 임명되어 큰 성공을 거두었다. 설교는 무려 2만 명을 끌어모아 변화를 불러일으키는 개인의 힘을 강조해 사회적 행동주의를 고무했다. 이 전도사들은 사회를 개선하기 위해 음주를 줄이려고 노력했던 금주 운동의 근원으로 여겨진다.

초월주의의 세 번째 신조인 개인 자율권의 개념은 아마도 가장 광범위한데, 이는 그것이 현대 미국 시민들에 의해 가장 높이 평가되는 믿음이기 때문이며, 그것은 집단의 권리보다 개인의 권리를 보호하는 오래 지속된 법률에서 준수된다. 18세기 중반 이전에, 미국 인구는 자신을 주로 미국 시민이 아닌, 그들이 속한 인종이나 정치 집단의 일부로서 인식하는 경향이 있는 이민자들로 구성되었다. ⁶그러나, 사후에 초월주의 세대라고 이름 붙여진 1792년에서 1821년 사이에 태어난 아이들은, 새로운 국가에서 자란 첫 번째 자손들을 대표한다.

성장함에 따라, 그들은 개혁가, 전도사, 캠퍼스 폭도들이 되어 압제적인 영국 정부로부터의 자유를 위해 싸웠다. 성인이 되어, 그들은 노예제 폐지 운동의 확고한 지지자로 성장했는데, 그것은 노예 해방이 영적으로 명령되었다고 주장했으며, 이는, 성경에 따르면 모든 사람이 지구의 평등한 관리자이기 때문이다. 말년에도 완고하게, 어떤 이들은 시, 문학, 그리고 다른 창조적인 일을 자신을 표현하는 수단으로 삼았지만, 무엇보다도, 그들은 자유를 위해 계속 헌신했다. 그들의 작품들 중 많은 것들이 현재 미국 역사상 가장 중요한 예술적 업적들 중 하나로 여겨진다. 초월주의 세대에 의해 옹호된 변화는, 실행되었든 아니든, 특히 북부의 문화적 지형에 깊은 영향을 미쳤다. 그 결과, 남부의 노예 소유자와 노예제 폐지론자들 사이에 갈등이 일어났고, 이것이 미국 남북 전쟁에 자극제를 제공했다.

frustrated 휑좌절한   activism 몡(정치적) 행동주의
enlightenment 몡깨달음   transcend 통초월하다
materialistic 휑물질주의적인   radical 휑급진적인
decimation 몡훼손, 대량 살상   civil disobedience 시민 불복종
holistic 휑전체론적인   custodian 몡관리자
evoke 통불러일으키다   empowerment 몡자율권
far-reaching 휑(효과가) 광범위한   posthumously 뷔사후에
staunch 휑확고한   abolitionist movement 노예제 폐지 운동
emancipation 몡해방   mandated 휑명령된
unyielding 휑완고한   impetus 몡자극제, 추진력

1 지문의 단어 "decimation"과 의미가 가장 비슷한 것은?

(A) 궁핍

(B) 변혁

(C) 열망

(D) 파괴

2 2단락에 따르면, 다음 중 에머슨에 관해 사실인 것은?

(A) 그에게는 부분들의 합으로서의 자연 개념보다 전체로서의 자연 개념이 중요했다.

(B) 시민 불복종의 실천은 그가 다른 평화 운동가들에게서 배운 방법이었다.

(C) 미국의 자연 그대로의 자연환경은 그가 그 자원의 산업적 이용을 옹호하도록 동기를 부여했다.

(D) 그가 쓴 수필은 전통 종교보다 초월주의의 우월성을 주장했다.

3 지문에서 글쓴이는 왜 "the Temperance Movement"를 언급하는가?

(A) 2차 대각성 운동에서 발달한 조직적인 활동을 설명하기 위해

(B) 애팔래치아산맥에서 설교한 전도사의 한 유형을 설명하기 위해

(C) 기독교 교육의 영향에 대한 예를 들기 위해

(D) 에머슨의 글이 어떻게 다양한 집단의 사람들을 끌어모았는지 보여주기 위해

4 3단락에 따르면, 미국 동부에 전도사들이 임명된 것은

(A) 자연에 대한 종교적 책임을 설명하는 교훈을 전하기 위해서였다

(B) 사람들이 차이점에도 불구하고 다른 사람들을 받아들이도록 격려하기 위해서였다

(C) 지역 주민들에게 음주를 하지 않도록 설득하기 위해서였다

(D) 교도소 및 의료 시설의 개선을 추진하기 위해서였다

5 아래 문장 중 지문 속의 음영된 문장의 핵심 정보를 가장 잘 표현한 것은? 오답은 문장의 의미를 크게 바꾸거나 핵심 정보를 생략한다.

(A) 현대의 규칙들은 일반 사회가 아닌 개인이 그들의 삶에 대한 통제권을 가져야 한다는 믿음을 반영하기 위해 만들어졌다.

(B) 초월주의의 가장 널리 인정되고 지속되는 신념은 여전히 법 체계에서 볼 수 있으며, 개인의 자유에 대한 강조이다.

(C) 시민들은 자신에 대한 독점적 권력이라는 초월주의의 신조를 기꺼이 받아들였는데, 이는 그것이 그들에게 더 많은 능력을 부여했기 때문이다.

(D) 개인의 역할을 강조하면서, 초월주의자들은 미국 법에 통합되지 않은 세 번째 이론을 발전시켰다.

6 다음 중 4단락에서 1792년에서 1821년 사이에 태어난 아이들에 관해 추론할 수 있는 것은?

(A) 가족과 떨어져 국가의 다른 지역으로 이주했다.

(B) 자신들을 초월주의 세대라고 부르지 않았다.

(C) 그들의 이민자 부모와 같은 가치와 도덕성을 공유했다.

(D) 자신들을 미국 시민이라고 인식하지 않았다.

7 지문의 단어 "staunch"와 의미가 가장 비슷한 것은?

(A) 확고한

(B) 실용적인

(C) 혁신적인

(D) 귀중한

8 지문의 단어 "impetus"와 의미가 가장 비슷한 것은?

(A) 개선

(B) 결과

(C) 입장

(D) 자극

9 네 개의 네모[■]는 다음 문장이 삽입될 수 있는 곳을 나타내고 있다.

그들의 작품들 중 많은 것들이 현재 미국 역사상 가장 중요한 예술적 업적들 중 하나로 여겨진다.

이 문장은 어디에 들어가는 것이 가장 적절한가?

10 지시: 지문 요약을 위한 도입 문장이 아래에 주어져 있다. 지문의 가장 중요한 내용을 나타내는 보기 3개를 골라 요약을 완성하라. 어떤 문장은 지문에 언급되지 않은 내용이나 사소한 정보를 나타내므로 요약에 포함되지 않는다. 이 문제는 2점이다.

> 초월주의 클럽의 설립은 전례 없는 철학적 개념의 확산을 초래했다.
>
> · (A) 변화를 선동하는 한 사람의 능력에 대한 강조는 많은 사람들이 주요한 사회적 조정을 추진하는 운동가가 되도록 자극했다.
>
> · (C) 에머슨의 작품에서 제시된 생각을 바탕으로, 인간과 자연환경의 조화가 그 철학에 차용되었다.
>
> · (E) 초월주의자들은 기독교인들에게 지구를 보호할 의무가 있다고 주장했고, 이는 영성주의에 대한 관심의 부활을 촉발시켰다.

(B) 1750년 이전에 미국으로 이주한 이민자들은 초월주의 철학을 지지하지 않았으나, 그렇게 하는 자녀들을 낳았다.

(D) 초월주의 세대의 구성원들의 선동은 노예제에 동의하는 사람들과 반대하는 사람들 사이의 무력 충돌로 이어졌다.

(F) 설교자들은 성경에서 선언된 대로 사람들에게 신에 대한 그들의 의무에 관해 말하기 위해 동부 전역을 여행했다.

Vocabulary Review

본문 p. 172

1 distinguished	2 antiquity	3 resemblance
4 immature	5 emancipation	6 insurmountable
7 (A)	8 (B)	9 (D)	10 (C)
11 (B)	12 (D)	13 (A)	14 (A)

CHAPTER 10
Category Chart

Example

본문 p. 175

1 Gradualism: (C), (D), (F)   Catastrophism: (A), (E)

공룡 멸종

과학에서 가장 큰 미스터리 중 하나는 약 6,500만 년 전에 있었던 공룡의 소멸로, 이 동물 집단이 2억 년 이상 동안 지구를 지배했었기 때문이다. 현재, 고생물학자들은 무엇이 이 대멸종을 초래했는지에 대해 의견이 분분하다.

점진주의라고 알려진 한 가설은 공룡을 멸종시킨 사건들이 오랜 기간에 걸쳐 일어났다고 주장한다. 기본적으로, 지지자들은 수수께끼를 풀

기 위해 판 구조론에 주목하고 있는데, 이것은 지각 아래 판의 이동이 점차 화산 활동을 증가시켰다는 것을 암시한다. 전 지구적 폭발로 인해 방출된 기체는 잦은 산성비를 촉발하여 동식물에 피해를 입혔을 것이다. 그 결과로 나타난 먹이사슬의 붕괴는 또한 많은 동물들이 그것들의 영양적 필요를 충족시키는 것을 점점 더 어렵게 만들었을 것이다. 그러나, 이 이론의 반대자들은 그것이 이 화석 기록에 의해 뒷받침되지 않는다고 지적하는데, 그것은 공룡의 소멸이 이러한 과정들에 의해 설명될 수 있는 것보다 더 급작스러웠음을 나타낸다.

대조적으로, 격변주의는 공룡의 멸종이 거대한 혜성이나 소행성의 충돌로 인해 빠르게 일어났다고 가정한다. 그 충돌의 즉각적인 피해를 넘어, 전 세계의 기후 체계가 근본적으로 바뀌었을 것이다. 숲과 다른 가연성 생태계가 불타오르는 것에서 비롯된 거대한 불 폭풍과 극도로 강력한 허리케인이 흔했을 것이다. 이러한 파멸적인 상황에서, 처음의 충돌에서 살아남은 대부분의 유기체들은 짧은 시간 안에 소멸했을 것이다. 공룡이 멸종했을 무렵에 생긴 멕시코의 거대한 분화구의 존재에 의해 이 설명이 뒷받침되는 것처럼 보이지만, 반대자들은 그것의 생성에 의한 파괴는 전 세계의 이 동물들을 죽이기에는 불충분했다고 주장한다.

approximately (부) 약, 대략　　paleontologist (명) 고생물학자
hypothesis (명) 가설　　gradualism (명) 점진주의
proponent (명) 지지자　　plate tectonics 판 구조론
unravel (동) 풀다, 해결하다　　flora and fauna 동식물
nutritional (형) 영양적인　　opponent (명) 반대자　　abrupt (형) 급작스러운
catastrophism (명) 격변주의　　postulate (동) 가정하다
flammable (형) 가연성의, 불에 잘 타는　　be set ablaze 불타오르다
catastrophic (형) 파멸적인, 대재앙의　　devastation (명) 파괴, 황폐화

1 지시: 주어진 선택지에서 적절한 어구를 선택하여 관계있는 이론에 연결하시오.

선택지	점진주의
(B) 대부분의 유기체에게 치명적인 유독가스의 방출을 촉발했다 (G) 지각판의 이동을 가속화했다	· (C) 다양한 유기체들에게 심각한 먹이 부족을 초래했다 · (D) 전 세계 화산 폭발의 증가에서 비롯되었다 · (F) 동식물에게 해로운 산성비를 초래했다
	격변주의
	· (A) 거대한 외계 물체와의 충돌을 수반했다 · (E) 강력한 폭풍과 산불의 발달로 이어졌다

Reading Practice 1
본문 p.176

1 (D)　　2 (B)　　3 (A)　　4 (A)
5 Maritime Temperate Climates: (C), (E), (F)
　Continental Temperate Climates: (A), (G)

온대 기후

지구 인구의 약 40퍼센트는 북반구에서는 북회귀선과 북극권 사이의 그리고 남반구에서는 남회귀선과 남극권 사이의 좁은 온대 기후 지역에 살고 있다. 지구의 온대인 비교적 작은 지역(육지 전체의 약 7퍼센트)에도 불구하고, 온대 지역은 인간의 생존에 최적의 조건을 제공한다. 이것은 대부분 온화한 기후, 풍부한 강수량, 적절한 토양 비옥도 때문이다. 이러한 조건들은 집약 농업에 적합하며, 온대 지역의 농부들은 다양한 작물을 재배할 수 있다.

[1]양호한 기후는 현지인들에게 충분한 식량 생산을 지원할 수 있으며, 다른 지역의 상품 및 서비스를 대가로 수출될 수 있는 잉여를 제공할 수 있다. [2]그러나, 온대 기후 지역 내에서는 어떤 종류의 기후 조건이 우세할지에 영향을 미칠 수 있는 약간의 차이가 있는데, 이는 보통 그 지역의 지리적 위치와 관련이 있다. 기후학자들은 이것을 해양성 온대 기후대와 대륙성 온대 기후대의 두 가지 주요 범주로 나누는 경향이 있다.

해양성 온대 기후대 또는 해양성 기후대는 일반적으로 중위도에 있는 주요 대륙의 서쪽 해안을 따라서 그리고 호주 남동쪽 가장자리에서 볼 수 있다. 극지방에의 인접성은 이 지역들을 끊임없는 한대 전선에 노출시켜 날씨가 자주 흐리게 된다. 이러한 구름의 범위는 일 년 내내 적절한 강수량을 허용한다. 흐릿한 하늘은 또한 같은 위도의 다른 기후대의 그것들보다 서늘한 여름으로 이어지며, 그 지역이 일 년 내내 그것의 많은 온기를 유지하기 때문에 겨울은 더 포근하다. 해양성 기후의 온도 범위는 −10도에서 25도 사이로 매우 좁지만, 여전히 모든 온대 지역의 특징인 뚜렷한 사계절을 유지한다. 게다가, 해양성 기후의 계절은 중온으로 간주되는데, 겨울은 일 년 내내 광합성을 하기에는 너무 춥지만 일정 기간 지속적인 적설량을 유지할 만큼 춥지는 않다.

[4]반면에, 대륙성 온대 기후대는 더 추운 겨울과 더 따뜻한 여름으로 알려져 있는데, 이는 거대한 북반구 대륙의 중위도 내륙의 특징이다. 그곳들은 대양의 완화 효과에 영향을 받지 않을 정도로 해안에서 충분히 멀리 떨어져 있거나 한대 전선이 내륙 쪽으로가 아니라 바다 쪽으로 부는 곳에 위치해있다. 대신, 이 지역들은 겨울에는 차가운 기단에 의해, 여름에는 따뜻하거나 뜨거운 기단에 의해 침투된다. 따라서, 그곳들은 두세 달 동안 더 따뜻한 기온을 얻을 수 있지만, 비슷한 위도의 다른 기후대보다 훨씬 더 시원해질 수 있고, 일정 기간의 안정적인 적설량을 유지할 수 있다.

대륙성 기후의 강수량은 연중 고르게 분포하지 않는다. 겨울과 봄에는 여름보다 훨씬 더 많은 비가 내리고, 여름은 다소 건조하다. 비가 거의 오지 않는 기간을 견딜 수 있는 낙엽수와 관목은 키가 큰 풀들이 그러하듯 흔히 대륙성 기후대에서 자란다. 이 지역의 농업은 가뭄 기간에 살아남을 수 있는 곡물과 뿌리채소에 집중하는 경향이 있다. 이 생산물들은 대륙성 온대 기후에서 번성하며 미국 중서부, 중국, 러시아의 많은 도시들에서 인구 호황의 토대가 되었다.

precipitation (명) 강수량, 강수　　adequate (형) 적절한
fertility (명) 비옥도　　intensive agriculture 집약 농업
favorable (형) (기후가) 양호한　　latitude (명) 위도　　proximity (명) 인접성
polar fronts 한대 전선, 극 전선　　overcast (형) (날씨가) 흐린
hallmark (명) (전형적인) 특징　　mesothermal (형) (기후가) 중온의
photosynthesis (명) 광합성　　impervious (형) 영향받지 않는
moderate (동) 완화시키다　　offshore (부) (육지에서) 바다 쪽으로
infiltrate (동) 침투하다　　air mass 기단　　comparable (형) 비슷한
deciduous tree 낙엽수

1 다음 중 2단락에서 온대 지역에 관해 추론할 수 있는 것은?

(A) 극한 기후 조건에도 불구하고 많은 인구를 부양한다.

(B) 종종 토양 비옥도가 좋지 않지만, 온화한 기후와 풍부한 강수량을 자랑한다.

(C) 일반적으로 집약 농업보다는 조방 농업에 더 적합하다.

(D) 인구가 소비할 수 있는 것보다 더 많은 식량을 생산할 수 있다.

2 지문에 따르면, 기후를 대륙성 또는 해양성으로 분류하는 것은 주로

(A) 그 지역의 집약 농업 지원 능력에 의해 결정된다

(B) 온대 기후대 내의 지역 위치에 의해 결정된다

(C) 각 지역의 인구 밀도에 의해 결정된다

(D) 뚜렷한 사계절의 존재에 의해 결정된다

3 지문의 단어 "impervious"와 의미가 가장 비슷한 것은?

(A) 영향받지 않는

(B) 배출된

(C) 불균형한

(D) 없어서는 안 될

4 4단락에 따르면, 대륙성 온대 기후의 특징은

(A) 광범위한 값의 기온 차를 포함한다

(B) 내륙 지방으로 부는 시원한 바람을 포함한다

(C) 기후 조건에 영향을 미치는 큰 수역을 포함한다

(D) 순식간에 녹는 많은 양의 눈을 포함한다

5 지시: 주어진 선택지에서 적절한 어구를 선택하여 관계있는 온대 기후의 종류에 연결하시오.

선택지	해양성 온대 기후
(B) 겨울에 폭설이 내리지만, 즉시 녹는다 (D) 집약 농업에 부적합한 토양을 제공한다	· (C) 한대 전선으로 인해 자주 흐린 상태로 특징지어진다 · (E) 여름과 겨울의 기온 차가 거의 없다 · (F) 일 년 내내 강수량이 풍부하다
	대륙성 온대 기후
	· (A) 여름보다 겨울에 강수량이 더 많다 · (G) 가뭄에 강한 작물을 재배하기에 좋은 환경을 조성한다

Reading Practice 2 　　　　　　　　본문 p. 178

1 (C)　　　2 (B)　　　3 (B)　　　4 (A)

5 Formalism: (A), (E)　Contextualism: (C), (D), (F)

시각 예술 해석하기

시각 예술을 어떻게 해석할 것인가에 대한 문제는 예술 이론가들의 주된 관심사이다. 비평가는 확립된 기준에 따라 개별 작품을 평가하는 반면에, 예술 이론가는 그 기준이 정확히 무엇이 되어야 하는지를 결정하려고 시도한다. 사실상, 그 목표는 특정 작품의 본질적인 예술적 가치를 결정하는 것이 아니라, 대신에 이것을 하기 위해 사용될 수 있는 개념적 체계를 개발하는 것이다. 현재, 예술이 해석되는 데는 형식주의

와 맥락주의라는 두 가지 주요 이론이 있다.

형식주의는 선, 형태, 색상, 질감, 구성이 관객에게 제공하는 심미적 경험을 결정하기 위해 작품 자체에 집중해야 한다고 주장한다. 사실, 형식주의라는 용어는 이러한 형식에의 강조에서 비롯된다. 작품의 분석은 오로지 시각적 특성에 기반해야 하며, 예술가의 동기나 그것이 창작된 환경과 같은 다른 요소들은 무시되어야 한다. 형식주의적 접근을 비판하는 사람들은 이러한 편협한 초점은 긍정적인 것이라기보다는 부정적인 것이라고 주장하는데, 그들은 그것이 그 작품을 누가 그리고 무슨 목적으로 창작했는지에 대한 타당한 고려를 즉각 무시한다고 주장한다. 그러나, 양식적 요소에만 관심을 기울이도록 주장함으로써, 형식주의자들은 관객들이 자세히 보고 나서 예술의 감각적인 특징에 대한 느낌으로 반응하도록 장려한다.

대조적으로, 맥락주의는 작품이 창작되었던 맥락에 관심이 있다. 이러한 형태의 해석은 예술 작품을 그것의 창작을 야기한 외부 요인들과 결부시켜 이해하고자 한다. 특히 관심이 있는 것은 그 예술가의 동기이다. 맥락주의자는 예술가의 사회적 지위, 사생활, 사회 및 윤리 문제에 대한 견해, 그리고 이것들이 창작 과정을 어떻게 자극했는지 알고 싶어 할 것이다. 또 다른 고려 사항은 연구되는 예술 작품과 같은 문화에서 나온 다른 작품들 사이의 관계이다. 이것은 그 예술가의 영향에 대한 통찰력을 제공한다. 마지막으로, 맥락주의적 분석 동안 후원이 검토된다. 그 예술 작품이 누구를 위해 만들어졌고, 왜 그것을 창작하도록 화가에게 지원이 제공되었는가? 이러한 요소들을 조사함으로써, 맥락주의적 분석은 예술 작품의 근본적인 목적과 기능을 결정하고 평가하는 것을 가능하게 해준다.

두 접근 방식의 차이는 구체적인 예술 작품에 적용될 때 명백하다. 빈센트 반 고흐의 그림 '밤의 카페'는 두 이론의 지지자들에 의해 집중적으로 연구되어 온 것이다. 형식주의적 해석은 반 고흐가 그 그림의 독특한 시각적 효과를 창조하기 위해 사용한 다양한 기술에 초점을 맞춘다. 예를 들어, 그는 그림의 여러 부분들에 있는 특정 사물에 매우 두꺼운 붓놀림을 사용했고 그것들을 두드러지게 하기 위해 검은 선으로 윤곽을 그렸다. ³이에 더해, 반 고흐는 강렬하면서도 거의 부조화스러운 분위기를 내기 위해 빨간색과 녹색 같은 대조색을 사용했다. 그러나, 맥락주의적 분석은 이 그림이 사회 및 경제적 약자들이 살았던 몹시 지저분한 환경을 드러내기 위한 반 고흐의 시도를 나타낸다는 점에 관심을 모은다. 그림에 묘사된 유형의 카페는 다른 갈 곳이 없는 노숙자들로 종종 가득 차 있었다. 반 고흐가 이것을 알고 있었다는 것은 그가 남동생에게 쓴 편지에서 그가 돈이 없는 사람들이 피난할 수 있는 장소를 묘사하고 싶다고 언급했다는 점에서 명백해진다. '밤의 카페'에 대한 그의 목적은 화랑을 자주 드나들며 미술품을 구매하는 부유층과 상류층 사람들에게 이러한 프랑스 사회의 면모를 보여주는 것이었다고 주장할 수 있다.

established ⑱확립된　intrinsic ⑱본질적인, 내재된
formalism ⑲형식주의　contextualism ⑲맥락주의
aesthetic ⑱심미적인　stem from ~에서 비롯되다
out of hand 즉각　valid ⑱타당한, 유효한　sensuous ⑱감각적인
patronage ⑲(예술가에 대한) 후원　apparent ⑱명백한
discordant ⑱부조화스러운　sordid ⑱몹시 지저분한
take refuge 피난하다　frequent ⑧자주 드나들다

1 지문의 단어 "stems"와 의미가 가장 비슷한 것은?

(A) 억제하다

(B) 해석하다

(C) 기원하다

(D) 무시하다

2 지문의 단어 "them"이 가리키는 것은?

    (A) 붓놀림

    (B) 사물

    (C) 부분들

    (D) 선

3 4단락에 따르면, 반 고흐는 '밤의 카페'의 분위기를

    (A) 검정 물감으로 사물의 윤곽을 그려 만들어냈다

    (B) 대비되는 색조를 사용하여 만들어냈다

    (C) 물감을 고르지 않게 발라 만들어냈다

    (D) 가난해 보이는 사람들을 묘사해 만들어냈다

4 4단락에서, 글쓴이는 왜 반 고흐가 쓴 편지를 언급하는가?

    (A) 반 고흐가 카페의 고객층을 알고 있었음을 증명하기 위해

    (B) 반 고흐가 재정적인 어려움을 겪었음을 암시하기 위해

    (C) 반 고흐가 가족 구성원에게 느꼈던 연결을 강조하기 위해

    (D) 반 고흐가 상류층의 일원이었다는 것을 보여주기 위해

5 지시: 주어진 선택지에서 적절한 어구를 선택하여 관계있는 예술 해석 이론의 종류에 연결하시오.

선택지	형식주의
(B) 다른 시각적 요소보다 구성에 초점을 맞춘다 (G) 내적 및 외적 요인이 동일하다고 가정한다	· (A) 관객이 예술에 감정적으로 반응하도록 장려한다 · (E) 작품의 외관만을 고려한다
	맥락주의
	· (C) 예술가의 근본적인 동기를 탐구한다 · (D) 작품이 누구를 위해 만들어졌는지 숙고한다 · (F) 같은 전통에서 나온 서로 다른 예술 작품들을 비교한다

Reading Practice 3 본문 p. 180

1 (A)   2 (C)   3 (A)   4 (D)

5 Residents: (A), (C)   Transients: (B), (D), (F)

범고래

Killer whale라고 흔히 알려진 범고래는 모든 해양 돌고래를 포함하는 수생 포유류군인 참고래과에서 가장 큰 고래목 동물이다. 2A/2B/2D 그것은 방대한 크기와 놀라운 속도를 협력적인 무리 전략과 결합해 먹이사슬에서 정점의 위치를 유지하는 다재다능하고 효율적인 포식자이다.

범고래는 정착형과 이주형으로 알려진 두 개의 뚜렷한 개체군으로 나뉘는데, 이것들은 서로에 대해 극도의 적대감으로 반응하며 상호 교배하지 않는다. 비록 단일 종을 구성하지만, 과학자들은 그것들이 10만 년 이상 동안 서로 고립되어 있었다고 추정한다. 3한 이론은 각 분류를

구분하는 포식 활동 및 사회 관계와 관련된 행동적 특이성이 실은 궁극적으로 유전적 비호환성을 초래할 지속적인 종 분화의 과정의 징후일 수 있다는 것을 시사한다.

정착형은 오징어와 물고기로만 이루어진 식단에의 의존이 그것들이 음식물을 찾아 지속적으로 그것들의 영역을 횡단하고 가끔은 하루에 100킬로미터만큼이나 이동하는 것을 필요로 함에도 불구하고, 그것들이 주로 연안 해역에 서식하며 보통 일 년 내내 같은 지역 안에 머무른다는 사실에 의해 이주형과 구분된다. 사냥할 때, 정착형은 그것들의 목표를 달성하기 위해 일련의 공동 작전을 펼친다. 먹이를 찾기 위해, 쭉 뻗은 선을 따라 고르게 간격을 둔 각 범고래들은 생물학적 수중 음파 탐지기로 작용하는 딸깍거리는 소음인 반향정위를 사용하면서 같은 방향으로 천천히 전진할 것이다. 범고래 한 마리가 물고기나 오징어 떼를 발견하면, 그것은 다른 범고래들이 먹이의 존재를 알 수 있도록 그것들과 음성으로 소통한다. 이 시점에, 그 무리는 많은 전략을 사용할 수 있는데, 이는 물고기 떼를 공 모양의 꽉 찬 덩어리로 만들기 위해 둘러싸는 것과 수월한 섭취를 위해 물고기를 얕은 물로 유인하는 것을 포함한다.

이러한 복잡한 포식 활동에 참여하기 위해 필요한 사회적 상호 작용의 정도는 평생을 긴밀히 맺어진 무리에서 생활하는 정착형의 지배적인 행동 특성이다. 기본적인 사회적 단위는 가족으로, 그것은 모계이고 어미와 새끼들로 구성된다. 범고래는 90년까지 사는 것으로 알려져 있기 때문에, 하나의 모계는 최대 5세대로 구성될 수 있으며, 암컷의 자손은 지속적으로 무리의 수를 늘린다.

이주형의 사회 조직은 정착형의 그것과 매우 유사하지만, 특히 수컷의 행동과 관련하여 훨씬 덜 엄격하다. 일반적으로, 수컷 자손이 청년기 이후에 흩어질 가능성 때문에, 이주형은 보통 정착형의 모계와 같은 크기에 도달하는 경우가 거의 없는 작은 무리로 이동하고 생활한다. 장남은 성숙기에 도달한 후에 거의 항상 어미와 함께 남아 있지만, 그 다음의 아들들은 완전히 자라면 홀로 살기 위해 흔히 가족을 떠날 것이다.

비교적 분열된 사회 구조에도 불구하고, 뿔뿔이 흩어진 무리와 개체들은 포식 활동에 참여할 때 자주 함께한다. 이주형의 주식은 참돌고래, 쇠돌고래, 바다사자, 바다표범, 때때로 고래와 같은 대형 수생 해양 포유류들이며, 충분한 양의 먹이를 위한 탐색은 범고래들로 하여금 알래스카에서 캘리포니아 남부 극단에 이르는 지리적 범위를 포함하는 먼 거리를 이동하게 만든다. 사냥을 성공적으로 완수하려면 긴밀한 협력이 필요하지만, 이 과정에서 방출되는 소리는 먹잇감에 의해 쉽게 감지될 수 있기 때문에 음성 소통은 드물다. 같은 이유로, 반향정위는 기피되며, 따라서 사냥은 침묵 속에서 이루어진다.

orca (= killer whale) 몡범고래   cetacean 몡고래목 동물
versatile 혱다재다능한   cooperative 혱협력적인
hostility 몡적대감   interbreed 통상호 교배하다
idiosyncrasy 몡특이성   manifestation 몡징후, 조짐
speciation 몡종 분화   incompatibility 몡비호환성
concerted 혱공동의, 협력의   maneuver 몡작전; 통유인하다
echolocation 몡(동물의) 반향정위, 음파 위치 탐지
sonar 몡수중 음파 탐지기   close-knit 혱긴밀히 맺어진
matrilineal 혱모계의   matriline 몡모계   disperse 통흩어지다
adolescence 몡청년기   solitary 혱혼자의   dietary staple 주식

1 지문의 단어 "versatile"과 의미가 가장 비슷한 것은?

    (A) 적응력이 있는

    (B) 실행 가능한

    (C) 일회용의

    (D) 내구성이 있는

2 지문에 따르면, 다음 중 범고래가 먹이 사슬의 꼭대기에 있도록 하는 것이 아닌 것은?

(A) 극도의 신속성
(B) 상당한 크기
(C) 긴 수명
(D) 사냥 전략

3 2단락에서 글쓴이가 정착형 및 이주형 범고래에 관해 암시하는 것은?

(A) 결국 두 개의 서로 다른 종이 될 수도 있다.
(B) 결코 서로 접촉하지 않는다.
(C) 이미 서로 번식할 수 없을지도 모른다.
(D) 수천 년 동안 유전적으로 달랐다.

4 지문에서 글쓴이는 왜 "resident matriline"을 언급하는가?

(A) 이주형과 관련된 행동 특성을 설명하기 위해
(B) 특정 종의 우수성을 강조하기 위해
(C) 이주형 수컷이 더 독립적이라는 것을 시사하기 위해
(D) 정착형과 이주형 무리의 크기를 비교하기 위해

5 지시: 주어진 선택지에서 적절한 어구를 선택하여 관계있는 범고래의 종류에 연결하시오.

선택지	정착형
(E) 주로 무리가 아니라 짝을 지어 이동한다 (G) 사회적 상호작용의 음성 형태를 사용할 수 없다	· (A) 먹이를 사냥하기 위해 발성에 의존한다 · (C) 일반적으로 특정 지역에서 이탈하지 않는다
	이주형
	· (B) 유연한 공동체 구조를 갖는다 · (D) 종종 대형 생물을 사냥한다 · (F) 집단에서 분리되는 수컷을 포함한다

iBT Reading Test 1

1 (B) 　　2 (B) 　　3 (C) 　　4 (C)
5 (A) 　　6 (C) 　　7 (B), (C) 　8 (D)
9 (C) 　　10 First Period of Industrialization: (B), (E)
　　　　　Second Period of Industrialization: (C), (D), (G)

독일의 철도 개발

독일의 산업 혁명은 역사가들에 의해 크게 두 개의 물결로 분류되어 왔다. 첫 번째 물결은 1770년부터 1871년까지, 번영하던 북동부 프로이센 왕국에서 주로 일어났다. 1871년부터 1914년까지 지속된 두 번째 물결은 프로이센과 27개 주가 합병하여 독일 국가를 탄생시킨 후 일어났다. 통일 이후 시기의 중요한 특징은 철도 활용으로 산업 기회를 열었다는 점이다.

처음에, 서로 다른 독일 주들 출신의 산업가들과 투자자들은 기술 발전

을 위해 산업 리더인 영국에서 수입된 장비에 의존했다. 그 결과, 그 지역의 산업화는 다른 유럽 국가들에 비해 뒤떨어졌지만, 독일 주들은 느리고 비효율적인 기술을 기피했기 때문에 더 높은 수준의 효율성을 달성했다. 예를 들어, 최초의 철도는 6개월마다 교체가 필요한 연철 선로를 사용했다. 1857년, 강철 철도가 영국의 금속공학자 로버트 무쉐트에 의해 발명되었다. 이 철도는 교체 없이 수년 동안 지속될 수 있었고, 더 많은 양의 화물을 실은 기차를 수용할 수 있었다. 그 결과, 독일 투자자들이 철도를 건설하기 시작했을 때, 그들은 강철 선로와 효율적인 기차 엔진을 사용했다.

안타깝게도, 독일의 주들은 대부분 분열되어 있었기 때문에, 철도 건설은 많은 경우에 너무 큰 비용이 들었다. [5]루르의 석탄 매장량과 실레지아 상부의 철 매장층을 포함하여 광물이 풍부한 지역은 철도 접근 없이는 개발이 불가능했기 때문에, 이는 그 지역의 경제 성장을 제한했다. 1871년 이전에 건설된 철도는 주들 간의 통신과 교통 속도를 높이는 데 유용했지만, 철도 노선이 산업 지역과 연결되어 있지 않았기 때문에 산업 진보를 일으키지는 않았다. [6]그러나 제한된 노선에도 불구하고, 1834년부터 1871년까지 주들은 '졸베라인', 즉 독일 관세 동맹을 통해 서로와의 무역을 성공적으로 수행했다. 이것은 그 지역에서 관세 및 세관 협정을 제정하고 독일 산업들을 오스트리아와 프랑스의 보호무역주의 정책으로부터 격리시키는 경제 연합의 역할을 했다. '졸베라인'은 통일을 위한 토대를 마련했고 이후 시기의 산업 성장을 촉진했다.

1870년까지, 11,000마일 이상의 철도가 건설되었다. 이 철도는 1871년 통일 이후 국유화되었다. 통일은 지역 상품의 새로운 시장을 개척했고 낙후된 지역에 투자를 유치했다. 독일의 정치인들과 경제학자들은 경제에서의 철도의 중요성을 인식했고, 그래서, 다른 유럽 강대국들과 달리 독일의 산업화는 철도를 우선시했다. **따라서, 산업 지역과 주요 항구를 연결하는 새로운 노선들이 건설되었다.** 통일 후 10년 내에, 독일 열차는 4만 3천 명의 승객과 3만 톤의 화물을 실어 날랐고, 프랑스와 다른 유럽 대륙 국가들이 수송하는 물량을 능가했다.

[7B/7C]한 국가 내의 부와 광물 자원의 통합은 빠른 운송과 결합되어, 전국적으로 산업화를 재점화했다. 독일 황제 대신 오토 폰 비스마르크 수상의 세심한 지도 아래, 독일은 강철 생산의 선두 국가가 되었고, 그것은 1885년 100만 톤에서 1905년 1000만 톤으로 증가했다. 석탄 채굴량은 1905년까지 영국 다음으로 많았다. 기계공학과 함께, 석탄과 철은 제2차 산업혁명의 두드러진 특징이 되었다.

두 번째 시기 내내, 정부는 산업, 경제, 군사 문제에서 영국과 경쟁하는 데 집중했다. 잘 통합된 철도 체계는 이러한 경쟁을 뒷받침했다. [8]앞서 가기 위한 시도로, 과학자들과 기술자들은 영국에 의해 연구가 덜 된 분야로 전환했다. 그 국가는 화학, 전기 공학, 모터 쪽으로 방향을 틀었다. 대체로, 그것은 다른 어느 국가보다 이 분야에 많은 투자를 했고, 이것은 중요한 발명과 발견을 낳았다.

prosperous 형 번영하는　　merging 명 합병
disparate 형 서로 다른, 상이한　　lag behind 뒤떨어지다
metallurgist 명 금속공학자　　fragmented 형 분열된　　tariff 명 관세
insulate 통 격리시키다　　protectionist 형 보호무역주의의
incubate 통 (성장을) 촉진하다　　nationalize 통 국유화하다
prioritize 통 우선시하다　　surpass 통 능가하다
consolidation 명 통합　　reignite 통 재점화하다, 다시 촉발하다

1 지문에서 1단락의 목적은?

(A) 독일의 국경을 확장시킨 요인들 기술하기
(B) 독일 산업 혁명의 연대기를 자세히 설명하기
(C) 독일에서 지역 발전의 영향 묘사하기

CHAPTER 10 | Category Chart **61**

(D) 독일 산업 혁명을 시작하기 위해 사용된 방법 설명하기

2 지문의 단어 "disparate"와 의미가 가장 비슷한 것은?

(A) 협력하는
(B) 다양한
(C) 자치적인
(D) 정당한

3 지문의 단어 "fragmented"와 의미가 가장 비슷한 것은?

(A) 패배한
(B) 정복된
(C) 분할된
(D) 지명된

4 지문의 단어 "they"가 가리키는 것은?

(A) 석탄 매장량
(B) 철 매장층
(C) 철도
(D) 주들

5 다음 중 3단락에서 루르와 실레시아 상부의 광물 매장량에 관해 추론할 수 있는 것은?

(A) 철도 건설 초기에는 이용되지 않았다.
(B) 프로이센에 의해 소유되기 전까지는 생산성이 높지 않았다.
(C) 해외 수출과 연결되기 전까지는 잘 알려지지 않았다.
(D) 국가에 의해 소유되기 전까지는 채굴되지 않았다.

6 3단락에 따르면, '졸베라인'은 어떻게 독일 주들에게 이익을 주었는가?

(A) 경제 불황에서 주들을 구해냈다.
(B) 구식 기술로부터 철도 체계를 방어했다.
(C) 주들 간의 무역을 규제했다.
(D) 외국 동맹국들과의 관계를 강화했다.

7 5단락에 따르면, 독일의 산업화를 다시 부흥시켰던 것은? 두 개의 정답을 고르시오.

(A) 값싼 강철의 수입
(B) 단일 국가의 설립
(C) 고속 수송의 발달
(D) 광산 안전의 향상

8 6단락에 따르면, 독일 과학자들은

(A) 영국 상품의 구매를 거부해서 영국 경쟁자들을 이기려 시도했다
(B) 외국의 연구 결과 복제해서 영국 경쟁자들을 이기려 시도했다
(C) 세계 최대 석탄 생산국이 되어 영국 경쟁자들을 이기려 시도했다
(D) 다른 연구 분야에 집중해서 영국 경쟁자들을 이기려 시도했다

9 네 개의 네모[■]는 다음 문장이 삽입될 수 있는 곳을 나타내고 있다.

따라서, 산업 지역과 주요 항구를 연결하는 새로운 노선들이 건설되었다.

이 문장은 어디에 들어가는 것이 가장 적절한가?

10 지시: 주어진 선택지에서 적절한 문장을 선택하여 관계있는 독일 산업화 시기에 연결하시오. **이 문제는 3점이다.**

선택지	첫 번째 산업화 시기
(A) 다양한 종류의 자재들이 철도를 건설하는 데 사용되었다. (F) 석탄 사용량이 대폭 감소했다.	· (B) 산업은 영국에서의 수입에 의존했다. · (E) 철도는 주로 주들 간 통신과 교통에 이용되었다.
	두 번째 산업화 시기
	· (C) 정부가 대부분의 철도 노선을 관리했다. · (D) 강철 생산이 10배 증가했다. · (G) 외세와 경쟁하는 데 초점이 맞춰졌다.

iBT Reading Test 2

본문 p.186

1 (B) 2 (B) 3 (B) 4 (A)
5 (C) 6 (A) 7 (A) 8 (D)
9 (B) 10 Essenes: (E), (F) Sadducees: (A), (G)
Jewish Refugees: (B)

사해 문서

[2]1947년, 사해의 북서쪽 해안에서 내륙으로 약 1마일 떨어진 건조한 고원에 위치한 작은 정착지인 쿰란 근처에서 베두인족 양치기는 동굴 속에서 아마포로 감싼 문서들이 들어 있는 고대의 도자기 모음을 발견했다. 고고학자들은 그 이후 이 장소에서 850여 점의 두루마리 조각을 발굴했는데, 그것들의 대부분은 11개의 다른 동굴에 흩어져 있던 점토 항아리에 숨겨져 있었다. 사해 문서라고 불리는 이 모음은 십계명의 사본을 포함한 최초의 알려진 성서 관련 문서들을 포함하기 때문에 20세기 가장 중요한 발견들 중 하나로 여겨진다. 그것은 또한 노래, 시, 귀한 보물이 있는 은닉처 목록, 고대 히브리 문화를 설명하는 다른 필사본들 같은 수많은 성서와 관련 없는 문서들로 구성되어 있다.

사해 문서의 논란의 여지가 있는 측면 중 하나는 그것들이 발견된 불분명한 장소와 그것들이 어떻게 그곳에 도달했는지이다. [3]이 문서들은 도심에서 멀리 떨어진 지역에서 발견되었으며 거의 2천 년 동안 훼손되지 않은 것으로 보였다. 이 시대의 많은 유대인 집단들이 로마인들에 의해 멸망되어, 그들의 문화에 대한 단서를 거의 남기지 않았기 때문에, 사해 문서를 그것들을 제작한 사람들과 관련 짓는 결정적인 증거는 결코 드러나지 않을 수도 있다.

쿰란의 지리에 대한 초기 조사 이후, 학자들은 그 정착지와 유대인 역사가 요세푸스가 제공한 그 지역에 대한 상세한 설명 사이에 연관성을 짓기 시작했다. 이 고대의 설명에 따르면, 서기 1세기에 그 동굴들 근처에서 마지막으로 살았던 사람들은 구약성서에 제시된 가르침을 따르는 일신교 집단인 에세네파였다. 학자들은 에세네파가 사해 문서를 작성했고 그것들을 보호하기 위해 동굴 속에 보관했을 것으로 추측한다. 그 무렵, 로마인들은 폭력적인 반유대주의적인 박해의 시대를 열었고, 많은 에세네파가 그 지역에서 도망치게 했다. 에세네파는 무사히 돌아갈 수 있을 때 그 두루마리를 되찾을 생각이었을지도 모르지만, 서기 68년에 집단 전체가 학살당해서, 그 숨겨진 경전에 대한 전래의 지식은 남기지 못했다.

탄소 연대 측정법을 사용한 두루마리의 이후 분석은 학자들로 하여금

그 장소가 다른 유대교 종파인 사두개파에 의해 운영된 수도원의 유적이라는 대안적인 이론을 고려하게 했다. 6B이 관점에 대한 지지는 에세네파가 이 지역에 거주하기 수년 전으로 연대가 추정되는 여러 개의 두루마리 조각을 중심으로 하며, 이는 이전 거주자인 사두개파가 그 경전을 썼음을 나타낸다. **학자들은 이 조각의 내용 중 일부가 사두개파 가르침의 내용과 아주 유사하다는 점에 주목했다.** 6C한 두루마리는 그들의 랍비들의 글과 동일한 정결법을 명확하게 설명한다. 6D추가로, 이 문서는 사두개파의 원칙을 따르는 달력을 재현하여, 사두개파에 의해 기념된 것으로 알려진 축제일들을 보여준다.

최근, 두 명의 이스라엘 고고학자가 세 번째이자 더 그럴듯한 이론을 주장했다. 여러 다른 언어로 쓰인 문서에서 제공되는 다양한 관점에 기초하여, 고고학자들은 그 두루마리가 한 종파의 것들이 아닌 유대인 난민들의 장서의 잔해를 나타낸다고 주장한다. 7그들의 가정은 유대인들이 달아나면서 예루살렘에서 경전을 가져갔다는 역사 기록들에 의해 뒷받침된다. 그들은 사해의 해안으로 내려오기 전에 쿰란 동굴들을 마주쳤을 것이다.

이 가설에 따르면, 쿰란의 중요성은 종교적이 아니라 실용적이었다. 서기 68년, 로마인들이 유대인 정착촌을 파괴했을 때, 그 지역은 지역 도자기 산업의 중심지였다. 동굴 안으로 물을 운반하기 위해 만들어진 독특한 물 운송 체계뿐만 아니라 버려진 토기 가마, 점토 그릇, 도공의 점토 퇴적물 등이 발굴되었다. 이 발견은 그 동굴들이 로마인들의 도착 전까지 도자기 공장의 역할을 했다는 것을 보여준다. 그 공장은 유대인들이 사해에 도달하기 전에 두루마리를 숨길 수 있었던 마지막 안전한 장소였을 것이다.

unearth 통발굴하다   cache 명은닉처, 저장소
controversial 형논란의 여지가 있는   obscure 형불분명한
undisturbed 형훼손되지 않은   conclusive 형결정적인
monotheistic 형일신교의   persecution 명박해
retrieve 통되찾다   massacre 통학살하다   sect 명종파
rabbinic 형랍비의   plausible 형그럴듯한   refugee 명난민
supposition 명가정   kiln 명(도자기를 굽는) 가마

1 지문의 단어 "caches"와 의미가 가장 비슷한 것은?

(A) 전시회
(B) 비축품
(C) 선택
(D) 예시

2 1단락에 따르면, 다음 중 쿰란에서 처음 발견된 도자기에 관해 사실인 것은?

(A) 그 중 일부는 동굴 밖에 있었다.
(B) 그것의 내용물은 천으로 싸여 있었다.
(C) 그것은 최소 850년 동안 숨겨져 있었다.
(D) 발견 당시 대부분이 파손되어 있었다.

3 2단락에 따르면, 쿰란에서의 발견이 이례적이었던 것은

(A) 그것이 도심의 실험실에서 확인되었기 때문이다
(B) 그것이 멀리 떨어진, 인구 밀도가 낮은 지역에 있었기 때문이다
(C) 그것이 종교의식에 사용되는 구조물을 포함했기 때문이다
(D) 그것이 중요한 도서의 목록을 포함했기 때문이다

4 아래 문장 중 지문 속의 음영된 문장의 핵심 정보를 가장 잘 표현한 것은? 오답은 문장의 의미를 크게 바꾸거나 핵심 정보를 생략한다.

(A) 에세네파는 아마도 두루마리를 되찾을 계획이었겠지만, 그 분파는 비밀 장소에 대한 정보를 전달하기 전에 살해되었다.

(B) 에세네파는 학살당했기 때문에 기록된 작품의 위치에 대한 단서를 남기지 않았다.
(C) 그 유대인 집단은 항상 현장으로 돌아와서 두루마리를 다시 얻을 계획이었지만 그렇게 하지 못했다.
(D) 에세네파가 문서를 되찾을 수는 없었지만, 고대 기록은 동굴 안에 안전하게 남아 있었다.

5 지문의 단어 "induced"와 의미가 가장 비슷한 것은?

(A) 상기시켰다
(B) 지시했다
(C) 유발했다
(D) 경고했다

6 4단락에 따르면, 다음 중 그 두루마리를 사두개파 종파의 것으로 보는 증거로서 언급되지 않은 것은?

(A) 사두개파 수도원의 유적에서 발견된 유사한 두루마리
(B) 에세네파의 그 지역 거주 이전 시점으로 연대가 추정되는 조각
(C) 사두개파 종교 교리와 일치하는 것으로 알려진 기록
(D) 사두개파 축제 일정을 상세히 기술한 문서

7 5단락에서 글쓴이가 암시하는 것으로, 그 두루마리들은

(A) 예루살렘 시에서 가져온 것이다
(B) 두루마리가 발견된 동굴 근처에서 가져온 것이다
(C) 쿰란의 정착지에서 가져온 것이다
(D) 사해의 해안 지대에서 가져온 것이다

8 글쓴이는 왜 "unique water-transport system"에 관해 논하는가?

(A) 유대 민족에게만 알려졌던 기술을 설명하기 위해
(B) 점토가 어떻게 외곽 지역에서 쿰란으로 수입되었는지 설명하기 위해
(C) 그 지역이 사해와 매우 가까웠다는 증거를 제공하기 위해
(D) 그 지역이 도자기 생산의 주요 장소였음을 보여주기 위해

9 네 개의 네모[■]는 다음 문장이 삽입될 수 있는 곳을 나타내고 있다. **학자들은 이 조각의 내용 중 일부가 사두개파 가르침의 내용과 아주 유사하다는 점에 주목했다.**

이 문장은 어디에 들어가는 것이 가장 적절한가?

10 지시: 주어진 선택지에서 적절한 어구를 선택하여 관계있는 사람들에 연결하시오. 이 문제는 3점이다.

선택지	에세네파
(C) 두루마리에 기록된 바와 같이 여러 신을 숭배했다 (D) 두루마리에서 발견된 노래들을 썼다	· (E) 안전한 보관을 위해 두루마리를 남겨둔 채 쿰란에서 도망쳤다 · (F) 서기 1세기에 로마인들에 의해 학살되었다
	사두개파
	· (A) 두루마리에 요약된 축제일을 기념했다 · (G) 세 집단 중 쿰란의 최초 거주자들이었다
	유대인 난민들
	· (B) 로마인들을 피하기 위해 예루살렘에서 두루마리를 가져왔다

1 sordid   **2** incubate   **3** frequent
4 conclusive   **5** supposition   **6** hallmark
7 (C)   **8** (A)   **9** (D)   **10** (A)
11 (B)   **12** (B)   **13** (C)   **14** (A)

Actual Test 1

Passage 1
본문 p.192

1 (B)   **2** (B)   **3** (A)   **4** (C)
5 (C)   **6** (C)   **7** (A)   **8** (D)
9 (B)   **10** (A), (B), (D)

수학의 역사

18,000년에서 20,000년된 것으로 추정되는 유물인 이상고 뼈는 인류에 의한 숫자 사용의 최초의 알려진 예이다. 길이는 대략 10센티미터로, 그 뼈 도구는 그것들이 장식적이 아니라 기능적임을 암시하는 방식으로 정렬된 세 열의 비대칭의 눈금들로 나뉜다. 왼쪽 및 오른쪽 열의 눈금들은 여러 개의 홀수 세트로 나뉘는데, 그것들의 합은 60이고, 중앙 열은 더하면 48이 된다. 비록 인류학자들은 단순한 계산기에서 원시적인 달력에 이르기까지 이 유물의 정확한 기능에 대해 의견이 분분하지만, 모두 그것이 큰 숫자를 인식하고, 세고, 정리하는 능력을 분명히 보여준다는 데 동의한다.

구석기 시대부터 신석기 시대까지, 현대 인류의 조상들은 기본적인 수 세기 기술의 발달에 있어 눈부신 발전을 이루었다. 추상적인 개념으로서의 숫자 발명 전, 초기 수렵 채집인들은 아마도 종종 자연의 주판이라고 일컬어지는 손가락과 엄지손가락을 기반으로 한 간단한 계산법을 사용했을 것이다. **이 계산법의 한계 때문에, 사람들은 양을 기록하기 위해 마침내 뼈나 나무에 표시를 내기 시작했다.** [4]중석기 시대쯤에는, 각 숫자를 표현하기 위해 특정 기호들이 사용되었으며, 신석기 시대로의 전환은 종교의식과 스톤헨지 같은 종교적인 건축물의 건설을 보조하기 위한 간단한 계산의 이용을 특징으로 한다. 이 시기는 인류의 지적 성장에 중요한 이정표를 세웠고, 인류 문명화의 과정에 영향을 미치고 형성할 고급 학문 발전의 토대를 마련했다.

이 초기 지식의 대부분은 비옥한 초승달 지대라고 알려진 지역에서 번성했던 문명 사회들에 의해 축적되고 통합되었다. [5A/5B/5D]티그리스 강과 유프라테스 강 사이에서 발달하기 시작한 다양한 민족들은 그들의 복잡한 도시 사회를 관리하기 위해 숫자를 광범위하게 사용했는데, 이는 세금과 상업 활동을 기록하기 위해서뿐만 아니라, 특히 주민, 식량, 물품의 목록을 작성하기 위함이었다. 이를 용이하게 하기 위해, 수학적 기록을 점토판에 새길 수 있게 해주는 새로운 숫자 표현 체계가 만들어졌다. (숫자 60에 기초한) 60진법을 사용하여, 복잡한 천문학적 자료가 기록되었고,이는 60분으로 이루어진 한 시간과 60초로 이루어진 일 분의 형태로 오늘날에도 여전히 사용되는 시간의 경과를 추적하는 정교한 수단의 개발로 이어졌다.

이 초기 발전들 중 다수는 이집트 문명에 의해 채택되었는데, 한 가지 주목할 만한 예외가 있었다. [6]60을 기준으로 사용하는 대신에, 이집트인들은 10을 중심으로 한 숫자 체계를 만들었는데, 이것은 알려진 최초의 미터법 사용이었다. 이것이 쉽게 계산될 수 있는 방정식의 범위를 크게 확장했기 때문에, 그들은 수학을 더 넓은 범위의 용도에 적용할 수 있었다. 특히, 그것은 공학 분야에서 큰 효율성을 발휘하여, 이집트인들을 알려지게 한 그 거대한 기념물들을 건설할 수 있게 해주었고, 그중 가장 인상적인 것은 기자 피라미드이다.

비록 이러한 초기 문명들에 의해 이뤄진 발전은 상당했지만, 실용적인 숫자 이용에서 현대 과학에 매우 중요한 추상적인 수 관련 학문으로의 전환을 이루어낸 것은 고대 그리스의 학자들이었다. 그리스인들의 수학에 대한 태도는 철학자 필로라우스에 의해 가장 잘 요약되는데, 그는 모든 것은 숫자로 표현될 수 있으며 우주는 이러한 숫자들 간의 관계가 파악되고 이해되어야만 이해될 수 있다고 주장했다. 이 전제의 한 예는 모든 상업 거래가 근본적이며 불변하는 방정식으로 쪼개어질 수 있다는 아리스토텔레스의 신념이었다.

비록 그리스 학자들은 기하학에서의 업적으로 가장 잘 알려져 있지만, 그들은 정수론, 복합 방정식, 초기 미적분을 포함한 다양한 분야에서 상당한 발전을 이루었다. 그리스의 철학적 사상과 기하학은 서로 밀접하게 연관되어 있으며, 각각은 이상화된 추상 형태의 분류와 표현에 중점을 두었다. 이 기법의 효과는 에라토스테네스의 연구로 입증되는데, 그는 그리스의 원칙을 지리학 연구에 적용했고, 지구의 곡률을 최초로 정확하게 계산했으며, 그 과정에서 경도와 위도의 현대적 체계의 전신을 고안해냈다.

artifact 몡유물   asymmetrical 휑비대칭의
functional 휑기능적인   decorative 휑장식적인
make strides 발전을 이루다   abacus 몡주판   disciplines 몡학문
accumulate 동축적하다   consolidate 동통합하다
inventory 동목록을 작성하다, 재고 정리하다   provisions 몡식량
sexagesimal system 60진법   passage of time 시간의 경과
metric system 미터법   equation 몡방정식   premise 몡전제
unvarying 휑불변하는   curvature 몡곡률
precursor 몡전신, 선구자   longitude 몡경도   latitude 몡위도

1 지문의 단어 "asymmetrical"과 의미가 가장 비슷한 것은?

(A) 과도한
(B) 불규칙한
(C) 일시적인
(D) 미완성의

2 지문의 단어 "it"이 가리키는 것은?

(A) 기능
(B) 유물
(C) 계산기
(D) 달력

3 지문에서 글쓴이는 왜 "Stonehenge"를 언급하는가?

(A) 건축물을 짓기 위한 수학 사용을 설명하기 위해
(B) 주목할 만한 중석기 건축물의 예를 제공하기 위해
(C) 초기 신념 체계의 발전을 강조하기 위해
(D) 신석기 시대 종교의식의 중요성을 보여주기 위해

4 다음 중 2단락에서 중석기 이전 인류에 관해 추론할 수 있는 것은?

(A) 10보다 큰 수를 셀 수 없었다.

(B) 방대한 숫자 관련 자료 기록을 새겼다.

(C) 정해진 숫자 표현을 사용하지 않았다.

(D) 식량을 찾을 때 기초적인 수학을 활용했다.

5 3단락에 따르면, 다음 중 비옥한 초승달 지대에서의 수학 사용의 가능한 예가 아닌 것은?

(A) 도시 주민 집계

(B) 지역 상업 통제

(C) 인구 증가 예측

(D) 물품 항목 정리

6 4단락에 따르면, 이집트인들과 초기 문명들의 주된 차이점은?

(A) 수학 방정식 계산 능력

(B) 인상적인 기념물을 세우려는 욕구

(C) 다용도 숫자 체계의 활용

(D) 응용 과학의 발명

7 지문의 단어 "premise"와 의미가 가장 비슷한 것은?

(A) 가정

(B) 모순

(C) 개념

(D) 쇠퇴

8 아래 문장 중 지문 속의 음영된 문장의 핵심 정보를 가장 잘 표현한 것은? 오답은 문장의 의미를 크게 바꾸거나 핵심 정보를 생략한다.

(A) 기하학 방정식을 사용한 에라토스테네스에 의한 지구 형태의 측정은 영속적인 체계의 개발로 이어졌다.

(B) 현재의 계산 방법은 중요한 지리적 현상을 측정한 에라토스테네스의 업적에 그 뿌리를 두고 있다.

(C) 에라토스테네스 방정식의 정확성은 기하학의 불변의 법칙을 이용하여 지리학의 영역을 확장할 수 있게 해주었다.

(D) 후기 지리학자들에게 영향을 준 에라토스테네스의 계산은 기하학에 대한 그리스식 접근법의 유용성을 보여준다.

9 네 개의 네모[■]는 다음 문장이 삽입될 수 있는 곳을 나타내고 있다.

이 계산법의 한계 때문에, 사람들은 양을 기록하기 위해 마침내 뼈나 나무에 표시를 내기 시작했다.

이 문장은 어디에 들어가는 것이 가장 적절한가?

10 지시: 지문 요약을 위한 도입 문장이 아래에 주어져 있다. 지문의 가장 중요한 내용을 나타내는 보기 3개를 골라 요약을 완성하라. 어떤 문장은 지문에 언급되지 않은 내용이나 사소한 정보를 나타내므로 요약에 포함되지 않는다. **이 문제는 2점이다.**

> **초기 문명들은 수학 분야에서 상당한 발전을 이루었다.**
> · (A) 이집트인들에 의해 사용된 미터법은 계산의 효용성과 다양성을 증가시켰다.
> · (B) 중동 문명들은 중요한 자료를 기록하고 별을 연구하기 위해 그들의 독특한 숫자 체계를 사용했다.
> · (D) 그리스 철학은 기하학 연구를 촉진했고, 과학의 실용적 응용에 대한 통찰력을 가져왔다.

(C) 비옥한 초승달 지대의 60진법은 현대의 시간 측정 방법에 통합되었다.

(E) 그리스의 기하학 발전은 상업 연구에 대한 새로운 과학적 접근법의 개발을 가져왔다.

(F) 이집트인들은 오래가는 건축물을 짓기 위해 초기 문명의 수학적 원리를 이용했다.

11 (B)	12 (C)	13 (B)	14 (D)
15 (D)	16 (B)	17 (D)	18 (A)
19 (B)	20 (A), (C), (E)		

사회적 동물

1859년에 다윈의 '종의 기원'이 처음 출간된 후, 생물학자들은 자연 선택이 종의 생존에 영향을 미치는 다양한 방식들을 조사하기 시작했다. 그러나, 많은 과학자들이 진화를 "적자생존"으로 간주하는 전통적인 관점이 종의 진화를 형성하는 모든 요소를 설명하기에 충분한지에 대해 점점 더 의문을 품기 시작했다. 특히, 만약 경쟁이 진화론의 바로 그 토대라면, 무엇이 그렇게 많은 유기체에서 목격되는 협력적인 행동을 설명할 수 있을까?

이후 1세기가 지나서야 생물학자 E. O. 윌슨은 그의 책에서 이타주의가 경쟁적 적합성만큼이나 생존에 중요하다고 주장했다. 따라서, 그것은 또한 자연 선택의 산물임이 틀림없다. 유기체의 사회적 행동 및 조직과 관련된 사회생물학의 관점에서, 개체 사이의 협력과 애정은 그것들이 서로 직접 경쟁하는 경우보다 각각 유전자 풀에 더 많이 기여하는 결과를 낳을 수 있다.

모든 사회적 동물들은 무리를 지어 살고, 연구원들은 동물들의 행동에 대한 통찰력을 얻기 위해 크기, 구성원 수를 제한하는 요인들, 무리의 형성으로 이어지는 원인들을 기록하려고 한다. ¹³에를 들어, 북극제비갈매기는 오랫동안 사회적 동물로 여겨져 왔으며, 포유류 포식자로부터 최대한 확실히 보호하기 위해 원형 배열의 중앙에 새끼를 숨긴다. 한 무리는 보통 50마리 이하의 새를 포함할 것이다. 이는 구성원 수의 상한선이 가용 자원에 의해 결정되며, 그것들은 북극 툰드라에서 극히 희박하기 때문이다. 하지만 생태계가 지탱할 만큼의 크기의 무리에서 사는 것은 제비갈매기에게 진화적으로 유리한데, 이는 주된 먹이가 고르지 않게 분포되어 있거나 찾기 어려울 때, 모험적인 개체들이 부차적인 공급원을 찾을 수 있기 때문이다. 그것들의 비행을 목격하거나 그것들을 따르는 구성원들은 이러한 대체 먹이에 대해 배우게 된다. 그러므로, 이 관점에서, 위험을 피하는 것과 정보를 공유하는 것 모두 군집 형성에 자극이 된다.

늑대는 떼라고 불리는 큰 무리를 지어 함께 사는 동물들의 또 다른 예가 되지만, 포식자로부터 자신을 보호하기 위해서가 아니라, 주로 성공적으로 먹이를 잡고 죽이기 위한 방법으로 그렇게 한다. 게다가, 그들은 진화를 통해 묘사되고 설명되는 생존을 위한 또 다른 기제인 텃세 행동을 발달시켰다. 늑대 떼의 구성원들은 그것들이 충분한 양의 먹이에 대한 접근하는 것을 확실히 하기 위한 방법으로, 몇 제곱킬로미터에서 수십 제곱킬로미터에 이르는 그것들의 영역을 지킨다. ¹⁴그것들은 도발이 없으면 침입자를 공격하기보다는 경고음을 낼 가능성이 높긴 하지만, 코요테, 낯선 늑대, 길들여진 개들이 그것들의 지역으로 들어온다면 그것들에게 공격적으로 행동할 것이다. 진화 생물학에 따르면, 늑대와 다른 동물에게서 텃세 행동이 발달한 것은 먹이를 보호하기 위한 필요성에서 기인한 것일 수 있다.

일단 먹이가 확보되면, 사회적 동물은 그것을 공동체의 다른 구성원들과 공유하려고 한다. 그러나, 진화적 관점에서, 먹이를 더 잘 구할 수 있는 무리 구성원들에게 보상해서 그것들이 사냥꾼이나 채집가로서의 역할을 계속 수행할 수 있도록 하는 것이 유리하다. 그러므로, 가장 유능한 사냥꾼과 채집가들은 종종 그것들을 건강하고 튼튼하게 유지하기 위해 불균형한 양의 먹이를 받으며, 이는 어려운 일을 수행할 수 있는 그것들의 능력을 향상시킨다. 시간이 지남에 따라, 이 건강한 사회 구성원들은 그만큼 건강하지 못한 구성원보다 더 권위 있는 지위를 차지하는 경향이 있으며, 무리 내에서는 계급이 발달한다. 예를 들어, 일반 침팬지의 무리는 도구 제작이나 사냥과 같은 특수한 기술을 가진 구성원들에게 높은 지위를 부여하고, 이 엘리트 무리는 먹이에 관한 한 우선권을 부여받는다.

사회생물학자들에 따르면, 동물에서 사회 계급의 발달은, 인간에서와 마찬가지로, 종의 진화에서 필연적인 단계로 간주될 수 있다. 이것은 인간과 계급 공동체에 사는 원숭이 같은 다른 영장류 사이의 밀접한 유전적 관계에 의해 입증된다. [18]인간과 다른 동물 간의 관계는 격렬한 논쟁의 문제로, 특히 사회학자들이 주장하듯이, 인간은 식량, 피난처, 생식 건강을 확보하는 것과 같은 생존의 필수 요소들을 넘어섰기 때문이다. 인간은 가장 복잡한 동물 공동체조차도 뛰어넘는 단계의 의식 수준을 발전시켜 왔다.

sufficient 휑충분한   altruism 몡이타주의   fitness 몡적합성
standpoint 몡관점   membership 몡구성원 수   glean 동얻다
sparse 휑(식생이) 희박한   impetus 몡자극, 원동력
cohabitate 동함께 살다   territorial 휑텃세의
trespasser 몡침입자   provocation 몡도발, 자극
territoriality 몡텃세 행동   disproportionate 휑불균형한
demanding 휑어려운   prestigious 휑권위 있는
hierarchy 몡계급   priority 몡우선권, 우선순위
when it comes to ~에 관한 한   essentials 몡필수 요소들
reproductive 휑생식의   consciousness 몡의식, 자각

11 지문의 단어 "it"이 가리키는 것은?

(A) 책
(B) 이타주의
(C) 적합성
(D) 생존

12 지문의 단어 "glean"과 의미가 가장 비슷한 것은?

(A) 제공하다
(B) 보여주다
(C) 얻다
(D) 묘사하다

13 3단락에 따르면, 북극제비갈매기가 무리 지어 사는 한 가지 이유는

(A) 배고픈 새끼들에게 추가적인 먹이를 공급하기 위해서이다
(B) 새끼들의 안전을 보장하기 위해서이다
(C) 포식자로부터 그것들의 영역을 방어하기 위해서이다
(D) 구성원들에게 교육받을 기회를 주기 위해서이다

14 다음 중 4단락에서 늑대에 관해 추론할 수 있는 것은?

(A) 먹이를 두고 싸울 때만 난폭하게 행동한다.
(B) 사냥 능력을 기반으로 구성원을 평가한다.
(C) 먹이가 적을 때 호전적으로 행동한다.
(D) 때때로 다른 떼의 영역에 들어간다.

15 아래 문장 중 지문 속의 음영된 문장의 핵심 정보를 가장 잘 표현한 것은? 오답은 문장의 의미를 크게 바꾸거나 핵심 정보를 생략한다.

(A) 일부 구성원들의 순종적인 성질 때문에, 더 공격적이고 지배적인 구성원들은 더 많은 먹이로 보상받을 것이다.
(B) 진화론은 보상이 집단의 구성원들로 하여금 사냥꾼이나 채집가로서의 역할을 더 잘 수행하도록 동기를 부여한다고 진술한다.

(C) 무리의 생존을 지키는 가장 좋은 방법은 대부분의 먹이를 얻을 책임이 있는 여러 명의 구성원을 두는 것이다.
(D) 유능한 포식자들이 노력을 지속할 수 있을 만큼 충분히 만족하도록 무리로부터 보상받는 것은 진화론적으로 타당하다.

16 지문의 단어 "disproportionate"와 의미가 가장 비슷한 것은?

(A) 공평한
(B) 불평등한
(C) 고의적인
(D) 비정상적인

17 지문에서 글쓴이는 왜 "the common chimpanzee"를 언급하는가?

(A) 일부 동물들이 성공적인 포식자가 될 수 있다는 증거를 제시하기 위해
(B) 일부 종들이 어떻게 도구 제작을 높이 평가하도록 진화했는지 보여주기 위해
(C) 먹이를 사냥하는 동물 종의 예를 들기 위해
(D) 고도로 숙련된 개체에게 권위를 부여하는 종을 명시하기 위해

18 지문에 따르면, 인간이 다른 동물들과 같은 방법으로 사회생물학자들에 의해 분석될 수 없는 것은

(A) 우리는 더 이상 생존의 기본적인 요소들에 몰두하지 않기 때문이다
(B) 우리는 계급으로 구조화된 공동체에서 사는 것을 그만두었기 때문이다
(C) 우리는 자신의 존재, 생각, 감정을 인식하게 되었기 때문이다
(D) 우리는 동물 행동학자에 의해 정확하게 관찰될 수 없기 때문이다

19 네 개의 네모[■]는 다음 문장이 삽입될 수 있는 곳을 나타내고 있다.

이것은 인간과 계급 공동체에 사는 원숭이 같은 다른 영장류 사이의 밀접한 유전적 관계에 의해 입증된다.

이 문장은 어디에 들어가는 것이 가장 적절한가?

20 지시: 지문 요약을 위한 도입 문장이 아래에 주어져 있다. 지문의 가장 중요한 내용을 나타내는 보기 3개를 골라 요약을 완성하라. 어떤 문장은 지문에 언급되지 않은 내용이나 사소한 정보를 나타내므로 요약에 포함되지 않는다. 이 문제는 2점이다.

> **진화론을 이용하여, 과학자들은 종의 진화를 촉진하는 동물의 행동을 평가할 수 있다.**
> · (A) 먹이에 더 잘 기여할 수 있는 구성원들이 보상받기 때문에 사회 계급이 발전한다.
> · (C) 홀로 사는 생물보다 무리로 살아남는 것이 더 쉬워질 때 개체들의 집합체가 형성된다.
> · (E) 텃세 행동은 동물이 같은 먹이를 얻기 위한 경쟁자들을 물리칠 필요성에서 기인한다.

(B) 힘든 일을 수행하는 공동체의 구성원들은 다른 구성원들보다 번식할 가능성이 더 높다.
(D) 에너지 자원에 대한 불균형한 접근은 일부 동물들이 다른 먹이 채집 전략에 정통하도록 자극한다.
(F) 다른 동물들에게 중요한 기구를 만드는 방법을 가르치는 동물들은 더 큰 사회적 지위를 얻을 수 있다.

21 (C) 22 (B) 23 (A) 24 (D)
25 (A) 26 (A) 27 (B) 28 (C)
29 (B) 30 (A), (B), (F)

지구의 나이

중세 시대 전반에 걸쳐, 유럽 학자들은 성경의 설명에 근거하여 지구의 연대를 측정하려고 시도했다. ²²관찰 가능한 지질학적 과정에 기초하여 훨씬 더 많은 나이를 제안할 만큼 대담했던 사람들은 잠재적으로 심각한 결과, 심지어 죽음에 직면했다. 그러나, 유럽의 계몽주의 시대는 이 문제에 대한 상당한 과학적 조사의 시작을 의미했다.

최초의 시도들 중 하나는 18세기에 에드먼드 핼리가 바다의 염도가 지구의 연대를 측정하는 데 사용될 수 있다는 이론을 세웠을 때 일어났다. 빗물이 결국 바다에 도달하기 전에 바위와 흙에서 작은 소금 조각들을 가져가는 것을 관찰하면서, 그는 해수면에서 물이 증발하기 때문에 이 과정이 바다의 염도를 점차 상승시키고 있다고 결론지었다. 처음에 바다가 담수로 형성되었다는 가정에서, 그는 지구의 나이가 현재의 해양 염도와 그것이 증가하는 속도에 기초하여 계산될 수 있다고 믿었다. 후속 연구자들은 그의 방법을 적용하여, 지구의 나이를 5천만 년에서 1억 5천만 년 사이로 추정했다.

비록 한때 영향력이 있었지만, 소금 이론은 몇 가지 본질적인 결함 때문에 결국 폐기되었다. ²⁴ᴬ우선, 과학자들은 바다의 원래 염도를 알지 못하기 때문에, 염도가 얼마나 상승했는지, 만약 조금이라도 상승했다고 해도, 알아낼 방법이 없다. ²⁴ᶜ그리고, 핼리가 믿었던 것과는 달리, 소금은 해수에서 영구적으로 용해된 상태로 남아 있지 않으며, 대신에, 그것 중 일부는 다른 광물들과 결합해서 퇴적물로서 해저로 떨어진다. ²⁴ᴮ그 결과, 비록 바다의 염도가 일시적으로 변동하지만, 그것은 시간이 지남에 따라 크게 상승하거나 하락하지는 않는다.

19세기에, 물리학자 켈빈 경은 지구의 온도를 연구함으로써 지구의 연대를 측정할 수 있다고 가정했다. 그의 이론은 지구가 녹은 암석으로 시작했다고 가정했다. ²⁵지각의 상부가 내부보다 더 차갑다는 그의 관찰에 기초하여, 켈빈은 열이 지표면과 우주로 빠져나가면서 지구가 점점 더 차가워지고 있다는 결론을 내렸다. 냉각 속도를 설정하기 위해, 그는 열이 땅에서 대기로 전달되는 속도를 연구했다.

냉각 이론은 그것이 잘못된 가정에 기반했다고 지적한 다른 과학자들에 의해 빠르게 비판받았다. 켈빈은 오로지 고체 암석을 통한 열의 전도를 기반으로 계산을 수행했지만, 사실 열은 액체의 이동에 의해서도 지구를 통과해서 전달되는데, 이는 지구 내부의 일부가 반액체이기 때문이다. ²⁶켈빈은 또한 열이 더해지지 않고 지구가 일정한 속도로 냉각되고 있다고 가정했지만, 이것은 논란의 여지가 있는 견해였다.

과학자들은 방사성 붕괴라고 알려진 과정으로 인해 암석이 자체적인 열을 발생시켜 지구가 냉각되는 속도를 정확하게 측정하는 것이 불가능하다는 것을 나중에 알게 되었다. 이 발견은 냉각 이론을 반증했을 뿐만 아니라 오늘날에도 여전히 사용되고 있는 방사성 연대 측정법의 발전으로 이어졌다. 방사성 원소가 일정한 속도로 점차 안정적인 원소로 분해되기 때문에 이 방법은 실행 가능하다. 일단 이 속도가 결정되면, 지질학자들은 암석 안에서 발견되는 다양한 원소의 양을 측정함으로써 암석의 나이를 계산할 수 있다. 따라서 오래된 암석에 방사성 연대 측정법을 적용하는 것은 지구의 나이를 연구하는 새로운 방법을 제시했고, 35억 년이 넘는 지질학적 물질들이 발견되었다. 그러나, 풍화 작용과 지구 지각판의 움직임 같은 과정으로 인해 암석들이 영겁에 걸쳐 함께 섞였기 때문에, 가장 오래된 암석들은 지표면 훨씬 아래에 숨겨져 있을 수 있다.

이 문제에 대한 해결책은 태양계의 다른 곳에서 유래된 물체들을 분석하는 것이었다. 태양계의 모든 부분이 거의 동시에 형성되었다고 여겨지기 때문에, 20세기 연구자들은 지구의 암석과 같은 지질학적 과정을 거치지 않은 외계의 물체에 방사성 연대 측정법을 적용했다. 이 접근법은 특히 운석에 대해 성공적이었는데, 그것들은 형성에서부터 지구에 충돌했을 때까지 변화를 거의 겪지 않았기 때문이다. **과학자들은 또한 이 방법을 달의 암석에도 적용하여 좋은 결과를 얻었다.** 1950년대에, 연구자들은 애리조나에서 발견된 운석의 연대를 측정하여 지구의 나이를 약 45억 년으로 추정했다. 이 수치는 수십 개의 운석과 달의 암석에 대한 분석이 유사한 결과를 산출한 이후 몇 년 동안 확증되었다.

potentially (부)잠재적으로   considerable (형)상당한
salinity (명)염도   evaporate (동)증발하다   assumption (명)가정
influential (형)영향력이 있는   discard (동)폐기하다
intrinsic (형)본질적인, 내재적인   permanently (부)영구적으로
sediment (명)퇴적물   fluctuate (동)변동하다
postulate (동)가정하다   conduction (명)전도
controversial (형)논란의 여지가 있는   radioactive decay 방사성 붕괴
disprove (동)반증하다   radiometric dating 방사성 연대 측정법
viable (형)실행 가능한   eon (명)영겁, 무궁한 시간

21 지문의 단어 "considerable"과 의미가 가장 비슷한 것은?
   (A) 사려 깊은
   (B) 중대한
   (C) 상당한
   (D) 조심하는

22 다음 중 중세 유럽의 학자들에 관해 추론할 수 있는 것은?
   (A) 그들 중 다수는 지구의 나이를 알아내는 것이 불가능하다고 생각했다.
   (B) 그들 중 일부는 지구가 성경에서 묘사된 것보다 더 오래되었다고 믿었다.
   (C) 그들 중 지구가 6천 년이 조금 넘었다고 받아들이는 사람은 거의 없었다.
   (D) 그들 모두가 자연적인 지질학적 과정이 얼마나 오래 걸리는지 이해하지 못했다.

23 지문의 단어 "it"이 가리키는 것은?
   (A) 빗물
   (B) 소금
   (C) 암석
   (D) 흙

24 3단락에 따르면, 다음 중 소금 이론의 결함이 아닌 것은?
   (A) 과학자들은 바다의 처음 소금 함량을 모른다.
   (B) 바다의 염도는 크게 변동하지 않는다.
   (C) 소금은 바닷물에 무한정 떠 있지 않다.
   (D) 바다의 많은 광물은 소금과 쉽게 결합하지 않는다.

25 4단락에 따르면, 켈빈으로 하여금 지구가 냉각되고 있다고 생각하게 했던 것은?
   (A) 지구의 내부는 외부보다 따뜻했다.
   (B) 지표면 온도가 시간이 지남에 따라 하락하고 있었다.
   (C) 그는 녹은 용암이 지표면으로 빠져나가는 것을 목격했다.

(D) 그는 원자가 계속해서 열을 잃고 있다고 믿었다.

26 5단락에 따르면, 켈빈은

(A) 시간이 지남에 따라 지구가 일정한 속도로 냉각된다고 가정했다

(B) 지구 내부의 일부가 반액체라고 가정했다

(C) 고체 암석 내부의 열의 양이 계산될 수 없다고 가정했다

(D) 원자가 엄청난 양의 잠재 에너지를 포함한다고 가정했다

27 지문의 단어 "disproved"와 의미가 가장 비슷한 것은?

(A) 파괴했다

(B) 반박했다

(C) 변형했다

(D) 입증했다

28 글쓴이는 왜 "weathering and the movement of the Earth's tectonic plates"를 언급하는가?

(A) 태양계에서 지구의 지질학적 과정이 독특하다는 것을 보여주기 위해

(B) 방사성 연대 측정 분야에서 지구의 암석을 사용하는 것에 대한 근거를 제공하기 위해

(C) 지구의 연대 측정에서 지구의 암석이 완전히 신뢰할 수는 없는 이유를 설명하기 위해

(D) 보다 정확한 지구의 연대 측정 방법으로 이끈 발견을 강조하기 위해

29 네 개의 네모[■]는 다음 문장이 삽입될 수 있는 곳을 나타내고 있다.

과학자들은 또한 이 방법을 달의 암석에도 적용하여 좋은 결과를 얻었다.

이 문장은 어디에 들어가는 것이 가장 적절한가?

30 지시: 지문 요약을 위한 도입 문장이 아래에 주어져 있다. 지문의 가장 중요한 내용을 나타내는 보기 3개를 골라 요약을 완성하라. 어떤 문장은 지문에 언급되지 않은 내용이나 사소한 정보를 나타내므로 요약에 포함되지 않는다. 이 문제는 2점이다.

> 역사 속에서, 과학자들은 지구의 나이를 측정하는 다양한 기술을 고안했고, 다양한 정도의 성공을 거두었다.
> · (A) 나중에 그가 틀렸다는 것이 입증되었지만, 켈빈 경은 열이 지구를 빠져나가는 속도를 계산함으로써 지구의 연대를 측정할 수 있다고 주장했다.
> · (B) 비록 나중에는 그것이 부정되었지만, 18세기에 에드먼드 핼리는 바다의 염도 상승을 연구함으로써 지구의 나이를 결정하는 과정을 개발했다.
> · (F) 현대 과학자들은 방사성 연대 측정법으로 알려진 과정을 적용하여 우리 행성의 나이가 약 45억 년이라는 결론을 내렸다.

(C) 에드먼드 핼리는 해저에서 발견되는 소금의 양을 측정하여 지구의 나이를 처음으로 추정했다.

(D) 켈빈에 의해 개발된 냉각 이론은 당시에는 논란의 여지가 많았지만, 나중에 과학자들은 그것이 정확하다는 것을 증명했다.

(E) 유성과 같은 외계 기원의 물체는 광물 구성이 손상되지 않은 채로 남아 있기 때문에 방사성 연대 측정에 특히 유용하다.

Actual Test 2

Passage 1
본문 p.204

1 (C) 2 (D) 3 (D) 4 (D)
5 (B) 6 (A) 7 (B) 8 (C)
9 (B) 10 Ecitoninae: (B), (F), (G)
        Dorylinae: (A), (D)

군대개미

개밋과는 흔히 개미라고 불리는 분류학상 곤충 군으로, 2만 개 이상의 별개의 종으로 이루어져 지구상 가장 다양한 생물과들 중 하나이다. 이 과 내의 종 분화 정도는 상당한 수준의 유전적 다양화를 가져왔다. 이는 그 곤충이 특히 도시 지역, 열대 우림, 사막, 산을 포함하는 다양한 생태학적 틈새에서 성공할 수 있도록 해주었다. 다양한 특화된 적응 형태들은 또한 개미가 이처럼 다양한 생태계에서 번성할 수 있도록 했다.

[4]지구의 많은 특화된 개미들 중에는 군대개미가 있는데, 그것들은 그것들이 서식하는 열대 정글에서의 생활에 특히 적합하게 해주는 여러 신체 및 행동 특성을 지닌다. 군대개미는 각각 수십 가지의 변종을 포함하는 두 개의 별개의 아과로 나뉜다. 남아메리카에 서식하는 것들은 에사이토니네이아과에 속하며, 아프리카의 상대는 가시방패개미아과로 분류된다. 비록 두 아과가 구별되는 특성을 가지고 있지만, 두 집단은 공통의 진화적 유전에 그것들의 뿌리를 둔 많은 특징을 공유한다. 사실 두 아과는 단일 조상의 후손이며, 각각에 의해 공유되는 복잡한 행동적 특징은 1억 년 이상 진화 정지 상태로 남아 있었다.

백악기 중기까지, 이 곤충의 현대 변종을 구분하는 주요 특성이 이미 확립되었다. [5A]예를 들어, 먹이를 찾아 한 지역 내에서 끊임없이 이동해야 하기 때문에, 모든 군대개미는 유목 생활을 한다. 그것들의 유목 생활 방식은 살 곳을 제공하는 매우 독특한 방법을 낳았다. 영구적인 둥지를 만드는 대부분의 개미 종들과 달리, 군대개미는 일개미들의 몸으로 형성된, 비부악으로 알려진 임시 거주지를 만든다. 이 살아 있는 몸의 더미는 잠재적인 포식자와 비바람으로부터 여왕개미를 보호한다. [5C]또 다른 공통적인 특징은 떼 짓기라고 알려진 활동으로, 그것에 의해 수백만 마리의 병사 개미가 먹이를 찾아 조직화된 대형으로 이동하며, 먹이에는 다른 곤충, 새, 도마뱀, 심지어는 큰 포유류가 포함될 수도 있다. [5D]양물 탐색은 군대개미의 두 아과 모두의 주요 초점으로, 이는 매달 4백만 개 이상의 알을 낳는 그것들의 여왕이 모든 개미들 중 가장 번식력이 높기 때문이다.

이러한 기본적인 행동 패턴을 공유함에도 불구하고, 각 아과는 포식에 참여할 때 자신만의 독특한 전략을 활용한다. 아프리카에서는, 운전사 개미라고도 알려진 가시방패개미아과는 그것들의 턱에 의존한다. [6]이것은 강력한 집게 역할을 하는, 개미들의 턱에 있는 긴 부속기관으로, 더 작은 먹이를 쉽게 죽이고 더 큰 동물의 살점을 제거할 수 있다.

아프리카 군대개미들은 사냥할 때 떼 전선을 이용하는데, 이는 먹이를 몰기 위해 지역을 휩쓸고 다니는 밀집된 습격자 무리를 필요로 하는 방법이다. 각 떼 전선에는 종종 2천만 마리 이상의 함께 일하는 개미가 있기 때문에, 그것은 모든 크기의 동물들에게 상당한 위협을 가한다. 심지어 인간도 늙거나, 아프거나, 다쳤다면 위협받을 수 있다. 이 전선 뒤쪽으로는 정해진 오솔길을 따라 이동하다가 마지막으로 비부악으로

되돌아가는 거대한 열로 합쳐지는 부채꼴 모양의 일개미 조직이 뻗어 있다. 일개미들이 먹이를 들고 오갈 때, 그것들은 길을 따라 살아 있는 방패를 형성한 병사들에 의해 보호받는다.

아프리카의 상대들과 달리, 에사이토니네이아과 군대개미는 먹이를 무력화하고 죽이기 위해 강력한 침에 의존한다. 그 남아메리카 종들은 단단한 물질을 삼킬 수 없기 때문에, 그것들의 독은 희생자들의 살을 소화 가능한 형태로 분해하는 조직 분해 효소를 포함하고 있다. 이 개미들은 무시무시한 턱을 가지고 있지만, 이것들은 가시방패아과 개미들의 것처럼 크지는 않다. 그것들은 작은 곤충과 도마뱀이 움직이지 못하게 되면 주로 절단하는 데 사용된다.

사냥할 때, 에사이토니네이아과는 군집이 여러 열로 이동하는 채집 집단으로 나뉘어 비부악에서 뻗어 나온 나무 같은 모양을 형성하는 전략을 사용한다. 개미들의 연속적인 양방향 흐름은 이 길을 따라 이동하여, 지속적인 먹이 공급이 비부악으로 돌아가는 것을 보장한다. 8이 종들은 자신들보다 훨씬 더 큰 생물들에게 위험을 끼치지 않으며, 사실 농업 활동을 방해하는 다른 곤충들을 제거하기 때문에 많은 농부들에게 호의적으로 여겨진다.

Formicidae 명개밋과　　taxonomic 형분류학상의
speciation 명종 분화　　diversification 명다양화　　niche 명틈새
subfamily 명아과(과의 하위 단위)　　counterpart 명상대, 대응물
attribute 명특성　　be descended from ~의 후손이다
evolutionary stasis 진화 정지　　nomadic 형유목 생활을 하는, 유목의
permanent 형영구적인　　elements 명비바람
sustenance 명자양물　　prolific 형번식력이 높은
mandible 명(곤충의) 턱　　appendage 명부속기관
in unison 함께, 일제히　　enzyme 명효소　　digestible 형소화 가능한
formidable 형무시무시한　　dismember 동절단하다
immobilize 동움직이지 못하게 하다

1 지문의 단어 "diversification"와 의미가 가장 비슷한 것은?
　(A) 지배
　(B) 독립체
　(C) 다양성
　(D) 성숙

2 지문에서 글쓴이는 왜 "urban areas, rainforests, deserts, and mountains"를 언급하는가?
　(A) 개미들의 적응력을 제한하는 요인들을 강조하기 위해
　(B) 수많은 개미 변종에 대한 이유를 제공하기 위해
　(C) 종이 가장 잘 적응할 수 있는 생태계를 밝히기 위해
　(D) 생물체에 의해 점유된 서식지의 예를 들기 위해

3 지문의 단어 "their"가 가리키는 것은?
　(A) 두 아과
　(B) 구별되는 특성
　(C) 두 집단
　(D) 많은 특징

4 2단락에 따르면, 다음 중 군대개미에 관해 사실인 것은?
　(A) 그것들의 구조와 생리에서 사실상 구분이 되지 않는다.
　(B) 세계적으로 약 12종으로 이루어져 있다.
　(C) 남아메리카로 퍼지기 전에 아프리카에서 기원했다.
　(D) 열대 지역의 정글에 매우 잘 적응되어 있다.

5 3단락에 따르면, 다음 중 군대개미의 두 아과가 공유하는 특징이 아닌 것은?
　(A) 정기적으로 무리 지어 이동하고자 하는 욕구
　(B) 영구적인 주거지를 지을 필요성
　(C) 집단적인 사냥 방법의 이용
　(D) 많은 수의 새끼 생산

6 다음 중 4단락에서 아프리카 군대개미에 관해 추론할 수 있는 것은?
　(A) 그것들보다 더 큰 동물들에게 위험을 제시한다.
　(B) 정해진 길이 있는 지역을 통해 이동하는 것을 선호한다.
　(C) 여러 마리의 여왕개미를 포함하는 큰 집단을 형성한다.
　(D) 개별적으로 사냥한 다음 그 먹이를 전체 군집과 공유한다.

7 지문의 단어 "immobilized"와 의미가 가장 비슷한 것은?
　(A) 제거되다
　(B) 마비되다
　(C) 다치다
　(D) 안정되다

8 7단락에 따르면, 많은 농부들은 왜 에사이토니네이아과를 유익하다고 여기는가?
　(A) 그것들은 접근하기 어려운 지역의 경작을 가능하게 해준다.
　(B) 그것들은 더 큰 생물들에게 위험하지 않다.
　(C) 그것들은 해충으로 여겨지는 벌레들을 죽인다.
　(D) 그것들은 수확에 피해를 줄 가능성이 낮다.

9 네 개의 네모[■]는 다음 문장이 삽입될 수 있는 곳을 나타내고 있다.
　심지어 인간도 늙거나, 아프거나, 다쳤다면 위협받을 수 있다.
　이 문장은 어디에 들어가는 것이 가장 적절한가?

10 지시: 주어진 선택지에서 적절한 어구를 선택하여 관계있는 군대개미의 아과에 연결하시오. 이 문제는 3점이다.

선택지	에사이토니네이아과
(C) 다른 군대개미 군집을 급습한다 (E) 다른 생물과 더불어 식물을 섭취한다	· (B) 독침이 있다 · (F) 살점을 녹이는 물질을 생성한다 · (G) 먹이를 찾을 때 작은 무리로 나뉜다
	가시방패개미아과
	· (A) 2천만 마리 이상 개체의 무리로 사냥한다 · (D) 먹이를 죽이기 위해 강력한 턱에 의존한다

Passage 2　　　　본문 p. 208

11 (D)　　12 (A)　　13 (C)　　14 (C)
15 (C)　　16 (B)　　17 (B)　　18 (C)
19 (D)　　20 (A), (B), (E)

조현병

조현병은 사회적 및 직업적 기능 장애, 현실 인식의 장애, 망상 또는 환청으로 특징지어지는 정신 질환이다. 진단은 주로 의료 전문가에 의한 이차적인 관찰에 추가하여, 환자 및 그들과 가까운 사람들의 개인적인 설명에 기초한다. 북아메리카 사람들 1,000명 중 약 8명이 모든 사회 경제적, 민족적, 인종적 경계를 넘나드는 이 질환에 걸리게 되며, 그것은 전국의 정신병원 입원의 주된 동기이다.

19세기 후반 동안, 의사들은 그 질환이 뇌의 전두엽의 부적절한 발달과 관련된 생리학적 질병이라고 믿었고, 다수가 전두엽 절제술이라고 알려진 정신외과적 방법으로 환자들을 치료하려고 시도했다. ¹²이 기술은 1890년 스위스 태생의 고틀리프 부르크하르트 박사에 의해 최초로 시행되었는데, 그것은 건강한 "분석적인" 쪽에서 제 기능을 못 하는 "감정적인" 쪽을 잘라내기 위해 뇌의 우반구와 좌반구의 분리를 수반했다. 그 수술은 납작한 금속 기구를 두개골의 윗부분에 박는 것에 의해 수행되었다. 처음에는, 거친 수술이 대중의 강한 의심에 부딪혔지만, 업적으로 노벨 의학상을 수상한 포르투갈의 신경학자 안토니우 에가스 모니스의 추가적인 개선은 그것이 조현병의 많은 증상을 완화시켰음을 보여주었다.

그러나, 수천 명의 사람들에게서의 전두엽 절제술의 입증된 성공에도 불구하고, 그 수술은 그것의 알려진 위험 때문에 계속 매우 논란이 많았다. ¹⁵윤리적으로 살아 있는 사람들의 뇌에 연구가 거의 이루어질 수 없었기 때문에, 의사들은 사망한 환자의 조직에 수행된 실험에 근거해서 자주 잘못된 가정을 했다. 이는 그 수술 자체의 섬세한 특성과 결합하여 수술 중에 빈번한 실수가 범해지는 결과를 낳았다. 일부 피실험자들은 영구적인 식물인간 상태에 빠졌으며, 일부는 더 이상 도움 없이 기능할 수 없었고, 다른 이들은 그 수술 후에 사망하기도 했다. 많은 의학계 종사자들은 정신 질환의 치료가 건강한 신경 조직의 파괴를 필요로 한다는 생각에 거부감을 느꼈고 대신 약물의 사용을 지지했다. 그러한 이유로, 클로르프로마진과 같은 항정신병 약물의 등장과 함께, 정신외과 시술은 급격히 줄어들었다.

조현병 치료에 대한 현대의 약리학적 접근은 뇌가 정상 기능을 유지하기 위해 자연적으로 생성되는 여러 호르몬을 관리해야 한다는 것을 보여주는 진보된 20세기의 신경학 연구를 기반으로 한다. 신경 화학물질이 비정상적인 양으로 있으면, 환자는 사소한 감정 기복에서부터 심한 우울증이나 조증에 이르는 감정 상태의 변화를 겪게 된다. 조현병 환자의 뇌에서는, 내재하는 화학수용체와 결합해 뇌의 다른 부위에서 전두엽으로의 정보 흐름을 촉진하는 것으로 알려진 호르몬인 도파민의 수치가 매우 높다. 따라서, 전두엽은 그것이 처리할 수 없는 데이터로 가득 차며, 기억력, 주의력, 문제 해결 기술이 악화된다. ¹⁶항정신병 약물은 도파민 대신 수용체에 결합하여 차단제로 작용하며 정신병 증상의 일시적인 완화를 제공한다. **이는 환자들로 하여금 많은 청각적 또는 시각적 정보 입력이 수반되는 상황에 더 잘 대처하게 해준다.** 정신 건강 전문가들은 이것이 치료제로 여겨져서는 안 된다고 주장하지만, 이 약물의 투여는 조현병을 앓는 많은 사람들이 병원 시설 밖에서 건강하게 살 수 있게 해주었다.

더 많은 환자들이 스스로 증상을 관리하는 것을 배우면서, 의학적 치료와 연계하여 작용하는 대안적 치료법이 이 사람들이 더 큰 사회에 완전히 통합될 수 있도록 돕는 방법으로서 등장했다. 상담은 생활 기술을 가르침으로써 자존감과 사회적 기능을 증진시키며 꽤 성공적인 것으로 나타났다. 추가로, 영양학자들은 조현병 환자의 식단을 생선과 일부 야채에서 자연적으로 발견되는 오메가-3 지방산으로 보충하는 것이 환자들이 그들의 환경을 더 잘 인지하고 정보를 더 잘 통합할 수 있도록 돕는다는 것을 발견했다.

이러한 대안들은 정신 질환의 개념을 전인적이고 비공식적이며 공동체 지향적인 치료를 필요로 하는 평생의 상태로서 강조한다. 흥미롭게도, 이 접근법은 환자의 자율성을 보장하고 조현병과 관련된 증상을 견딜 수 있도록 더 잘 준비시킴으로써 질병의 의학적 치료보다 훨씬 더 성공적인 것으로 입증되었다.

schizophrenia 몡조현병, 정신분열증　　dysfunction 몡기능 장애
impairment 몡장애, 손상　　delusion 몡망상
auditory hallucination 환청　　frontal lobe 전두엽
psychosurgical 혱정신외과적인　　lobotomy 몡전두엽 절제술
sever 통잘라내다, 절단하다　　malfunctioning 혱제 기능을 못 하는
vegetative 혱식물인간의　　repulse 통거부감을 느끼게 하다
pharmaceutical 몡약물, 약　　antipsychotic 혱항정신병의
psychosurgery 몡정신외과　　pharmacological 혱약리학적인
functionality 몡기능　　neurochemical 몡신경 화학물질
mood swing 감정 기복　　depression 몡우울증　　mania 몡조증
be inundated with ~으로 가득 차다　　psychosis 몡정신병
in conjunction with ~과 연계하여　　supplement 통보충하다
holistic 혱전인적인, 전체론적인　　autonomy 몡자율성

11 지문의 단어 "malfunctioning"과 의미가 가장 비슷한 것은?

　(A) 불쾌한

　(B) 불합리한

　(C) 믿을 수 없는

　(D) 작동하지 않는

12 2단락에 따르면, 부르크하르트 박사가 그의 정신외과적 방법으로 달성하기를 원했던 것은?

　(A) 뇌의 소위 감정적 영역과 분석적 영역을 분할하는 것

　(B) 뇌의 두 반구 사이의 관계를 더 잘 이해하는 것

　(C) 환자들이 환각과 물리적 현실을 구분할 수 있게 하는 것

　(D) 다른 과학자들에게 그것이 다양한 질병을 치료하는 데 사용될 수 있다는 것을 증명하는 것

13 지문의 단어 "others"가 가리키는 것은?

　(A) 실수

　(B) 수술

　(C) 피실험자들

　(D) 상태

14 지문에서 글쓴이는 왜 "chlorpromazine"을 언급하는가?

　(A) 정신외과적 방법으로 대체되는 약의 종류를 기술하기 위해

　(B) 의사들이 이용할 수 있는 광범위한 약물을 설명하기 위해

　(C) 정신병을 치료하기 위해 사용되는 약물의 예를 들기 위해

　(D) 신경 조직을 치료하는 데 가장 효과적인 약을 명시하기 위해

15 3단락에 따르면, 반복적인 수술 실수의 주된 원인은 무엇이었는가?

　(A) 뇌는 수술하기에는 너무 연약한 장기였다.

　(B) 의사들은 일반적으로 그들의 분야에 훈련되지 않았다.

　(C) 실험에 근거한 추측은 종종 오류가 있었다.

　(D) 살아 있는 환자에게 종종 실험이 실시되었다.

16 4단락에서 글쓴이가 항정신병 약물에 관해 암시하는 것은?

　(A) 반복 투여하면 그것의 효과가 떨어진다.

　(B) 그것의 효과는 적용 중단 후에 감소할 것이다.

　(C) 정신질환을 치료할 수 있는 그것의 능력은 상당히 제한적이다.

　(D) 그것의 강도는 신경 수용체의 수와 직접적으로 관련 있다.

17 아래 문장 중 지문 속의 음영된 문장의 핵심 정보를 가장 잘 표현한 것은? 오답은 문장의 의미를 크게 바꾸거나 핵심 정보를 생략한다.

(A) 조현병 환자는 그들의 식사에서 지방의 양을 늘림으로써 전반적인 사회통합과 뇌 기능을 향상시킬 수 있다.

(B) 조현병 환자에게 식이 보충제를 주는 것이 그들의 인지 및 이해 능력을 증대하는 것으로 밝혀졌다.

(C) 조현병 환자에 의해 섭취된 물질은 그들이 자신을 인식하는 방식에 영향을 미칠 수 있다.

(D) 식단에서의 생선과 채소의 부족은 조현병 환자들이 새로운 장소와 사실에 대처하는 경향을 감소시킬 수 있다.

18 지문의 단어 "autonomy"와 의미가 가장 비슷한 것은?

(A) 도움
(B) 확신
(C) 독립
(D) 강조

19 네 개의 네모[■]는 다음 문장이 삽입될 수 있는 곳을 나타내고 있다.

이는 환자들로 하여금 많은 청각적 또는 시각적 정보 입력이 수반되는 상황에 더 잘 대처하게 해준다.

이 문장은 어디에 들어가는 것이 가장 적절한가?

20 지시: 지문 요약을 위한 도입 문장이 아래에 주어져 있다. 지문의 가장 중요한 내용을 나타내는 보기 3개를 골라 요약을 완성하라. 어떤 문장은 지문에 언급되지 않은 내용이나 사소한 정보를 나타내므로 요약에 포함되지 않는다. 이 문제는 2점이다.

> 조현병은 여러 방법으로 치료되어 온, 널리 퍼진 정신 질환이다.
>
> · (A) 의학 조사는 이 질환이 신경 화학물질의 불균형에 의해 유발되며, 이는 항정신병 약물 사용으로 도움을 받을 수 있다는 것을 밝혔다.
> · (B) 이 질환에 대한 초기 연구는 그것이 뇌의 제 기능을 못 하는 부분에 의해 발병하며 외과적 수술에 의해 치료될 수 있다고 결정했다.
> · (E) 환자의 사회에 대한 더 나은 적응성과 관련된 전인적인 치료에 대한 증가된 강조는 식생활의 변화와 지속적인 상담 치료를 포함한다.

(C) 많은 과학자들은 전두엽 절제술이 사람의 뇌를 영구적으로 손상시킬 수 있다고 우려하여 덜 심각한 치료법 사용을 선호했다.

(D) 제약 산업이 발전하면서 특별히 정신 질환을 해결할 수 있는 신약이 시중에 판매되기 시작했다.

(F) 과학자들은 조현병이 치료 가능한 질병인지 아니면 다양한 방법으로 치료되어야 하는 평생의 고통인지에 대해 열렬히 논쟁해왔다.

Passage 3

21 (B)　　22 (A)　　23 (C)　　24 (A)
25 (B)　　26 (D)　　27 (B)　　28 (A)
29 (C)　　30 (D), (E), (F)

오리온성운

태양의 나이는 대략 45억 년이며 그것의 헬륨이 탄소로 완전히 융합될 때까지 40억 년에서 50억 년 정도 더 탈 것으로 예상된다. 일단 이

것이 발생하면, 그것의 가스는 흩어져서 성간 입자의 분산된 집합체인 행성상 성운을 생성할 것이다. 별 진화라고 불리는 이 과정은 우주의 모든 별에 영향을 미치는데, 그것들은 끊임없이 형성되고, 화학적 조성이 허락하는 한 오래 번성한 다음 사라진다. 별 진화의 증거는 오리온자리의 벨트 바로 아래에 위치한 녹색빛 구름인 오리온성운에서 관찰될 수 있다. 수백 년 동안, 초기 천문학자들은 우주의 전반적인 구조에 대한 단서를 찾기 위해 처음에는 맨눈으로, 그다음에는 원시적인 망원경으로 이것을 연구했다.

그 주제에 관한 가장 유명한 역사적 저작 중 하나는 1755년에 임마누엘 칸트에 의해 쓰였다. 그 독일 태생의 철학자는 뉴턴의 중력 법칙에 근거하여 별은 성운 구름이 천천히 회전하면서, 중력 압력 때문에 점차 납작한 원반으로 붕괴하면서 형성된다고 제시했다. 이 원반으로부터, 엄청나게 많은 뜨거운 태양 가스의 집합체들, 즉 젊은 별들이 형성된다. 나머지 입자들은 미행성, 즉 충분한 질량을 부착해서 결국 원시행성으로 커지며 모두 중력에 의해 뭉쳐지는 작은 덩어리로 합쳐진다. 따라서, 오리온성운은 별들의 탄생지일 뿐만 아니라, 전체 태양계의 요람이었다.

[24]그러나, 칸트의 천체 물리학 연구는 철학적일 뿐 실제 자료가 거의 포함되어 있지 않았기 때문에, 처음에는 과학자들에 의해 무시되었는데, 그들은 그 이론에 신빙성을 많이 부여하지 않았다. 따라서, 이 발상들이 천문학 분야에서 받아들여지기까지는 40여 년이 걸렸고, 프랑스의 수학자 피에르 시몽 라플라스가 칸트의 명제에 과학적 방법론을 적용하고 별의 형성에 관한 자신의 논문을 발표한 후에야 비로소 그러했다. [25A]그는 중력 인력이 정말로 태양계 형성의 원동력이며, 일단 어린 별이 형성되고, 냉각되고, 수축되면, 각운동량은 자전 속도의 급상승을 초래하고, 입자들을 바깥쪽으로 밀어내는 반면 중력은 그것들을 중앙으로 끌어당긴다고 주장했다. [25C/25D]그 힘이 마침내 균형을 이룰 때, 가스와 먼지의 수많은 적도 고리가 남겨지고 각각은 행성으로 합쳐질 것이다. 칸트의 예측과 결합된 이 모델은 현재 칸트-라플라스의 성운설로 알려져 있으며, 이후 100년 동안 별 진화에 대한 정통 모델로 여겨졌다.

그럼에도 불구하고, 그 가설에 대한 여러 반론이 있었는데, 즉 19세기 후반 영국의 물리학자 제임스 클러크 맥스웰에 의해 표명된 것들로, 그의 중력 계산은 라플라스의 논문이 틀렸음을 입증했다. [26]대신, 그는 만약 알려진 행성을 구성했다고 여겨지는 모든 물질이 한때 태양 주위에 원반 모양의 구름으로 분포했다면, 중력은 이 물질 모두를 태양 쪽으로 즉시 끌어당겨 별개 행성의 형성을 방해했을 것이라고 주장했다.

맥스웰의 지지자들과 칸트-라플라스 가설의 지지자들 사이의 논쟁은 1990년에 정교한 성간 천문대인 허블 우주 망원경이 발사될 때까지 격렬하게 이어졌다. 허블은 주요 렌즈 기둥에 부착된 두 개의 거울 기구에서 가시광선, 자외선, 적외선이 반사되는 것을 기록하도록 설계되었다. **그 망원경은 또한 중요한 자료를 포착하기 위한 광범위한 적응형 광학 필터를 포함한다.** 이 정보를 이용하여, 그것은 폭이 3광년 이상인 우주 영역의 고해상도 합성 이미지를 그린다.

허블 망원경의 수석 과학자 로버트 오델은 오리온성운의 그러한 사진 한 장을 이용하여 천체 형성에 대한 더 많은 해답을 찾아냈다. 처음에, 여러 계에 대한 그의 분석은 칸트-라플라스 가설을 뒷받침하는 것처럼 보였는데, 중심점에 각각 원시별이 있는 어린 계 또는 원시 행성계는 예측한 대로 원반 모양으로 나타났다. [28]그러나, 더 자세히 관찰한 결과, 허블 망원경의 이미지는 원반이 끝부분에서 약간 오목한 구조로 접혀 있다는 것을 밝혀냈다. 그는 이것이, 점진적인 별의 진화가 그 별이 일련의 원시 행성 고리로 둘러싸이게 되는 지점까지는 발생하지만,

Actual Test 2 71

어떻게든 입자들을 모으기 위해 중력에 의존하는 대신, 행성들이 같은 구역 내의 다른 원시 행성 고리들과 파괴적인 충돌에 의해 형성되며, 이는 그 가설에 대한 반론을 충족시킨다고 주장했다. 주변에 수백 개의 계를 가지고 있는 오리온성운에서는, 대변동의 행성 형성이 일어날 가능성이 더 높다. 흥미롭게도, 이것은 또한 생명체를 부양할 수 있는 행성이 형성될 가능성을 높인다.

disperse ⑧흩어지다   planetary nebula 행성상 성운
diffuse ⑲분산된   interstellar ⑲성간의, 행성 간의
with the naked eye 맨눈으로   a plethora of 엄청나게 많은
planetesimal ⑲미행성   accrete ⑧고착시키다
astrophysics ⑲천체 물리학   credence ⑲신빙성
methodology ⑲방법론   proposition ⑲명제   treatise ⑲논문
attraction ⑲인력, 끌어당기는 힘
angular momentum 각운동량(회전 운동하는 물체의 운동량)
equatorial ⑲적도의   coalesce into ~으로 합쳐지다
orthodox ⑲정통의   invalidate ⑧틀렸음을 입증하다
composite ⑲합성의   morphology ⑲형태, 형태론
epicenter ⑲중심점   concave ⑲오목한
catastrophic ⑲파괴적인   cataclysmic ⑲대변동의
feasibility ⑲가능성, 실현 가능성

21 지문의 단어 "this"가 가리키는 것은?

(A) 증거
(B) 구름
(C) 벨트
(D) 별자리

22 지문에서 글쓴이는 왜 "Newton's Law of Gravity"를 언급하는가?

(A) 칸트가 그의 명제를 공식화하기 위해 사용한 기본 이론을 설명하기 위해
(B) 칸트가 그의 저작에서 어떤 규칙을 따라야 했는지를 보여주기 위해
(C) 칸트가 자신의 논거를 주장하기 위해 사용한 인정된 개념을 반박하기 위해
(D) 칸트의 전제에 의해 반증된 저작의 예를 들기 위해

23 지문의 단어 "plethora"와 의미가 가장 비슷한 것은?

(A) 부재
(B) 정확성
(C) 풍요
(D) 인정

24 3단락에 따르면, 칸트의 저작은 왜 전문가들에 의해 대부분 무시되었는가?

(A) 자료보다는 추측을 포함했다.
(B) 다른 이론들과 양립할 수 없었다.
(C) 과학 용어를 포함하지 않았다.
(D) 사실 같지 않은 정보를 포함했다.

25 다음 중 칸트-라플라스 가설이 제시하지 않은 것은?

(A) 별들은 열을 발산하고 그 후에 그것들의 축에서 회전한다.
(B) 중력은 태양 중심으로부터 여분의 입자들을 떼어놓는다.
(C) 고리는 안정된 환경에 달성된 후에 형성된다.
(D) 먼지와 가스가 결합하여 행성을 형성한다.

26 4단락에서, 맥스웰의 중력 계산이 암시하는 것은?

(A) 별은 라플라스가 예측한 것만큼 실제로 빨리 회전하지 않는다.
(B) 젊은 태양계의 미행성들 사이에 충돌이 자주 일어난다.
(C) 원시 행성 덩어리들을 고정시키는 중력은 약하다.
(D) 태양의 중력은 미행성에 의해 가해지는 힘보다 강하다.

27 지문의 단어 "feasibility"와 의미가 가장 비슷한 것은?

(A) 절차
(B) 가능성
(C) 매력
(D) 기대

28 6단락에 따르면, 어떤 발견이 로버트 오델로 하여금 칸트-라플라스 가설에 의문을 품게 했는가?

(A) 납작한 원시 행성계의 가장자리가 구부러져 있었다.
(B) 그 계들은 중앙에 하나 이상의 원시별을 포함했다.
(C) 미행성의 근접성에 의해 충돌의 확률이 증가했다.
(D) 원시 행성 물질의 고리는 존재하지 않았다.

29 네 개의 네모[■]는 다음 문장이 삽입될 수 있는 곳을 나타내고 있다.

그 망원경은 또한 중요한 자료를 포착하기 위한 광범위한 적응형 광학 필터를 포함한다.

이 문장은 어디에 들어가는 것이 가장 적절한가?

30 지시: 지문 요약을 위한 도입 문장이 아래에 주어져 있다. 지문의 가장 중요한 내용을 나타내는 보기 3개를 골라 요약을 완성하라. 어떤 문장은 지문에 언급되지 않은 내용이나 사소한 정보를 나타내므로 요약에 포함되지 않는다. **이 문제는 2점이다.**

> 오리온성운 관측은 별과 행성 형성 과정에 대한 통찰을 제공해 왔다.
> · (D) 전체로서, 칸트와 라플라스의 연구는 한때 널리 받아들여졌던 별 진화의 성운 가설로 이어졌다.
> · (E) 허블 망원경으로 이루어진 관측은 별 형성의 특정 측면과 행성들이 어떻게 형성되는지를 밝히는 데 도움을 주었다.
> · (F) 칸트-라플라스 가설은 새로운 연구에 의해 이의가 제기되었고, 이는 오랜 논쟁으로 이어졌다.

(A) 지구에서 가장 가까운 성운은 허블 망원경에 의해 그려진 합성 이미지로 증명되었듯이, 폭이 3광년 이상이다.
(B) 중력에 의해 생성된 압력은 성운이 함몰되어 얇고 둥근 형태를 띠게 한다.
(C) 서로 충돌하는 물질의 띠는 전형적인 태양계의 중심에 있는 각 새로운 별 주위에 형성된다.

APEX
READING
for the
TOEFL iBT® Expert

Answer Book